Smart Grids and Internet of Things

Scrivener Publishing
100 Cummings Center, Suite 541J
Beverly, MA 01915-6106

Publishers at Scrivener
Martin Scrivener (martin@scrivenerpublishing.com)
Phillip Carmical (pcarmical@scrivenerpublishing.com)

Smart Grids and Internet of Things

An Energy Perspective

Edited by

P. Sanjeevikumar
Rajesh Kumar Dhanaraj
Malathy Sathyamoorthy
Jens Bo Holm-Nielsen

and

Balamurugan Balusamy

Scrivener
Publishing

WILEY

This edition first published 2023 by John Wiley & Sons, Inc., 111 River Street, Hoboken, NJ 07030, USA and Scrivener Publishing LLC, 100 Cummings Center, Suite 541J, Beverly, MA 01915, USA
© 2023 Scrivener Publishing LLC
For more information about Scrivener publications please visit www.scrivenerpublishing.com.

Wiley Global Headquarters
111 River Street, Hoboken, NJ 07030, USA

For details of our global editorial offices, customer services, and more information about Wiley products visit us at www.wiley.com.

Limit of Liability/Disclaimer of Warranty
While the publisher and authors have used their best efforts in preparing this work, they make no representations or warranties with respect to the accuracy or completeness of the contents of this work and specifically disclaim all warranties, including without limitation any implied warranties of merchantability or fitness for a particular purpose. No warranty may be created or extended by sales representatives, written sales materials, or promotional statements for this work. The fact that an organization, website, or product is referred to in this work as a citation and/or potential source of further information does not mean that the publisher and authors endorse the information or services the organization, website, or product may provide or recommendations it may make. This work is sold with the understanding that the publisher is not engaged in rendering professional services. The advice and strategies contained herein may not be suitable for your situation. You should consult with a specialist where appropriate. Neither the publisher nor authors shall be liable for any loss of profit or any other commercial damages, including but not limited to special, incidental, consequential, or other damages. Further, readers should be aware that websites listed in this work may have changed or disappeared between when this work was written and when it is read.

Library of Congress Cataloging-in-Publication Data

ISBN 9781119812449

Front cover images supplied by Stockvault.com
Cover design by Russell Richardson

Set in size of 11pt and Minion Pro by Manila Typesetting Company, Makati, Philippines

Printed in the USA

10 9 8 7 6 5 4 3 2 1

Contents

9 Significance of Block Chain in IoTSG - A Prominent and Reliable Solution

S. Vinothkumar, S. Varadhaganapathy, R. Shanthakumari and M. Ramalingam

14 Utilization of Wireless Technologies in IoTSG for Energy Monitoring in Smart Devices 395

S. Suresh Kumar, A. Prakash, O. Vignesh and M. Yogesh Iggalore

Preface

As editors, we feel privileged to have been asked to edit the 1st edition of *"Smart Grids and Internet of Things: An energy perspective"*. Internet of Things (IoT) is a self-organized network which consists of sensors, software and devices. The data is exchanged among them with the help of the internet. Smart Grids (SG) is a collection of devices deployed in a larger area to perform continuous monitoring and analysis in that region. It is highly responsible for balancing the flow of energy between the servers and consumers. SG also take care of transmission and distributing power to the components involved. The tracking of the devices present in SG is achieved by IoT framework. Thus, assimilating IoT and SG will lead to a betterment in developing solutions for many real time problems.

The book also presents information about various wireless communication protocol which helps in data transmission between the devices involved in IoTSG. The cloud and fog computing which helps to process the edge servers with low latency and avoiding congestion between the devices which are geographically dispersed is also discussed. The efficient big data analytics procedure which will avoid computation overhead and saves energy of the devices deployed in IoTSG is also presented in this book. Incorporation of Machine learning (ML) techniques which helps to automate the things in a sensible way for real time applications by using IoTSGs are discussed briefly. The variety of security threats, privacy issues, cyber-attacks which are very prevalent among the internet related applications are addressed in this book. Multifaceted block chain assimilated with IoTSG which will develop fault tolerant network with enhanced energy is also discussed.

At the end of each chapter, authors have clearly identified important research gaps and needs for future research related to IoTSG. This book includes chapters that provide the latest scientific knowledge on requirements for internet of things, smart grids, integrating IoT with smart grid, communications and security framework in IoTSG, utilizing blockchain technologies in IoTSG, along with their issues and challenges. Authors also have included case studies involving energy trading markets, and energy exchange platforms that will benefit the readers in understanding the application of IoTSG in energy sector. We believe the authors have done an outstanding job in presenting the latest information in their respective fields and hope this edition will bring about a prospective shift in energy market globally.

Sanjeevikumar Padmanaban
Esbjerg, Denmark
Jens Bo Holm-Nielsen
Esbjerg, Denmark
Rajesh Kumar Dhanaraj
Delhi, India
Malathy Sathyamoorthy
Tamilnadu, India
Balamurugan Balusamy
Delhi, India

Introduction to the Internet of Things: Opportunities, Perspectives and Challenges

F. Leo John[1]*, D. Lakshmi[2] and Manideep Kuncharam[3]

*[1]Department Computer Science and Information Technology,
Prowess University, Delaware, Wilmington, USA*
*[2]School of Computing Science and Engineering, VIT Bhopal University,
Madhya Pradesh, India*
*[3]Department of Information Technology, B.V. Raju Institute of Technology,
Narasapur, Telangana, India*

Abstract

The Internet of Things (IOT) and its security is an important role in the modern era of intelligent computing and its applications. The IOT advantages support the individuals and organizations from the remote regions to complete the tasks, operations and services and make their decisions in an effective manner. Providers of services and manufacturers of equipment primarily concentrate on the provision of information and pay little attention to the protection and privacy of the information provided. The IOT integrates a range of innovations and plans through standard communication protocols and special solution schemes to integrate a variety of smart artifacts. As the rising emphasis and major global investments show, green IOT, IOT security, self-configuration, self-adaptation and interoperable communication are the main topics for study. Sensors have been used by different industries to gather data, however their control systems are kept purposely isolated in order to prevent cyberattacks. The deployment of IOT security issues poses the entire evolution of smart objects. The capacity of IOT is extended to connecting devices, machines and applications to the Internet. IOT allows all the connected devices and things to exchange data or even control each other. The different types of current IOT platforms, IOT protocol threats, and IOT layers are discussed in this paper. Experts forecast that after the existence of 5G technology

Corresponding author: f.leojohn@gmail.com

P. Sanjeevikumar, Rajesh Kumar Dhanaraj, Malathy Sathyamoorthy, Jens Bo Holm-Nielsen
and Balamurugan Balusamy (eds.) *Smart Grids and Internet of Things: An Energy Perspective*,
(1–34) © 2023 Scrivener Publishing LLC

to the extent almost 50 billion devices or things are connected to the internet. This book chapter will be useful for developing IOT applications for organizations, with a better approach and provides a key factor in the decision-making process.

Keywords: IOT security, threats, privacy, IOT platforms

1.1   Introduction

It has now become a buzzword for everyone working in this field of research, with the rapid development of the Universal Object Interaction (UOI or IOT). IOT is the global "intelligent" versioned network for regular physical objects. Its ability to carry out its activities automatically by means of integrated computer hardware, cameras, sensors, actuators, control units and applications. Figure 1.1 illustrates the various layers and its protocols that get connected in the IOT environment. The 21st century is for IOT, which is seen as a physical devices network from electronic and software sensors. The network of around 27 billion physical devices on IOT is now available and the list is expanding. These devices (car, fridge, TV, etc.) can be uniquely recognized by an interconnected computing system and can be linked from anywhere to gain more services and value through effective information and communications technologies. The "THING" in IOT is everywhere around us, like health care equipment, houses, computers, mobiles, livestock, agriculture, humans, energy, industry, logistics etc. Today, intelligent health services, intelligent houses, intelligent traffic and intelligent home appliances are using this technology for greater digital use. Figure 1.1 shows the overview of the IOT environment.

It is possible to classify IOT applications into two categories:

- **IOT-based tracking systems:** These applications regularly capture and send data to the cloud from attached sensors or computers. Examples include home control, hospital security and intelligent measurements. They also provide online control and data analytics.
- **Applications for IOT control-oriented:** The program uses sensor data to track linked actuators in real time. For eg, autos, industrial robots and remote operation. The latency, accuracy and usability criteria which differ depending on the application situation. The most common application of IOT devices is data processing. For the calculation of such parameters, most IOT devices have single or multiple

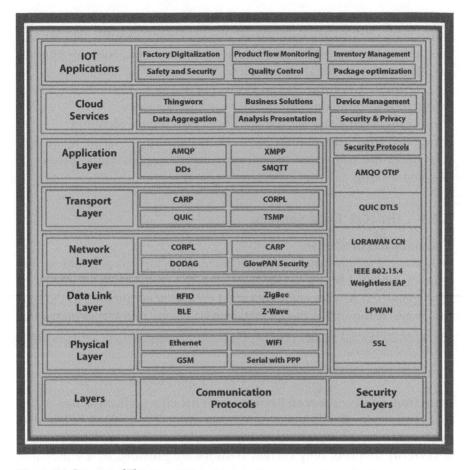

Figure 1.1 Internet of Things environment.

sensors. Every device involved in IOT represents a risk, and it is a major threat to an organization about the confidentiality of the data collected and the dataset integrity. Connecting low-cost IOT devices with minimal security mechanisms will face ever-increasing potential security threats. IOT applications pose a variety of security issues.

The major characteristics of IOT are:

Self-Adaptation: The capability of an IOT system needs to adapt with the operating conditions and changing contexts.

Self-Configuration: This feature enables several IOT or IOT devices to work along with larger numbers of devices simultaneously. IOT devices should have the capability of configuring the network, software upgrade with lesser or no manual intervention.

Interoperable Communication Protocols: This feature allows communication with all other devices within the infrastructure.

Unique Identity: Every IOT device has its own unique identifier.

Integrated into Information Network: Data from the larger number of IOT nodes are connected to aggregate the data, analyze and predict or decision making.

1.1.1   The IOT Data Sources

Classification of Sensors

Data sources are growing enormously in terms of formats and volume. The scale of data will be incredibly high with the connectivity of numerous IOT connected devices and anticipated billions of sensors too in the near future too. A sensor is a device that detects changes in the environment. A sensor is worthless by itself, but it plays an essential part in using it in the electronic device.

The various types of data sources are given below:

Data from passive sources: Passive sensor data is less effective, low-power and needs to be allowed, generating data only when advised before data can be collected and transmitted. For example, when the readable machine is correctly invoked, only current statistics are provided by a sensor that measures ground-water saturation. These sensors are typically small, durable and used in hazardous, and remote places. Usually, these sensors are lightweight, rugged and used in hazardous and remote areas.

Real time data: Active sensor data streams the data continuously (Example: a jet engine). For easy receipt and extraction of insights from data sources, data capture, processing platforms and infrastructures must therefore be available.

Dynamic source (fog devices) Data: Here sensor data is collected from physical, mechanical, electrical and electronic components attached to the sensors. These sensors can be used to allow IOT devices to transmit data. These sensors possess the inherent resources and capacity to conduct communication with IOT applications based on business, the web and cloud using all types of IOT devices.

Features of Sensors

A node of the sensor, also called a mote, which is a node in a network of sensors that can process, collect sensory information and connect to other linked nodes in the network. A mote is a node, but a node is not a mote every time. The sensors deployed heavily can be the temperature, pressure removal, long-range communication, short-range communication.

The three characteristics for a strong sensor is as follows:

> ➤ It should be sensitive to the condition or phenomenon that it measures.
> ➤ It should not be vulnerable to other physical conditions or environment.
> ➤ During the measuring process, it should not alter the calculated phenomenon or condition.

Properties of Sensor

The most important thing is that a sensor can be defined by different properties:

> **Range:** The initial and final values of the phenomenon or condition that the sensor can measure.
> **Sensitivity:** the minimum parameter change that induces a measurable signal change.
> **Resolution:** The minimal change in the sensor's phenomenon or condition.

There are a wide variety of sensors that we can use to monitor almost any physical aspect surrounding us. Below are some common sensors commonly used in daily life:

Electronic Sensors

Temperature Sensor: Used to measure temperature in the physical environment. For example: thermocouple.

IR Sensor: It is used to detect obstacles and controls direction in the robotic vehicle. Eg.- Device having photo chips with photocell, Tv remote.

Ultrasonic Sensor: It is used to detect high frequency sound waves and measure the distant object. Ex: Transducers, SONAR, and Radar.

Touch Sensor: Touch Sensors are nothing but switches used in electric stove.

IOT Sensors
Proximity Sensor: It is used to find the properties of the existing or non-existing objects. It is mainly used in retail to track the number of particular products sold.
Chemical Sensors: Used to detect any changes in the liquid or air. Eg.-chemi resistor.
Gas Sensor: It is very similar to gas sensors but used in multiple domains such as agriculture, health, manufacturing industries and so on. Ex: Ozone Monitoring Type.
Humidity Sensor: Used to measure vapor in the atmosphere.

Robotics Sensor
Acceleration Sensor: For acceleration measurement an accelerometer is primarily used. These sensors can be used in many configurations. The selection form depends on the industry's requirements.
Sound Sensor: These sensors are typically microphones used to detect the sound and to deliver the required voltage level based on the sound level detected.
Light Sensor: Light sensors are kinds of transducer systems used to detect light and create a voltage shift identical to the light intensity of the light sensors.
Tactile Sensor: This is a sensor form that specifies the interaction between the sensor and the target. In everyday scenarios including in lamps, touch sensors are most likely implemented with dim or improve luminosity by pressing their base and lifting buttons.

1.1.2 IOT Revolution

In comparison with the current global Internet, the benefits of exploring IOT technology are immense. But because several devices can interact with one another using IOT services independently of human interference, there are enough safety problems linked to this innovative communication process. IOT environment devices are exposed to higher degree external attackers analyzed on the Internet. In the future as a result of technological revolution, everything is a service. There is a drastic change in technology space, process space, infrastructure space and architecture space.

Space for Technology: There are a variety of interruptive, super-important and new technologies such as integration of micro services, nanotechnology and devices, as well as real time analyzes that lead to interfacing, knowledge engineering, actionable insights, dissemination, etc.

Space for Process: With the aid of advanced technology, services and software, big data, converging, scalable and immediate infrastructure, and trendy smartphones entering common IT, new process restructuring and integration, management frameworks, process revolution, process law, and regulation and re-engineering are emerging and evolving.

Space for Infrastructure: The newly-seen technology, which integrates, centralizes, federates, automates and methods for sharing, explicitly demonstrates that in the days to come, the highly-critical and undesirable infrastructure environment will hit higher and green. The system for measuring, contacting, organizing, evaluating and displaying is making a great deal of improvements. The physical infrastructure has been transformed and built so that a transparent and discoverable network can be connected, and that the programmable, virtual and well-structured infrastructure can be controlled remotely.

Space for Architecture: Event-driven architecture (EDA), model-driven architecture and Service-oriented architecture (SOA) are the key architectural trends that simplify and streamline enterprise, embedded, mobile and cloud IT (MDA). Considering the unparalleled and rising demand from the service-orientation model, both products are perceived and prescribed as a product. This ensures that all is provided with its logical interface to allow other systems and resources to identify, bind and benefit from various skills and competencies. In this group, IT inventions and revolutions are shown in Table 1.1.

Table 1.1 The innovations of internet paradigm.

In terms of access and technology	In terms of content and operation
<ul><li>Computer's Internet</li><li>The Device's Internet</li><li>Services Internet</li><li>The Internet for Things</li><li>Energy's Internet</li></ul>	<ul><li>Internet 1.0 - (The easy online world read only)</li><li>Internet 2.0 - (Workshops for social media)</li><li>Site 3.0 - (Web Information discovery and distribution of correct human perception information)</li><li>Internet 4.0 - (The intelligent Web-Entertainment and distribution of realistic perspectives into human use)</li></ul>

Literature Review

In the literature on IOT security threats a small spectrum of work has been investigated. This section addresses the works of numerous researchers to the whole of IOT protection. The security related issues and privacy issues and the relevant methods of resolution, as taken from the work of numerous researchers in this area, were discussed in [1]. As IOT or "IOT" (Internet of Things) implementations are rising, there would be a huge demand for the IOT sensors and actuators in the market. In [2], various IOT platforms are discussed. Usage of ThingSpeak platform was presented in [3]. IBM Watson platform pros and cons are discussed in [4].

In [5], various cloud IOT platforms are discussed. Limitations of the exiting platform and various new IOT platforms with enhanced features are discussed in [6, 7] In [8], the authors conducted a survey of various issues related to IOT protection and user privacy. IOT standards and communication protocol comparisons are discussed [9–13]. In [14], various IOT security considerations are presented in the design of the IOT framework. The authors presented in [15] and [16] the different communication protocol schemes, the need for IOT and the mechanism to be used to reduce the different IOT threats.

1.2   IOT Platform

An IOT device is linked to multiple devices by an Internet transmission protocol. Every IOT infrastructure has two key divisions: front end and back end. Sensors and drives (actuators) will be on the front end. The communication network and IOT platforms are at the back end [17]. The bulk of IOT processes are used for sensors. There are a large number of IOT platforms available for business and the markets [18].

Both platforms' implementations and requirements differ slightly. The IOT platform needs to be easy, safe and stable, because if the platform fails, it could cost millions or even fails [19]. For users, on the other hand, an IOT platform failure can be an inconvenience. The new IOT channels described below in Table 1.2 are the popular IOT cloud platform created by the software giants. The demand for sensors expands as IOT applications, but for an IOT application it is important to choose the right sensor and the right IOT platform.

Table 1.2 Shows the some of the existing IOT platforms and its services, drawbacks and possible threats.

S. no.	IOT platform	Service	Drawbacks	Possible threats
1.	Thing Speak [4, 9]	Storage service	Limited Uploading Data	Insider Threat, Lack of Confidentiality
2	IBM Watson [5, 6, 9]	Exchange, collection of data and service of the weather data	Cost, Integration and difficult to maintain	Key management
3	Amazon web services IOT [7–9]	Sensors can be conveniently connected to different applications from vehicles to turbine and intelligent home lights	Complex usage of services less secure for hosting critical enterprise applications	Advanced Intrusion Detection
4	Microsoft Azure IOT [8 , 9]	Faster connection between device and cloud	Log Security Events are not available	Denial of Service, false data injection
5	Google Cloud Platform [8, 9]	Fully managed cloud services	Monitoring is not implemented to track sensor data	Side channel attacks, malicious-sensor commands
6	Cisco IOT Cloud	Mobile Cloud based service	Does not support heterogeneous IOT devices	Location inference
7	Thingworx 8 IOT Platform	Industrial companies and faster connectivity	Hard to manage complex system	Hello flood attack and wormhole attack

(Continued)

Table 1.2 Shows the some of the existing IOT platforms and its services, drawbacks and possible threats. (*Continued*)

S. no.	IOT platform	Service	Drawbacks	Possible threats
8	Salesforce IOT	Customer service by gathering data from websites, devices and applications etc.,	Flexibility is limited. Security liability	Denial of Service, Unauthorized access
9	Oracle IOT	Fast Messaging Service in user devices	User Interface is difficult	Malware attacks
10	Kaa IOT	A complete middleware end to end IOT development smart devices	Less hardware modules supported	Black hole attack, wormhole attack

1.3   IOT Layers and its Protocols

The Internet of Things (IOT) keeps changing everything. Sadly, at the height of a safety nightmare several industries, consumer and industrial device owners and infrastructure operators are fast identified. Therefore, IOT security is not the subject of a single platform, a static collection of meta-security regimes as implemented in networked applications and hosts. Every IOT computer participating system and system, it requires a unique application IOT security depends on the application of the device to the affected or controlled device's physical process or state and sensitivities. Figure 1.2 depicts the IOT layers. The architecture of IOT Security comprise of three distinct layers:

    i)   Sensing or Physical or Perception Layer
    ii)   Networking or Gateway Layer
    iii) Data Processing Layer
    iv)   Application or Session Layer

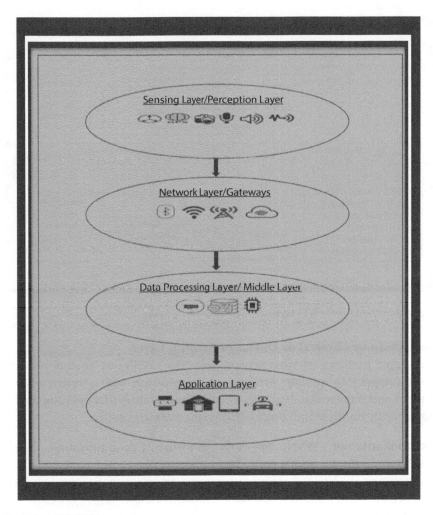

Figure 1.2 IOT layers.

Flow of Data in IOT Layers

Raw sensory data may be viewed as the lowest stages in the process of information hierarchy, where many IOT sensors accumulate a significant volume of data in terms of Exabyte or more than that in the course of time. The following layer processes the raw data in order to receive organized, filtered and comprehensible system knowledge ready for processing. The third layer gives us the intelligence by exposing the occult information from the organized data for smart intervention. Figure 1.3 shows the data row in IOT layers.

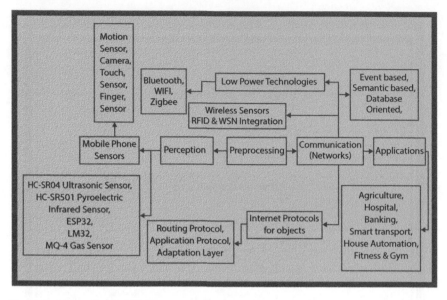

Figure 1.3 Data flow in IOT layers.

Perception or physical or Device or Sensing Layer

This layer involves wireless sensor networks (WSN) as an independent node category to include wireless communication with a restricted frequency and bandwidth. It acts as a central base station that operates a relay device with multiple hub links between the base and source.

Components of WSN Network Module: Communication Stack, Hardware, Software and Secure Data Collection.

Elements of WSN: The various components of WSN are Sensor, Memory, Transceivers and Batteries, and detector controllers

Limitations of WSN: Network discovery, power management, collaborative signal and information processing. Control and routing, tasking, queering and security.

Common Attacks in WSN: Fake node, node replication (Sybil Attack), confidentiality, integrity, black whole routing attacks, Denial of Service (DoS), physical damage/unauthorized application, availability, freshness, autonomy and authentication of an organization or enterprise.

DoS attacks on various layers: WSN devices can be targeted (DoS) on various network layers, including:

> Physical layer attacks are jamming, node tampering.
> Link layer Attacks are Battery exhaustion, collision, unfairness.

Network layer Attacks are hello flood, homing, spoofing, black hole, sybil, wormhole acknowledgement flooding.
Transport layer threats are flooding, de-synchronization
Application layer threats are traffic congestion generation

Counter Measures of WSN: The most appropriate technique for sensors and small electronic devices is the lightweight encryption technique. Therefore, lightweight encryption has allowed sensors to improve the safety and privacy of data stored in the sensor. Most of the issues caused by unauthorized users in the system can be solved by the node authentication mechanism.

Middleware/Processing Layer
In IOT, middleware is often used to connect with "cloud technology, federated overlays, or distributed systems." The list of providers for middleware is as follows:

Event-based: Events where events function under unique parameters which relate to state change all components of middleware communicate among themselves. Security capabilities are offered in some middleware applications.
Service-based: Middleware Service-based implementations are the same as in a service-based computer system (SOC), which depends more on service-based architecture (SOA). They have security attributes and are vulnerable to security threats at the same time.
Virtual (VM) driven machine: Middleware applications that use virtual networks for secure results are referred to as Virtual machine (VM) applications. The individual modules that interact with VM on a network node are included in each device. In order to block malicious network propagation programs, Mate, a middleware system, includes a special security function that is managed.
Agent-based: Agent-based middleware provides a security risk analysis for responsible mobile operators.
Tuple spaces: Tuple space middleware includes modules with a registry called tuple spatial components that, as such, do not support a security framework.
Relevant application: As required by the application, this middleware concentrates on resource management for various applications.

Communication/Networking/Transport Layer
The transmitting layer transmits the information of a sensor to the perception layer through networks such as 3G, LAN, Bluetooth, Wireless,

RFID, and NFC. It operates or stores, tests and executes enormous chunks of transport layer files. A multitude of tools can be managed and used in the lower layers. It utilizes diverse infrastructure such as databases, cloud computing and computer processing units. The business Intelligence layers operates the IOT framework as a whole, including games, business models and benefit and privacy for users. Hence, we do not discuss it further.
Application layer: It provides global governance of the applications provided, taking into account knowledge about objects handled in the layer of middleware.

Transport Security
Datagram Transport Layer (DTLS) can share information in a timely manner to avoid eavesdropping, tampering or forging datagram-based applications. The DTLS type depends mostly on the TLS safety rules and is built to provide the same security guarantees. This implementation has to do with a packet reordering, depletion of the data graph and data of larger scale than that of a datagram network packet in the DTLS protocol datagram.

Figure 1.4 gives an outline of some of the most well-known protocols which can be used to form a full communication stack by IOT devices. A broad variety of protocols can be used to facilitate the transmission and coordination of messages within an IOT system and its host network. Based on the operating cases and security specifications of any particular device, the required message stack and communication protocol selection would depend. The following are the few list of protocols in various layers and its features.

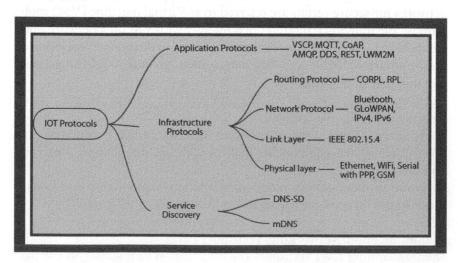

Figure 1.4 IOT protocols in each layer.

Transfer Control Protocol (TCP)
Layer: Transport/Network
Model/Architecture: Request/Response
Working Procedure: TCP is the most common protocol for the underlying secure transport of today's web-based communications.
Limitations: In restricted network environments with high latencies or limited bandwidth, TCP is often not suitable for use.

User Datagram Protocol (UDP)
Layer: Transport/Network
Model/Architecture: Request/Response
Working Procedure: The UDP provides a lightweight transport mechanism for connectivity-free communication. For real-time services, such as computer games, voice and video communication, UDPs and many IOT sensor devices, live conferences are very limited.

Benefits: For both throughput and bandwidth UDP is much more efficient. It also supports multiple transmissions.
Limitations: Possibility of Data Corruption, no compensation for lost packets, no congestion control.

Message Queuing Telemetry Transport (MQTT)
Layer: Application
Model/Architecture: Publish/Subscribe
Working Mechanism: Three key components are included in the working mechanism structure: marketers, subscribers and brokers. From an IOT standpoint, publishers are simply linked to the broker's lightweight sensors to return to sleep where possible. Subscribers are services that include a certain subject or sensory data in such a way that link to notify brokers before fresh information is obtained. Brokers are responsible for sorting and sending subscribers sensory information.

Uses: Protocol to collect and relay system data to servers. It is most suited for TCP networks. It targets large networks of small devices controlled from the cloud. Examples: Stock Price Tickers, Temperature updates, mobile notifications, oil pressure feeds
Benefits: Works in low latency device and unreliable network
Limitations: Scalability and security is not guaranteed along with transmission delay and packet overhead.
Constrained Application Protocol (CoAP)
Layer: Application

Model/Architecture: Request/Response

Working Mechanism: The architecture of the CoAP divides into two major sub layers: signaling and request or response. The sub layer of messaging is important for the accuracy and replication of communications while the sub layer of Request or Response is in-charge for communication. Four types of communications or notifications are available at CoAP: piggyback, authenticated, unconfirmed and confirmed. Confirmable and non-confirmable modes represent precise and inconsistent transmissions while other modes of request or response are used. Piggyback is used for direct communication between client and server in which the sends the server response immediately after receipt of the request. CoAP uses PUSH, DELETE, GET, Place and generating, updating, extracting and deleting message programs.

At CoAP, there are four types of communications or notifications: piggyback, authenticated, unconfirmed and independent. Confirmable and non-confirmable modes are transmissions that are reliable and unreliable, the other one is request or response modes.

The CoAP supports both confirmable and non-confirmable modes. represent precise and inconsistent transmissions while other modes of request or response are used. The CON message is sent from one node to another for reliable communication, and the sender needs an ACK response. Whereas unreliable communication uses NON messages that do not require any receiver ACK. Piggyback is used to communicate directly between the client and the server, where the server sends its response immediately after the request has been sent. CoAP uses PUSH, Edit, GET, Position, and programs to generate, update, extract and delete messages.

Uses: It is an optimized protocol for server-communicated UDP clients. In particular for sensors, valves and other related components for minor power reduction that have to be remotely controlled and tracked via the same restricted network. In machine to machine communication, it is commonly used.

Benefits: Reduces packet overhead and provides reliability along with multicast support.

Limitations: Does not have guaranteed authentication and data protection.

Secure Message Queuing Telemetry Transport (SMQTT)

Layer: Application

Model/Architecture: Publish/Subscribe

Working Mechanism: An enhancement to MQTT is a stable MQTT (SMQTT) that uses lightweight encryption based on attributes. The broadcast encryption function, which encodes and transmits one message to several other nodes, is the main benefit of doing this. Usually, the algorithm consists of four main initialization, encoding, publishing and decryption levels. Customers and service providers register with the broker during the configuration process and get a master secret key. The data is encrypted, published and shipped by a courier to subscribers when the content is posted, and then decrypted using the same master key.

Uses: A protocol used by secured communication devices
Benefits: Works in low latency device and unreliable network
Limitations: Encryption and Key generation algorithms are not norm.
Advanced Message Queuing Telemetry Transport (AMQP)
Layer: Application
Model/Architecture: Publish/Subscribe
Working Mechanism: It's all MQTT-like. The greatest contrast is that the broker has two essential parts: trade and queues. Based upon predefined roles and conditions, the exchange accepts and distributes messages to a publisher. Tails are mainly subjects and subscribed by subscribers who, as soon as they are in the queue, receive sensory information.

Uses: A queuing structure is designed to link servers to each other. AMQP is a dual protocol for wire that is intended for data communication or data exchange between two separate vendors. Companies such as JP Morgan use it to handle thousands of messages a day. NASA achieves this for Nebula cloud computing. It is used by Google to process complex events. Here are a few more AMQP cases and connections:

> ➢ It is being used in India's Aadhar project, one of the world's largest biometric databases, home to 1.2 billion identities.
> ➢ The project gathers eight terabytes per day of data from the architecture of ocean observers.
> ➢ Everything about the queues at AMQP. It transmits messages to servers about transactions. It can manage thousands of right-wing queued transactions as a message based middleware from the banking sector.

Benefits: It has better security, reliability and interoperability.
Limitations: If most of the smart devices are mobile. Owing to complex network conditions in various areas. It is difficult to communicate with

cloud servers because of their changing location. Mobility issue arises with scalability.

Extensible Messaging and Presence Protocol (XMPP)
Layer: Application
Model/Architecture: It supports both publish/subscribe and Request/ Response.
Working Procedure: XMPP uses XML text in its native format, which naturally facilitates contact between individuals. It works like MQTT over TCP. XMPP enables a device to be quickly accessed. This is incredibly useful if such information runs between distant and largely irrelevant points, including person-to-person.

Uses: It is a message protocol originally developed to chat and transfer messages. Most systems only use polling or tracking on demand for notifications.
Benefits: Its strength lies in the management, security and scalability of the IOT framework for customers.
Limitations: Packet overhead, High Power Consumption and does not support device to device communication

Data Distribution Service (DDS)
Layer: Application
Model/Architecture: Publish/Subscribe
Working Procedure: This method is a fast bus for intelligent system integration. The DDS aims at machines using machine data specifically. The primary objective of the DDS system is to bind devices to other machines. It distributes information. This is a middleware quality, high-performance, data-centered, rooted in manufacturing and embedded applications. The DDS provides multiple parallel receivers with millions of messages per second. The pub or sub-pattern will be enforced by DDS. It integrates system components together, provides low-latency, very stable access to data and a scalable architecture that IOT requires to be marketed and mission-critical.

Uses: The DDS provides the flexibility, reliability and speed that are required for the development of complex, real-time applications for high-performance embedded computer systems. The deployments include defense systems, wind turbines, healthcare integration, diagnostic imaging, vehicle monitoring and protection and property surveillance systems.
Benefits: The preferred UDP is. Message broker and data center elimination simplifies implementation, minimizes latency, maximizes scalability, increases efficiency, decreases costs and complexity. It also has rigorous

Table 1.3 IOT communication protocols.

Protocol	Layer	Signal spread	Network	Security	Benefits	Limitations
IEEE 802.15.4	Data Link	DSSS (Direct Sequence Spread Spectrum)	WPAN	AES Encryption	Low cost with better security and reliability	Low speed vulnerable to eavesdropping, jamming [11].
IEEE 802.11AH	Data Link	MIMO-OFDM (Multiple-input, multiple-output orthogonal frequency-division multiplexing)	WLAN	-	Uses low frequency spectra with less bandwidth and also less cost	Communication range is not specified vulnerable to impersonation attacks [11].
WirelessHART(Highway Addressable Remote Transducer Protocol)	Data Link	FHSS and DSSS	WPAN	AES Encryption	Cost effective and high performance best suited for greenfield projects and operates on low battery without wires	It lacks in security such as non repudiation, accounting, secure multicast and so on [18]

(Continued)

Table 1.3 IOT communication protocols. (*Continued*)

Protocol	Layer	Signal spread	Network	Security	Benefits	Limitations
Z-wave	Data Link	FHSS(Frequency-hopping spread spectrum)	WPAN	AES Encryption	Low power consumption, easy to control from remote	Tampering the hard coded key in the device prone to packet injection attacks [11]
Bluetooth LE	Data Link	FHSS	WPAN	AES Encryption	Cheap, Free to use	Short range communication a only and it connects only two devices at a time
ZigBee smart Energy	Data Link	DSSS	WPAN	AES Block cipher	Mesh network, Direct communication, low power consumption	Costly, works with low speed in small distance

(*Continued*)

Table 1.3 IOT communication protocols. (*Continued*)

Protocol	Layer	Signal spread	Network	Security	Benefits	Limitations
HomePlug	Data Link	Binary Phase Shift Keying(BPSK), Quadrature Phase Shift Keying(QPSK), 16Quadrature-Amplitude-Modulation(QAM), 64 QAM, 128QAM, 256 QAM	WPAN	AES Encryption	Low power and cost-reliable communications	Not compatible with certain power strips and vulnerable to entry of outer signals
Wireless Fidelity Wi-Fi	Data Link	DSSS, Complimentary Coding Key(CCK), OFDM	WPAN/ P2P	RC4 Stream Cipher and AES Block Cipher	Easy to add or remove Wi-Fi clients, data connection is fast up to 300Mbps	Scalability and security still needs to be improved
Long Term Evolution Advanced (LTE-A)	Data Link	MIMO, 64 QAM	WWAN	AES Encryption	Efficient delivering of data	Costly, DDOS and DOS attacks are possible

(*Continued*)

Table 1.3 IOT communication protocols. (*Continued*)

Protocol	Layer	Signal spread	Network	Security	Benefits	Limitations
Long Range Radio Wide Area Network (LoRaWAN)	Data Link	Chirp spread spectrum or depends on end device	WWAN	End to end encryption	Low cost, mobility, security and reduced power consumption	Suitable for sending only small packets of data every couple of minutes
Routing Protocol for Lo-Power and Lossy Networks (RPL)	Network Layer Routing Protocols		WWAN	No Encryption	Low power consumption and High Scalability, low memory usage	Security
IPv6 over Low Power Wireless Personal Area Networks (6LoWPAN)	Network Encapsulation protocols	DSSS	WPAN	AES Encryption	Offers interoperability, security and management	scalability

quality management of operation, multi-packages, configuration reliability and robust redundancy.

Limitations: Mobility and maintainability is always hard to overcome for any heterogeneous IOT environment.

The above table indicates very few protocols commonly used to fulfill the internet's requirements. The network layer contains two distinct sub-layers: a routing layer to relay data to base station and a packet encapsulation layer.

A variety of exciting innovations can support the IOT vision for multiple forms of applications. This section seeks to present and compile the most relevant IOT technologies. The Figure 1.5 illustrates the gathered IOT technologies which rely on an architectural perspective to present the aspects and qualifications of each technology.

The demands of the CIA. This ensures that security, honesty and availability must adhere to IOT traffic. Privacy is designed to ensure safe IOT flow. Only open to unique users from Confident Users. Honesty focuses primarily on stopping or modifying IOT traffic. Integrity in IOT communication can be enforced via end-to-end encryption. IOT traffic can also be handled by firewalls, but it does not ensure security high computing power endpoints on IOT computers. IOT consists of data exchange between

IOT Protocol Challanges	Data Link Layer Protocols	Network Layer Encapsulation Protocols	Network Layer Routing Protocols	Security in IOT Protocols	LPWAN Standards	Existing Technologies
Enabling a Complex sensing environment	WirelessHART	IPV6 Over NFC	RPL	MAC 802.15.4	IEEE	3GPP/LTE-A/GSM
Evolving architecture	DASH7	6LoWPAN	CORPL	6LoWPAN	ETSI(LTN)	Thread
Multiple Connectivity options	LTE-A	Ipv6 over BLE	AODV	RPL	IETF	NFC
Security of Information exchange within IOT	LoRaWAN	Ipve6 over ULE	CARP	CORPL	Weightless SIG	Dash7
Complexity of IOT	HomePlug	ZigBee Ip	LOADng and AODv2	CARP	LoRa Alliance	SigFox

Figure 1.5 Taxonomy of technologies.

users and objects or between objects. Such protection standards should be enforced in this setting.

IOT security is further classified into three layers. They are sensing layer security, communication security and service layer security.

Sensing Layer Security

The layer of devices contains products, sites, and stuff, such as light bulbs or devices such as medical equipment that are complicated. During the design, IOT protection should be considered and proper encryption should be done to ensure integrity and safety. Devices should be manipulated and the requisite software upgrades should continuously be performed. Some of the open challenges in sensing layer are listed below:

The IOT system has exposed a pervasive security issue.

- Web device unreliable
- Failure to authenticate/authorize
- Network vulnerability
- Failure to encrypt transport
- Concerns over privacy
- Smartphone apps are insecure
- Cloud interface is insecure
- Configuration with inadequate defense
- Unclear Firmware/Software
- Personal Layer Protection

Communication Layer Security

Protection of the gateway layers means messages between the devices and other networks enabled by the Internet. The gateway layer must take into account protection in protocol correspondence to maintain secrecy and honesty. Gateway or communication layer security open challenges are shown in Figure 1.6.

Service Layer Security

The protection of service layers reflects operations in IOT management such as policy and rules and system automation. It must concentrate on the role-based management of access and trail of system or user changes. In the case of an abnormal activity, data management should be carried out to detect infected computers.

Common Security Issues in IOT

In order to guarantee that customer's interactions are handled in a secure environment, IOT should be installed. IOT faces various security problems to deter an unauthorized person from accessing private data.

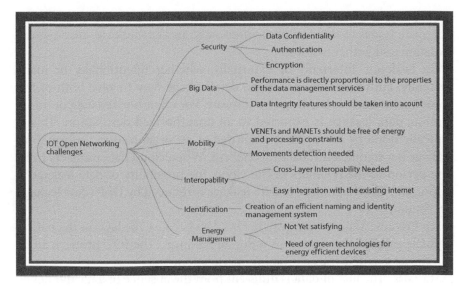

Figure 1.6 Open IOT domain network security issues.

The following problems should be addressed by IOT research:

- Intelligent/self-conscious event-driven agents should be made available.
- Networked computer behavior.
- Heterogeneous system sets privacy-preserving technologies.
- Decentralized authentication and confidence templates.
- Energy-efficient encryption and technology for data safety.
- Cloud storage reliability and faith.
- Property of records.
- Questions of legislation and accountability.
- Data storage archive.
- Access and usage privileges, value-added sharing rules.
- IOT solutions for artificial immune systems.
- Protected inexpensive equipment.
- Management of Privacy Policy.

Attacks on Different Layers

Shift is the only constant thing and end users are trying to grow. Software to satisfy their specifications. Threats have grown and increased security precautions which must be taken into account. Various attacks on four layers of IOT are discussed below.

Perception or Sensing Layer

The main issues in the data perception stage are data leakage, sovereignty, violation and authentication.

Data Leakage: Internally or externally, whether intentionally or inadvertently, authorized or malicious, data leakage may involve both of the combination such as hardware or software. For unauthorized data or information, data leakage is exported to an unauthorized destination. This is typically done by an internal employee of an organization. Information leakage is a significant reliability concern. When cloud data transfers from one person to many others in the cloud, the possibility of data leakage is important. The magnitude of data leakage is reduced by DLP (data leakage prevention).

Data Privacy: Data sovereignty means data because the laws of the nation regulate information stored in a digital medium. The IOT protects all in the universe and is thus entitled to jurisdiction.

Data Loss: The loss of data is different from the absence of data and hence is like a vengeance employer operation or administrator activity. The other reasons for the data loss are natural disasters and any part of the infrastructure failure too.

Data Authentication: Data will at any time be obtained from any unit. They are intruders that they can forge. It must be assured that only expected or legitimate users receive perceived data. In addition, it is compulsory to confirm that during transit the data were not updated. Authentication of data may include completeness and originality.

Availability attacks: One of the main assets is availability for the planned customers. Denial of Service (DDoS) is an overload situation triggered by multiple attackers. However, this is not the only requirement for data centers to make it difficult to reach their intended customers. Here we examine the spectrum of threats causing DCs to freeze malicious traffic:

- **Attacker's Flooding:** DDoS means that attackers flood malicious or incompatible packets DCs. Matchboard Profiler can quickly identify this kind of overload threat. The user will be filtered on the firewall if the attacker's characteristic is detected.
- **Flash Crowd Flooding:** Flash crowds are overwhelmed due to the fact that large numbers of legal users concurrently request the DC services. This can be overcome by buffering excess demands such that this overload state is only alive for a period of time.

- **Spoofing Attacker's Flooding:** This is the product of impersonation and can be understood by each one Application and management of sequence numbers of the internet protocol (IP) address demands and petitioners.
- **Aggressive legitimate flooding:** Aggressive lawyers are individuals who make similar demands that in a short period of time make them restless. This implies that with requests to slow down their DC performance, the legal users overload the server. These risks are hard to detect due to their legal functionality. It is possible to classify such attacks by calculating the time between data packets and the back-off time values.

Responsive data alteration: Data can be retrieved, updated and transmitted to the node during transit from the sensors. It is not necessary to modify complete data; part of the message is adequate to serve the purpose. Changes are made in three ways: (1) the material is altered; Part of the details was changed; (2) sequence changes which have interrupted data transmission, pointless message; and (3) time changes which may lead to replay attacks.

For instance, with the telemedicine diagnosis if a virtual communication ECG study were changed, the result will be several other problems for the patient. In road traffic, it may also lead to another tragedy, provided traffic disorder or collision is not expected.

1.4   Architecture and Future Problems for IOT Protection

The IOT is not limited to a single architecture. Various models and users follow their own layers. Generally, four layers of the IOT are assumed. IOT security thus does not require applying a single, rigid set of meta-security guidelines to networked computers and host networks. For each system and system in which IOT devices participate, a specific program is needed. IOT protection challenges should be broken down to the basis of anonymity, ethics and technologies. With respect to IOT computer protection issues, separate scholars share their own opinions. In such a big heterogeneous world, protection provisioning for different devices like IOT is extremely difficult.

Attacks from Architecture View

External Attacks: Protection problems must be resolved to make good use of the advantages of IOT first addressed. The main issue is the trust of the cloud service provider. In order to access resources, companies willfully unload confidential and insensitive data. But you don't know where to process or store your files. This information can be exchanged by the provider or used for malicious acts by the provider itself.

Attack of Wormhole: In ad hoc networks, wormhole intrusion is very common. IOT connects fixed, dynamic, and vehicle-specific objects, from wristwatches and fridges. There is also a heterogeneous relation between the objects, whether wired or wireless, depending on the geographic place. In this scenario, no hosts in the network need be affected by the attacker. The attacker only tracks and transmits the data to the other node and from that node. Wormhole attacks are very odd and hard to spot.

Selective attack for routing: Malicious nodes pick and discard packets; that is, filter and make the remainder of those packets selectively. Dropped packets could require further analysis of critical data.

Attack of Sinkhole: Sensors that remain on the network unattended for a long time are responsive to sinkhole attacks. The node affected attracts data from all the nodes surrounding it. The attacker then carries out other attacks, including selective routing, development and modification.

Sewage pool invasion: Using this method, the malicious user's aim is to drag all data pertaining to communication and operations in a targeted area against it and then swap a base station node for less powerful targeted attacks.

Heads of Witch: The malicious node profits from a genuine node malfunction. The truthful connection takes diversion by the malicious if the legal node fails Node, resulting in data loss, with all its possible correspondence.

Addressing all the IOT issues: Another big security issue is the spoofing of virtual machine (VM) IP addresses. There are circumstances where attackers can obtain the VMs' IP address and install or attach malicious devices to intervene in any of the hacking activities. Hacking is prevented, and attackers can exploit and use customers' private data for malicious purposes. The cloud technology offers on-demand technology and supports multi-tenancy, it is also used for malicious purposes. They are more vulnerable to attacks using DDoS. The target will be steadily invested in managing the flood message as the intruder begins to flood. The provider is running out of money and will not even serve legitimate clients within a certain time span. If Data Leakage Prevention (DLP) agents are in the cloud due to the multi-variance and the issue of data leakage will continue, regular access by users in the cloud environment.

Attack IP spoof: Spoofing is an attack where the attacker seems to be another human being with restricted resources to access or hack data. Such an intrusion can take different forms; for example, an attacker can mimic an authenticated user's IP address to access their account. Spoofing IP means the creation of so-called spoofing IP addresses for fashioned IP sources to conceal the identity of the person sending or transmitting a particular computer device. Three forms of spoof attacks are: hiding attack, impersonation, and an assault on reflection. Traffic delays in any network is a hazard if the amount packets obtained surpass the maximum size. The element to be influenced by the overpowering time is congestion.

Spoof Attack Types

- **Hiding Attack:** Attackers send at the same time a great number of modified packer headers otherwise called spoofed packets. It is also possible by generating a random IP address using software. In DC, where unique packets are to be processed as legal shipments, this causes confusion.
- **Impersonation Attack:** Attackers even can send the data packets with the modified IP address header. The source IP address can be sent to some unknown legitimate user and act as legit users. It refers to a man in the middle attack. Malicious attacker accepts customer requests, spoofs IP and sends datacenter requests to act as a legal user of data center. Again, datacenter (DC) responses are processed and instantly distributed to customers. This leads to questions about confidentiality and the misuse or destruction of DC information.
- **Reflection Attack:** Attackers send spoof packets to some anonymous person, including the victim's source IP address. This allows unintended reactions from unfamiliar users to hit the victim.

Physical protection: In order to identify threats, a safe checkpoint should be regularly audited for the hardware used to serve customers.

Software Security: Threatened issues will affect many customers who rely on a particular user or interface in application programming and related interfaces to apps to corrupt or alter the software of the application.

Protection of the network: latency threats like service denial (DoS) and distribution service denial (DDoS) can result in severe network traffic delay as well as obstruction of communication that affects routine operations.

Issues pertaining to legal services standard (LSL): SLAs must meet the legal criteria between consumers and service providers for various countries, cyber regulations vary. Failure to comply can lead to enforcement problems.

Spying or Eavesdropping: Eavesdropping is an intercept for illegal access for network traffic.

This can lead to secrecy failure. The person in the center is also available. The attack creates a link with the two victims, let you think you speak specifically but infect the conversation between them.

Attack replay: The intruder intercepts, stores, and sends old messages later links to illegal services from the participants.

Back door: A "hind door," such as an asynchronous external modem and bypass control mechanisms, allows the assailant access to the network login.

Unfinished deletion of data: Incomplete data elimination exact data destruction is not feasible so copies are not possible. The data is preserved in the closest replica but not available.

Byzantine default: Byzantine failure is an act that jeopardizes a server or group of cloud output loss repositories.

Context Sensitivity: This function involves an accurate recognition of the fundamental aspect of the context of an object.

Digital computer relation and physical world: The processor has to be coupled to the physical environment to calculate different information.

IOT Identification: It is necessary to provide an identity for every layer of the IOT protocol stack since in the sense of IOT a vast number of applications will operate.

System authentication: Intelligent devices based on data collection and aggregation sensors within an IOT environment a variety of laws are regulated authorizing the exchange of information between these sensors.

Combination of data: IOT's software heterogeneity leads to different types of data generated by various devices. In order to produce usable information, such data must be combined, which then enables unique security protocols to be implemented.

IOT Scalability: More and more devices will be introduced to the IOT ecosystem by ongoing developments, which enable the creation of connectivity habits between such devices and rigorous environmental conservation measures to be implemented.

Stable Configuration and Set-up: To address the scalability problem in IOT, a protected set-up process that is privately accessible must also be provided.

IOT and critical infrastructure (CI): In vital infrastructure, such as tele-communications, electricity etc, IOT threats and privacy issues have been identified. You ought to approach things in the best way possible.

Contrary user interests: IOT is a more dynamic and multi-source environment, and so correlated personal data needs to be safeguarded.

IOT with Internet Growth: The continuous development of the digital Internet specifically impacts IOT, requiring the provision of data protection and privacy to numerous IOT environment components.

Esteem between IOT and humans: A clear degree of confidence between human and IOT elements must be assured. Human privacy still needs to be maintained in accordance with the comfort level of IOT machines.

Data management: The data protection can be carried out on IOT using cryptographic methods and protocols, and exclusive policies should be specified for this purpose.

Longevity of IOT devices: It should be taken into account, during IOT protection deployment, that any person on IOT has a restricted and strictly short life cycle.

Figure 1.7 shows various layers of security threats and countermeasures to overcome those threats.

Mobility: If mobile was the smartest device. Owing to their changing location, cloud data center connectivity is difficult due to changing network requirements in different locations.

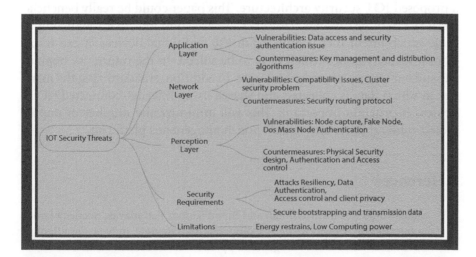

Figure 1.7 IOT security threats.

IOT Security Solution

Many steps must be taken and protection considered during the design process itself, to address different safety problems. The construction process building protection begins on the level of the operating system and then on the aircraft, and can be extended before real device launch. In order to design, companies, the best employees at the workplace should be equipped with adequate access privileges and clear data privacy measures should also be implemented. The unit and its output assessment should be constantly tracked. IOT includes personalized security in the general view, and many studies must be conducted in the field of IOT security.

1.5   Conclusion

The Internet of Things (IOT) will link billions of devices to the Internet as a development of the global network Internet worldwide. The enormous scalability features that manage heterogeneous intelligent devices provide efficient communication through sensors and actuators between these devices. Making communication environments secure is more important than data collection and aggregation. Provisioning security for the IOT dimensions and the heterogeneity of the embedded systems is an extremely difficult activity. When providing protection is feasible, both security vulnerabilities and flaws related to this advanced technology need to be considered. In the updated literature, we have aimed to analyze security problems and performed a thorough review of the work with reference to a proposed IOT security architecture. This paper could be really beneficial for IOT safety researchers. However, we are conscious that the incomparable scalability of IOT is growing due to additional devices, it can result in new security issues which have to be solved. In the future, we hope to expand our survey towards this target. In addition, standardizing the manner in which data is collected and shared using Internet-connected (IOT) devices is urgently important. This will minimize the number of unpredicted vulnerabilities and related non-homogeneous platforms.

References

1. Mohammad Reza, Hosenkhan and Binod Kumar Pattanayak, Security Issues in Internet of Things (IOT): A Comprehensive Review, in:New Paradigm in Decision Science and Management, pp. 359-369, 2018.

2. Losavio, M., Chow, K., Koltay, A. and James, J., The Internet of Things and the Smart City: Legal challenges with digital forensics, privacy, and security. Security and Privacy, 1(3), p.e23, 2018.
3. Maureira, M. G. "ThingSpeak – an API and Web Service for the Internet of Things." 2014.
4. G.Mogos, N.S Mohmd Jamail, Critical Security Issues on Internet of Things, International Journal of Engineering Research and Technology, Vol.12(1), pp.113-118, 2019.
5. Kumar, D. R., Krishna, T. A., & Wahi, A. (2018). Health Monitoring Framework for in Time Recognition of Pulmonary Embolism Using Internet of Things. Journal of Computational and Theoretical Nanoscience, 15(5). 1598–1602
6. Ray, "A survey of IOT cloud platforms", Future Computing and Informatics Journal, vol. 1, no. 1-2, pp. 35-46, 2016. Available: 10.1016/j.fcij.2017.02.001.
7. "Gackowiec, P. and Podobińska-Staniec, M., IOT platforms for the Mining Industry: An Overview. Inżynieria Mineralna, 1(1), 2021.
8. D. Mendez Mena, I. Papapanagiotou and B. Yang, "Internet of things: Survey on security", Information Security Journal: A Global Perspective, vol. 27, no. 3, pp. 162-182, 2018. Available: 10.1080/19393555.2018.1458258 [Accessed 11 February 2021].
9. Ibrahim, Q. and Lazim, S, An Insight Review of Internet of Things (IOT) Protocols, Standards, Platforms, Applications and Security Issues. International Journal of Sensors, Wireless Communications and Control, 10, 2020.
10. Dhiviya, S., Malathy, S., & Kumar, D. R. (2018). Internet of Things (IOT) Elements, Trends and Applications. Journal of Computational and Theoretical Nanoscience, 15(5), 1639–1643.
11. T. Salman and R. Jain, "A Survey of Protocols and Standards for Internet of Things", Advanced Computing and Communications, 2017. Available: 10.34048/2017.1.f3.0
12. J. Dizdarević, F. Carpio, A. Jukan and X. Masip-Bruin, "A Survey of Communication Protocols for Internet of Things and Related Challenges of Fog and Cloud Computing Integration", ACM Computing Surveys, vol. 51, no. 6, pp. 1-29, 2019. Available: 10.1145/3292674.
13. " Nabati, R. and Taheri, S, The internet of things (IOT) a survey. Turkish Online Journal of Design, Art and Communication, Vol. 6, pp.725-739, 2016.
14. S. Raza, A. Slabbert, T. Voigt and K. Landernäs, "Security considerations for the WirelessHART protocol, " 2009 IEEE Conference on Emerging Technologies & Factory Automation, Mallorca, 2009, pp. 1-8, doi: 10.1109/ETFA.2009.5347043.
15. A. Triantafyllou, P. Sarigiannidis and T. Lagkas, "Network Protocols, Schemes, and Mechanisms for Internet of Things (IOT): Features, Open

Challenges, and Trends", Wireless Communications and *Mobile Computing*, vol. 2018, pp. 1-24, 2018. Available: 10.1155/2018/5349894.

16. M. Liyanage, I. Ahmad, A. Abro, A. Gurtov and M. Ylianttila, Comprehensive guide to 5G security, 2019.

17. Woungang, I., Dhurandher, S. and Visconti, A., Internet of Things Design, Architectures and Protocols. Internet of Things, 14, p.100267, 2021.

18. Elazhary, H., Internet of Things (IOT), mobile cloud, cloudlet, mobile IOT, IOT cloud, fog, mobile edge, and edge emerging computing paradigms: Disambiguation and research directions. Journal of Network and Computer Applications, 128, pp.105-140, 2019.

19. Lalitha, K., Kumar, D. R., Poongodi, C., & Arumugam, J. (2021). Healthcare Internet of Things – The Role of Communication Tools and Technologies. In Blockchain, Internet of Things, and Artificial Intelligence (pp. 331–348). Chapman and Hall/CRC.

Role of Battery Management System in IoT Devices

R. Deepa[1]*, K. Mohanraj[2], N. Balaji[2] and P. Ramesh Kumar[3]

[1]Department of EIE, Bannari Amman Institute of Technology, Tamilnadu, India
[2]Department of ICE, Sri Sairam Engineering College, Tamilnadu, India
[3]HCL Technologies, Karnataka, India

Abstract

The battery is the most crucial component in any device and proper battery maintenance is needed for it to work effectively. Previously, the lead acid batteries were widely used in the battery backup systems and other electrical systems; however, the lithium batteries are now preferred, and it should be monitored effectively. As a result, a systematic battery management system must be introduced such that the battery's output can be monitored continuously. The battery management system is a part of a system that keeps track of the operating system, output, and battery life, as well as the charge and discharge processes. This system is made up of measuring devices that keep track of temperature, voltage and current in the battery. The state of charge (SOC) and state of health (SOH) can be determined using the values of the battery. The IoT based battery management system detects battery output by using an IoT power calculator to estimate battery life and analyse IoT Processors sleep modes.

Keywords: Lithium battery, Internet of Things, battery life, battery management system

*Corresponding author: rangarajdeepa@gmail.com

P. Sanjeevikumar, Rajesh Kumar Dhanaraj, Malathy Sathyamoorthy, Jens Bo Holm-Nielsen and Balamurugan Balusamy (eds.) *Smart Grids and Internet of Things: An Energy Perspective*, (35–66) © 2023 Scrivener Publishing LLC

2.1 Introduction

The Battery has become an important component of our daily lives. Consider Smartphone powered by a small lithium-ion battery, which is insufficient to charge, so we need a strong battery that can power our appliance for a reasonable amount of time. But you will still look for a battery that charges quickly and provides a performance that lasts at least a day after a complete charge period. The same concept applies to battery powered IoT devices. A simple computer that has been connected to the internet in order to exchange data is known as an Internet of Things (IoT) system. Each IoT device necessitates a different level of power. A basic sensor node can be powered by an AA battery or even a coin cell with a 3V output voltage. On the other hand, an IoT gadget that has to control a motor would require more current. As a result, a battery with a current capacity of up to 2 amps, such as a sealed lead acid battery with a 12V output voltage, is required. The battery-operated devices and systems include a thorough review of battery design and applications, as well as new technical advancements. The most recent developments are covered in this chapter, particularly in the field of lithium-ion batteries, which are widely used. It focuses on battery-powered devices and systems' power usage, as well as the effects of battery life and runtime. The area of battery management has received a lot of attention, particularly in terms of charging methods and battery selection criteria.

This chapter would be useful for researchers interested in battery-powered devices and systems. This work may be of interest to graduates working in research institutes, universities, and enterprises dealing with power sources and energy conversion, as well as civil, electrical, and transportation engineers and chemists.

2.1.1 Types of Lithium Batteries

The chemistry, voltage, and specific energy of a battery are the three main characteristics. Here the types of batteries are determined by the number of factors [1]. Some systems, for example, others need a continuous supply of electricity, requiring small bursts of power. Others need a lot of current to function, while others may function with very little.

Batteries differ depending on the application and must be carefully chosen, especially in the field of IoT, where battery life is crucial. There are several batteries available, some of which are listed below.

2.1.1.1   Lithium Battery (LR)

It comes in a wide variety of size and shape. The most well-known formats for IoT applications are buttons and coins.

2.1.1.2   Button Type Lithium Battery (BLB)

It is made of lithium alloy and carbon monofluoride gel. When discharged, the voltage of this cell type drops to 2.2 V. The BLB with low self-discharge rate, makes a suitable device that need to operate for longer periods of time while using less fuel. RTC and memory backup systems frequently use them. Models that are commonly used include: BR1225 (48 mAh), BR2032 (190 mAh) and others.

2.1.1.3   Coin Type Lithium Battery (CLB)

As compared to button type lithium cells, lithium cells of the coin type (CR) have a faster discharge rate. They are used in devices with higher pulse current requirements that don't need to operate for long periods of time. The cathode in CR cells is Manganese Dioxide, which decreases the battery's internal impedance. It is used in remote controls, small wireless devices, and flashes, where the pulse current is needed. CR2032 (225 mAh) and CR2025 (165 mAh) are two common versions are used.

2.1.1.4   Lithium-Ion Battery (LIB)

In this battery, the lithium ions pass between a negative and positive electrode. When discharging, they change to the positive from the negative electrode, and in charging, they switch to negative electrode from the positive electrode. The electrolyte is a lithium compound that has been intercalated and works as an electrolyte.

2.1.1.5   Lithium-Ion Polymer Battery (LIP)

It is the most common type of battery that humans experience in our everyday lives. The LIP batteries are rechargeable batteries with a semi-solid or gel-like polymer electrolyte that has a high conductivity. In cases where size and weight are important, these batteries are used.

2.1.1.6   Lithium Cobalt Battery (LCB)

Cobalt is the major active ingredient in this type of Lithium-ion battery. It contains a graphite carbon anode and a cobalt oxide cathode. The Lithium ion flows from the anode to cathode while discharging, and it has a layered structure. The shorter lifetime and weaker thermal stability are the major drawbacks.

2.1.1.7   Lithium Manganese Battery (LMB)

This battery supports fast charging and high current discharging, as well as strong thermal stability and low internal cell resistance [5]. The battery efficiency is moderate, and the power is less when compared to the cobalt model. The reliability of the LMB battery is higher than cobalt model. The battery used in addition to other active metals is to improve a quality, such as power or energy.

2.1.1.8   Lithium Phosphate Battery (LPB)

The LPB battery has very low nominal voltage. Furthermore, the real energy of the cobalt model is lower. The cold has a negative impact on results. This battery has a faster self-discharge rate. This battery voltage discharge curve is very smooth. It has a small amount of storage space. It is the best Lithium-Ion battery in the market in terms of protection.

2.1.1.9   Lithium Titanate Battery (LTB)

The graphite anode is substituted by Lithium Titanate in this battery. It can discharge a significant amount of current while conductivity. It is also easy to charge this battery. Other Lithium-ion batteries cannot operate at lower temperatures than this one. The high cost of this battery is a drawback. It is also one of the most secured Lithium-Ion batteries on the market.

2.1.2   Selection of the Battery

Before deciding on which battery to use, the following considerations should be considered:

1. Nominal Voltage
2. Total operating time

3. Amount of time, the battery has been recharged and discharged
4. Time taken for charging the device
5. Battery cut off voltage
6. Physical dimension of the battery-powered device
7. Environmental and electromagnetic factors that have a direct or indirect impact on the battery's life expectancy
8. Total Cost

2.1.2.1 Nominal Voltage

The device can function with the lowest voltage. The selected battery must have a minimum voltage that is equal to or less than the device's minimal voltage.

2.1.2.2 Operating Time

The device provides an estimate of battery power. The power of a battery is calculated in Watt-Hour or Ampere-Hour. The milliampere-hour (mAh) is another common unit. The 1000th of an ampere-hour provides a milli-ampere-hour (Ah).

2.1.2.3 Time for Recharge and Discharge

When assessing the battery's life, the number of times it can be recharged, the charge retention, and the solution to retreat charging must all be considered [3].

2.1.2.4 Cut Off Voltage

A circuit is designed with a cut-off voltage that is only disconnected when the battery reaches a certain voltage level.

2.1.2.5 Physical Dimension

The battery's physical characteristics are also significant. A wearable IoT device, for example, may require a very small and thin battery, but battery size would be negligible on a larger scale, such as smart home automation.

2.1.2.6   Environmental Conditions

Moisture resistance, corrosion resistance, overheating resistance, bloating resistance, shock resistance, and damage resistance are all factors to consider in the environment.

2.1.2.7   Total Cost

The Cost is the major consideration. If the overall cost of the device is low, then battery cost, is a major factor.

The comparison of the battery types with the nominal voltage and the full charge voltage is shown in Figure 2.1.

Generally, the types of batteries classified under the category of rechargeable and non-rechargeable batteries. The non-rechargeable batteries are referred to as primary batteries because they can only be used once. These batteries are not rechargeable and cannot be used again. The examples are the button type and coin type battery. The rechargeable batteries are often referred to as secondary batteries because they can be recharged and reused [4]. Though they are expensive, they can be recharged and reused, and when properly used and charged, they have a long-life span [2, 26]. Lithium-ion battery, Lithium Cobalt, Lithium Phosphate and Lithium Titanate are the rechargeable batteries. The applications of the lithium batteries are given in Table 2.1.

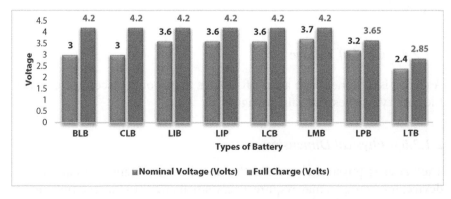

Figure 2.1 Batteries with nominal voltage and full charge voltage.

Table 2.1 Application of lithium batteries.

Battery type	Applications
Button type	Wrist Watches and Pocket Calculators
Coin type	Electronic Watches, Calculators and Electronic Translators
Lithium-Ion	Laptops and Electric Vehicles
Lithium-Ion Polymer	Video Game Consoles and Power Banks
Lithium Cobalt	Cameras, Cell Phone and Laptops
Lithium Manganese	Toys, Medical Devices and Health Appliances
Lithium Phosphate	Power Tools, Electric Vehicles and Medical
Lithium Titanate	Electric Vehicles and Grid Storage

2.2   Internet of Things

The Internet of Things is a network, which uses both wireless and wired internet connections to connect physical things to the Internet. RFID, NFC, Wi-Fi, Bluetooth, and ZigBee will be used for local area communications by these sensors. Wide-area networking technologies such as GSM, GPRS, 3G, and LTE can also be used by sensors [12, 16]. The Internet of Things (IoT) would be able to:

1. **Link both inanimate and living objects:** The first tests and implementations of the Internet of Things were based on connecting industrial equipment. The vision of the Internet of Things has expanded to include anything from heavy machinery to commonplace things. Gas turbines, automobiles, and power metres are all on the list. Plants, farm animals, and humans are examples of living species. The Cow Tracking Project in Essex, for example, monitors cows for disease and tracks herd behaviour using data from radio positioning tags. People are interacting in the Internet of Things environment owing to wearable computing and digital fitness gadgets like the Nike+ Fuel band and Fitbit. The Internet of Everything (IoE), which covers people, places, artefacts, and things, is now included in Cisco's definition of

IoT. In today's connected ecosystems, anything that can be connected to a sensor and network can be included.

2. **Collect data from Sensors:** One or more sensors will be present in each linked physical object. Position, vibration, motion, and temperature are just a few of the parameters that each sensor may track [11]. The sensors will be associated with one another and the network that can analyse and convey information from the sensor's data feeds as part of the Internet of Things. Both the company's systems and its personnel will benefit from the fresh information provided by these sensors.

3. **Update the types of items that communicate over an IP network:** People and computers used to communicate with one another in the past. Consider how different your life would be if all of your gadgets could communicate with one another. What do you think? People, software systems, and other devices will be able to communicate with IoT-enabled objects about their health and the environment. This information can be exchanged or compiled and transmitted at regular intervals. In future, everything will have digital identity and will be able to recognise, track, and communicate with objects.

IoT data is not just about conventional computing data. The data may be limited in size and sent daily. The network connected devices, or nodes, in IoT is also greater than the traditional computing. Intelligence and machine-to-machine communications are extracted from the devices and network would permit businesses to automate simple tasks without relying on central or cloud-based software and resources [6]. The characteristics make it possible to collect an extensive range of data, and they also present challenges in terms of data networking and security. The use of a battery to power devices is needed in many IoT applications. Suitable networks could be tough to come all over in the real world, whether the installation is deep inside a commercial freezer or atop a towering wind turbine.

The rising rate of growth of battery-enabled consumer electronic devices, the popularity of the Internet of Things (IoT), and governments' persistent efforts to raise public consciousness about the need to save power and reduce carbon emissions are all major factors driving global demand for smart batteries [9]. One of the largest contributors to global carbon emissions is the power generation industry. As a result, efforts to develop energy-efficient goods will help to reduce the world's carbon footprint.

2.2.1   IoT – Battery Market

Figure 2.2 depicts the world-wide IoT battery market, which is projected to grow at a CAGR of 11.6 % from 2020 to 2025, from USD 9.2 billion in 2020 to USD 15.9 billion in 2025.The market's growth is being fuelled by a multifold increase in IoT use and adoption of IoT - enabled devices, increases the international demand for the wireless communication, a boom in Research and Development accomplishments to improve the advanced, lightweight, thin batteries, and an increase in request for flexible batteries used.

During the forecast period, lithium batteries are predicted to have the largest share of the IoT battery market. Wearables, home control systems, retail, aerospace, and security are only a few of the IoT devices that use lithium batteries [7]. Furthermore, properties like high energy density are a major component in its development when compared to other batteries.

The Primary battery used in device, that does not need a great deal of power and have a short life cycle. Because they have a shorter self-discharge period than rechargeable thin-film batteries, these batteries have seen increased use in sectors such as home electricity, smart cards, pharmacy, smart packaging, and medical and cosmetic accessories [10]. As a result, the primary battery markets are expected to grow at the quickest rate throughout the forecast period.

The North American region is a major hub for IoT-enabled device batteries. It is home to some of the world's most powerful multinational

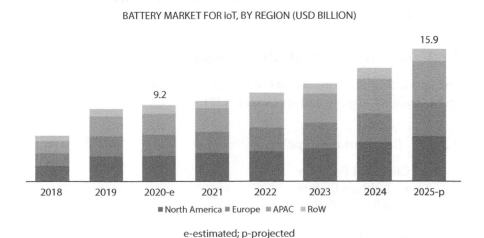

Figure 2.2 IoT - battery market by region.

corporations, including Intel (US), Texas Instruments (US), and Cisco Systems (US). In addition, a number of North American firms are working on batteries for wearables, smart cards, smart packaging, medical devices, and wireless communication systems. The battery market in this sector is being propelled forward by increased demand for wearable and medical devices. As a result of improvements in the packaging sector in North America, smart sensors, RFID tags, and smart labels have all been integrated into products. Printed thin batteries are used in smart packages. The thin-film and printed battery sectors of the IoT battery market in North America are likely to develop due to an increase in demand for smart packaging [25]. Demand for thin-film and printed batteries is predicted to expand in North America as Internet of Things becomes widespread in medical devices and wireless gadgets get smaller.

Duracell Inc. of the United States, Energizer Holdings Inc. of the United States, Samsung SDI Co. of South Korea, LG Chem Ltd. of South Korea, Panasonic Corporation of Japan, ST microelectronics N.V. of Switzerland and Cymbet of the United States are few of the leading industry participants in the IoT battery market.

Cymbet is a global pioneer in the IoT battery industry, supplying batteries to a wide variety of industries. PowerFab, the company's patented manufacturing technology, uses semiconductor fabrication processes to create rechargeable energy storage products that don't contain any liquids, gels, or toxic chemicals. The company's EnerChip batteries and integrated solutions enable the development and implementation of innovative sensor, industrial control, and RFID tag concepts, as well as communication, portable, medical, and electronic devices. Cymbet has employed joint ventures and partnerships to strengthen its market position.

2.2.2   IoT - Battery Marketing Strategy

The marketing strategy for IoT batteries has been segmented by type, rechargeability, region, and application [27].

2.2.2.1   Based on the Type

- Chemical Batteries
  - Lithium Battery
  - Alkaline Battery

- Printed Battery

- Thin film Battery
- Solid State Chip Battery

2.2.2.2   Based on the Rechargeability

- Primary Batteries
- Secondary Batteries

2.2.2.3   Based on the Region

- North America
- Europe
- Asia Pacific
- Japan, etc.

2.2.2.4   Based on the Application

- Home Automation
- Wearable Device
- Healthcare
- Banking Sector
- Industrial Sector
- Agriculture
- Aerospace
- Retail
- Consumer Electronics

2.3   Power of IoT Devices in Battery Management System

According to the Battery Management Device Industry, the projected market size in 2019 is USD 5.2 billion, with a CAGR of 19.5% forecast to hit USD 12.6 billion in 2024. The growing demand for battery monitoring in renewable energy systems, as well as the need for efficient electric grid management, are anticipated to boost this market forward [14, 17]. As a result of continued device development, the power management IC (PMIC) market is expected to keep expanding.

Since maintenance and battery replacement are not cost-effective methods of energising a large range of IoT devices, developers of IoT solutions rely on power management solutions to efficiently handle the power needed to energise a wide range of IoT devices. There are many power management solutions on the market today, and due to power conversion and control choices, one power management solution may be better suited for a specific application based on its characteristics. By optimising the battery life of Internet of Things devices, the power management integrated circuit (PMIC) incorporates several functions.

The technology used in battery management integrated circuits is very advanced. Its integration process is much too complex, necessitating the use of highly trained technicians in order to produce it. Hundreds of integrated circuits are manufactured at the same time on a single, thin slice of silicon, and broken apart into individual IC chips [13]. The entire manufacturing process takes place in a cleanroom, which is a highly regulated space. Assembling the entire circuit often involves a high degree of experience, slowing down the operation, which is a problem for the battery management ICs industry.

2.3.1   Power Management

Power becomes a problem when we realise that there will be billions of sensors and edge devices, many of which will be used in very remote locations. In IoT sector, the sensors are submerged underwater or implanted in tangible constructions, complicates the power sources even further. The chapter defines the fundamentals of power management and energy harvesting. Equally notions is critical to the success of the IoT project.

The term "power management" refers to a wide range of topics that include both software and hardware. Understanding the importance of power management in an IoT implementation, as well as to control the remote devices and other devices, are critical. For the device, the planner must create the massive budget, which includes:

- Active sensors
- Data collection frequency
- Wireless radio communication strength and power
- Communication Frequency
- Microprocessor or microcontroller power as a function of core frequency
- Passive power component
- Energy loss from leakage or insufficient power supply
- Power reserve for actuators and motors

Budget is balance of the power contributors minus power source (battery). Battery power does not act in a linear fashion over time. When a battery is discharged, the voltage drops curvilinearly as the battery's energy content is depleted [8, 15]. As a result, wireless networking systems are struggling to keep up. If the battery voltage is less than a specific voltage, a radio or CPU will not pass the threshold voltage and it blows out.

The TI Sensor Tag C2650, for example, has the power characteristics:

- Standby mode is of 0.24 mA
- Running with all sensors disabled at 0.33 mA
- LEDs
- Barometric sensor: 0.5 mA
- Light sensor: 0.56 mA
- Accelerometer and gyros: 4.68 mA
- Temperature sensor: 0.84 mA
- All sensors are on at 100 ms/sample data rate and broadcasting BLE at 5.5 mA:

A 240 mAh CR2032 coin cell battery powers the TI Sensor Tag. As a result, the maximum lifespan is estimated approximately of 44 hours. In contrast, the rate of decline for battery-powered devices varies and is not linear.

Clock gating modules are used to reduce processor or microcontroller clock speeds, adjust the sensing frequency and broadcast frequency, reduce contact pressure using back-off methods, and use varying levels of sleep modes. In silicon, clock gating modules are not employed. These methods are often used in computing technology as a general method.

2.3.2   Energy Harvesting

The Energy harvesting is critical for the Internet of Things to function. Any system that reflects a state change (such as radio signals or light, hot to cold) can transform the energy into electrical energy in general. Some gadgets are entirely powered by energy, while others are hybrids that rely on harvesting to complement or extend the battery's life. For systems to work, they must be able to capture and store energy. As a result, more sophisticated power management will be needed.

When the piezoelectric mechanical harvesting system is installed in a footway, it must reward for the lack of foot activity in order to keep the machine functioning. Regular contact with energy harvesting equipment will degrade the battery's capacity even more.

To avoid a total lack of functionality, these IoT implementations will almost always employ advanced power management techniques. Low-standby currents, low-leakage loops, and clock throttling are all common techniques. According to the architect, the machine must not be under-powered or overloaded.

In general, harvesting systems have low energy capacity and conversion efficiency. An architect should consider energy harvesting in situations, where a considerable amount of untapped waste energy, like industrial areas.

2.3.3   Piezo-Mechanical Harvesting

Piezoelectric effects can be used in sensors as well as in power genera-tors. Vibration, motion, and sound is used to turn the mechanical stress into energy. Even when implanted in concrete, these harvesters could be employed in smart highways and infrastructures to harvest and change the systems based on the traffic flow. These devices generate milliwatt-level currents, making them ideal for energy collecting and storage in microsys-tems. MEMS piezo-mechanical devices, electrostatic systems, and electro-magnetic systems will all be used in this process.

According to Faraday's law, the magnetic flux moving through a coil of wire produces an electric current. This law enables electrostatic harvesting. In this case, the vibration is either coupled to the coil or to a magnet. The vibration can either connected to the coil or to a magnet in this situation. Unfortunately, this system does not have adequate voltage for rectification in the case of IoT sensors.

The change in the distance between two capacitive plates kept at con-stant voltage or the charge is used in electrostatic systems. As the distance between the plates changes due to vibration, the following model can be used to harvest energy (E).

$$E = \frac{1}{2}QV^2 = \frac{Q^2}{2C}$$

In the preceding equation, the C represents capacitance, Q represents the constant charge and V represents constant voltage. Based on the plate length L_w, the relative static permittivity ε_0, and the distance between plates d, the capacitance can be calculated is shown:

$$C = \varepsilon_0 \frac{L_w}{d}$$

Electrostatic conversion is versatile and cost-effective to generated using micromachining and semiconductor fabrication.

The ultimate mechanical-to-electrical conversion process is piezo-mechanical method. Energy processing follows the same general theory. The oscillations will be transformed into an electrical current as the piezo-mechanical MEMS mechanism tries to reduce the mass attached to the device.

When collecting and transmitting vibration or mechanical energy, another concern is the ability to condition the energy before using or storing it. For conditioning, a passive rectifier along with large value capacitor is commonly utilised. Additional types do not involve in much planning.

2.3.4   Batteries Access to IoT Pioneers

Choosing the appropriate battery for the smart device is a complex thing that is influenced by a variety of factors. The battery will not only be light and small in size to fit into miniaturised designs, but it must be stable for a long period of time (good charge retention). Another important feature of the battery is its ability to perform in a wide range of temperatures (for both indoor and outdoor use) while maintaining a consistent output voltage over the device's lifetime.

The most popular types of batteries are primary (non-rechargeable) and secondary (rechargeable). The biggest difference between the two is that the chemical reaction in secondary batteries can be reversed to recharge the battery.

Li-ion batteries have become the chosen power source in most applications, since they deliver the best combination of power per unit mass and volume. It is the most effective one in terms of coulometric efficiency. To put it another way, you get the most power out of a Li-ion battery for every Watt you put into it. Finally, a single Li-ion cell has a nominal voltage of 3.7V. This is higher than 3.3V, which is one of the most widely used logic levels in today's electronics.

2.3.5   Factors for Powering IoT Devices

There are certain factors for consideration, when powering the IoT devices are discussed below.

2.3.5.1   Temperature

Temperature is one of the most significant factors in battery life. The chemistry of the battery starts to slow down at lower temperatures, decreasing the available capacity. Most batteries cannot provide the same amount of power at room temperature, but not all battery chemistries feel this the same way.

Lead-acid batteries are still commonly utilised in the automotive and grid storage industries because they have more energy at lower temperatures than lithium-ion batteries. Low-temperature processing is best suited to nickel-cadmium batteries. They are, however, susceptible to high self-discharge, as are other nickel-based batteries. It is also a good idea to avoid charging any battery at low temperatures, as this can cause permanent harm.

Similarly, batteries can overheat and enter thermal runaway when exposed to high temperatures and/or loads. If the gas release mechanism is defective, it is unlikely that a battery will burst into flames or combust, but explosions can and do happen in extreme circumstances. More than likely, it would spew a cloud of highly poisonous gas, which is clearly bad news for everyone involved.

There are certain methods to maintain batteries within reasonable operating temperature ranges at either end of the temperature range. However, a large amount of energy can be expended on heating or cooling the batteries themselves, this eventually decreases overall device performance.

2.3.5.2   Environmental Factors

Depending on the design of an IoT application, a product may be exposed to additional environmental factors [18]. For deployments near the sea, salt sprays and humidity are the major concerns.

Chemicals or other liquids may be used as part of the production process that the electronics is regulating in some situations. The chemicals could be directly hazardous to the battery's materials, or they could be conductive enough to short the battery terminals. Thermal runaway may occur as a result of any of these events.

2.3.5.3   Power Budget

The most significant element in power source selection is the application's power requirements. This decision is affected by factors such as the cost and availability of various power sources. Other power sources should be considered if, for example, the device is costly for its intended application due to the high cost of the battery required to generate power. Lithium-ion batteries or energy harvesting are much more viable options if versatility is necessary. If both AC mains are unavailable but versatility is not a problem, such as for remote backup grid storage for a solar power network, lead-acid batteries become more desirable, owing to their lower initial cost and better low-temperature performance.

2.3.5.4   Form Factor

The mechanical size and mass of the product are essential to consider for a given a set of environmental and power constraints. In automotive applications, a larger battery may normally be used to control electronics in a low-power mode before they are recharged.

There are also other areas in the application where you can lose weight. However, in a cell phone or laptop, days or even hours of battery life are needed in something that is held in a person's pocket or bag. The dimensions and weight are extremely important. To take it to its logical conclusion, many sensor applications only have enough space for the electronics and power source needed to track a specific property, such as temperature, and send the data to a hub. Coin cell batteries, such as the regular CR2032, are always the best option in this situation.

2.3.5.5   Status of the Battery

Overcharging or discharging a battery can be harmful to its overall health as well. Overcharging a battery can cause corrosion and gas formation. When a battery is overcharged, plating forms on the electrodes, slowing reaction rates and leading to increased internal resistance. This can greatly reduce a battery's projected lifespan.

It is best to keep an eye on the battery's state of charge (SOC) in order to get the most out of your power solution. There are two options for accomplishing this. Tracking SOC over time will help with more accurate prediction of the battery's overall state of health (SOH) if done correctly.

Monitoring the battery voltage is a simpler and more cost-effective approach. This is analogous to checking the level of water in a water tower to see how much is left. It tends to be less accurate, and improving accuracy can be costly. It can, however, be necessary in certain circumstances where you need to start something that will then recharge the battery.

2.3.5.6   Shipment

Finally, notice that battery shipping is a vital consideration. New transportation guidelines governing lithium and lithium-ion batteries have been enacted and are currently being reviewed. Certain battery packs must undergo additional testing in order to be shipped as non-hazardous material, and certain batteries must undergo additional testing in order to ship at all. There are also rules and regulations in existence that require special labelling for the shipping of such battery packs or battery-related equipment. Make sure to check the latest transportation regulations with the appropriate national and international agencies.

Two relevant issues in battery are battery life and power utilization. Estimating them at the start of the design process can really be difficult. Evidently, battery life and power consumption are influenced by nearly every aspect of a system, including its hardware, battery, firmware, use case, and climate. Even if every one of these device aspects can be tested more or less correctly on its own, putting them together in the same design space is a difficult challenge.

A lot of considerations involved in the design of an IoT system. Temperature, pressure, and humidity sensors, as well as communication protocols, are the examples. Energy use is being put to the test by the growing demand for high-performance products.

2.4   Battery Life Estimation of IoT Devices

The Internet has changed the way most electronic devices are designed, with everything from bus stop signage to complex production processes now relying on connectivity to function. The implementation of sensor systems that gather data and send it to the cloud is perhaps the most important change. This includes everything from home temperature monitoring and heating control to logistics company location-tracking systems [19, 20]. These small "things," unlike many larger connected systems, often lack access to mains power.

Energy harvesting seems to be the most efficient technique for several applications. Since the energy needed by the machine is taken from the environment using technologies ranging from solar panels to devices that use the energy from motion or even the push of a switch, energy harvesting allows the possibility of limitless operation if the device can be designed to use less power than is accessible by energy harvesting.

Even though a growing number of applications can now be produced at the ultra-low power levels needed for energy harvesting, far more are not suitable. Perhaps the amount of power needed to process data on the system is too high, the communication technology's specifications are too strict, or therefore it is not a good source of energy to harvest. In this case, the device must be powered by batteries.

Unlike energy harvesting devices, which would either need less power than the available and therefore batteries need to be replaced at some stage. Since the cost of replacing batteries is often higher than the cost of the IoT device itself, calculating lifetime is important.

2.4.1 Factors Affecting the Battery Life of IoT Devices

The battery life of an IoT device is calculated using a basic formula: the battery capacity divided by the average rate of discharge. Minimizing the device's energy consumption or increasing the battery capacity would extend the battery's life and lower the product's overall cost of ownership.

However, the device can be configured to achieve the requisite lifetime using a variety of processors, communications technologies, and software algorithms. Since batteries are often the most expensive component of an IoT sensor device, engineers have a small number of options. Since the cost of replacing a battery is so high, many IoT sensors are designed to run for their entire life on the original battery [21].

2.4.2 Battery Life Calculator

Since battery life is such an essential aspect of IoT design, Premier Farnell, The Development Distributor, has developed an IoT Power Calculator to assist developers of Internet of Things (IoT) projects in calculating the planned battery life of their IoT products, as well as enabling them to experiment with various components and software algorithms to see how they affect battery life [23].

The calculator allows you to input parameters for your processor, communications device, sensor, and battery, as well as explain how your programme works, and then calculates the battery life of your design, as shown in the Figure 2.3.

This powerful tool provides an instant prediction to see how well the IoT design is practical. It will also recommend trying out various methods, demonstrating the impact of different processors, communications technologies, battery types, and software algorithms. The IoT Battery Life Calculator assures that you don't waste time on products that didn't last

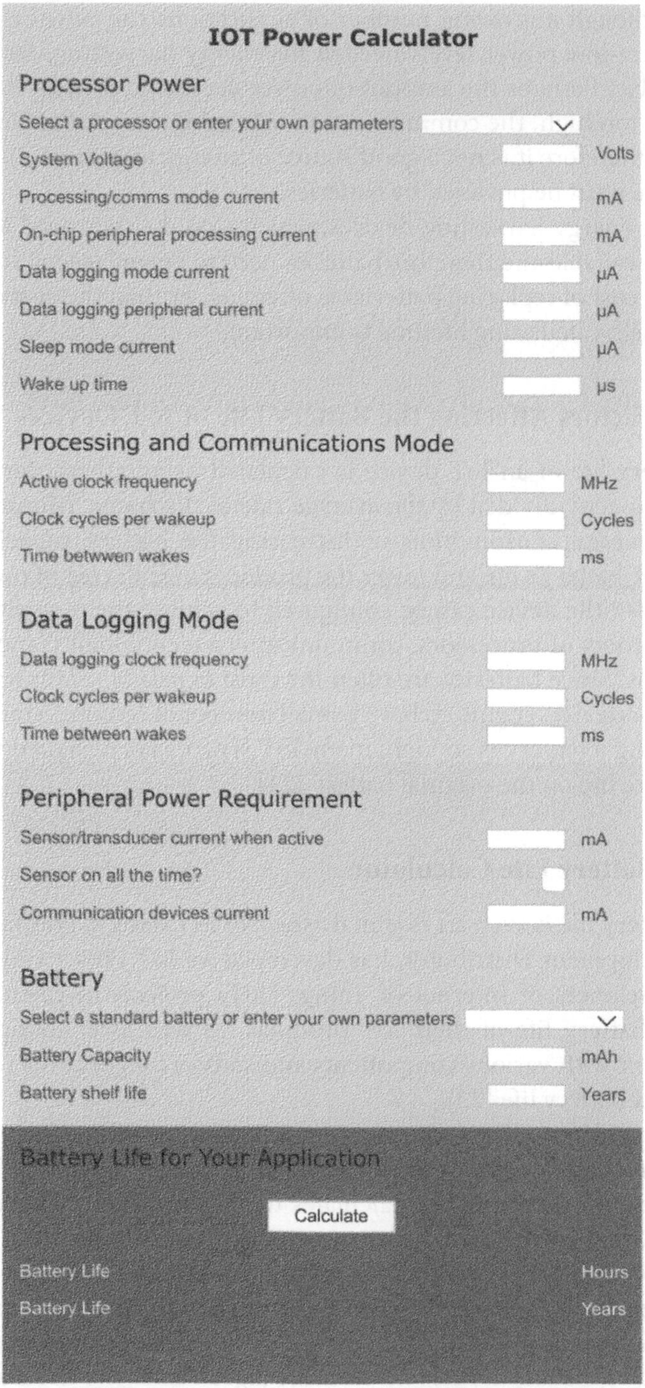

IOT Power Calculator

Processor Power

Select a processor or enter your own parameters	⌄
System Voltage	Volts
Processing/comms mode current	mA
On-chip peripheral processing current	mA
Data logging mode current	µA
Data logging peripheral current	µA
Sleep mode current	µA
Wake up time	µs

Processing and Communications Mode

Active clock frequency	MHz
Clock cycles per wakeup	Cycles
Time betwwen wakes	ms

Data Logging Mode

Data logging clock frequency	MHz
Clock cycles per wakeup	Cycles
Time between wakes	ms

Peripheral Power Requirement

Sensor/transducer current when active	mA
Sensor on all the time?	
Communication devices current	mA

Battery

Select a standard battery or enter your own parameters	⌄
Battery Capacity	mAh
Battery shelf life	Years

Battery Life for Your Application

Calculate

Battery Life	Hours
Battery Life	Years

Figure 2.3 IoT power calculator.

forever [22, 24]. This chapter explains how to make use of the calculator and how to make even more precise calculations, while also pointing out areas where the calculator does not accurately reflect reality.

2.4.3   Sleep Modes of IoT Processors

This section includes the sleep modes of Arduino and the TI processor. The easiest way to create an IoT application with Arduino, ESP8266, and other compatible devices is to use the code in the loop () process. We may use the delay (.) method to decide how long the device can wait before restarting and performing the same tasks, for example, when collecting data from a sensor at regular intervals. When it comes to power control, this approach is not the most ideal one. To enhance our results, we may take a number of approaches.

An ESP8266 device, for example, has four different battery-saving modes:

- No sleep
- Modem sleep
- Light sleep
- Deep-sleep

2.4.3.1   No Sleep

This is an inefficient way to use this device. It is still turned on.

2.4.3.2   Modem Sleep

When the ESP8266 is connected to Wi-Fi, the modem sleep is allowed. Between two DTIM Beacon intervals, the ESP8266 switches off the Wi-Fi module in this mode. Before the next Beacon, the ESP8266 restarts the Wi-Fi module.

2.4.3.3   Light Sleep

This mode resembles Modem-sleep mode in appearance. In this mode, the ESP8266 disables the clock rather than suspending the CPU. This mode is stronger than the previous one. In Light-sleep mode, the ESP8266 should be woken up using a GPIO pin.

2.4.3.4   Deep Sleep

In deep sleep mode, except for the RTC (Real Time Clock), everything is switched off, so that the ESP8266 can be turned on and off at will. This is the most efficient way of providing service. The deep-sleep mode can be used in situations where the machine must submit data at regular intervals. A sensor-based application like this is an example. The app collects sensor data, sends the results, and then goes into deep sleep mode [28].

Ultra-low power sleep modes are available on processors optimised for IoT applications. The processor is designed to remain in this state for the vast majority of the time, only waking up to gather or process data or relay information to the network.

2.4.4   Core Current Consumption

The TI CC2650MODA – Wireless MCU, STM32L51xD – Arm Cortex M3 MCU and NXP JN516x – Wireless Microcontroller are the ultra-low power devices used in IoT Processors. Consider CC2650MODA, is the simple link uses wireless MCU and the amount of current consumed in various states are shown in Table 2.2. From shutdown to active service, power consumption varies by six times higher.

Shutting down the processor has few benefits unless the data is sampled less often. Too much circuitry and code would be needed to restart, which would increase both the cost and the complexity. Furthermore, the standby modes consume less than $3\mu A$, implying that completely discharging the battery would take at least eight years, much longer than the lifespan of many IoT devices and the shelf life of a CR2032 battery. Consequently, fully turning off the processor usually has little benefit.

It is critical to choose the appropriate standby mode. While the lowest power standby absorbs more than a third of the current used by the highest power standby, it saves very little processor state. Although some IoT applications will need the lowest-power sleep modes, many will opt to keep the cache in order to reduce the amount of cycles needed to process data in active mode.

It is a trade-off to process in active mode. Because of the CMOS technology used in IoT processors like this one, power consumption increases linearly with clock frequency, as shown in Table 2.2. Faster clock speeds may appear to indicate shorter battery life, but given that the "base" current is 1.45mA, the shorter wake time needed to run the same algorithm at faster clock speeds may indicate that slowing the clock is a false economy that reduces battery life.

Table 2.2 Core current consumption of CC2650MODA.

Parameter		Test conditions	Min	TYP	Max	Unit
I_{core}	Core Current Consumption	Reset. RESET_N pin asserted or VDD below Power-on-Reset threshold		100		nA
		Shutdown. No clocks running, no retention		150		
		Standby. With Cache. RTC, CPU, RAM and (partial) register retention. RCOSC_LF		1		µA
		Standby. With Cache. RTC, CPU, RAM and (partial) register retention. XOSC_LF		1.2		
		Standby. With Cache. RTC, CPU, RAM and (partial) register retention. RCOSC_LF		2.5		
		Standby. With Cache. RTC, CPU, RAM and (partial) register retention. XOSC_LF		2.7		
		Idle. Supply systems and RAM powered.		550		
		Active. Core running CoreMark		1.45 mA + 31 µA/ MHz		
		Radio RX		6.2		mA
		Radio TX, 0-dBm output power		6.8		
		Radio TX, 5-dBm output power		9.4		

However, the estimation is not as straightforward as it appears: switching from one mode to another requires a finite amount of wake time. The CC2650MODA takes 151 micro-seconds to switch from standby to active mode. The processor wakes up at its fastest clock frequency of 48MHz,

Table 2.3 Peripheral current consumption of CC2650MODA.

Parameter		Test conditions	Min	TYP	Max	Unit
Peripheral current consumption						
I$_{peri}$	Peripheral Power domain	Delta current with domain enabled		20		µA
	Serial power domain	Delta current with domain enabled		13		
	RF Core	Delta current with power domain enabled, clock enabled, RF Core Idle		237		
	µDMA	Delta current with clock enabled, module idle		130		
	Timers	Delta current with clock enabled, module idle		113		
	I²C	Delta current with clock enabled, module idle		12		
	I2S	Delta current with clock enabled, module idle		36		
	SSI	Delta current with clock enabled, module idle		93		
	UART	Delta current with clock enabled, module idle		164		

ensuring that more than 7000 clock cycles are used. Slowing the clock to swap a longer code execution time for lower power during wake-up is likely to prolong battery life in applications where only a small amount of code is needed. Similarly, reducing the number of wakes and completing as many tasks as possible before going back to standby will extend the battery's life.

2.4.5 Peripheral Current Consumption

Modern IoT devices are highly complex products that incorporate a range of peripherals to provide a single-chip solution for a variety of needs. Many IoT devices, particularly simple sensors, do not require this feature, so it is important to turn off any peripherals that are not in use.

The power consumption of the peripherals available on the CC2650MODA family is shown in Table 2.3. Disabling the various instruments, even if the current consumed by them is in the tens or low hundreds of μA, may have a major effect. A total of 318μA can be saved when serial connectivity is not required. Although this does not seem to be a huge amount of current, it can significantly affect battery life and may be used to increase the clock speed by 10MHz, reducing the amount of time spent in battery-draining active mode.

2.5 IoT Networking Technologies

The device specifications are often used to decide the best communications technology. This always ensures using an RF connection for battery powered IoT systems: wired communications will lose all of the advantages of using battery power to remove wires.

Increased coverage or higher data speeds in wireless communications typically necessitate higher power consumption, so the lowest-power communications system that can satisfy these demands is always the obvious option [29]. Some devices would become impractical if the unit was powered by batteries: for example, considering larger batteries and advancements in cellular technology for IoT, a CR2032 would not be able to support a 3G modem.

There are many common technologies for IoT sensors. For example, LoRa may be used to create a low-power, long-range WAN that can span several kilometres, whereas Bluetooth Low Energy (BLE) can only communicate over short distances and uses considerably less power [30].

Additional aspect is whether an on-chip communication interface or a separate communication chip should be used. Although on-chip power consumption is often lower, it is not possible to find an integrated solution at all times, therefore a distinct system is the one and only possibility. Because even low-power communications technologies quickly deplete a battery, and processing needs are typically higher than those of the RF stage, the communications interface must be handled with care. Take the CC2650MODA, for example, the transmission circuit requires 9.4mA to power the circuit and supports the BLE, IEEE802.15.4, and two ultra-low-power communication standards. The current required is three times more than the CPU draws after it runs at maximum speed.

Some IoT systems will perform some pre-processing and data collection to save battery power by only waking the communications circuits when they have enough data to make transmission worthwhile. The IoT battery life calculator makes calculating the impact of aggregating data to reduce transmission frequency easy [31].

2.5.1   Selection of an IoT Sensor

Sensors could have a substantial impact on an IoT system's battery life, as many IoT systems are designed primarily to collect environmental data [34]. It is important to choose the right technologies and mode of service.

Take, for example, a temperature sensor. The resistance of an RTD (resistance temperature detector) like the Honeywell HEL-777 or a thermistor like the Honeywell 135-104LAF-J01 varies with temperature. A voltage divider can be used in simple applications where accuracy is not important, but high-precision systems need a current source, which requires more power.

Integrated temperature sensors, such as the LM35DZ, are a reasonable choice for a variety of applications: at room temperature, the device is accurate to ±¼°C and draws just 60µA. It is important that whatever sensor is chosen only draws power while it is in operation. Even the low-power LM36DZ draws about 30 times the current of the CC2650MODA processor in standby mode, so powering the sensor when the processor is not taking measurements wastes battery energy.

2.5.2   IoT - Battery Technologies

For IoT applications, a variety of batteries are popular. The CR2032 "coin cell" is becoming increasingly popular because it has a small form factor and enough ability to keep IoT devices running for years.

The minimal data available for several batteries are noticed. The capacity is often the only other parameter defined in addition to the physical dimensions and output voltage. The battery capacity is obviously important, since it defines how much energy your IoT device can use.

The power of a battery is influenced by its efficiency. Simply specifying a CR2032 cell risks buying a low-cost device, reducing the IoT device's battery life, and accumulating potential battery maintenance costs. Different chemistries can be available in the form factor selected, which can have a considerable impact on battery life.

The Premier Farnell IoT calculator equipped with two CR2032 batteries, both uses Lithium Manganese Dioxide chemistry. One battery, on the other hand, stated to have around 10% less power than the other, but this can be justified for certain applications because it costs less than half as much as the higher-capacity battery [32].

2.5.3 Battery Specifications

It is reasonable to think batteries are simple devices based on the brief data sheets provided with many of devices. The IoT calculator takes a similar approach, assuming that the battery capacity is set, which is clearly not valid in practice: consider the Multicomp CR2032. Figure 2.4 depicts how capacity varies as a function of load and temperature.

The first thing you note is that the 210mAh capacity is dependent on ideal conditions. The lifetime is greatly shortened if the load needs more current [33]. More significantly, in some applications, such as monitoring the temperature of refrigerated products, the battery's power decreases dramatically as the temperature drops.

Current is drawn in pulses by IoT applications. For a brief period of time, the processor and sensor could draw several milliamps before switching to a low-power mode for an extended period of time. The output voltage

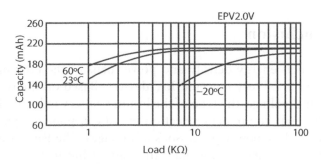

Figure 2.4 Capacity of CR2032 battery.

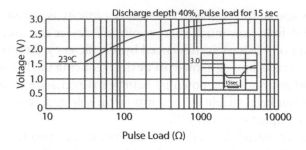

Figure 2.5 Pulse discharge of CR2032 battery.

decreases as current is drawn in pulses [37]. Figure 2.5 shows how a 2mA pulsed load causes a CR2032's output to drop from 3V to about 2.2V.

2.5.4 Battery Shelf Life

Since many IoT applications provide years of operation from a single battery, shelf life is an important factor.

The shelf life and self-discharge are two requirements that decide how long a battery lasts when not in use. A CR2032 battery's self-discharge is usually only 1-2 percent per year when stated, but this does not indicate that the battery has a shelf life of 50 to 100 years; most batteries have a shelf life of just seven or eight years [35, 36]. The non-linear behaviour of the battery chemistry is to account for this apparent inconsistency.

The IoT battery life calculator makes a broad assumption: the battery leaks its entire charge linearly over the specified shelf life. While fact differs, it makes no difference to the calculation's output whether the IoT device under consideration has a battery life of fewer than a few years, and it ensures that the calculator produces a conservative battery life if the model is designed to run for periods approaching the battery shelf life.

2.6 Conclusion

Due to the high energy density and power density, the lithium batteries are employed in battery powered IoT devices. Based on the requirement of the nominal voltage, the type of the lithium battery to be used with IoT device. Although component selection is critical, poor design decisions can negate the low-power processor's advantages. The Farnell IoT power calculator is used here to calculate the battery life in hours and years, which is dependent on the processor and power consumption. The trick to maximising battery life is to hold the processor as much as possible in low-power standby mode and to avoid using wireless communications. The sensor interfaced with the IoT device estimates the IoT battery life calculator allows it easy to formulate hypotheses on how different algorithms, materials and communication technologies affect battery life.

References

1. Yoshio, Masaki, Ralph J. Brodd, and Akiya Kozawa, Lithium-ion batteries, Vol. 1, 2009.
2. Zubi, Ghassan, Rodolfo Dufo-López, Monica Carvalho, and Guzay Pasaoglu, The lithium-ion battery: State of the art and future perspectives, Renewable and Sustainable Energy Reviews, Vol.89, p.292, 2018.
3. Lahiri, Kanishka, Anand Raghunathan, and Sujit Dey, Efficient power profiling for battery-driven embedded system design, IEEE Transactions on computer-aided design of integrated circuits and systems, Vol.23, p.919, 2004.
4. Gaines, Linda, The future of automotive lithium-ion battery recycling: Charting a sustainable course, Sustainable Materials and Technologies, Vol.1, p.2-7, 2014.
5. Podder, Shuvankar, and Md Ziaur Rahman Khan, Comparison of lead acid and Li-ion battery in solar home system of Bangladesh, 5th International Conference on Informatics, Electronics and Vision (ICIEV), p. 434-438, 2016.
6. Adhikaree, Amit, Taesic Kim, Jitendra Vagdoda, Ason Ochoa, Patrick J. Hernandez, and Young Lee, Cloud-based battery condition monitoring platform for large-scale lithium-ion battery energy storage systems using internet-of-things (IoT), IEEE Energy Conversion Congress and Exposition (ECCE), p. 1004-1009, 2017.
7. Sathya, K., & Kumar, D. R. (2012, February). Energy efficient clustering in sensor networks using Cluster Manager. 2012 International Conference on Computing, Communication and Applications (ICCCA). https://doi.org/10.1109/iccca.2012.6179177
8. Haldar, Suman, Supratim Mondal, Arindam Mondal, and Rajib Banerjee, Battery Management System Using State of Charge Estimation: An IoT Based Approach, National Conference on Emerging Trends on Sustainable Technology and Engineering Applications (NCETSTEA), p. 1-5, 2020.
9. Friansa, Koko, Irsyad Nashirul Haq, Bening Maria Santi, Deddy Kurniadi, Edi Leksono, and Brian Yuliarto, Development of battery monitoring system in smart microgrid based on internet of things (IoT), Procedia engineering, Vol.170, p. 482-487, 2017.
10. Aydın, İlker, and Özgür Üstün, A basic battery management system design with IoT feature for LiFePO4 batteries, 10th International Conference on Electrical and Electronics Engineering (ELECO), p. 1309-1313, 2017.

11. Karumbaya, Athena, and Gowri Satheesh, IoT empowered real time environment monitoring system, International Journal of Computer Applications Vol.129, no. 5, p.30-32, 2015.

12. Madakam, Somayya, Vihar Lake, Vihar Lake, and Vihar Lake, Internet of Things (IoT): A literature review, Journal of Computer and Communications, Vol. 3, no. 05, p.164, 2015.

13. Chatzakis, John, Kostas Kalaitzakis, Nicholas C. Voulgaris, and Stefanos N. Manias, Designing a new generalized battery management system, IEEE transactions on Industrial Electronics, Vol.50, no. 5, p.990-999, 2003.

14. Rahimi-Eichi, Habiballah, Unnati Ojha, Federico Baronti, and Mo-Yuen Chow, Battery management system: An overview of its application in the smart grid and electric vehicles, IEEE Industrial Electronics Magazine, Vol.7, no. 2, p: 4-16, 2013.

15. Pop, Valer, Henk Jan Bergveld, Dmitry Danilov, Paul PL Regtien, and Peter HL Notten, Battery management systems: Accurate state-of-charge indication for battery-powered applications, Vol. 9, 2008.

16. Li, Shancang, Li Da Xu, and Shanshan Zhao, The internet of things: a survey, Information Systems Frontiers, Vol.17, no. 2, p.243-259, 2015.

17. Xiong, Rui, Jiayi Cao, Quanqing Yu, Hongwen He, and Fengchun Sun, Critical review on the battery state of charge estimation methods for electric vehicles, IEEE Access, Vol.6, p.1832-1843, 2017.

18. Al-Sarawi, Shadi, Mohammed Anbar, Kamal Alieyan, and Mahmood Alzubaidi, Internet of Things (IoT) communication protocols, 8th International conference on information technology (ICIT), p. 685-690, 2017.

19. Blaauw, D, D. Sylvester, P. Dutta, Y. Lee, I. Lee, S. Bang, and Y. Kim, IoT design space challenges, Circuits and systems, Symposium on VLSI Technology (VLSI-Technology): Digest of Technical Papers, p. 1-2, 2014.

20. Patel, Keyur K, and Sunil M. Patel, Internet of things-IoT: definition, characteristics, architecture, enabling technologies, application & future challenges, International Journal of Engineering Science and Computing, Vol. 6, no. 5, 2016.

21. Ramakrishnan, R., K. Sasikala, and M. Nithya, Challenges, Issues of Energy Efficiency in IoT devices and an analysis of battery life power consumption in IoT devices and Applications, Vol.7, p.478-484, 2020.

22. Fafoutis, Xenofon, Atis Elsts, Antonis Vafeas, George Oikonomou, and Robert Piechocki, On predicting the battery lifetime of IoT devices: experiences from the sphere deployments, In Proceedings of the 7th International Workshop on Real-World Embedded Wireless Systems and Networks, p. 7-12. 2018.

23. Lucero, Sam, IoT platforms: enabling the Internet of Things, White paper, 2016.

24. Li, Jin, Wei Liu, Tian Wang, Houbing Song, Xiong Li, Fang Liu, and Anfeng Liu, Battery-friendly relay selection scheme for prolonging the lifetimes of

sensor nodes in the Internet of Things, IEEE Access, Vol.7, p.33180-33201, 2019.

25. Barsukov, Yevgen, Battery selection, safety, and monitoring in mobile applications, In Texas Instrument, 2006 Portable Power Design Seminar, 2005.

26. R. K. Dhanaraj, L. Krishnasamy, O. Geman and D. R. Izdrui, "Black hole and sink hole attack detection in wireless body area networks," *Computers, Materials & Continua*, vol. 68, no.2, pp. 1949–1965, 2021. doi:10.32604/cmc.2021.015363

27. Kiehne, Heinz Albert. Battery technology handbook. Vol. 118. CRC Press, 2003.

28. Kodali, Ravi Kishore, Govinda Swamy, and Boppana Lakshmi, An implementation of IoT for healthcare, IEEE Recent Advances in Intelligent Computational Systems (RAICS), p. 411-416, 2015.

29. Hanes, David, Gonzalo Salgueiro, Patrick Grossetete, Robert Barton, and Jerome Henry, IoT fundamentals: Networking technologies, protocols, and use cases for the internet of things, Cisco Press, 2017.

30. Qian, Zhi-Hong, and Yi-jun Wang, IoT technology and application, Acta Electronica Sinica, Vol.40, no. 5, p.1023-1029, 2012.

31. Chen, Shanzhi, Hui Xu, Dake Liu, Bo Hu, and Hucheng Wang, A vision of IoT: Applications, challenges, and opportunities with china perspective, IEEE Internet of Things journal Vol.1, no. 4, p. 349-359, 2014.

32. Marano, Vincenzo, Simona Onori, Yann Guezennec, Giorgio Rizzoni, and Nullo Madella, Lithium-ion batteries life estimation for plug-in hybrid electric vehicles, IEEE Vehicle Power and Propulsion Conference, p. 536-543, 2009.

33. Takei, K, K. Kumai, Y. Kobayashi, H. Miyashiro, N. Terada, T. Iwahori, and T. Tanaka, Cycle life estimation of lithium secondary battery by extrapolation method and accelerated aging test, Journal of Power Sources, Vol. 97, p.697-701, 2001.

34. Deepa, R, and Lakshmipriya, Theft Detection System in Shops, International Journal of Engineering and Advanced Technology, Vol.8 (2S), p.384-387, 2018.

35. S., Benini, Luca, Giuliano Castelli, Alberto Macii, Enrico Macii, Massimo Poncino, and Riccardo Scarsi, A discrete-time battery model for high-level power estimation, In Proceedings of the conference on Design, automation and test in Europe, p. 35-41, 2000.

36. Wu, Ji, Chenbin Zhang, and Zonghai Chen, An online method for lithium-ion battery remaining useful life estimation using importance sampling and neural networks, Applied energy, Vol.173, p.134-140, 2016.

37. Keeli, Anupama, and Ratnesh K. Sharma, Optimal use of second life battery for peak load management and improving the life of the battery, IEEE International Electric Vehicle Conference, p. 1-6, 2012.

3

Smart Grid - Overview, Challenges and Security Issues

C. N. Vanitha[1*], Malathy S.[1] and S.A. Krishna[2†]

[1]*Computer Science and Engineering, Kongu Engineering College, Erode, Tamil Nadu, India*
[2]*Department of Mechatronics Engineering, Kongu Engineering College, Erode, Tamil Nadu, India*

Abstract

An electrical grid which acts smartly to control various operations of electronics and manage energy using energy measures is known as smart grid. Smart grid is used in home appliances in response to the demand. Distribution boards, control switches and circuit breakers are integrated into smart grid. The energy sources are renewed and batteries are recycled using the energy storage. Production control, conditioning of electronic power and distribution of power are the major features of smart grid. Smart grid is mainly evolved to build infrastructure for dual communication. Smart grid has many challenges to improve efficiency of the usage and to improve transmission, distribution, sustainability and reliability of the electricity. As Smart grids are greatly used in the field of electronics, it is vulnerable for attacks also. The attacks are happened by changing and monitoring information when the smart grid are in communication. The data passed between the smart grids are sensitive and high in volume. The attacks are highly minacious while traversing the environment as they intercept, manipulate and collect the data in transit. The chapter reveals the concept of smart grid and how the challenges, security issues are handled by smart grid in detail.

Keywords: Smart grid, security, power plants, energy market, electricity, electric vehicles, attacks, economy

Corresponding author: rushtovanitha@gmail.com
†*Corresponding author*: krishna.arunvijay08@gmail.com

P. Sanjeevikumar, Rajesh Kumar Dhanaraj, Malathy Sathyamoorthy, Jens Bo Holm-Nielsen and Balamurugan Balusamy (eds.) Smart Grids and Internet of Things: An Energy Perspective, (67–90) © 2023 Scrivener Publishing LLC

3.1 Introduction to the Chapter

In this chapter we are going to discuss about Smart grid and its uses in this modern world. Now-a-days smart grids are used everywhere like transportation, weather forecasting, etc. In this we are going to see the smart grid uses, and how it is used in electric vehicles and in power stations.

"Smart grid" another phrasing originally presented in 2005 by the 21st century innovation to the new age of clients. The expression "grid" alludes to the electrical grid that gives energy to the end buyer. "Smart" then again is like "smart telephones" or "smart TV", it implies that the article contains an underlying working framework, with further developed figuring and estimating capacities.

In Figure 3.1, the uses of smart grid is shown. The smart grid is used in Wind Generator, Photovoltaic, Electric vehicle, Cities & Offices, Hydraulic Power Generation, Home appliances, Factories, Nuclear Power Plant and Thermal Power Plants. A smart grid is nothing but an electrical grid which incorporates an assortment of activity as well as power measures together with smart meters, smart machines, environmentally friendly power assets, and energy productive assets. Electronic force molding and manage the conception and dissemination of power are significant parts of the smart grid.

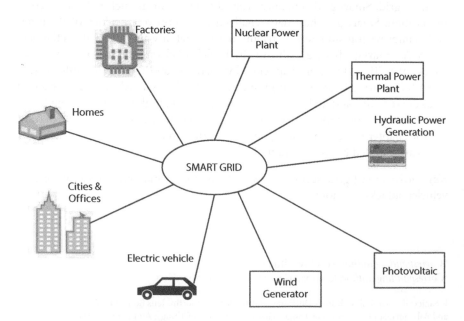

Figure 3.1 Uses of smart grid.

3.2   Smart Grid and Its Uses

Smart network is nothing but an electric network which incorporates a diversity of functions in addition to computing the power together with smart meters, smart tools, renewable energy resources, and capable power resources [1]. Smart network is a part of IoT structure [26], which can be used to distantly observe and supervise the whole thing starting at illumination, traffic signals, traffic jamming, parking places, highway warnings and premature recognition of belongings like power influxes as the consequence of tremor and tremendous climate.

In previous try at managing, measuring and observing has done for developing the smart network technology. For observing the loads in 1980s, mechanical meter analysis was used for observing the enormous clients and progressed into AMI (Advanced Metering Infrastructure) in 1990s, with measures that may hideaway how force was used at uncommon period in the daytime. Smart meters add constant cooperation's so that noticing can be made at real moment and can be used as an admittance to specify affirmation proficient apparatus, and "smart attachments" in the home.

Checking and synchronization of broad spot web were changed in the untimely 1990s when the Bonneville Power Administration expanded its smart network examination with model finders that has the capacity of snappy assessment of deviation in force greatness in overabundance of incredibly tremendous ecological zone [2]. The end of this work was the underlying prepared wide territory estimation framework (WAMS) in 2000. The IoT computerization and morals has a huge impact in this methodology.

Uses:

- Self-recuperating network
- Fault insurance
- Outage the executives
- Dynamic control of wastage
- Weather information mix
- Advanced detecting
- Automated feeder reconfiguration.

In Figure 3.2, the distribution of electricity to smart home is explained. The electricity is stored from the solar PV Module and it is distributed to smart home by crossing the isolator, inverter and AC Breaker. The Net meter/smart meter measures the loads given to smart home. An assortment of difficulties face the strength venture that its interchanges framework is not, at this point by and by coordinated to address [3].

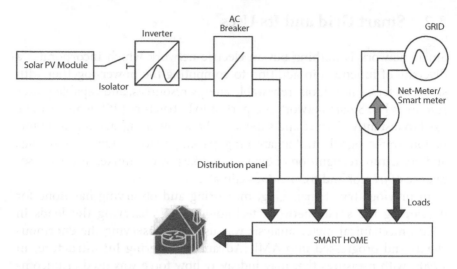

Figure 3.2 Electricity distribution to smart home.

Figure 3.3 explains the working principle of smart grid. The grid controls the smart meter which transmits the loads to the controller and to the consumer. A Power gadget utilizing worked in electrical and interchanges machine structure should be as per the following:

- Self-recuperating and versatile, utilizing mechanized purposes for insurance, flaw discovery, issue area, sectionalization, and computerized supplier reclamation over broad regions of the supplier domain.

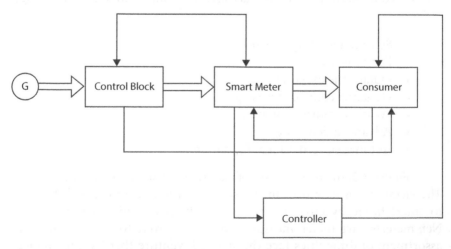

Figure 3.3 Working principle of smart grid.

- Interactive with customers and markets, empowering genuine time estimating, strength exchanging, and load the board.
- Optimized to utilize maturing hardware, staff from two or three associations, and various sources in a forceful climate.
- Predictive, planning redesign ahead of time of time to thwart as a substitute than just responds to crises.
- Distributed, permitting activities, for example, age, metering, load planning, and diverse to be without trouble helped out at particular spots and through exceptional associations.
- Integrated, blending the in the past isolated highlights of observing, control, security, upkeep, strength the executives, circulation the board, business, and friends realities innovation.
- Secure, protecting significant framework from digital or real assault.

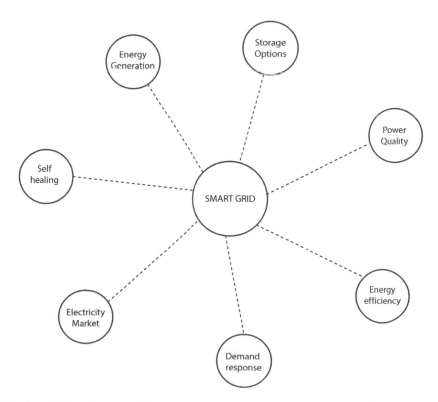

Figure 3.4 Uses of smart grid.

In Figure 3.4, the uses of smart grid are explained in diagrammatic representation. Though these features are carried out these days via a variety of utilities, there is plenty version in the stage of implementation, and they are normally no longer carried out on broad ample scale to tackle the stage of troubles confronted with the aid of the grid today.

A wonderful many smart grid definitions exist: some useful, some mechanical, and a few favorable circumstances situated. A continuous factor to most definitions is the product of prevalent sensor innovations, two-way interchanges, and dispensed preparing to the strength grid, making data buoy and records organization key to the astute grid.

3.3   The Grid as it Stands-What's at Risk?

In Figure 3.5, the challenges and risk in the smart grid is denoted. There is a big demand in getting the electricity the place it desires to go through the broadcast and circulation; moreover, proscribing the grids competence and dependability. While lots of hundreds of high-voltage broadcast

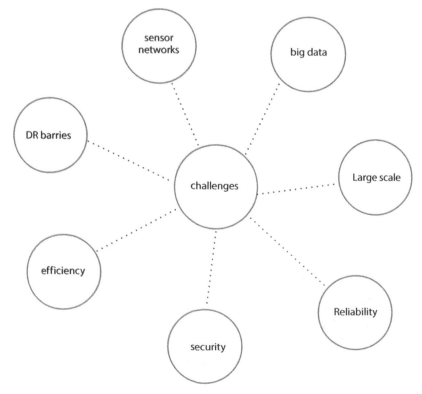

Figure 3.5 Challenges in smart grid.

strains direction at some stage in the United States, solely 668 extra miles of throughway broadcast comprised and constructed given that 2000 [4]. Since an outcome, scheme constraints deteriorate at an event when outages and electricity eminence troubles are projected to outlay American exchange greater than $100 billion on well-known each year.

Based on twentieth century sketch requirements and having developed in duration whilst growing the grid was once the solitary desire and visibility surrounded by using the structures was once restricted, in previous the grid in contains the solitary task, i.e., observance the illumination on.

Energy efficiency? A minor issue all things considered grand while strength used to be – as the precept went – "excessively minimal effort to meter".

Natural effects? Essentially now not a basic issue when the current grid was once arranged.

3.3.1   Reliability

Over the point of reference forty years, there are 5 monster power outages out of that three of which are came upon in past 9 years. More power outages and brownouts are happening because of the moderate noting age of robotized switches, be brief of modernized investigation, "pitiable perceivability" - a "be brief of situational readiness" on the factor of grid administrators [5]. This subject of power outages has serious more extensive ramifications than essentially prepared for the lights to show up on. Envision plant development shut, consumable suppers ruin, site guest's lights obscure, and FICO assessment card associations delivered ended. Such are the exceptional outcomes of in any case a dainty close by power outage.

As of now, the incongruity is extraordinary: In a human advancement the spot skill rules most noteworthy, America is depending on a midway planned and illegal foundation molded principally through the time of chip that forestall our flexibility and spots us at chance on a few genuine fronts.

3.3.2   Efficiency

When the grid is environment friendly for 5% then the power is equal to banish the gas continuingly and equal for releasing of fuel from fifty-three million vehicles in greenhouse. : If every American household restores in modern times one luminous tuber (Edison's pleasure and joy) with a dense glowing tuber, the world will become more efficient and over three million residences would be lit saving energy and thereby facilitate an accumulation of close to $600 million annually. Obviously, there are many opportunities for energy conservation and enhancement.

3.3.3 Security

When the blackout of 2003 occurred–the biggest in US archives – tragedy struck Americans causing a monumental disaster. With loss of power millions of dollars of business is lost and criminal activity skyrockets. Creating sound energy grids is imperative to national and state security; otherwise the weak grid infrastructure could be open to terrostic threat. And no longer without cause. The grids weakened structure leaves the U.S. open to assault. Indeed if one grid system fails its possible to create a domino effect and hence other connecting electric grids could also fail. Such energy grid failures are likely to impact industries relying on electricity to operate, in theory. It would be harmful to security and banking industries as well as others.

3.3.4 National Economy

The numbers are prominent and represent themselves:

- A planned power outage all through Silicon Valley added up to $75 million in misfortunes.
- In 2000, the one-hour blackout that hit the Chicago Board of Trade came about in $20 trillion in exchanges deferred.

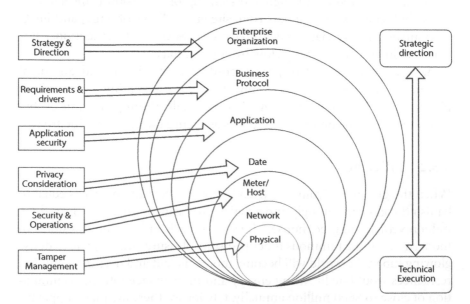

Figure 3.6 Smart grid layered approach to security considerations.

- Sun Microsystems gauges that a power outage costs the organization $1 million each and every moment.
- The Northeast power outage of 2003 brought about a $6 billion monetary misfortune to the locale. Intensifying the issue is a financial gadget tenaciously become computerized.

In Figure 3.6, the security considerations of smart grid in layer view is presented. During the 1980s, electrical burden from touchy advanced gear, for example, chips (mechanized frameworks, homegrown devices and hardware) and robotized producing was once when restricted. During the 1990s, chip share developed to generally 10%. Today, load from chip used sciences and modernized assembling has ascended to 40%, and the heap is anticipated to protract to expanded than 60% with the valuable asset of 2015 [6].

3.4   Creating the Platform for Smart Grid

In Figure 3.7, the smart grid architecture is presented creating a clever grid is slated to fee between $476 and $880 billion, and it will take years to achieve. But new Internet of Things (IoT) [30, 31] digital technological

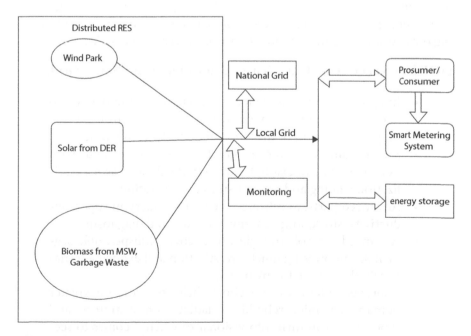

Figure 3.7 Smart grid architecture.

know-how can "smarten" today's grid quicker and at a decrease cost. It can additionally join all the players—electricity producers, customers, and transmission and distribution companies—providing non-stop comments to assist them make extra sustainable options now.

Businesses may additionally opt for to hire land to a wind farm, use photo voltaic panels throughout organization buildings, or run fleets of electric powered automobiles that each use and shop energy. Similarly, shoppers are an increasing number of shopping for photo voltaic panels and electric powered vehicles to be greater sustainable, as nicely as the use of clever meters and analytics to reveal and decrease consumption. Both of these agencies are probable to save and promote extra strength lower back to the grid. While in its infancy, the prosumer market is predicted to take off in the close to future. Mass adoption of self sustaining automobiles may advocate this movement [7].

3.4.1 Consider the ATM

It is accessible certainly anywhere. Every unit facets a comparable person interface, comprehensible whether you comprehend the nearby language. Users don't provide it a second thought. It genuinely works. Yet the reality that the ATM exists at all was once made feasible solely by means of industry-wide settlement on a multitude of frequent standards, from verbal exchange to safety to commercial enterprise rules. Fortunately, the agendas of utilities, regulators and automation carriers are unexpectedly aligning and motion towards figuring out and adopting Smart Grid requirements is gaining velocity.

DOE lists 5 crucial applied sciences that will force the Smart Grid:

- Integrated correspondences, associating components to open construction for ongoing realities and control, permitting each segment of the lattice to each 'talk' and 'tune in'.
- Sensing and size innovations, to help speedier and extra exact reaction, for example, far away checking, season of-utilization valuing and request side administration.
- Advanced parts, to rehearse the current query in superconductivity, stockpiling, energy hardware and diagnostics.
- Advanced control strategies, to uncover indispensable segments, empowering quick investigation and explicit alternatives unbelievable to any match.
- Improved interfaces and choice help, to settle on greater human dynamic, rebuilding lattice administrators and supervisors can turn into visionaries when it comes to seeing into their frameworks.

3.5   Smart Grid in Power Plants

Smart grid, a secure, integrated, reconfigurable, electronically managed device used to supply electric powered energy that operates in parallel with a regular energy grid. Although many of its aspects had been developed, and some implemented, all through the early twenty first century, as of 2016 no clever grid used to be but completely complete. In Figure 3.8, the smart grid in power plants is denoted in pictorial view. Simply defined, an electric powered electricity grid is a community of wires, transformers, substations, and machines that connects strength flowers with customers. In such a typical energy grid, electrical energy is disbursed in one direction, from strength plant to customers, thru a community that has few abilities of monitoring its transit and delivery.

By distinction to this "dumb grid," a "smart" energy grid would encompass an array of sensors, communications networks, manipulate systems, and computer systems that would enhance the efficiency, security, and reliability of the end-to-end system. In particular, a clever grid may want to react to and limit the affect of unexpected events, such as electricity outages, giving the grid an exceptional "self-healing" capability. Utilities would be in a position to cost clients variable quotes based totally on fluctuations in provide and demand, and buyers should programmatically regulate their use of electrical energy in order to decrease costs [8].

Finally, a more suitable and smarter grid should do a higher job of integrating wind energy and photo voltaic electricity into the electrical energy supply, and it ought to guide a device for charging plug-in electric powered vehicles.

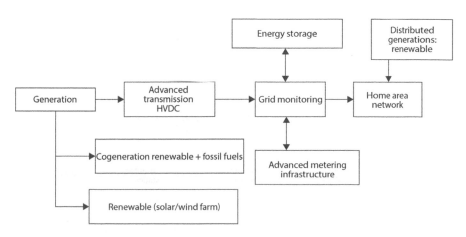

Figure 3.8 Smart grid in power plants.

3.5.1   Distributed Power Flow Control

Distributed power/gas float manage Power go with the flow manipulate units hooked up on energy traces can manipulate the go with the flow of energy within. These units aid increased use of renewable power through imparting greater consistent, real-time manage over how that strength is routed inside the SEG [9].

The science utilized through the created MAS for changing the strength line reactance comprises of an armada of DPFCs. Every framework has the usefulness of infusing a positive confirmation of inductance or capacitance into the line. Facilitated oversee of these units opens up bendy lattice based oversee inclinations via moving energy streams in agreement to Ohm's Law when set up in succession with the line.

The mechanical ability has been first acquired 2006 at Georgia Tech. First control establishments have been demonstrated in 2012 and 2013 with up to 100 contraptions known as Distributed Series Reactors (DSRs).

In Figure 3.9, the communication process of the smart grid from generating station to consumers is explained. DSRs are snared immediately on the actual conductors. The DSRs are fruitful of infusing up to 50 μH of inductance on order and may also be turned on consecutively to give the necessary phase of impedance at any time [10].

Simply nowadays' more prominent successful styles of the DSR-type and a Static Synchronous Series Compensator-type (SSSC) have been presented. The SSSC can substitute push power away from the over-burden line or draw strength onto a pitifully stacked line. By coupling a principle or slacking 90° voltage into the line the SSSC can supply the presentation of an assortment reactor and an arrangement capacitor. Every one of these units is snared on

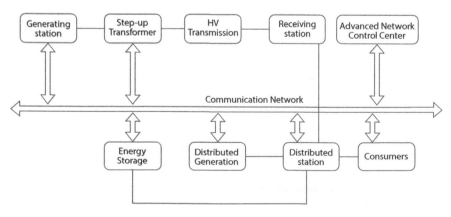

Figure 3.9 Communication network of smart grid.

the line towers, or are assembled on explicit pinnacles or help structures at the substation. The secluded chart of all DPFC styles allows quick establishment, customized setup and gathering as pleasantly as re-sending on various strength follows when load specifications change solidly.

All styles of DPFCs utilize the equivalent control and interchanges structure: The DPFCs on a strength line are connected among each unique by utilizing radio distant and are distributed to a regulator interface which speaks with the guide of IEC 60870-5-104 convention with the matrix control framework. Toward the IDEAL mission the DPFCs are overseen distantly by means of the MAS. This favors composed and quick changes of line impedances in a fit framework with numerous branches.

3.5.2   Power System Automation

Power-system automation is the act of routinely controlling the energy gadget by way of instrumentation and manages devices. Substation automation refers to the usage of information from Intelligent digital gadgets (IED), manipulate and automation competencies inside the substation, and manage instructions from far off customers to control power-framework gadgets. Since substation mechanization relies upon substation reconciliation, the expressions are consistently utilized full reciprocally [11].

Force framework robotization comprises of approaches related with age and transportation of force. Observing and oversee of energy transporting structures in the substation and on as far as possible the predominance of blackouts and abbreviate the length of blackouts that do happen. The IEDs, interchanges conventions, and specialized strategies, work by and large as a contraption to work power-framework mechanization. The time-frame "power framework" portrays the arrangement of contraptions that make up the real designs that produce, communicate, and convey power. The time span "instrumentation and oversee (I&C) framework" alludes to the arrangement of units that screen, control, and gatekeeper the power framework. Much force framework robotization is observed with the guide of SCADA.

3.5.3   IT Companies Disrupting the Energy Market

Smart grid offers IT-based options which the typical energy grid is lacking. These new options pave the way of new entrants that have been historically no longer associated to the electricity grid. Technology groups are disrupting the normal strength market gamers in various ways. They enhance complicated distribution structures to meet the extra decentralized strength era due to micro grids [12]. Additionally is the enlarge in statistics series bringing many new chances for technological know-how agencies as deploying transmission grid sensors at a person degree and balancing device reserves. The technological know-how in micro grids makes strength consumption more cost-effective for households [13] than shopping for from utilities.

Additionally, residents can control their strength consumption simpler and greater efficiently with the connection to clever meters. However, the performances and reliability of micro grids strongly rely on the non-stop interplay between electricity generation, storage and load requirements. A hybrid imparting combining renewable strength sources with storing power sources as coal and fuel is displaying the hybrid supplying of a micro grid serving alone.

3.6   Google in Smart Grid

Google, long a benefactor of sustainable power projects, server farm effectivity and homegrown force organization innovation, is currently plunging into the power framework itself. Google has been getting into framework perspective energy hardware as of late — shutting month, it dispatched a $1 million prize for more modest, more astute inverter plans by its Little Box Challenge [14]. In any case, it's in any case far from being a whole lattice science seller, rather than monsters like General Electric, Siemens, ABB, Schneider Electric and Alstom.

So the spot Google should plan to fill in the holes in the sharp network scene? Here's an overview of a portion of its unpracticed power and power organization endeavors in progress to date, to give us an encounter of the spot it has been and the spot it very well might be going:

- Google has put more noteworthy than $1 billion in photograph voltaic and wind strength errands in the past 5 years, making it a critical partner in the difficulty of how that irregular unpracticed power is inherent into the lattice.
- Google is also a partner in cutting edge lattice projects. It holds a 37.5 rate stake in the Atlantic Wind Connection, a conscious $5 billion transmission spine to join 7,000 megawatts of seaward wind power by utilizing a high-voltage, direct-momentum 250-mile transmission course between southern Virginia and northern New Jersey.

- Google has just been laying the foundation for extra exuberant investment in the network. In 2010, it obtained endorsement from the Federal Energy Regulatory Commission to advance and buy electrical energy like a utility. The pass gave Google additional adaptability by they way it dealt with its on location age, organized its solidarity purchase arrangements, and bridled electrical energy for its records habitats.
- Google as of now has a fundamental traction in the shrewd matrix zone with the guide of Google Maps, which fills in as the premise of a large group of new GIS structures for lattice planning and the executives. Last yr Google dispatched an organization with General Electric to blend Google Maps with GE's Small world electric, telecom and pipeline local area organization programming.
- Google has been extracting effectively from its realities offices throughout recent years, giving it discernment into how to control processing stuff and framework comparable to the network.

At long last, Google's homegrown force organization endeavors are subsequent to slowing down without its unsuccessful Power Meter project, which have grown tremendously with the $3.2 billion purchase of cunning indoor regulator creator Nest Labs. That allows Google 1 million and reported the purchase of the smart home-products startup Nest Labs was to "**capitalize on the development of devices and mobile software for the connected home**" and compete with companies such as Apple.

3.7   Smart Grid in Electric Cars

Smart grid query should consider consolidating sustainable power sources into the power local area and the provisioning of electric fueled vehicles. In a real astute lattice, electric fueled vehicles will at this point don't exclusively be competent to attract on electrical energy to run their engines, anyway they will furthermore be skilled to do the opposite: send electrical energy saved in their batteries again into the network when it is required.

- A mixture or gas versatile vehicle, which creates strength from storable fuel, utilizes its generator to deliver power for a utility at stature electrical energy use times [15]. Here the

engines fill in as a dispensed time framework, creating
strength from customary petroleum derivatives or hydrogen.

- A battery-controlled or module half and half vehicle, which
  utilizes its extra battery-powered battery capacity to outfit
  energy to the electric fueled matrix in light of extensive load
  requests. These vehicles would then be able to be revived for
  the term of off-top hours at more savvy costs while helping to absorb additional dead night age. Here the vehicles
  fill in as a dispensed battery stockpiling machine to support
  power.

- A photograph voltaic vehicle, which utilizes its extra charging
  ability to supply solidarity to the electric fueled matrix when
  the battery is altogether charged. Here the vehicle solidly
  will turn into a little inexhaustible power strength station.
  Such designs have been being used because of the reality the
  Nineteen Nineties and are consequently utilized on account of
  monster vehicles, extraordinarily sun based controlled boats.

3.7.1   Vehicle-to-Grid

The transmission of power from the smart grid which is fixed in vehicles to
grid is explained in Figure 3.10. Electric vehicles need to be respected now
not exclusively for their bodies anyway furthermore for their cerebrums.
As per Pike Research, the 2d rush of EVs and module electric controlled
vehicles are probably to be considerably more astute than the first as auto-
makers are improving their telematics highlights. Vehicle-to-grid (V2G)
depicts a contraption wherein module electric controlled cars (EVs. For
example, battery electric fueled vehicles and module half and half electric
controlled vehicles, talk with the strength framework to advance interest
reaction contributions both through giving over electrical energy into the
network or by methods for choking their charging rate [16].

Since most vehicles are left a basic of 95 level of the time, their batteries
ought to be utilized to allow electrical energy to float from the auto to the
power strains and back, with a cost to the utilities of up to $4,000 per yr
per vehicle. V2G is a model of battery-to-matrix strength used to vehicles.

There are three varieties of the vehicle-to-grid idea:
Smart network query should consider fusing sustainable power sources
into the strength local area and the provisioning of electric controlled vehicles. In a real smart matrix, electric fueled cars will now not exclusively be
in a situation to attract on electrical energy to run their engines; anyway,

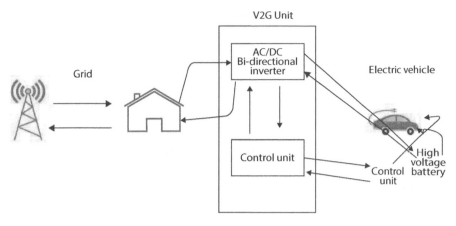

Figure 3.10 Smart grid in vehicle to grid.

they will moreover be in a situation to do the opposite: transport electrical energy saved in their batteries lower once more into the framework when it is required [17].

Overall, American vehicles get pushed for essentially one hour consistently. Most vehicles will have a lot of more battery limit. Energizing the total vehicle armada would allow extra than three occurrences the power created in the United States. On the other hand, it's vital for make certain people are currently not charging at the extremely top time, as late evening when the electrical energy matrix is weighted down through necessities like air-conditioning [18].

3.7.2   Challenges in Smart Grid Electric Cars

Perhaps the biggest test for the mass selection of electric fueled vehicles through customers is fluctuate uneasiness. Having pushed standard vehicles, the spot foundation for refueling is richly settled, customers are wary of the dead vehicle situation that an EV would perhaps present. Even though EV OEMs and battery makers are ceaselessly attempting to upgrade battery range, the connected presented costs with the all-inclusive change represent a threat for mass reception too. In the short run, shift anxiety might be tempered by utilizing creating financially savvy, long reach batteries by means of consistent query and by utilizing setting up an enough open charging smart lattice framework. In agreement to Frost and Sullivan, the answer is that OEMs and providers must work together for related contributions as a response [19].

electric car

Figure 3.11 Electric car.

The model of the electric car is given in Figure 3.11. Electric vehicles (EVs) are getting more famous, and this implies that traditional inner ignition vehicles will be supplanted by EVs soon. While EVs can have different advantages, opionions vary. For example, some experts argue the EVs are more efficient in energy consumption because they cause less metropolitan air contamination, and so on. Yet, one might ask, "where does the electricity come from. Therefore it could be possible that a misuse of EVs could occur without setting up a legitimate framework of responsible energy sources. Hence, a wholesome energy grid would prompt diverse bothersome results. The difficulties and outcomes incorporate, yet are not restricted to the following:

Force framework unwavering quality issues
Major issues in power generation and satisfying power need
Charging foundation

3.7.3   Toyota and Microsoft in Smart Electric Cars

Toyota and Microsoft dispatched a $12 million mission in 2011 to convey telematics to Toyota's vehicle by the cloud, and thus allowing owners to join to information contributions and control the batteries in their electric vehicles [20, 27]. They will make a global local area dependent on the Windows Azure distributed computing stage. Furthermore, growing a device through which vehicles like the moving toward RAV4 EV and module Prius talk with and draw energy from the network. We'll see it first in the electric fueled and module crossovers Toyota welcomed on a restricted scale in 2012.

3.8   Revisit the Risk

3.8.1   Reliability

A Smart Grid that foresees, distinguishes, and reacts to inconveniences quickly decreases wide-territory power outages to towards strength autonomy from abroad power sources, which themselves may furthermore be targets for assault, open air of our wellbeing and control. The smart grid utilizes applied sciences, for example, country assessment, that improve deficiency location and grant self-mending of the local area aside from the intercession of professionals. This will make certain greater dependable furnish of electricity, and decreased vulnerability to herbal failures or attack [21].

Albeit several courses are promoted as an attribute of the astute matrix, the noteworthy framework also included more than one courses. Starting power follows in the network have been built the utilization of an outspread model, later availability was once guaranteed by more than one course, alluded to as a local area structure. Nonetheless, this made another issue:

In the event that the cutting-edge float or related outcomes all through the local area surpass the restrictions of any remarkable local area

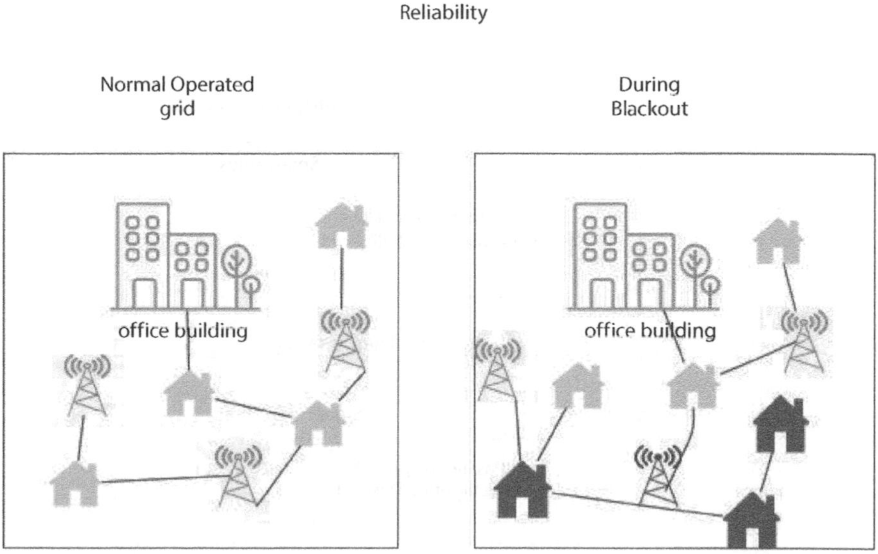

Figure 3.12 Blackouts in reliability.

component, it should fall flat, and the current day would be shunted to various local area components, which in the end may moreover flop additionally, incurring a domino impact. See Figure 3.12 for the blackouts in reliability. See strength blackout. A technique to hinder this is load shedding through intentional power outage or voltage rebate (brownout) [22].

3.8.2 Efficiency

It is assessed that huge number of bucks will be saved gratitude to request reaction applications that supply quantifiable, power monetary reserve funds and require no human mediation or lead change.

In Figure 3.13, the energy efficiency in smart grid is represented. The dramatically decreased want to construct extra electricity flowers and transmission traces help, too. Numerous contribution to general enhancement of the effectively of strength infrastructure are predicted from the deployment of clever grid technology, in unique consisting of demand-side management, for instance turning off air conditioners throughout momentary spikes in electrical energy price, decreasing the voltage when viable on distribution traces thru Voltage/VAR Optimization (VVO), getting rid of truck-rolls for meter reading, and lowering truck-rolls via multiplied outage administration the usage of information from Advanced Metering Infrastructure systems. The common impact is much less redundancy in

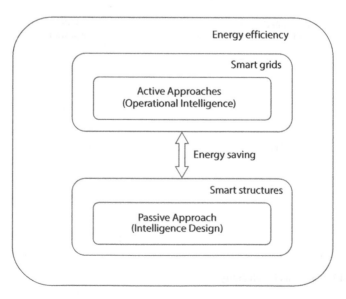

Figure 3.13 Energy efficiency in smart grid.

transmission and distribution lines, and larger utilization of generators, main to decrease energy prices.

3.8.3   Security

The Smart Grid will be greater resistant to assault and herbal disasters. So fortified, it will additionally pass us towards power independence from overseas strength sources, which themselves can also be goals for attack, outdoor of our safety and control. While modernization of electrical grids into clever grids approves for optimization of everyday processes, a clever grid, being online, can be susceptible to cyber-attacks. Transformers which expand the voltage of electrical energy created at energy vegetation for long-distance travel, transmission strains themselves, and distribution strains which supply the electrical energy to its shoppers are in particular susceptible [23].

These structures be counted on sensors which collect records from the subject and then supply it to manipulate centers, the place algorithms automate evaluation and decision-making processes.

These choices are dispatched lower back to the field, the place present tools execute them. Hackers have the viable to disrupt these computerized manipulate systems, severing the channels which enable generated electrical energy to be utilized. This is referred to as a denial of carrier or DoS attack.

They can additionally launch integrity assaults which corrupt facts being transmitted alongside the device as properly as desynchronization assaults which have an effect on when such records is delivered to the fabulous location. Additionally, intruders can once more get right of entry to by using renewable power era structures and clever meters related to the grid, taking gain of greater specialized weaknesses or ones whose safety has no longer been prioritized.

Because a clever grid has a giant wide variety of get admission to point, like clever meters, defending all of its susceptible factors can show difficult. There is additionally difficulty on the safety of the infrastructure, specially that involving communications technology.

Concerns especially middle round the communications technological know-how at the coronary heart of the clever grid. Designed to enable real-time contact between utilities and meters in customers' properties and businesses, there is a hazard that these competencies should be exploited for crook or even terrorist actions.

One of the key skills of this connectivity is the capacity to remotely change off energy supplies, enabling utilities to shortly and effortlessly stop or alter resources to clients who default on payment. This is absolutely a big boon for power providers; however, additionally raises some giant safety issues.

Cybercriminals have infiltrated the U.S. electric powered grid earlier than on several occasions. Aside from laptop infiltration, there are additionally worries that laptop malware which focused SCADA structures which are extensively used in industry, ought to be used to assault a clever grid network [24].

3.8.4   National Economy

Opening the grid to advancement will permit markets to create liberated and development to prosper. For the wellbeing of correlation, consider the market-production effect of the kickoff of the PDA undertaking during the 1980s [25]. With incomes of $33 billion at that point, the resulting multiplication of purchaser driven product and contributions changed over it into a $117 billion market starting at 2006.

3.9   Summary

Conventional force grid can be redesigned into smart grids by fusing two-way coordinated interchanges and smart processing capacities for improved productivity, dependability, and choice help.

Smart grid empowers us to utilize both customary fuel source for example carbon-based powers and sustainable power source for example wind and sunlight-based energy. Carbon fuel-based force plants can help out environmentally [28, 29] friendly power plants to diminish the carbon fuel utilization and contamination brought about by it.

A smart grid conveys power among provider and shopper utilizing two-way advanced innovation. To build dependability, straightforwardness and to lessen cost and save energy smart grids can be utilized.

It joins modernization of customary power network by giving continuous checking of force utilization which encourages customers to limit their cost on ordinary energy by changing their home apparatuses activity to maintain a strategic distance from top hours and use the sustainable assets.

References

1. Zahra, M. (2013) Smart Grid Technology, Vision, Management and Control. WSEAS TRANSACTIONS on SYSTEMS, 12, 11-21.
2. Isere, M., Saunter, T. and Hung, J.Y. (2010) Future Energy Systems: Integrating Renewable Energy Sources into the Smart Power Grid through Industrial Electronics. IEEE Industrial Electronics Magazine, 4, 18-37.

3. Dr.U.Niehage, "Pathways to a Smart Grid," Power Transmission and Distribution—Siemens, November 8, 2007. http://www.smartgrid.eu/documents/2ndGA/Niehage.pdf

4. S. Rahman, "The Smart Grid and Its Impact on the Integration of Distributed Energy Resources," Southeast University, Nanjing, April 2, 2009.

5. P. F. Ruiz, "Towards Smart Power Networks," Lessons Learned from European Research FP5 projects- European Commission in 2005, 2005. http://ec.europa.eu/research/energy.pdf/towards

6. IBM, "Smart Grid Overview—IBM," International Exhibition and Conference—Gridtech 2009, New Delhi, January 29-30, 2009.

7. D. P. Kothari and I. J. Nagrath, "Modern Power system Analysis," 3rd Edition, McGraw Hill, New York, 2006.

8. Rajesh Kumar, D., & Shanmugam, A. (2017). A Hyper Heuristic Localization Based Cloned Node Detection Technique Using GSA Based Simulated Annealing in Sensor Networks. In Cognitive Computing for Big Data Systems Over IoT (pp. 307–335). Springer International Publishing.

9. V. C. Gungor and F. C. Lambert, —A survey on communication networks for electric system automation, Comput. Networks, vol. 50, pp. 877–897, May 2006.

10. S. Paudyal, C. Canizares, and K. Bhattacharya, —Optimal operation of distribution feeders in smart grids, IEEE Trans. Ind. Electron., vol. 58, no. 10, pp. 4495–4503, Oct. 2011.

11. D. M. Laverty, D. J. Morrow, R. Best, and P. A. Crossley, —Telecommunications for smart grid: Backhaul solutions for the distribution network, in Proc. IEEE Power and Energy Society General Meeting, Jul. 25–29, 2010, pp. 1–6.

12. L. Wenpeng, D. Sharp, and S. Lancashire, —Smart grid communication network capacity planning for power utilities, in Proc. IEEE PES, Transmission Distrib. Conf. Expo., Apr. 19–22, 2010, pp. 1–4.

13. Y. Peizhong, A. Iwayemi, and C. Zhou, —Developing ZigBee deployment guideline under WiFi interference for smart grid applications, IEEE Trans. Smart Grid, vol. 2, no. 1, pp. 110–120, Mar. 2011.

14. C. Gezer and C. Buratti, —A ZigBee smart energy implementation for energy efficient buildings, in Proc. IEEE 73rd Veh. Technol. Conf. (VTC Spring), May 15–18, 2011, pp. 1–5.

15. R. P. Lewis, P. Igic, and Z. Zhongfu, —Assessment of communication methods for smart electricity metering in the U.K., in Proc. IEEE PES/IAS Conf. Sustainable Alternative Energy (SAE), Sep. 2009, pp. 1–4.

16. Dhiviya, S., Malathy, S., & Kumar, D. R. (2018). Internet of Things (IoT) Elements, Trends and Applications. Journal of Computational and Theoretical Nanoscience, 15(5), 1639–1643.

17. M. Y. Zhai, —Transmission characteristics of low-voltage distribution networks in China under the smart grids environment, IEEE Trans. Power Delivery, vol. 26, no. 1, pp. 173–180, Jan. 2011.

18. V. Paruchuri, A. Durresi, and M. Ramesh, —Securing powerline communications, in Proc. IEEE Int. Symp. Power Line Commun. Appl., (ISPLC), Apr. 2–4, 2008, pp. 64–69.

19. Q.Yang, J. A. Barria, and T. C. Green, —Communication infrastructures for distributed control of power distribution networks, IEEE Trans. Ind. Inform., vol. 7, no. 2, pp. 316–327, May 2011.

20. T. Sauter and M. Lobashov, —End-to-end communication architecture for smart grids, IEEE Trans. Ind. Electron., vol. 58, no. 4, pp. 1218–1228, Apr. 2011.

21. K. Moslehi and R. Kumar, —Smart grid—A reliability perspective, Innovative Smart Grid Technologies (ISGT), pp. 1–8, Jan. 19–21, 2010.

22. Southern Company Services, Inc., —Comments request for information on smart grid communications requirements, Jul. 2010.

23. R. Bo and F. Li, —Probabilistic LMP forecasting considering load uncertainty, IEEE Trans. Power Syst., vol. 24, pp. 1279–1289, Aug. 2009.

24. Krishnasamy, L., Dhanaraj, R. K., Ganesh Gopal, D., Reddy Gadekallu, T., Aboudaif, M. K., & Abouel Nasr, E. (2020). A Heuristic Angular Clustering Framework for Secured Statistical Data Aggregation in Sensor Networks. Sensors, 20(17), 4937

25. G. Bumiller, —Single frequency network technology for fast ad hoc communication networks over power lines, WiKuWissenschaftsverlag Dr. Stein 2010.

26. S.Malathy, Dr.C.N.Vanitha, "Secure Integration of Cyber Security and Internet of Things in Addressing its Challenges", International Journal of Recent Technology and Engineering, ISSN: 2277-3878,Volume 8, Issue 4, November 2019.

27. K.Vanitha, C.N.Vanitha, M.Mohamed Musthafa, S.Malathy, "Efficient Semantic Interrogation Scheme over Cryptographic Data in Cloud" IEEE Xplore Digital Library, DOI:10.1109/ICICT48043.2020.9112383, June 2020.

28. Dhanaraj, R.K., Islam, S.H. & Rajasekar, V. A cryptographic paradigm to detect and mitigate blackhole attack in VANET environments. Wireless Netw., (2022). https://doi.org/10.1007/s11276-022-03017-6

29. Das, B., Mushtaque, A., Memon, F., Dhanaraj, R. K., Thirumalaisamy, M., Shaikh, M. Z., Nighat, A., & Gismalla, M. S. M. (2022). Real-Time Design and Implementation of Soft Error Mitigation Using Embedded System. In Journal of Circuits, Systems and Computers. World Scientific Pub Co Pte Ltd. https://doi.org/10.1142/s0218126622502802

30. Dhiviya, S., Malathy, S., & Kumar, D. R. (2018). Internet of Things (IoT) Elements, Trends and Applications. Journal of Computational and Theoretical Nanoscience, 15(5), 1639–1643. https://doi.org/10.1166/jctn.2018.7354

31. Dhanaraj, R. K., Rajkumar, K., & Hariharan, U. (2020). Enterprise IoT Modeling: Supervised, Unsupervised, and Reinforcement Learning. In Business Intelligence for Enterprise Internet of Things (pp. 55–79). Springer International Publishing. https://doi.org/10.1007/978-3-030-44407-5_3

4

IoT-Based Energy Management Strategies in Smart Grid

Seyed Ehsan Ahmadi[1]* and Sina Delpasand[2]

[1]*Northumbria University, Electrical Power and Control Systems Research Group, Ellison Place NE1 8ST, Newcastle upon Tyne, UK*
[2]*Faculty of New Sciences and Technologies, University of Tehran, Tehran, Iran*

Abstract

The Internet of things (IoT) enable advanced technologies mostly on the basis of advanced metering infrastructure and intelligent devices. In order to balance energy between generation and consumption sides and to realize the economic, reliable, and robust operation of energy systems with Smart Grid (SG) applications, an Energy Management System (EMS) should be established. Therefore, several models can be assigned for the EMS to handle the energy exchange and data communication among the participants to guarantee their privacy and self-sufficiency in the decision-making process. Accordingly, the IoT enables to analysis, share, and utilization of data gathered from different levels of an EMS. Furthermore, demand side management (DSM) programs as an imperative feature of EMSs can be proposed to enhance systematic application of network resources and reduce peak load demands. Based on the mentioned motivations, this chapter comprehensively reviews the energy management strategies in SG. The application of IoT facility for energy management in SGs is presented considering diverse types of EMS at the SG, i.e., smart home EMS and smart building EMS. Besides, network operator, data and communication technologies, and aggregators are reviewed as the participants of EMSs. Various distributed energy resources such as renewable energy sources, plug-in electric vehicles, and energy storage systems are also addressed. Moreover, the uncertainty management methods, power quality management, and DSM programs are reviewed to address vital factors in EMS implementation in SG.

Keywords: Energy management, smart grid, Internet of Things, distributed energy resources, demand response, optimization approaches

Corresponding author: ehsanahmadi94@gmail.com

P. Sanjeevikumar, Rajesh Kumar Dhanaraj, Malathy Sathyamoorthy, Jens Bo Holm-Nielsen and Balamurugan Balusamy (eds.) *Smart Grids and Internet of Things: An Energy Perspective*, (91–126) © 2023 Scrivener Publishing LLC

4.1   Introduction

The increased utilization of alternative Renewable Energy Sources (RES) creates the major issue for reliable and flexible scheduling of the Smart Grid (SG) [1]. Thus, integration of renewable-based communication frameworks including Wind Turbine (WT) and Photovoltaic (PV) can establish a more intelligent, interconnected, efficient, and reliable power grid [2]. A smart communication mostly consists of Internet of things (IoT) authorized advanced technologies mainly based on advanced metering infrastructure (AMI) and intelligent devices. An intelligent facility is required for the effective processing of big data [3, 4]. An Energy Management System (EMS) for the SG can help to sustain the energy balance between generation and consumption, assuring whole grid constraints to realize the economic, reliable, and robust scheduling of the energy system. It can be mentioned that optimization can guarantees the reduced energy cost. Accordingly, an EMS minimizes the energy cost requested for a particular employment by cooperating with all systematic proceedings [5]. Many researchers have considered various management strategies in SGs including smart home EMS, smart building EMS, and EMS aggregator, but some of them have investigated the model of uncertainties, optimization methods, and solution approaches applied in EMS. The centralized, decentralized (or distributed) and hierarchical EMS framework can be proposed for controlling and managing the participants in the SGs. The major participants of an EMS include generation, transmission, distribution, and end-users. Accordingly, many models can be assigned for the EMS to deal with the energy exchange and data communication among the participants to ensure their privacy and independence in decision-making objectives [6].

The majority of the data flow in the SG structure is bi-directional. This feature ensures decision-making process to Distributed Energy Resources (DER), energy users, Plug-in Electric Vehicle (PEV) owners, aggregators, and various agents, particularly for programs such as Demand Response (DR) and Demand-Side Management (DSM), which allows consumers to participate through enabling services for the reliable and flexible scheduling of the network. Accordingly, IoT enables to analysis, share, and use of data collected from diverse levels of an EMS [7, 8]. Novel procedures have supported the energy network to become more intelligent but introduce various uncertainties such as RES-based uncertainty in the generation, and uncertainty in the forecasted load. Diverse approaches to deal with the uncertainties can be classified into probabilistic, fuzzy, robust, etc. [9]. On the other hand, DR and DSM are two imperative features of EMSs that cooperate to enhance systematic application of network resources and decrease peak load demands. It ensures the reliable scheduling of the system, higher performance, and reduction of voltage adjustment issues. Both DR and DSM programs are proposed to maximize the employment of available resources, enhancing performance, reliability, adjusting the load profile, and other advantages [10].

In this chapter, the energy management strategies in SG are investigated comprehensively. Initially, for a closer look at the basics of the issue, the application of IoT for energy management in SGs is presented. The EMS is significantly reviewed, in which the objectives of EMS and the three control frameworks of EMS containing centralized, decentralized, and hierarchical approaches are discussed. Then, the types of EMS at the SG, i.e., smart home EMS and smart building EMS are presented to cover the SG applications. In another section, the participants of EMS are investigated. The network operator, data and communication technologies, and aggregators are reviewed separately in this section. Besides, the DER scheduling such as RES, PEVs, and Energy Storage Systems (ESSs) are also addressed. Later, important factors for EMS establishment are comprehensively studied. Also, the uncertainty management methods, Power Quality Management (PQM), and DSM and DR programs are reviewed to address vital factors in EMS implementation in SG. For a further investigation, the solution approaches for EMS are discussed.

4.2   Application of IoT for Energy Management in Smart Grids

The data developed in a SG is extremely high compared to the existing electrical network. The massive processing of data is for the sake of the continuous bi-directional communication between main grid (central controller) and Smart Meters (SMs) or local controller established at the local areas. Smart framework is required for the effective management of massive information. If an appropriate structure is not ensured for the mentioned bi-directional communication, it can impede the implementation of the SG. Accordingly, the IoT facility undertakes an important role. The IoT facility comes to the aid of narrowing down the transfer of massive information among the main grid and the consumers through a proper IP (Internet protocol). The application of IoT in SG is important where there is a power deficiency in the system. It supports the required backup generating units to compensate for the power deficiency.

Figure 4.1 demonstrates the main layers of IoT application in SGs. The IoT facility is also desired to perform effectual communication between the SMs established at the placement of user and the placed sensors to switch the equipment regarding the demand profile. By use of SMs with internet

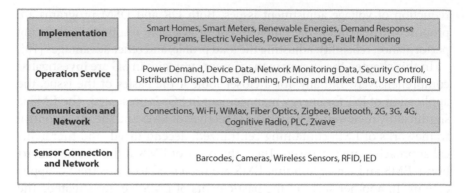

Figure 4.1 Main layers of IoT application in SGs [11].

Table 4.1 Sections of IoT application in SG [11].

Section	Illustrative cases
Energy Supply and Peak Load	SM Reading; EMS for Smart Transmission and Distribution Networks; Online Monitoring of Power Generation Units (Unit Commitment).
Residential, Commercial, and Industrial	Home EMS; Charging/Discharging of PEVs; Model of DR Program.
Users/Utilities	Reading of Diverse Energy Forms in SMs (Electricity, Gas, etc); Management of Finances; Distributed Generations.

connection for all users, the network monitors and obtains the load profile constantly. Table 4.1 shows requirement of IoT facilities in different sections of SGs. Furthermore, gathered information from a SM could be employed to develop fault detection and restoration in the energy networks [11].

4.3 Energy Management System

4.3.1 Objectives of EMS

A single objective or multiple objectives can be assigned for the EMS with technical, economic, techno-economic, ecological, and socio-economic approaches. Technical objectives contain device efficiency and power quality constraints. Investigation of technical objectives ensures the higher efficiency of the network, higher power supplying, and enhance life-time. Utilization of RES-based units, ESSs, and PEVs without appropriate cooperation may result in system aberration from its expected performance, e.g., inconvenient PEV charging, and discharging may increase temperature of transformers, and also inconvenient utilization of RES-based units leads aberration in power and other considerable problems. By establishing relevant EMS strategy, technical objectives and corresponding constraints should be considered in the problem. Economic objectives imply total operation cost, energy cost to the users, revenue increase of parking lot owners and aggregators, etc. Notably, without taking into account technical constraints, the optimization of EMS may ensure the optimal profit. Ecological objectives include emission reduction to generate low carbon energy scheduling diverse fossil-based and renewable-based generations. Socio-economic objectives are investigated to regulate the social activities including different programs in which consumers and generation units can actively participate to meet optimal economic solution [12].

4.3.2   Control Frameworks of EMS

The performance of EMS highly is dependent on the management frame work, and the proposed solution procedure, mainly applied frameworks are centralized, decentralized (or distributed), and hierarchical approaches. The mentioned management frameworks are reviewed below in detail for figuring out the advantages and disadvantages of employing them to SG.

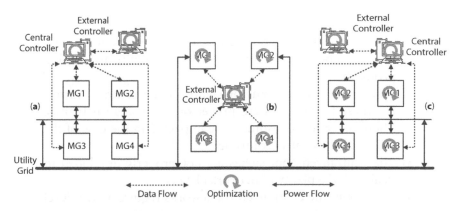

Figure 4.2 Overview of EMS frameworks: (a) centralized; (b) decentralized; (c) hierarchical.

Figure 4.2 illustrates the control frameworks of EMS in the network with Multi-Microgrids (MGs) [13]. The control frameworks of EMS shown in Figure 4.2 are discussed below in detail.

4.3.2.1   Centralized Approach

The centralized management framework is identified through a controlling center with an affective data processing system and a reliable communication structure to control energy consumption. In centralized framework, all participants will individually collaborate and associate exclusively with a controlling center. The controlling center should be able to verify, collect, and evaluate real-time information and ensure all devices with applicable management commands [14].

The centralized frameworks have been widely applied in SGs due to the significant coordination potential within DERs. Real-time monitoring capability and straightforward application are the main features of centralized approaches. Besides, private information can be protected inside the controlling center. The mentioned features mean that EMS requires to be effective to handle large data while making an appropriate decision [15]. The centralized framework ensures optimal global performance, but it has its proper share of imperfections as well. Due to the growing penetration of DERs and prosumers/consumers, the centralized algorithms are no longer efficient, because they are impotent in monitoring and controlling SGs. Although the centralized frameworks are comprehensively applied for controlling of numerous energy networks in past years, they cannot be an appropriate option for IoT applications. Furthermore, it implicates a single point of failure. The main reasons behind this can be mentioned as follows [16]:

1) Centralized frameworks are not straightforward to develop and are not suitable for SGs as they require to develop promptly.
2) Due to the single point of failure of the central controller, these frameworks are proper only for small networks. Therefore, a few consumers are impacted in the case of the failure of the central controller.
3) The centralized approaches are not properly developed to deal with the plenty of network players.
4) Last point, the centralized frameworks require a great level of connection since each agent should directly communicate with the central operator.

generation and consumption for a flexible and stable performance of the SGs. The EMS is one of the practical methods to effectively decrease energy consumption in SGs. The EMS enables the ability to energize device if needed. One of the main objectives of the EMS in SG is to control energy flow by determining the optimal energy distribution. By introducing the EMSs, the average energy consumption of the manufacturing companies is reduced from 5% to 15%, depending on the company's energy level of quality [19]. In this section, the smart home and smart building EMSs a~ reviewed to identify their applications in SGs.

4.4.1   Smart Home EMS

The idea of smart home has made much attention am~ researchers due to the covering diverse sorts of er~ storages, and managing appliances to regularly a~ EMS in residential places are enabled with h~ local and remote controllable loads, RES-~ tery ESSs to establish an autonomou~ system. However, considering unce~ energy prices, a residential cons~ ate his/her local energy con~ viously, the EMS can be a~ or management sche~ residential place t~ decrease opera~ tem. Comm~ dential plac~ units is stron~ identified as an a~ take into account u~ applied in the system t~

A typical smart hom~ Common energy resource~ sented. The EMS of smart h~ PEV batteries, and various types~ is a decision-making design that ca~ casts alternation of current power p~ local information of energy demand fro~ sumption behavior. This system (as demons~ for daily scheduling, in which on/off state ot~ planned in the previous day [21].

4.3.2.2   Decentralized Approach

The decentralized framework is identified through the distributed operating structure with each local area having a self-sufficient communication and management facilities. Therefore, the decentralized framework with increasing extensibility, nates imperfections of centralized framework, and preventing single-point fail-enabling higher reliability of connection support procedure of whole net-ure. Specifically, if connectivity of several controllers among units are lost, the whole network can keep sustained. The decentralized EMS framework does not necessitate a high level of connection. The decentralized framework is majorly relying on the local parameters. Besides, decentralized EMS framework does not require going via entire decisions support procedure of whole net-work by utilizing one central controller; thus, it is not constrained by a huge calculation burden. According to the level of decentralization pro-vided, the decentralized framework can be classified into three scheduling modes including fully self-sufficient, partially self-sufficient, and com-pletely dependent. In the completely dependent scheduling mode, the local controllers interact with each other through a central management system.

Although the interaction between local controlling devices is constrained on a central management system, solution is obtained by themselves and not centralized management system. As previously mentioned, the cen-tralized EMS provides global optimization; thus, ensures lower total oper-ating cost, however, local energy management in decentralized framework cannot ensure an optimal operation and is more reliable compared to the centralized framework guarantees fast response cost. Noting that the decentralized framework in SG applications are impactful factors for controlling systems in SGs with IoT facility because:

- IoT facilities in SGs are s~ ~tion ~ance and promote framework over multiagent over

- IoT facility is apportioned between multiagent over adaptivity.

- Calculated profit is apportioned between multiagent over the IoT facility.

- IoT cannot be influenced by a single-point failure.

- IoT cannot be influenced by dynamic structure.

- IoT confirms real-time feature.

4.3.2.3   Hierarchical Approach

According to the decentralized framework, the hierarchical manage-ment strategy is investigated for a single microgrid or interconnected

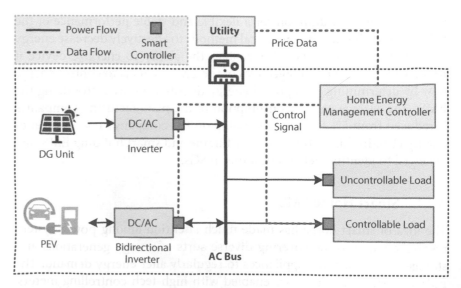

Figure 4.4 Smart home EMS architecture [21].

The main objectives of these management systems are to manage and optimize power flow and energy consumption. The EMS of smart homes have substantial utilizations in generation, transmission, and distribution sides of power network, and these systems can have an important role at the SGs. The main notable features among the applications contain supervised control and collective information with the EMS functional capabilities. Accordingly, DSM and DR programs which are taken into account to provide proper resolutions to network operator, have promoted drive for more smart EMS. Generally, EMS of smart home provides either of these capabilities: 1) A profitable outline of diverse illustrative types of energy consumption information; 2) Enhanced responsibilities contain data, technology, and management via a controlling center; 3) Joint systems with all properties of developed operations and potential for predicting and operating of local demands; 4) Intelligent functions ensure user decision to realize preferences of residential device. Like any other EMSs, the smart home EMS has the final objectives to maintain energy, reduce operation cost and enhance user's comfort [22].

4.4.2 Smart Building EMS

Smart building EMS is the data-processing system that manages electrical and mechanical devices in buildings. The smart building EMS connects

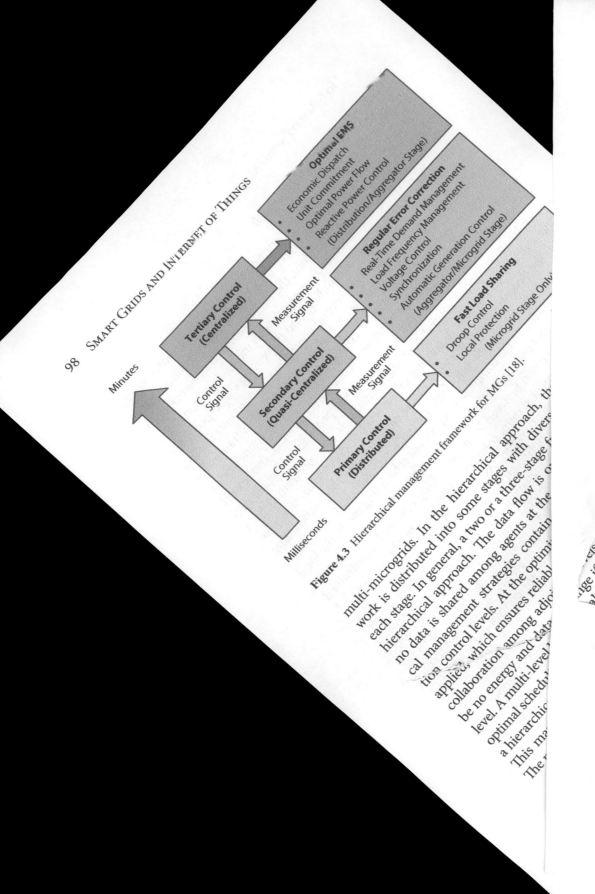

Figure 4.3 Hierarchical management framework for MGs [18].

multi-microgrids. In the hierarchical approach, the work is distributed into some stages with diverse each stage. In general, a two or a three-stage hierarchical approach. The data flow is o no data is shared among agents at the tion control strategies contain applied, which ensures reliab collaboration among adji be no energy and data level. A multi-level optimal schedu a hierarchic This the building devices to a control center to provide controlling commands of on/off times, humidity, temperatures, etc. The smart building EMS also enables monitoring, control systems, and required alarm signals and provides the operators to optimize the building efficiency. The smart building EMS is a crucial component for controlling energy consumption, particularly in huge complex buildings and multi-building areas. Input commands transferred to EMS of smart building can control the rates of temperature, humidity, etc. Then, outputs transfer commands from centralized control center to implemented components including pumps, valves, fans, etc. to set their required settings or to switch appliances on/off. The smart building EMS can be applied to manage nearly all devices and to control urgent devices simultaneously [23].

A smart building EMS is an actual tool for controlling the energy in buildings, therefore, an expert operator can apply the smart building EMS to optimize the required adjusting to enhance energy profits without ignoring essential functions. The smart building EMS can greatly improve entire management and efficiency of buildings, enhancing comprehensive approach to managing schedule feedback. It can be mentioned that power and energy savings of about 10–20% can be realized by implementing a proper smart building EMS compared to the individual controllers for each operating system. However, the smart building EMS cannot compensate for improperly designed systems, inaccurate maintenance, or unsatisfactory management. The smart building EMS is generally ideal for enabling the management of multi-building areas. A smart building EMS requires to be properly established and designed with excellent documentation. Also, it is feasible to attain acceptable management by applying autonomous controls for various types of energy demands in small buildings. In this case, the controlling system may be a less expensive option than a thorough smart building EMS. Accordingly, the smart building EMS can be investigated for energy managing any size of the buildings, however, the enhancement in control system extremely becomes noticeable in large, distributed building areas. Providing proper consumer interfaces with a smart building EMS is important.

The architecture of the smart building EMS is demonstrated into Figure 4.5. The left section is related to the graphical user interface employed principally to manage the energy performance. Accessibility via interfaces and dynamic displays offers online scheduling and enables remote control and monitoring devices. The middle section is the local zone networks interface which helps users to entirely access data from the smart building and its settings anyway. The right section is related to the control systems and the corresponding sensors throughout the building. Amount of

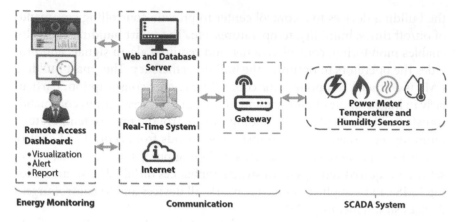

Figure 4.5 Architecture of smart building EMS.

energy consumption and values temperature and humidity of the residential buildings can be measured applying diverse sensors, and required data can be sent via web browsers through Internet infrastructure to switch on/off mechanical and electrical equipment including air conditioners, control heating system, boilers, pumps, etc. Required signal is sent to the controllers via Internet infrastructure and essential command is issued. Based on the set points, each controller will continue its function until it reaches desired state, and updated data can be also monitored via Internet infrastructure and browsing diverse devices. Providing suitable access routes enables the operator of building to apply EMS of smart building as an optimization tool.

The monitoring capability of a smart building EMS provides controlling of device status and power consumption with a real-time scheduling procedure. These facilities ensure recognition of issues which may be insignificant. Smart building EMS can enhance management data collection by reporting system efficiency. The main advantage of a smart building EMS implementation is that consumers can assess the efficiency of the controls and appropriately can make regulations [24]. Other benefits of smart building EMS can be noted as follows:

> The Precise management of ecological status;
> Ensuring improved support for residents;
> Energy-saving management objectives that will decrease energy bills;
> Capability to record and archive data for management objectives;

Providing prompt information on generation units status;
Automated initiation of alarms during system faults or alternation of expected status;
Detection of both scheduled and unscheduled maintenance provisions;
The convenience of development to control other devices, areas, or buildings.

4.5   Participants of EMS

In this section, the network operator, data and communication technologies, and aggregators are reviewed as the key factors of the EMS at the generation and consumption sides of the SG. The main participants of EMS are the utility grid, the DNO, the Transmission System Operator (TSO), the low-level prosumers (means both consumers and producers), etc. Each participant has their operational constraints established in EMS algorithms. Participants of the SG are mainly linked with communication frameworks to exchange vital data. The required data of computation and control are

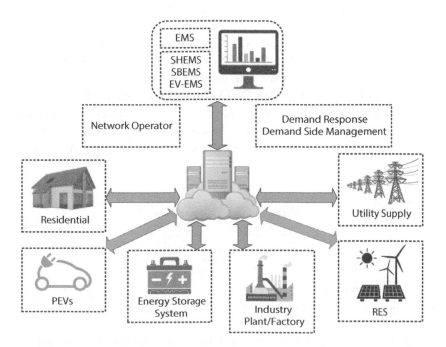

Figure 4.6 Participants of EMS in SG environment.

exchanged via the ICT interface. Figure 4.6 demonstrates diverse participants of the EMS with the bidirectional communication framework. The
proposed bi-directional data flow ensures decision support to RES-based
units, prosumers, PEV owners, local aggregators, and agents, particularly
for DSM and DR programs. This framework provides prosumers to effectively participate in the EMS to present active services for a flexible and
reliable SG scheduling. Accordingly, IoT and big data monitoring enable
to investigate, exchange, and apply data collected from various levels of the
EMS [25].

4.5.1   Network Operator

Each SG has its hierarchical structure for network operations. The network
operator's function is to provide sustained supply and demand balance
cost-effectively with a particular level of flexibility and reliability with the
lowest environmental effects. The Independent System Operator (ISO) has
its assignment and commitment at the transmission level such as establishing stability and balance among generating units and distribution level
since the power supply at low voltage side is key function of DNOs. Figure
4.7 demonstrates assignment of each network participants. The function of
the network operator is to handle the problems of congestion, overloading,
etc.

The expeditious increase of RES-based units and ESSs in the energy and
electricity section requires the employment of a moderator, where TSOs
or DNOs play an important role to establish optimal performance. The
major responsibility of TSO or DNO is to control assets, network potential,
and performance of network participants. It can be noted that centralized
prevalent sources and various RES-based units can give their ancillary services straightaway to TSO and get the scheduling commands back from

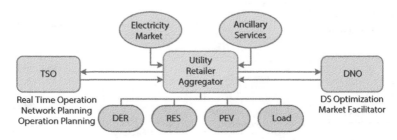

Figure 4.7 Assignment and commitment of transmission and distribution system
operators.

them, while the distributed energy sources and prosumers (or consumers) give their services to and get the scheduling commands back from the DNO. The DNO can promote free access to the local and general electricity markets, allows users to act as prosumers at high levels, and control the utilization of distributed sources for ensuring reliable, ecological, and cost-effective power supply [26].

4.5.2   Data and Communication Technologies

Information and Communications Technologies (ICTs) present an important feature in effective application, development, and operation of the EMS. Smart, reliable, and prompt communication framework is important for communication among the wide range of distributed resources, i.e., DGs, ESSs, and local consumers, to provide real-time information exchange and other required data for network management. Accordingly, a strong communication framework is required for providing an enhancement referring to performance, dependability, resilience, and financial support for all network participators in a management system. The communication technologies applied for powerful EMS performance can be generally classified into wired and wireless groups. Categorized wired and wireless technologies are illustrated in Figure 4.8. Besides, the different wired and wireless technologies regarding transfer protocols and ranges, applications, advantages, and disadvantages are compared in Table 4.2 [7].

It can be mentioned that the communication necessity of an EMS relies on style of EMS application. The centralized framework involves determined and resilient communication structure. For example, Programmable Logic Controller (PLC), Supervisory Control and Data Acquisition (SCADA), and optical fiber are illustrious classical technologies, however, they are still favored technologies for wired connection infrastructure in centralized framework. A SCADA system is fundamentally a centralized controlling system on a wide scale. SCADA is not an online controller

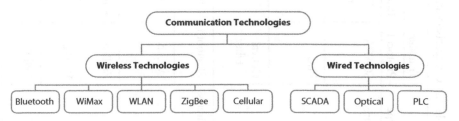

Figure 4.8 Wired and wireless communication technologies [7].

Table 4.2 Comparison among wired and wireless communication technologies [7].

| Type | Transfer | | Application | Advantages | Disadvantages |
	Protocol	Range			
Wired	SCADA	≈ Thousand mile	Desired for centralized EMS	Ability to handle huge data, enables sensor connections, RTU connection feasible, faster response	Need experienced operator, further cost, more complex
	PLC	≈ 200 Km	Suitable for centralized EMS	Simple interfacing, simple in programming	Much complex for setup, complicated in error troubleshooting
	Optical Fiber	≈ 100 Km	Best for distributed and centralized EMSs	Large bandwidth, fast rate, inexpensive, low signal degradation, long life	Insufficient employment, brittleness, repeater required for long-distance
Wireless	Bluetooth	≈ 100 m	Appropriate for HEMS	Efficient, low interference	Low security, disturbance from RF, energy usage
	WLAN	≈ 100 m	Desired for home automation	Fast, accurate, and flexible	Better connection decreased information transfer rate, narrow bandwidth
	ZigBee	≈ 10-100 m	Home automation utilizations	low energy usage, efficient, flexible, and self-heal	lower privacy, less transmission rate, and range
	WiMax	≈ 50 Km	Appropriate for AMI	Ability to handle hundreds of consumers, long-distance	Sensitive to weather, disturbance issue, costly
	Cellular	≈ 5-100 Km	For automation utilizations	Useful in nature, simple upgrade, wireless connection	Endangered in nature, major setup cost

but is set beside the online controllers for managing procedures external to SCADA. PLC or Remote Terminal Unit (RTU) automatically operates the primary control procedure. A PLC applies power transmission lines to send radiofrequency waves of 30 kHz to 0.5 MHz. Data protection of this kind of communication technology is significantly high. Optical fiber technology has developed to a suitable level where accessible fibers have losses lower than 0.4 dB/km. The improvement of applicable lasers and optical detectors enables engineers to investigate optical fiber technologies for networks up to 120 km or more without any repeaters [27].

The developments in diverse wireless communication protocols have significantly enhanced the IoT capabilities of in SGs. For decentralized framework, distributed communication links are applied with a shorter transfer range in protocols such as ZigBee, WLAN, and RF. The further components desired for connection in smart home EMS and smart building EMS are Home Area Network (HAN), SMs, control devices, sensors, and smart appliances. Wired communication infrastructures are still favored communication technologies for the EMS based on their higher range of information transmission, but the corresponding investment costs are still a problem. On the other hand, wireless communication infrastructures are desirable for distant areas with low information of transmission and lower costs, however, disturbance is still a problem for wireless infrastructures. Based on the latest developments in implementation of management system, more local controlling devices, sensors, and SMs are required to be applied for diverse objectives of management. Accordingly, IoT controllers are becoming a more crucial component in monitoring and controlling energy applications. However, collaboration and system security are serious issues for communication technologies to preserve the privacy of users [28, 29].

4.5.3   Aggregators

Due to the enhanced penetration of DERs, consumers have the opportunity to become more proactive participants in the SG to generate energy locally or engage in DR schemes. Besides, they ensure various facilities that result in an effective and reliable network. Moreover, the participation of prosumers may lead to a more complicated grid. Accordingly, the EMS aggregator plays an essential role to deal with the issues such as price fluctuation and imbalance in supply and demand. The management systems of aggregators are novel kinds of electricity agents presented to enhance energy balance for a particular type of users by generating power and retailing surplus power. The term "aggregator" can be considered as an admissible unit that provides a possibility to tackle the resilience of low-demand

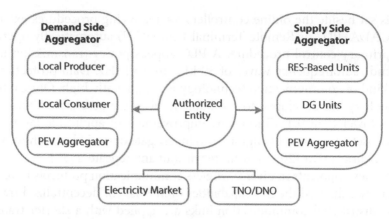

Figure 4.9 Supply- and demand-side aggregators [7].

users by enhancing their real-time connection to the retail markets to trade energy and obtain profits. Aggregator which contains with EMS aggregator, decreases network operator concerns with direct interaction with consumers. The EMS aggregator provides higher power system management requested by the network operator to meet generation and consumption by controlling demand or applying local feasible RES-based generations. Diverse groups of aggregators for conducting EMS strategies are suggested by many researchers, namely, EMS aggregators, DER aggregators, PEV aggregators, local demand aggregators, and MG aggregators. An aggregator can be defined as an authorized agency which is able to participate in the local/global power and energy market. As it is clear, small generation facilities such as PV, WT, DG, etc., and the end-users cannot participate directly in energy market for buying/selling power, hence, aggregator has a key factor as moderator to contribute in energy market.

Figure 4.9 demonstrates collaboration among designed aggregators at both generation and consumption sides regarding energy market and network operators. The responsibility and function of the aggregator are to abbreviate such small generators and prosumers (consumers who can generate and share surplus energy with the main utility and other energy users) in an acceptable amount to contribute in energy market. Finally, generated revenues are shared among generation units, end-user consumers, and local aggregators [7, 30].

4.6   DER Scheduling

RESs are nowadays more important to realize the energy requirement. Renewable energies may often lose to supply required power as a consequence of probabilistic nature of RES-based units and the corresponding uncertainties. For this reason, renewable systems have a direct effect on MGs and SGs. Figure 4.10 illustrates the EMS architecture in presence of the RES-based generations. Local loads are supplied using DG and they are majorly controllable. The feasible power generation may also inconstant at different periods. Moreover, the ESS provides energy support and makes it possible to store energy during high generation times. Accordingly, an EMS with sufficient operational constraints can realize an appropriate scheduling for DGs units, RES-based generations, and controllable loads ensuring optimal power flow and unit commitment [31].

Short-term generation scheduling is an important issue for the RESs. Scheduling approaches for production-side containing RESs such as grid-connected WTs and PVs must know the feasible energy supply to illustrate a proper estimation of power generation profile. Due to the existing uncertainties on the demand-side and variable inherent of RESs, establishing a communication platform among energy users and main grid is also necessary. The major issue in scheduling of PVs and WTs is that they cannot be operated similar to the regular centralized generators since they include climatic aspects including solar irradiation and wind speed. Accordingly, RESs require mitigation techniques to realize a sustainable power generation in the network. As mentioned previously, scheduling issues corresponding to the RESs can be relieved through properly applying on-site ESSs [32]. The benefits of on-site ESS can be highlighted as follows:

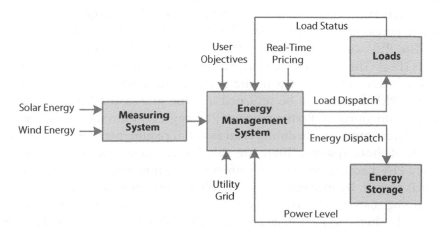

Figure 4.10 EMS connections in the SG application in presence of the RES-based generations.

1. Reducing the requirement capacity of transmission lines and generation units;
2. Enhancing controlling strategies;
3. Ensuring required reserve;
4. Improving voltage, frequency, and power factor of the network, and
5. Sidelong environmental benefits regarding to an increased application of RES-based units.

Many researches have been conducted on the modeling of increased ability of PEV aggregator for ensuring more ancillary services and applying PEVs as mobile storage that can resolve some problems of the distribution system. In SGs, the employment of PEVs in transportation grids has developed as a novel concern to decrease value of fossil fuels and carbon emissions. By utilizing plenty of PEVs with an appropriate controlling strategy, a considerable amount of power capacity can be stored for enhancing flexibility of the SGs. The PEVs can ensure prompt and accurate feedbacks for frequency adjustment. Besides, with optimal power scheduling, a PEV could act as a DG or ESS for participating in DR programs as well as smoothing the intermittency and unpredictability of RES-based generations such as wind, solar, and wave. Therefore, energy from a PEV to the grid has the potential to support grid operation and management. PEV aggregator is chargeable for supplying required energy and regulating charging profile of vehicle's daily driving under its contracted area. Since huge integration of PEVs can seriously influence scheduling of the network, from power generation to grid capacities, as well as the price of supplying energy. Accordingly, the improvement of PEV charging strategies is much necessary which can have a limited impact on the SGs [33].

The PEV can be effectively charged/discharged in available Parking Lots (PLs). The PLs can be considered as authorized entities in which electric vehicles can connect with the grid and charge/discharge. The charge of the PEV battery can be returned into the grid as the Vehicle to Grid (V2G) functionality. Participation of PEV aggregators in the power market points that optimal scheduling is an essential requirement for the employment of these systems. There are valuable economic incentives to owning a PEV because owners can gain incomes through the V2G while their car is parked. By managing and controlling the charge of the PEV battery, charging costs for PEV owners can be reduced. The Grid to Vehicle (G2V) mode is when energy storage is charging and PEV receives required power from the electricity grid. In this mode, the PEV acts as a local electric load. Besides, the PEVs in V2G mode can ensure significant benefits by providing

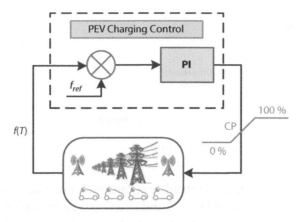

Figure 4.11 The scheme of PEVs charging power control [34].

enhanced system flexibility. As mentioned previously, the optimal scheduling of the V2G facility presents significant benefits to all participants in the grid. However, there are several challenges in the implementation of such a facility that must be addressed. One of the challenges is the regulation and reserve capacity suggestions with the unidirectional V2G which are much less than the cases suggested for the bidirectional V2G facility. The PEVs can be considered as a supporting agent integrated to the primary control of frequency. The control scheme, as shown in Figure 4.11, determines the frequency fluctuation in SG to control the PEVs charging energy by reducing charging level [34, 35].

4.7 Important Factors for EMS Establishment

4.7.1 Uncertainty Modeling and Management Methods

Given the large changes in the consumption patterns over 24 hours a day and the uncertainty of renewable energy sources, including wind power plants and photovoltaic systems, it is necessary to come up with solutions that can be used to optimize the power grid in the face of the differences in generation and consumption. Hence, uncertainty management is a significant issue in planning and scheduling of power systems. Accordingly, probabilistic forecasts play a vital role in dealing with uncertainty. Probabilistic nature of power and energy systems imposes stochastic techniques to investigate network reliability and performance. Due to various uncertainty in the power and energy systems, deterministic techniques are

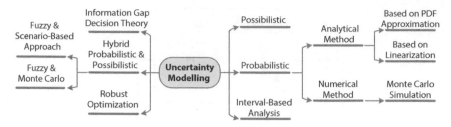

Figure 4.12 Uncertainty modeling overview.

not appropriate to employ. Instead of considering exact data of parameters (i.e., solar irradiation, wind speed, and power consumption), random allocations are calculated as inputs of stochastic approach to figure out probabilistic nature of RES [36].

The prevalent methods for handling uncertainties of the system can be categorized into three major approaches. The main purpose of these approaches is to examine effect of import parameters with uncertainty on export variables of power system. The variation between these approaches can be expressed in the definition of the uncertainty in the input parameters. In first method, uncertain parameters are simulated via Probability Density Functions (PDFs) and can be conducted through diverse probabilistic techniques including Monte Carlo Simulation (MCS) and Scenario-Based Analysis (SBA) as probabilistic approaches. In second method, uncertain parameters are indicated via fuzzy Membership Functions (MFs) and are conducted through fuzzy algorithms as possibilistic approaches. The third method contains hybrid probabilistic-possibilistic method in which uncertain data are indicated via PDFs and can be conducted through probabilistic techniques, while other data are indicated via fuzzy MFs and can be conducted with possibility concept [37, 38].

Figure 4.12 illustrates uncertainty modeling methods in power systems including probabilistic approaches [39], possibilistic approaches [40], hybrid possibilistic-probabilistic approaches [41], interval analysis [42], Information Gap Decision Theory (IGDT) [43], and robust optimization [44].

4.7.2   Power Quality Management

Power quality is generally recognized as the ability of power network for providing a reliable power flow as a feasible permanent energy supply. The power flow must be a perfect sine waveform with determined voltage and frequency margins. The PQM has closely corresponded to quality control or purity of AC sine wave of the electric power supply. The necessity of power quality is a subject that is becoming proliferating to electrical power users with diverse consumptions. Sensible components and non-linear load profiles are regular in industrial and residential environments. Accordingly, increased consciousness of power quality is enhancing. Power quality is a significant factor of SGs with a straightforward impact on performance, safety, and flexibility [45].

The term "power quality" is utilized equivalently with service quality, supply resilience, and current/voltage quality. Based on different descriptions, power quality is mainly meant to indicate quality of current/voltage. Accordingly, it is described as quantity and quality of bus voltage to sustain a perfect sine at nominal frequency. Also, power quality is much important for SG's functionality. The good performance of the SG grid needs a balance between two main aspects, namely, efficiency and reliability. In most scheduling cases, reliability takes priority over performance, but it is not always guaranteed. Power quality guarantees the needful adaptability between the sensitive electrical and electronic components,

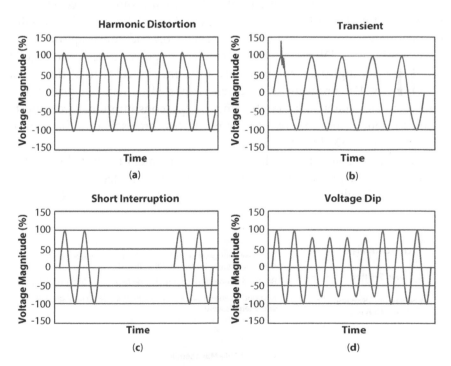

Figure 4.13 Waveform demonstrating (a) harmonic distortion, (b) impulsive transient event, (c) short interruption, and (d) voltage dip.

which can make sure an uninterrupted and high-quality supply of electricity in the future. Accordingly, the power quality is a vital aspect of the flexible and efficient scheduling of the current grid as well as the future SGs. Furthermore, cost and energy saving are due to good power quality. Besides, reactive power tariffs can save the cost of consumers directly [46, 47]. Power quality is an issue thoroughly interconnected with disturbance sources that effects management approaches. Recognizing power quality disturbances can help to reduce undesirable effects and achieve the best scheme for power quality management. Hence, PQM is usually connecting with the issues such as harmonic distortion, transients, short interruption, voltage dips, and current and voltage instability as thoroughly shown in Figure 4.13 [47].

4.7.3   DSM and DR Programs

The DSM is a program that enables energy users to manage functions based on their energy consumption. For example, DSM encourages end-users to shift their consumption within peak hours for utilizing less power to off-peak periods to shave (or smooth) their load profile. Moreover, DSM relieves network contingencies, increases dependability and flexibility, reduces power outages, and balances generation and consumption in the network. Besides, DR program is decrement of power usage from regular usage responding to an enhancement in energy price. One of the major functions of DR program is to lessen requested demand in peak hours and increase capability of controlling energy consumption according to available generation. Figure 4.14 demonstrates three schemes that can be applied in the DSM [48, 49].

The DR programs persuade the active consumers to shift their determined demand profile in response to time-varying electricity tariffs or economic stimulus. Besides, large-scale assumptions of such DR schemes

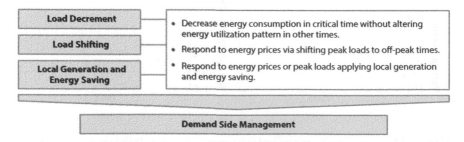

Figure 4.14 Three main schemes used in the DSM approaches [48].

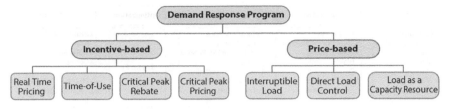

Figure 4.15 Classifications of DR programs.

and building EMS in neighboring areas can result in rebound peaks when electricity is in the lower prices. The DR programs can be generally classified into incentive-based and price-based programs as illustrated in Figure 4.15.

In the incentive-based DR program, energy users participate in a motivation program that lets the main utility frequently control and manage their electrical devices when required energy demand is high. In SG application, when load shedding is necessary to ensure the system stability, Direct Load Control (DLC) program can directly control home appliances by the implemented control center and prefers some of them to be interrupted. Price-based approaches of DR programs ensure dynamic signals of energy price to control power consumptions during peak-hours when corresponding energy price is higher than other times. Accordingly, when energy prices are increased by the market, energy users are expected to decrease their consumption. Besides, energy users can be supplied based on energy prices to shift their required load from peak hours to periods with reduced energy prices, therefore, cost of consuming energy will be decreased [50, 51].

4.8   Optimization Approaches for EMS

In recent years, various programming approaches and optimization algorithms of EMS are developed for the networks including Energy Storage (ES), PEV, RES, and responsive loads. Primary purpose of EMS approach is to optimize objective function containing fuel cost, energy efficiency, reliability, power quality, losses, power dispatch, etc. Figure 4.16 demonstrates procedure to solve an EMS problem considering feasible inputs, economic objectives, technical constraints, and intended output. The optimization methods can be categorized into exact and approximate approaches. The exact approaches of optimization ensure optimal operation, but the calculation difficulty rises then [7]. As shown in Figure 4.17, the optimization

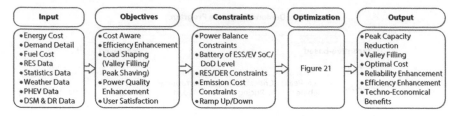

Figure 4.16 Procedure for solving an EMS problem [7].

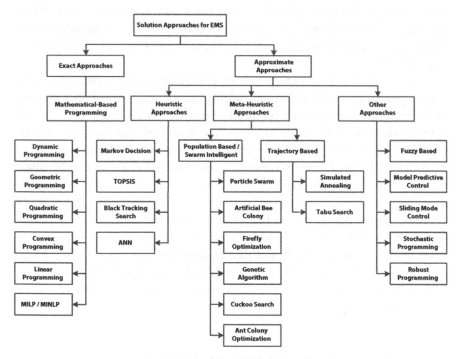

Figure 4.17 Optimization approaches applied to the EMS [7].

methods can be classified into four groups including mathematical programming, heuristic programming, metaheuristic programming, and
other optimization approaches. Mathematical programming refers to
exact approaches of optimization. Thus, they are not suggested for real-
time employment. Although approximate approaches of optimization do
not ensure optimal operation, they provide a solution within an acceptable
period with the best approximate result. The heuristic or metaheuristic
optimization approaches refer to approximate methods that give the result
at an optimum value within the acceptable period and can be utilized to

real-time optimization problems. The optimization approaches to EMS are reviewed in detail in the following subsections.

4.8.1   Mathematical Approaches

According to the type of objective function and corresponding constraints, mathematical-based programming approaches can be classified as Dynamic Programming (DP), Geometric Programming (GP), Quadratic Programming (QP), convex programming, and linear and nonlinear programming. Optimization problem formulated by mathematical-based programming approaches allocate regular assets, for instance, they can

Table 4.3 Comparison of mathematical optimization approaches [7].

Approach	Advantage	Disadvantage
Dynamic Programming	High computational ability	Offline programming, Complicated problem formulation, Computational issue
Geometric Programming	Easy to operate and implement	The complexity level is high
Quadratic Programming	Prompt convergence, Convenient to online scheduling	Online application not feasible
Convex Programming	Reliable, Effective, Proper for real-time scheduling	Higher difficulty
Linear Programming	Acceptable for online application	Only works with linear variables, Unsuitable to more than two variables
MILP	Accuracy greater than non-linear programming	Reduced modeling ability in comparison to non-linear programming
MINLP	Greater in simulation ability	Enhanced calculation time and reduced quality of solution

be indicated in mathematical provisions and can apply discrete or continuous variables. Accordingly, thorough consideration of modeling term is requested by mathematical optimization problem, and the reliability should be assigned in the model descriptions. The main concept of DP is suggested by Bellman based on the optimality concept. DP approach can be implemented for any mixed-integer nonlinear optimization problems. QP and convex programming approaches are extensively proposed by researchers. QP method optimizes quadratic functions with linear problem constraints. It can be mentioned that the computing time of QP method is relatively lower in comparison with DP method. In convex approaches, objective function is a convex framework for minimization problems or a concave framework for maximization problems with entire convex constraints for both groups [7, 52].

Table 4.3 shows comparison among diverse mathematical-based programming approaches.

4.8.2   Heuristic Approaches

The Heuristic method is a primary technique for ensuring approximate results to considered optimization objective according to the assigned constraints. The heuristic-based approaches are properly developed for the EMS to lessen the computational difficulty for the associated objectives [7, 53].

Table 4.4 represents a comparison among heuristic-based programming approaches.

Table 4.4 Comparison of heuristic optimization approaches [7].

Approach	Advantage	Disadvantage
Markov Decision	The best method for making a proper decision	Only applicable for linear programming
TOPSIS	Easy to implement, low requirements	Hardly reliable for optimal operation
Backtracking Search	Intelligent approach, Easy to apply	Incapable for many sections, Huge data processing is needed
ANN	An appropriate method to predict and make a proper decision	Parallel data processing is needed, Unascertained performance

4.8.3   Metaheuristic Approaches

Major metaheuristic approaches including Particle Swarm Optimization (PSO) algorithm, bee colony optimization, Genetic Algorithms (GAs), Simulated Annealing (SA), ant colony optimization, and many other approaches, are stochastic and are stimulated by the natural world, physical, or biological origin. The majority of the metaheuristic-based approaches are based on the population and are a beneficent algorithm. These metaheuristic-based methods are computationally robust but do not impose objective to be convex [7, 54].

Table 4.5 shows a comparison of diverse metaheuristic approaches applied for EMS.

4.8.4   Other Programming Approaches

In addition to the mathematical programming, heuristics programming, and metaheuristics programming, some other optimization methods have been investigated to improve optimization model and to realize computational interests in problem results. Optimization approaches including

Table 4.5 Comparison of metaheuristic optimization approaches [7].

Approach	Advantage	Disadvantage
GA	Easy to apply, Probabilistic method	Computing period is much
PSO	Easy to apply, Bounded input parameter is needed	Computing period is much, Difficult for online application
Tabu Search	Resilient in nature, Flexible memory	Computational difficulty
Artificial Bee Colony	Easy to implement, Robust, Flexible	The high complexity of the algorithm for the serial procedure
SA	The less computational time needed	Checking the optimality of result
Firefly	Handle extremely nonlinear problems, Intermodal solution	Possible to trap local minimum results

fuzzy, Model Predictive Control (MPC), Sliding Mode Control (SMC), stochastic and robust programming are also proposed by many researchers. Among the mentioned optimization approaches, stochastic and robust programming is more applicable for uncertainty modeling.

Table 4.6 demonstrates a comparison among other approaches used in EMS.

Preference of the optimization approaches requires utilizing criteria before applying it to the programming or before modeling optimization functions. Some of the above-mentioned optimization functions require high computing time and huge data storage. The mathematical-based approach needs more computing time compared with heuristic programming and metaheuristic programming methods. Most of the metaheuristic approaches are on the basis of population, and they meet optimal result with lower computing complication. Moreover, heuristic approaches are on the basis of knowledge, which presents approximate result for the optimization function. Besides, history data of programming is needed as well as specific presumptions to realize optimal solutions with lower computing

Table 4.6 Comparison of other optimization approaches [7].

Approach	Advantage	Disadvantage
Fuzzy	Simple to implement, Manage incomplete data, Flexible	Greater computational time
Model Predictive Control	Predictive approach, Best performance with large data	High-cost implementation, Greater skill required
Sliding Mode Control	Suitable for nonlinear problems, Robust to uncertain parameters	Intelligent switching, Restricted to a single input data
Stochastic	Manage uncertain parameters well, Ideal to make a proper decision	High data processing is required, Data allocation is needed
Robust	Eliminate various disturbances, No need for history data	Greater skills required for online programming

time for heuristic approaches. Besides, MPC, SMC, stochastic, robust, etc are more complex to apply [7, 55].

4.9   Conclusion

The enhancing application of IoT concept in EMS presents issues corresponding to managing huge data processing, its administration, and its communication framework. Despite cloud computing are becoming a favorable solution, the issues corresponding to data security, flexibility, interoperability, and connectivity of IoT systems necessitate consideration. Hence, there is a requirement to concentrate on the standardization of IoT systems to provide network adeptness and sufficiency. To provide an appropriate scheduling of DERs, ensuring requested demand, and increasing the efficiency of system in SG application, it is essential to apply suitable energy management strategies. Objectives of these strategies will define the performance of the entire system. Wonderfully, the EMS provides optimal application of the DER to ensure the cost-effective, reliable, and flexible operation of the SGs. As diverse types of optimization algorithms have their advantages and disadvantages, responsibility of the designer is to opt for the suitable algorithm considering problem objectives, constraints, demand profile of users, market energy prices, optimization scenarios, etc. Development of economical SGs with flexible and resilient communication frameworks is highly important. Also, an appropriate modeling of uncertainty is an issue that requires to be perfectly investigated.

Important notes can be also highlighted as: 1) Advanced communication infrastructures are the major essentials for integration of RES-based generations into the SGs; 2) The smart home and smart building EMS are important for optimal assignment of DERs in the SGs; 3) Computational difficulty requires to be considered while performing EMS objective; 4) The safety and privacy of the user's information require to be guaranteed with the applying of proper adjustments and policies.

References

1. A. Hasankhani, S. Mehdi Hakimi, M. Shafie-khah, and H. Asadolahi, "Blockchain technology in the future smart grids: A comprehensive review and frameworks," *International Journal of Electrical Power & Energy Systems*, vol. 129, p. 106811, 2021/07/01/ 2021, doi: https://doi.org/10.1016/j.ijepes.2021.106811.

2. A. Jafari, T. Khalili, H. G. Ganjehlou, and A. Bidram, "Optimal integration of renewable energy sources, diesel generators, and demand response program from pollution, financial, and reliability viewpoints: A multi-objective approach," *Journal of Cleaner Production*, vol. 247, p. 119100, 2020/02/20/ 2020, doi: https://doi.org/10.1016/j.jclepro.2019.119100.

3. S. Sharda, M. Singh, and K. Sharma, "Demand side management through load shifting in IoT based HEMS: Overview, challenges and opportunities," *Sustainable Cities and Society*, vol. 65, p. 102517, 2021/02/01/ 2021, doi: https://doi.org/10.1016/j.scs.2020.102517.

4. A. Prasanth and S. Jayachitra, "A novel multi-objective optimization strategy for enhancing quality of service in IoT-enabled WSN applications," *Peer-to-Peer Networking and Applications*, vol. 13, no. 6, pp. 1905-1920, 2020/11/01 2020, doi: 10.1007/s12083-020-00945-y.

5. S. E. Ahmadi, N. Rezaei, and H. Khayyam, "Energy management system of networked microgrids through optimal reliability-oriented day-ahead self-healing scheduling," *Sustainable Energy, Grids and Networks*, vol. 23, p. 100387, 2020/09/01/ 2020, doi: https://doi.org/10.1016/j.segan.2020.100387.

6. F. J. Vivas, A. De las Heras, F. Segura, and J. M. Andújar, "A review of energy management strategies for renewable hybrid energy systems with hydrogen backup," *Renewable and Sustainable Energy Reviews*, vol. 82, pp. 126-155, 2018/02/01/ 2018, doi: https://doi.org/10.1016/j.rser.2017.09.014.

7. S. K. Rathor and D. Saxena, "Energy management system for smart grid: An overview and key issues," *International Journal of Energy Research*, https://doi.org/10.1002/er.4883 vol. 44, no. 6, pp. 4067-4109, 2020/05/01 2020, doi: https://doi.org/10.1002/er.4883.

8. A. Prasanth and S. Pavalarajan, "Implementation of Efficient Intra- and Inter-Zone Routing for Extending Network Consistency in Wireless Sensor Networks," *Journal of Circuits, Systems and Computers*, vol. 29, no. 08, p. 2050129, 2020/06/30 2019, doi: 10.1142/S0218126620501297.

9. A. Zakaria, F. B. Ismail, M. S. H. Lipu, and M. A. Hannan, "Uncertainty models for stochastic optimization in renewable energy applications," *Renewable Energy*, vol. 145, pp. 1543-1571, 2020/01/01/ 2020, doi: https://doi.org/10.1016/j.renene.2019.07.081.

10. B. E. Sedhom, M. M. El-Saadawi, M. S. El Moursi, M. A. Hassan, and A. A. Eladl, "IoT-based optimal demand side management and control scheme for smart microgrid," *International Journal of Electrical Power & Energy Systems*, vol. 127, p. 106674, 2021/05/01/ 2021, doi: https://doi.org/10.1016/j.ijepes.2020.106674.

11. S. S. Reka and T. Dragicevic, "Future effectual role of energy delivery: A comprehensive review of Internet of Things and smart grid," *Renewable and Sustainable Energy Reviews*, vol. 91, pp. 90-108, 2018/08/01/ 2018, doi: https://doi.org/10.1016/j.rser.2018.03.089.

12. M. S. Aliero, K. N. Qureshi, M. F. Pasha, and G. Jeon, "Smart Home Energy Management Systems in Internet of Things networks for green cities

demands and services," *Environmental Technology & Innovation*, p. 101443, 2021/02/20/ 2021, doi: https://doi.org/10.1016/j.eti.2021.101443.

13. Z. Cheng, J. Duan, and M. Chow, "To Centralize or to Distribute: That Is the Question: A Comparison of Advanced Microgrid Management Systems," *IEEE Industrial Electronics Magazine*, vol. 12, no. 1, pp. 6-24, 2018, doi: 10.1109/MIE.2018.2789926.

14. J. B. Almada, R. P. S. Leão, R. F. Sampaio, and G. C. Barroso, "A centralized and heuristic approach for energy management of an AC microgrid," *Renewable and Sustainable Energy Reviews*, vol. 60, pp. 1396-1404, 2016/07/01/ 2016, doi: https://doi.org/10.1016/j.rser.2016.03.002.

15. D. Espín-Sarzosa, R. Palma-Behnke, and O. Núñez-Mata, "Energy Management Systems for Microgrids: Main Existing Trends in Centralized Control Architectures," *Energies*, vol. 13, no. 3, 2020, doi: 10.3390/en13030547.

16. H. Pourbabak, T. Chen, and W. Su, "1 - Centralized, decentralized, and distributed control for Energy Internet," in *The Energy Internet*, W. Su and A. Q. Huang Eds.: Woodhead Publishing, 2019, pp. 3-19.

17. S. Xu, H. Pourbabak, and W. Su, "Distributed cooperative control for economic operation of multiple plug-in electric vehicle parking decks," *International Transactions on Electrical Energy Systems*, https://doi.org/10.1002/etep.2348 vol. 27, no. 9, p. e2348, 2017/09/01 2017, doi: https://doi.org/10.1002/etep.2348.

18. F. Shahnia, R. P. S. Chandrasena, S. Rajakaruna, and A. Ghosh, "Primary control level of parallel distributed energy resources converters in system of multiple interconnected autonomous microgrids within self-healing networks," *IET Generation, Transmission & Distribution*, vol. 8, no. 2, pp. 203-222. [Online]. Available: https://digital-library.theiet.org/content/journals/10.1049/iet-gtd.2013.0126

19. P. Thollander, M. Karlsson, P. Rohdin, J. Wollin, and J. Rosenqvist, "13 - Energy management," in *Introduction to Industrial Energy Efficiency*, P. Thollander, M. Karlsson, P. Rohdin, J. Wollin, and J. Rosenqvist Eds.: Academic Press, 2020, pp. 239-257.

20. A. Akbari-Dibavar, S. Nojavan, B. Mohammadi-Ivatloo, and K. Zare, "Smart home energy management using hybrid robust-stochastic optimization," *Computers & Industrial Engineering*, vol. 143, p. 106425, 2020/05/01/ 2020, doi: https://doi.org/10.1016/j.cie.2020.106425.

21. X. Kong, B. Sun, D. Kong, and B. Li, "Home energy management optimization method considering potential risk cost," *Sustainable Cities and Society*, vol. 62, p. 102378, 2020/11/01/ 2020, doi: https://doi.org/10.1016/j.scs.2020.102378.

22. Y. Liu, B. Qiu, X. Fan, H. Zhu, and B. Han, "Review of Smart Home Energy Management Systems," *Energy Procedia*, vol. 104, pp. 504-508, 2016/12/01/ 2016, doi: https://doi.org/10.1016/j.egypro.2016.12.085.

23. D. Mariano-Hernández, L. Hernández-Callejo, A. Zorita-Lamadrid, O. Duque-Pérez, and F. Santos García, "A review of strategies for building energy

management system: Model predictive control, demand side management, optimization, and fault detect & diagnosis," *Journal of Building Engineering,* vol. 33, p. 101692, 2021/01/01/ 2021, doi: https://doi.org/10.1016/j. jobe.2020.101692.

24. A. G. Hossam, "Building Energy Management Systems (BEMS)," in *Energy Conservation in Residential, Commercial, and Industrial Facilities*: IEEE, 2018, pp. 15-81.

25. P. Gupta, R. Kandari, and A. Kumar, "Chapter 1 - An introduction to the smart grid-I," in *Advances in Smart Grid Power System*, A. Tomar and R. Kandari Eds.: Academic Press, 2021, pp. 1-31.

26. M. Jalali, K. Zare, and H. Seyedi, "Strategic decision-making of distribution network operator with multi-microgrids considering demand response program," *Energy,* vol. 141, pp. 1059-1071, 2017/12/15/ 2017, doi: https://doi. org/10.1016/j.energy.2017.09.145.

27. D. J. Marihart, "Communications technology guidelines for EMS/SCADA systems," *IEEE Transactions on Power Delivery,* vol. 16, no. 2, pp. 181-188, 2001, doi: 10.1109/61.915480.

28. H. Elkhorchani and K. Grayaa, "Novel home energy management system using wireless communication technologies for carbon emission reduction within a smart grid," *Journal of Cleaner Production,* vol. 135, pp. 950-962, 2016/11/01/ 2016, doi: https://doi.org/10.1016/j.jclepro.2016.06.179.

29. M. Faheem *et al.*, "Smart grid communication and information technologies in the perspective of Industry 4.0: Opportunities and challenges," *Computer Science Review,* vol. 30, pp. 1-30, 2018/11/01/ 2018, doi: https:// doi.org/10.1016/j.cosrev.2018.08.001.

30. P. Sheikhahmadi and S. Bahramara, "The participation of a renewable energy-based aggregator in real-time market: A Bi-level approach," *Journal of Cleaner Production,* vol. 276, p. 123149, 2020/12/10/ 2020, doi: https://doi. org/10.1016/j.jclepro.2020.123149.

31. k. Ismail El, B. Rachid, L. Abdellah, and A. My Othman, "Power Scheduling for Renewable Energy Connected to the grid," *E3S Web Conf.,* 10.1051/ e3sconf/20186408008 vol. 64, // 2018. [Online]. Available: https://doi. org/10.1051/e3sconf/20186408008.

32. G. J. Osório, M. Shafie-khah, J. M. Lujano-Rojas, and J. P. S. Catalão, "Scheduling Model for Renewable Energy Sources Integration in an Insular Power System," *Energies,* vol. 11, no. 1, 2018, doi: 10.3390/en11010144.

33. M. Alipour, B. Mohammadi-Ivatloo, M. Moradi-Dalvand, and K. Zare, "Stochastic scheduling of aggregators of plug-in electric vehicles for participation in energy and ancillary service markets," *Energy,* vol. 118, pp. 1168-1179, 2017/01/01/ 2017, doi: https://doi.org/10.1016/j.energy. 2016.10.141.

34. N. Kesorn, A. Pichetjamroen, S. Dechanupaprittha, and C. Jamroen, "Optimal PEVs charging control for frequency stabilization considering communication delay in remote microgrid," in *TENCON 2017 - 2017 IEEE*

Region 10 Conference, 5-8 Nov. 2017 2017, pp. 1469-1474, doi: 10.1109/TENCON.2017.8228089.

35. E. Sortomme and M. A. El-Sharkawi, "Optimal Scheduling of Vehicle-to-Grid Energy and Ancillary Services," *IEEE Transactions on Smart Grid,* vol. 3, no. 1, pp. 351-359, 2012, doi: 10.1109/TSG.2011.2164099.

36. A. R. Jordehi, "How to deal with uncertainties in electric power systems? A review," *Renewable and Sustainable Energy Reviews,* vol. 96, pp. 145-155, 2018/11/01/ 2018, doi: https://doi.org/10.1016/j.rser.2018.07.056.

37. M. Aien, A. Hajebrahimi, and M. Fotuhi-Firuzabad, "A comprehensive review on uncertainty modeling techniques in power system studies," *Renewable and Sustainable Energy Reviews,* vol. 57, pp. 1077-1089, 2016/05/01/ 2016, doi: https://doi.org/10.1016/j.rser.2015.12.070.

38. S. E. Ahmadi and N. Rezaei, "A new isolated renewable based multi micro-grid optimal energy management system considering uncertainty and demand response," *International Journal of Electrical Power & Energy Systems,* vol. 118, p. 105760, 2020/06/01/ 2020, doi: https://doi.org/10.1016/j.ijepes.2019.105760.

39. P. Kayal and C. K. Chanda, "Optimal mix of solar and wind distributed gen-crations considering performance improvement of electrical distribution network," *Renewable Energy,* vol. 75, pp. 173-186, 2015/03/01/ 2015, doi: https://doi.org/10.1016/j.renene.2014.10.003.

40. I. J. Ramirez-Rosado and J. A. Dominguez-Navarro, "Possibilistic model based on fuzzy sets for the multiobjective optimal planning of electric power distribution networks," *IEEE Transactions on Power Systems,* vol. 19, no. 4, pp. 1801-1810, 2004, doi: 10.1109/TPWRS.2004.835678.

41. A. Soroudi, "Possibilistic-Scenario Model for DG Impact Assessment on Distribution Networks in an Uncertain Environment," *IEEE Transactions on Power Systems,* vol. 27, no. 3, pp. 1283-1293, 2012, doi: 10.1109/TPWRS.2011.2180933.

42. X. Liao, K. Liu, Y. Zhang, K. Wang, and L. Qin, "Interval method for uncertain power flow analysis based on Taylor inclusion function," *IET Generation, Transmission & Distribution,* vol. 11, no. 5, pp. 1270-1278. [Online]. Available: https://digital-library.theiet.org/content/journals/10.1049/iet-gtd.2016.1344

43. S. E. Ahmadi and N. Rezaei, "An IGDT-based robust optimization model for optimal operational planning of cooperative microgrid clusters: A normal boundary intersection multi-objective approach," *International Journal of Electrical Power & Energy Systems,* vol. 127, p. 106634, 2021/05/01/ 2021, doi: https://doi.org/10.1016/j.ijepes.2020.106634.

44. M. Diekerhof, F. Peterssen, and A. Monti, "Hierarchical Distributed Robust Optimization for Demand Response Services," *IEEE Transactions on Smart Grid,* vol. 9, no. 6, pp. 6018-6029, 2018, doi: 10.1109/TSG.2017.2701821.

45. D. Thomas, G. D'Hoop, O. Deblecker, K. N. Genikomsakis, and C. S. Ioakimidis, "An integrated tool for optimal energy scheduling and power

quality improvement of a microgrid under multiple demand response schemes," *Applied Energy*, vol. 260, p. 114314, 2020/02/15/ 2020, doi: https://doi.org/10.1016/j.apenergy.2019.114314.

46. R. Naidoo, P. Pillay, J. Visser, R. C. Bansal, and N. T. Mbungu, "An adaptive method of symmetrical component estimation," *Electric Power Systems Research*, vol. 158, pp. 45-55, 2018/05/01/ 2018, doi: https://doi.org/10.1016/j.epsr.2018.01.003.

47. P. D. Surya Santoso, F. M. Mark, C. D. Roger, and H. W. Beaty, *Electrical Power Systems Quality, Third Edition*, 3rd ed. ed. New York: McGraw-Hill Education (in en), 2012.

48. H. Dagdougui, A. Ouammi, and R. Sacile, "Chapter 8 - Towards a Concept of Cooperating Power Network for Energy Management and Control of Microgrids," in *Microgrid*, M. S. Mahmoud Ed.: Butterworth-Heinemann, 2017, pp. 231-262.

49. N. Nikmehr, S. Najafi-Ravadanegh, and A. Khodaei, "Probabilistic optimal scheduling of networked microgrids considering time-based demand response programs under uncertainty," *Applied Energy*, vol. 198, pp. 267-279, 2017/07/15/ 2017, doi: https://doi.org/10.1016/j.apenergy.2017.04.071.

50. M. Daneshvar, M. Pesaran, and B. Mohammadi-ivatloo, "7 - Transactive energy in future smart homes," in *The Energy Internet*, W. Su and A. Q. Huang Eds.: Woodhead Publishing, 2019, pp. 153-179.

51. J. Contreras, M. Asensio, P. M. de Quevedo, G. Muñoz-Delgado, and S. Montoya-Bueno, "Chapter 4 - Demand Response Modeling," in *Joint RES and Distribution Network Expansion Planning Under a Demand Response Framework*, J. Contreras, M. Asensio, P. M. de Quevedo, G. Muñoz-Delgado, and S. Montoya-Bueno Eds.: Academic Press, 2016, pp. 33-40.

52. M. Elkazaz, M. Sumner, and D. Thomas, "Energy management system for hybrid PV-wind-battery microgrid using convex programming, model predictive and rolling horizon predictive control with experimental validation," *International Journal of Electrical Power & Energy Systems*, vol. 115, p. 105483, 2020/02/01/ 2020, doi: https://doi.org/10.1016/j.ijepes.2019.105483.

53. S. Umetani, Y. Fukushima, and H. Morita, "A linear programming based heuristic algorithm for charge and discharge scheduling of electric vehicles in a building energy management system," *Omega*, vol. 67, pp. 115-122, 2017/03/01/ 2017, doi: https://doi.org/10.1016/j.omega.2016.04.005.

54. E. G. Morquecho, S. P. Torres, and C. A. Castro, "An efficient hybrid meta-heuristics optimization technique applied to the AC electric transmission network expansion planning," *Swarm and Evolutionary Computation*, vol. 61, p. 100830, 2021/03/01/ 2021, doi: https://doi.org/10.1016/j.swevo.2020.100830.

55. S. Huang, Y. Lin, V. Chinde, X. Ma, and J. Lian, "Simulation-based performance evaluation of model predictive control for building energy systems," *Applied Energy*, vol. 281, p. 116027, 2021/01/01/ 2021, doi: https://doi.org/10.1016/j.apenergy.2020.116027.

5

Integrated Architecture for IoTSG: Internet of Things (IoT) and Smart Grid (SG)

Malathy S.[1]*, K. Sangeetha[1], C. N. Vanitha[1] and Rajesh Kumar Dhanaraj[2]

[1]Computer Science and Engineering, Kongu Engineering College, Erode, India
[2]Computer Science and Engineering, School of Computing Science & Engineering, Galgotias University, Greater Noida, India

Abstract

IoT is a new reality, affecting the energy industry with its cutting-edge advancements and real-time applications. It gathers actionable insights from sensor devices and gateway connectivity, then uses them to create cutting-edge services for increased productivity. It enhances overall experiences, complicated operability, and real-time decision-making even more. A power plant that uses sensor technology can automate process execution and provide better, more error-free services. IoT technology is a clever idea that guards against excessive resource use and supports consistency. IoT enables intelligent process monitoring that provides data on every aspect of the plant-process. Through IoT processing, the data is transformed into pertinent information and saved on a cloud platform for easy access. IoT also offers real-time quality monitoring, which aids in locating process nonconformities. Thus, it empowers managers to take timely, relevant actions and modify processes to raise quality and lower waste. A fundamental change is being brought about by the electricity industry's sensor-based operation. It makes use of cutting-edge processes to produce goods of high quality and satisfy corporate needs. The use of advanced analytics in business is benefiting industrialists most. In order to gather data from the assets and improve upon previous decisions, it employs sensor-enabled data. The power sector uses data analytics to optimize planning and generation. Additionally, when analytics and smart

*Corresponding author: ksmalathy@gmail.com

P. Sanjeevikumar, Rajesh Kumar Dhanaraj, Malathy Sathyamoorthy, Jens Bo Holm-Nielsen and Balamurugan Balusamy (eds.) *Smart Grids and Internet of Things: An Energy Perspective*, (127–156) © 2023 Scrivener Publishing LLC

metres are combined, it makes it easier to foresee precise consumption patterns that are utilized to balance supply and demand. As a result, it lessens energy waste and wasteful energy use. Along with newer and more sophisticated concepts, IoT opens up new business prospects. It entails sensor hardware, gateway connectivity, and communication protocols that come together to create IoT architecture for various enterprises. IoT technology allows for the implementation of smart strategies for increased production and growth. IoT integrated with smart grid is a cutting-edge technology that equips companies with real-time monitoring capabilities, intelligent data management, and analytics. In order to give improved strategies for effective energy usage, new IoT applications integrated with smart grid technologies are now being implemented.

Keywords: Internet of Things, smart grid, IoT architecture, smart metering, IoTSG architecture, data acquisition systems, IoTSG safety concerns, security measures of IoTSG

5.1   Introduction

The Internet of Things (IoT) is a commonly accepted technology that connects everyday objects to the internet to provide convenience and a variety of functions, and the Smart Grid (SG) is characterized as a power grid that is integrated with a broad network of ICT. The SG is made up of billions of smart items such as smart appliances, smart meters, actuators, and sensors, among other things. In [1] the various layers and the components involved in the IoT architecture has been discussed. Finding a dependable supplier of IoT solutions makes it simpler and more efficient to pact with the broad range of factors that affect architecture of IoT. This decision would result in a substantial decrease in the amount of money expended on the architecture development [2, 24, 25].

In general, there are three layers available in IoT architecture as shown in Figure 5.1:

1. The client's perspective
    a. Devices used by the end users are present in this layer
2. The server's perspective
    a. Operators and service providers are present in this layer
3. A link between devices and operators

    a. It acts as an interface between devices used by the end users and service providers

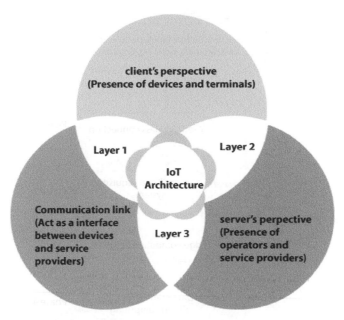

Figure 5.1 IoT architecture and its layers.

IoT architecture will be used successfully for most of the applications if it possesses the following features.

- Functionality
- Scalability
- Availability
- Maintainability

The consequence of IoT architecture without resolving these conditions is failure.

5.1.1   Designing of IoT Architecture

Though the process of developing software can be understood easily, the functional implementation of its four stages involves too many complex steps. To make the designing process a simple one, the building phase has been divided into 4 stages as follows.

1. Devices utilized (Example 1: Sensors and actuators)
2. Data gathering and analog-to-digital conversion systems
3. Edge computing devices
4. Data analysis, management, and storage

Figure 5.2 shows a more accurate representation of these phases.

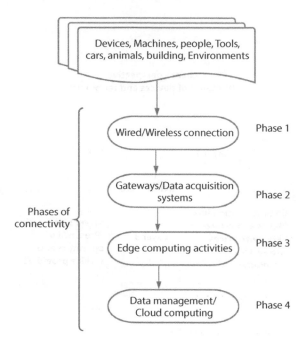

Figure 5.2 Phases of connectivity in IoT architecture.

The following are the components [3] present in the different stages of IoT architecture as illustrated in Figure 5.3.

1. Sensors and actuators
2. Data Acquisition Systems and Internet getaways
3. Edge computing devices
4. Data analysis, management, and storage

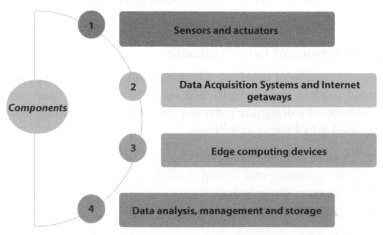

Figure 5.3 Components of IoT architecture.

Sensors and Actuators

The sensors possess a distinguished ability which translates the information gathered from the outside world into a formatted data that can be used for analysis purposes. The inclusion of devices utilized in 4 stages of IoT architecture is important because they are responsible for obtaining information in a form that can be processed.

The process is even more advanced for actuators, as these devices can intervene in physical reality. For example, sensors having the ability to switch on/off the light based on the presence/absence of human beings in a room. As a result, the identification and activation stage cover and changes everything required in the physical environment in order to obtain the information needed for analysis.

Data Acquisition Systems and Internet Getaways

The presence of various gateways [3] and data gathering systems is noted in stage 2. But the IoT design still requires working in close proximity with sensors and actuators. The data gathering systems pave a way for connecting the sensor network to the internet and aggregate performance, while Internet getaways use the technologies such as wireless (Wi-Fi) connection and wired connection (LANs) and carry out additional processing.

This stage is critical in that it processes the massive amount of data gathered in the earlier stage and reduces it to a manageable size for further processing. Aside from that, this is where the appropriate timing and structure conversion takes place. In a nutshell, Stage 2 digitizes and aggregates data.

Edge computing Devices

The prepared data is transmitted to the IT world during this stage of the IoT architecture. Edge IT systems specifically performs improved analytics and pre-processing during this stage [4, 26, 27]. Machine learning and visualization technology are employed during this phase. In addition to this, some supplementary processing will take place in this stage before moving on to the subsequent phase of the process.

Similarly, this phase is intertwined with the earlier stages in the creation of an IoT architecture. As a result, the position IT systems used in the verge of an architecture is similar to that of sensors and actuators, resulting in the creation of a wiring closet. It is also possible to work from remote offices at the same time.

Data Analysis, Management, and Storage

- In the final stage of IoT architecture, the core processes take place in the data center or cloud [5, 28, 29]. It allows for in-depth processing as well as a follow-up revision for input. Both Information technology and operational technology specialists are required in this situation.

- To put it another way, the process already requires the highest-level analytical abilities, from both the human and digital realm. As a result, data from other sources may be included here to ensure a thorough review.
- The knowledge is returned to the physical world after meeting all the quality criteria and specifications, but in a processed and precisely analyzed state.

Looping of Commands to the Devices

In reality, an extra stage is needed while developing a most viable IoT architecture. It refers to giving a user control over the structure — provided, of course, that the result does not require complete automation. Visualization and management are the most important activities performed in this stage. When Stage 5 is included practically, the device becomes a loop in which a user sends commands to sensors/actuators as aforementioned in stage 1 to accomplish certain acts. And then the process will be repeated through other subsequent stages.

5.1.2   IoT Characteristics

The following are the salient characteristics of IoT in [6].

1. The ability to connect

The most important feature to consider in the case of IoT is connectivity. It is impossible to implement any accurate business use case without unified communication among the components which are connected in the IoT ecosystems (eg. sensors, computational engines, data centers etc.). The technologies such as Bluetooth, radio waves, Li-Fi, Wi-Fi, and other technologies can be used to connect IoT devices. We can use various internet communication layer protocols to optimize efficiency and create generic connectivity across IoT ecosystems and industry. In some cases, the IoT ecosystem may be built either on institutional premises or within an intranet.

2. Observation

We humans have a natural ability to comprehend and analyze our surroundings grounded on our previous practices with several things or circumstances. To get the most out of IoT, we need to recite the analogue signal and change it in a manner that allows us to develop expressive insights from it. To collect data based on a specific problem, various types of sensors such as pressure sensors, light sensors, temperature sensors and so on [7] are used. Light detection sensors, as well as pressure, velocity, and imagery sensors, are used in automotive applications. We must select the appropriate sensing paradigm to make a use case fruitful.

3. Active Engagements

An IoT (internet) device establishes an active engagement between several products, hybrid platform technologies, and facilities in order for them to work together. We integrate cloud computing technology with block-chain to create lively engagements between IoT components present in an IoT application [30]. Raw analogue data must be acquired, pre-processed, and rescaled as per business capability, if the IoT solutions are upgraded up to the industry standard. Carriers must understand the potential needs of handling such a large-scale data to meet the enhanced business needs when developing the IoT ecosystem. It's easy to conflate the requirement for active arrangements with scale; in practice, this means that the systems must handle large amounts of data from a variety of technologies, networks, goods, industries etc.

4. Scale

Internet devices are constructed in a method that allows them to be quickly increased up or down on claim. Internet (IoT) is being used in a wide range of applications, from smart home applications to systematizing massive factories and workstations, so the use cases are diverse [8]. A carrier's IoT infrastructure should be based on their current and potential interaction scale.

5. Nature's Dynamic

The first and most important move is to collect and transform data in such a way that it can be used to make business decisions. Throughout this operation, various IoT components must change their states on a regular basis. A temperature sensor's input, for example, can change over time as weather conditions change [7]. This is something that should be kept in mind while building the various IoT devices or applications.

6. Psychic abilities

The information is used to gain valuable market insights and make critical business decisions. On top of this vast data, we build deep learning models to gain useful insights. The analogue signals are pre-processed and translated to a format that can be used to train machine-learning models. We must choose the appropriate data infrastructure grounded on requirements gathered from business clients.

7. Vitality

The entire ecosystem requires a lot of resources, from front end devices to networking as well as the analytics layers. We must follow design methodology when creating an IoT ecosystem so that energy consumption is kept to a minimum.

8. Safety

Protection is one of the most important aspects of the IoT ecosystem. Via networking components, critical data is transferred from sensors to the analytics layer. When designing an IoT framework, we must consider adequate security procedures and also the firewalls to protect data from mismanagement and exploitation. Any part of an IoT ecosystem that is compromised will ultimately cause the entire system to fail.

9. Incorporation

IoT assimilates various inter domain models to enhance the user experience. It also sticks on the fact that the maintenance and operating costs are properly balanced.

5.2 Introduction to Smart Grid

- A smart grid is an energy distribution network that uses digital communication to identify local changes in power demand and reacts automatically without the need for human intervention [9].

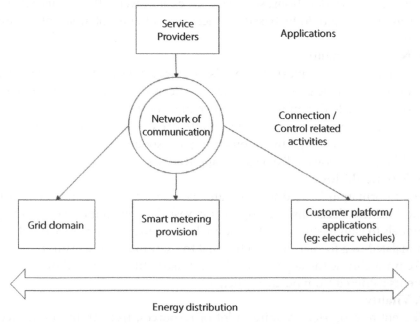

Figure 5.4 Components of smart grid architecture.

- It makes use of smart meters and appliances, as well as renewable and energy-efficient tools.
- The machine uses two-way wireless communication to deliver electricity [10, 23]. It helps users to communicate with the grid. Consumers, power companies, and government entities all profit from the smart grid, which eliminates many of the disadvantages of conventional electrical grids.

Figure 5.4 shows various reference points for generic Smart Grid Network Architecture components or modules. The components of a typical smart grid network are shown below.

- Grid-based domain (Operations include bulk generation, distribution, transmission)
- Meters that are smart
- Consumer domain (which includes smart appliances and other devices connected to a home network)
- Communication network (connects smart meters to customers and the power company for energy tracking and control operations; includes zigbee, Wi-Fi, HomePlug, cellular (GSM, GPRS, 3G, 4G-LTE), and other wireless technologies.
- Suppliers of third-party services (system vendors, operators, web companies etc.)

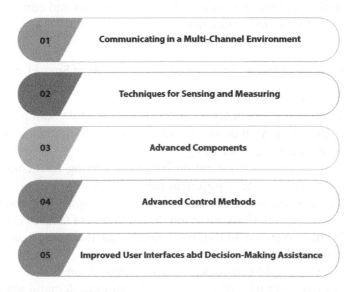

Figure 5.5 Smart grid technologies.

5.2.1   Smart Grid Technologies (SGT)

The Smart Grid systems are derived from five fundamental technologies identified by the US Department of Energy as shown in Figure 5.5. These technologies are combined to create a smart grid that is more effective and dependable than the current grid [11].

- **Communicating in a Multi-Channel Environment**
  Components are linked to open architecture to provide real-time information and power, allowing any part of the grid to speak and listen.
- **Techniques for Sensing and Measuring**
  To aid quicker and more precise responses, various sensing and measuring technologies are used for remote control, demand-side management, and bill generation.
- **Advanced Components**
  The new research in power electronics, storage, superconductivity, and diagnostics uses a variety of components.
- **Advanced Control Methods**
  Advanced methods are used to monitor critical components, diagnose problems quicker, and provide specific solutions in response to any incident.
- **Improved User Interfaces and Decision-Making Assistance**
  Improved smart systems are being used to enhance human decision-making, transforming grid operators and administrators into virtual futurists.

Advantages
The following are some of the advantages or benefits of Smart Grid:

- It reduces electricity theft.
- It cuts down on energy waste (transmission, distribution etc.)
- It saves money on power, meter reading, T&M activities, and repairs, among other things.
- Due to automatic operation based on varying load conditions, it eliminates equipment failures [12].
- Demand-Response decreases the burden on smart grid assets during peak periods, lowering the likelihood of failure [13].
- It cuts down on long-term outages and the costs that go along with them.
- The smart grid provides people with protection.
- A smart grid will satisfy increased customer demand without requiring additional infrastructure.

Disadvantages

The following are the Smart Grid's drawbacks or disadvantages:

- A reliable communication network should be accessible at all times.
- In a smart grid environment, network congestion or performance are major challenges during an emergency.
- In unusual circumstances such as a windstorm, heavy rain, or lightning, cellular network providers do not guarantee coverage.
- It is possible to hack certain smart meters, which can be used to increase or decrease power demand.
- Installing a smart meter is costlier than installing a traditional old electricity meter.

Figure 5.6 shows the Smart Grid Architecture for an energy company's smart metering application. Smart meters are built in homes, offices, and factories [9]. These smart meters communicate with the DCU (Data

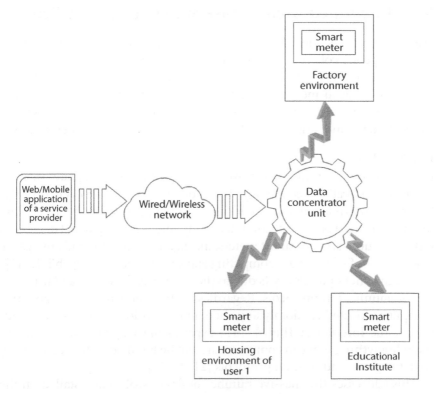

Figure 5.6 Smart grid architecture for smart metering application.

Concentrator Unit), which is located near the residential layout on an electric pole [2]. Instantaneous consumptions, accumulated energy, and time of day energy data are all parameters that meters can provide.

- The energy consumption and other parameters related to meter status are collected by the data concentrator units installed in the field. These collected data are wired or wirelessly transmitted to data servers at the service provider or at a third-party location.
- DSL, fiber optics, or a cellular network may all be used as a mode of transport (2G, GPRS, 3G, 4G-LTE etc.).
- Using a laptop, mobile device, phone, or PC, the entire smart grid network information can be updated/monitored through a web site or web portal. For data collection and retrieval, the web portal interacts with DCUs in real time. It detects tampering with meters, billing records, energy consumption, and load status, among other things.

5.3   Integrated Architecture of IoT and Smart Grid

The smart grid relies heavily on automatic meter reading systems. It is a device that intelligently collects, processes, and monitors power consumption information in real time. IoT (Internet of Things or IoT) enables automated data collection, irregular measurement, tracking of electricity quality, and analysis of usage patterns. In addition, the system allows for information release, distributed energy monitoring, and data sharing between smart power devices.

IoT Based SG

In comparison to a traditional power grid, the smart grid integrates Internet and Communication Technology [10] across the entire chain of energy originating from producers to the end users through across-the-board deployment of various types of detecting, activating, and other implanted devices, as well as the utilization of smart meters, intelligent appliances, and emergence of e-cars, all of which share computing and communication capabilities [2].

The Internet's popularity is due to the widespread use of standard TCP/IP communication protocols. Regardless of their access technologies, two computers located randomly anywhere in the world could easily communicate. The Internet of Things (IoT) expands the scope of the Internet to include anything that can communicate and be handled individually, using structured communication protocols [21, 26, 27].

This addresses the massive number of devices/objects installed on the SG has a critical need to establish a real time communication with the nearby devices, with the help of either the standard communication protocols such as TCP/IP stack, or by using the proprietary solutions such as Zigbee v1 module, (W)HART and Z-Wave technologies [14].

It would be interesting for energy suppliers to obtain energy usage remotely from SMs to bill the consumers, as well as detect attempts at

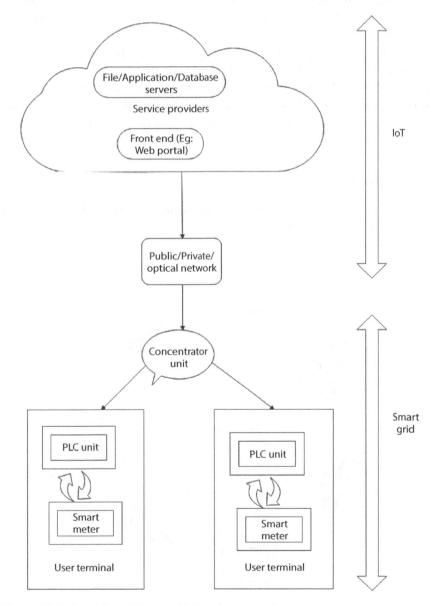

Figure 5.7 Integrated architecture of IoT and smart grid.

interfering using SMs (for example, energy stealing). End-users would also be interested in receiving latest rates (eg. dynamic pricing) in order to better control their consumption, as well as receiving early warnings about planned disconnection.

IP based communication protocols are responsible for bidirectional communication, end-to-end communication, as well as public relations infrastructures. They do so in order to make them more accessible and reduce prompted costs.

The idea of incorporating Internet and Communication Technology [10] with the smart grid paves a way for new security issues which does not exists at present. These security concerns and challenges will be hindrance for IoT-based SG's quick deployment and fast adoption by the users. Figure 5.7 illustrates an integrated architecture for Internet of Things and Smart Grid technology.

5.3.1   Safety Concerns

The IoT-based SG will face many security issues as a cyber-physical system as presented in Figure 5.8.

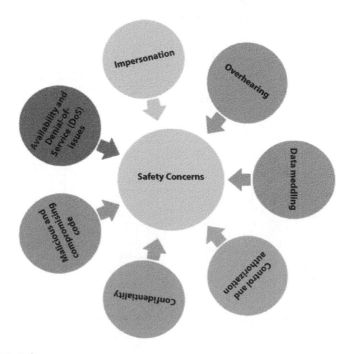

Figure 5.8 Safety concerns.

- **Impersonation:** This type of attack attempts to communicate pretending as an authentic organization in an illegal manner by impersonating it. An intruder may impersonate the identity of a smart meter to trick it into repaying as per its energy usage.
- **Overhearing:** Since IoT (IoT)-based SG devices interact with the help of the public internet, an invader can simply gain access to the data they exchange. An intruder can learn about a household's energy consumption easily.
- **Data meddling:** An invader may alter traded data (eg. changes in OLA transportation cost of rides during peak hours) to make them the minimal prices possible. As a result, instead of reducing their consumption (charging e-cars, for example), households could increase it, resulting in an encumbered power network.
- **Control and authorization:** Since certain devices, such as smart meters or field installed sensors and actuators used in the substations, can be controlled and configured remotely, an intruder or an enraged employee may attempt to obtain unauthorized right of entry, exploit them, and damage physical assets (such as transformers) or cause power wastages.
- **Confidentiality:** The fine-grained data available in smart appliances could compromise the user's confidentiality by revealing details of the activities (sleeping and wake up times, dinner times etc.,), whether they are available at home or abroad, whether they are on holiday, and so on.
- **Malicious and compromising code:** Since SG objects can compute and communicate, they are vulnerable to physical or remote compromise. Furthermore, since they execute on various software, they may be infected with different types of software or malevolent code which will monitor and exploit them (eg. Smart appliances in the home). The activity of physical compromise is more prevalent due to the light weight of the IoT devices.
- **Availability and Denial-of-Service (DoS) issues:** In the traditional power grid approach particularly if it was implemented on a large scale, it was difficult to estimate the availability of resources. In the SG, ICT would be incorporated even into the power grid's critical properties, allowing them to be targeted and rendered partially or completely inaccessible because of a DoS attack [15].

5.3.2   Security Issues

While designing an IoT-based SG there are several challenges must be dealt [16] in terms of security policies and procedures which are described as follows:

- **Mobility:** IoT devices are movable in nature (eg. e-cars). Since the environment is continuously changing, frequent authentication is needed in order to establish safe communication.
- **Positioning of devices:** SG has the potential to cover the entire world because of its distributive feature of objects/devices in large numbers. Such devices can operate even though they are unattended and can be installed in remote locations with a little distance of perimeter, allowing them to be easily accessed. Any attempt to tamper with security solutions should be detected.
- **Legacy systems:** The hardware and software are implemented with little connectivity, or via private communication networks. Most of them are built upon proprietary solutions. Due to this, legacy systems and devices might have little or no security support. Integrating legacy systems with an IoTSG is a difficult task.
- **Limited Resources:** a number of SG devices/objects, particularly those that are widely deployed, have limited resources. When designing security solutions, extra caution must be taken to ensure that the solutions can fit within their limited resources.
- **Heterogeneous nature of devices:** Due to differences in the resources of the devices/objects on the SG (eg. memory, time-sensitivity, computation, bandwidth), as well as differences in the usage of protocols on non-IP devices [17] obtaining safe communication among them is a difficult task that often necessitates the compatibility with the existing technologies or the use of gateways.
- **Collaborative communication:** Legacy systems and non-IP devices which could not support the TCP/IP stack (for example, Zigbee v1, HART) are unable to communicate with IP-based systems and devices. Without the help of gateways, establishing a safe and collaborative communication among those categories of system is impossible. The two

possible collaborative communication possible between IP and non-IP based system are:

1. Providing complete support, and
2. Providing partial support (eg. DTLS with/without certificate support)

- **Reliability:** It is necessary to create a substantial amount of trust among the devices in order to initialize a communication among them. In a large-scale network, it is practically difficult to manage the trust among the various devices deployed in IoTSG.
- **Timing constraints:** Certain devices in SG must respond to events and messages in real time. SCADA systems used in substations for communication and sharing purpose [18], must reply immediately to the dynamic changes in the electricity's current, voltage, or frequency values, as well as other meteorological factors. To keep the assets securely and also to avoid abnormalities from spreading outages to other sections of the power grid, various types of smart devices are included.

5.4   Smart Grid Security Services Based on IoT

The major security solutions to be included for an IoT-based SG are presented in Figure 5.9 are as follows.

- **Authentication:** The ability to verify or confirm the uniqueness of any communication device present in IoTSG [8]. For example, in order to bill for the right customer, an energy supplier must authenticate each smart meter.
- **Data Integrity:** The process of ensuring that the data received has not been altered in any way. Smart meters, for example, must maintain the integrity of software updates as well as the source of updates.
- **Confidentiality:** The process of providing the information only to those who have need as well as the proper privileges. End-user energy consumption will be available only to the SG's operator and the energy provider.

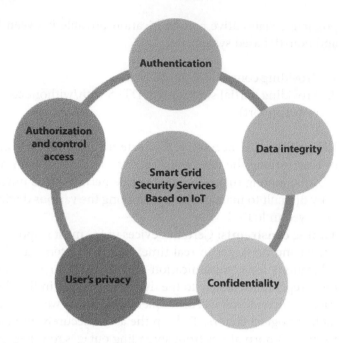

Figure 5.9 Smart grid security services based on IoT.

- **User Privacy:** Ensures that all data relating to the user whether brute, implied, or generated – cannot be accessed without his or her consent explicitly, and that it will be used only for the purposes intended. For example, billing data on energy usage could not be used for any other analysis purpose.
- **Authorization and Control Access:** Ensures that a legitimate person has been given the required rights to access certain services or is allowed to perform certain tasks. Field agents require authorization and access control rights to perform manual configuration on a smart meter.

Steps for Implementation

It is mandatory to know what is to be implemented rather than how to implement it. This ensures that IoT improves the profit in terms of current services offered, products utilized and for an additional cost incurred for the production process also. It may also improve the quality of your current goods and services by upgrading the features and options. The stage by stage implementation of IoT is given in Figure 5.10 and the steps for effective implementation is illustrated in Figure 5.11.

Step 1: Clear and precise definition of business goals

- Fix the goals clearly from the user requirements.
- Try with short-term investment which could be afforded.
- Work in a team and compare the returns and solutions with the older one.
- Determine a clear technique which supports both the near future and long run of IoT based SG.
- IoT can be more effectively introduced in stages, limiting the amount of capital you can spend on process optimization per month or year as shown in Figure 5.10.

Step 2: Investigate and Test Use Case on IoT
After recognizing the goals and issues, the readily available and most popular use case which will be most appropriate must be chosen [8]. Such an approach will help us to maintain the following features.

- **Preventive measures:** Continuous monitoring on the amount of wear, component loss, and oxidation in order to avoid permanent or expensive damage.
- **Automated refills:** keeping track of fuel levels and also the nature of the filter will help us to automate the refilling as well as the change of the filter process.
- **Periodical monitoring of resources:** Monitoring energy, water, and gas usage on a regular basis will help us for effective utilization of resources and it will reduce wastage.

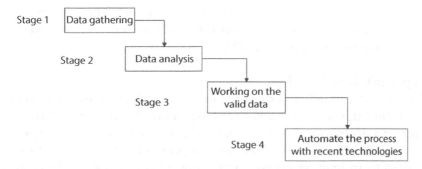

Figure 5.10 Stage by stage approach for effective IoT implementation.

- **Monitoring assets:** It entails tracking assets, such as objects, vehicles, and even people, as the name implies. Environmental monitoring entails gathering information about the external factors such as moisture, emissions, soil nutrient level and temperature.
- **Integration towards IoT:** A new product focused on customers, businesses, or industries has to be integrated towards the IoT network.
- **Access control:** Controlling access either in physical means or by digital means in order to develop an effective IoT based SG system is known as access control and security.
- **Process Control & Optimization:** gathering data on process performance and using it to improve it;

Choosing an appropriate and also the readily available use case will reduce the cost of testing.

Step 3: Choose an appropriate hardware

- Identifying the components involved in implementation is another important step.
- It will provide a basic understanding about the network infrastructure.
- The basic type of software will be sensors which will provide data on temperature, humidity, volume etc.
- The data collected by the sensors must then be transmitted over the internet to a destination.
- At this stage communication devices, which are used to link the data-gathering devices, are also needed.
- For some applications, a small change with an existing equipment is needed whereas for some applications a complete replacement of an existing hardware is needed to make the IoT devices compatible.

Step 4: IoT Tool Selection

The internet and IoT (Internet of Things or IoT) devices complement each other. The Internet is the backbone of IoT. In turn IoT devices will make the internet a useful one. Both Internet and IoT should be used effectively to improve the efficiency of your business operation. Any computer that can connect to an internet network and perform the functions as data gathering, processing and send it to an appropriate end terminal is considered

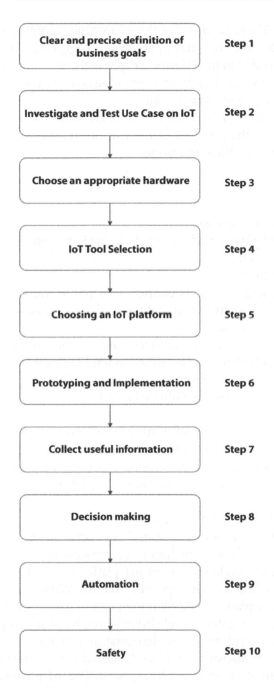

Figure 5.11 Steps for implementation.

an IoT device. They also monitor the environment continuously and send a message to the specified terminal when a triggering event occurs. The knowledge provided in the "Hardware" phase focuses on converting popular devices into IoT devices by incorporating sensors and other IoT terminals, such as the prototyping IoT kit.

Nowadays, more IoT-oriented devices are available which allows the system to "learn" the behavior of the user, anticipating their desires and alerting them if a problem is detected.

Examples:

1. Smart thermostats
2. Smart lights (Switch on/off the lights in presence/absence of human beings)
3. Smart locks
4. IP cameras (cameras connect to a phone via internet and send and receive video data as well as commands to adjust the camera's focus)
5. Drones (possessing self-stabilization with internet connectivity and also incur an ability to send the captured data and also it can be controlled automatically) [19]
6. Voice assistants (eg. Google Home)

All these applications are interesting from a manufacturing perspective, several companies have found innovative applications for them, such as Amazon's investments in autonomous drone delivery. IoT cameras can ensure protection within a physical business premises.

Step 5: Choosing an IoT Platform
The program that controls and centralizes every part of the IoT network and its connected devices, including the process of sending and receiving data/commands is known as an IoT platform. It can be made to order in-house or purchased from a specialist vendor. Whatever method is used to choose an IoT platform, networking plays a major role. It is not necessary to consider the feature of reliability before building the prototype, but it is mandatory for future IoT implementation activity.

When an IoT framework is replaced, the majority of the software aspects of the implementation must also be replaced: The IoT platform determines how everything interacts and how data is treated. It is a very expensive method to change it. After choosing an IoT platform, once the setup is ready, implementing IoT becomes much easier. All that is required is to set up links and protocols necessary for communication by following the guidelines of the chosen IoT platform.

Step 6: Prototyping and Implementation
Form a team of people from different departments to think thoroughly before beginning implementation. Since IoT includes several different systems communicating with one another, you'll need people with a variety of skills at all stages of the project, including conception, design, prototyping, implementation, and incrementation. The experts present in the IoT team are illustrated in Figure 5.12.

- **Computer engineer:** The person who is responsible for designing and implementing firmware programs for embedded systems which enables the transmission and reception of sensor data.

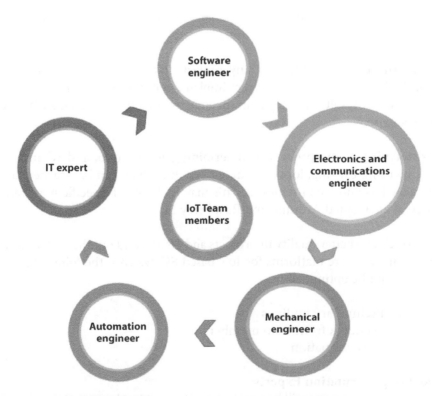

Figure 5.12 IoT base SG team.

- **Software Engineer:** The person who creates and implements computer programs that are connected with the network, APIs, and data collected.
- **Electronics engineer:** He is responsible for designing the circuit boards used in IoT based SG.
- **Mechanical Engineer:** A person who understands machines and other mechanical parts, as well as their restrictions.
- **Mechatronics Engineer:** A person who knows how to link IoT devices and the internet, with a focus on sensor applications.
- **Automation Engineer:** The person who is responsible for the management and computerization of manufacturing processes.
- **IT Expert:** He is responsible for the internet setup
- **Manufacturing Expert:** To direct the team to your needs based on their expertise in the manufacturing processes, needs, and limitations.
- **Telecommunications expert:** To work with a wide range of protocols, middle wares, and modern tools for IoT data transfer subscription models.

Commitment is essential for any project. IoT technology implementation is also similar to other project implementations. Acquire information based on the result, carefully plan the implementation, and evaluate it with a prototype.

Prototyping is the process of determining what works and what does not by using existing, loosely coupled systems which can be attached and detached as and when required. This may include IoT-specific hardware, such as an adapted Arduino and Raspberry Pi.

To achieve better quality in projects and also to find out the better hardware and software platforms for IoT based SG systems, the following factors should be optimized.

1. Preliminary findings
2. Feedback from team members
3. Cost estimation

Post Implementation Experts:
The following experts will help us to tune the post implementation process.

- **Information expert:** To handle data storage, an expert in information systems is needed.
- **Data scientist:** A person who extends his support to analyze the information gathered.
- **Statistician:** A person plays a vital role to help with data processing and quality control.
- **Security Officer:** An expert who is responsible for internal and external governance.
- **Computer scientist:** This kind of expert is needed to introduce an automation based techniques in IoTSG applications.

Step 7: Collect useful information

To keep track of everything in an environment [7], more sensors are deployed which complicates the entire network infrastructure. This entails producing terabytes of data continuously for each and second, minute and an hour. When dealing with large amounts of data, the natural inclination is to delete anything gathered as soon as it is used.

To store all the information gathered by the sensors, a lot of storage space is needed which will substantially increase the cost of IoT implementation. In the conventional methods, after processing the gathered data, it will be deleted from the storage. By using recent technologies such as big data and cloud storage facilities [22], there is no need to discard or delete any processed data from the storage. It can be saved and used to improve the processes even more.

In an ideal world, the information obtained will be collected, interpreted, and stored in a database for a fixed period of time. Data analysts will use the software to collect, compile and analyze the data. Such software will ensure process consistency and performance, identify potential problems, and discover the ways to improve them.

Since every sensor has a different type of output port as well as different output formats, practical implementation becomes difficult [17]. Before sending the data to the server, the person/device who is responsible for collecting the data must convert it to a particular format. Such a format will vary depending on the various platforms, IoT management apps, database sort, and technician's skill set. Based on the requirement of an application, data will be collected and stored on a continuous basis and also synchronized with time if needed.

Example: Logistics

1. The raw data from the sensors, combined with time data, can be used to determine how long it takes to transport a component of a machinery or product between targeted locations and compare it with the previous transportation time.
2. In the same way, GPS data can be gathered. From this, the traffic data can be generated [2]. This will be very useful in business for detecting bottlenecks and identifying ways to make the entire transportation as well as the manufacturing process more effective.
3. If the positions of machines are to be adjusted in the future, this will be a good initiative to check whether the hauling has been improved or deteriorated and suggest ways to improve it better.

Step 8: Decision making

There will be two different types of decision making as shown in Figure 5.13.

1. Lazy decision making
2. Automated decision making

Lazy decision making

The process of decision making based on the long term is known as "Lazy decision making". In this process, all the data gathered by the sensors are converted by the computers but it will be used later for analysis purposes.

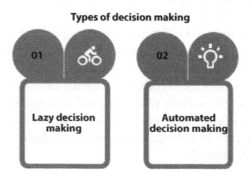

Figure 5.13 Types of decision making.

All will be saved indefinitely and could be evaluated and reanalyzed at any time.

This data can be used to track the status of your products, personnel, and systems, which also includes the data currently being collected. Data scientists and machine learning software analysis will determine what needs to be improved to make everything more effective.

Automated decision making
The process of decision making based on real-time is known as "Automated decision making". Such decisions will be carried out by automated systems rather than humans.

Automated decision making is widely used for safety purposes. If anything goes past a certain degree of safety, everything might have to be shut down at the same time. Such a logic should be pre-programmed into edge computing systems or on circuit boards, to ensure the shortest possible time between measurement and intervention.

Step 9: Automation
Machine learning is a form of artificial intelligence (AI) that is developed to analyze data in real time, finding trends in it and based on the code implemented, action will be taken.

AI will replace or complement the role of data scientist. It performs data analysis to predict the need for human behavior, maintenance among other things, simply by finding trends in the data [20].

Example:
Siemens' Internet of Trains in which machine learning and IoT were used to perform preventive maintenance on trains and rail tracks.

Step 10: Potential safety
The General Data Protection Regulation (GDPR), a regulation in EU law specifies some rules on ensuring safety of data available in IoT based SG systems.

- How should personal data be stored by an organization?
- How should that data be treated?
- How should that data be secured?

This law was adopted in 2018 by the European Commission, in part to avoid breaches like Equifax's and to mitigate the consequences if one breaks the rules.

References

1. Babar, M., *et al.*, *Secure and resilient demand side management engine using machine learning for IoT-enabled smart grid.* 2020. **62**: p. 102370.
2. Suresh, A., *et al.*, *Industrial IoT Application Architectures and Use Cases.* 2020: CRC Press.
3. Bansal, S. and D.J.I.J.o.W.I.N. Kumar, *IoT ecosystem: A survey on devices, gateways, operating systems, middleware and communication.* 2020: p. 1-25.
4. Sha, K., *et al.*, *A survey of edge computing-based designs for IoT security.* 2020. **6**(2): p. 195-202.
5. Jamali, M.A.J., *et al.*, *IoT Architecture.* 2020: p. 9-31.
6. Mocnej, J., *et al.*, *Quality-enabled decentralized IoT architecture with efficient resources utilization.* 2021. **67**: p. 102001.
7. Ullo, S.L. and G.J.S. Sinha, *Advances in smart environment monitoring systems using IoT and sensors.* 2020. **20**(11): p. 3113.
8. Liyanage, M., *et al.*, *IoT security: Advances in authentication.* 2020: John Wiley & Sons.
9. Dileep, G.J.R.E., *A survey on smart grid technologies and applications.* 2020. **146**: p. 2589-2625.
10. Sathish, R., & Kumar, D. R. (2013, April). Dynamic Detection of Clone Attack in Wireless Sensor Networks. 2013 International Conference on Communication Systems and Network Technologies (CSNT 2013).
11. Ahmadiahangar, R., *et al.*, *Challenges of smart grids implementation,* in *Demand-side Flexibility in Smart Grid.* 2020, Springer. p. 1-15.
12. Diahovchenko, I., *et al.*, *Progress and challenges in smart grids: distributed generation, smart metering, energy storage and smart loads.* 2020: p. 1-15.
13. Shewale, A., *et al.*, *An overview of demand response in smart grid and optimization techniques for efficient residential appliance scheduling problem.* 2020. **13**(16): p. 4266.
14. Gupta, T. and R. Bhatia. *Communication Technologies in Smart Grid at Different Network Layers: An Overview.* in *2020 International Conference on Intelligent Engineering and Management (ICIEM).* 2020. IEEE.
15. Xu, J., *et al.*, *Bayesian adversarial multi-node bandit for optimal smart grid protection against cyber attacks.* 2021. **128**: p. 109551.
16. Khan, F.A., *et al.*, *Blockchain technology, improvement suggestions, security challenges on smart grid and its application in healthcare for sustainable development.* 2020. **55**: p. 102018.
17. Nguyen, C.T., *et al.*, *Framework and Roadmap for Smart Grid Interoperability Standards Regional Roundtables Summary Report.* 2020.

18. Ferrag, M.A., *et al.*, *Cyber security for fog-based smart grid SCADA systems: Solutions and challenges.* 2020. **52**: p. 102500.

19. Nayyar, A., B.-L. Nguyen, and N.G. Nguyen. *The internet of drone things (iodt): Future envision of smart drones.* in *First International Conference on Sustainable Technologies for Computational Intelligence.* 2020. Springer.

20. Kaur, M.J., V.P. Mishra, and P. Maheshwari, *The convergence of digital twin, IoT, and machine learning: transforming data into action*, in *Digital twin technologies and smart cities.* 2020, Springer. p. 3-17.

21. S.Malathy, Dr.C.N.Vanitha, "Secure Integration of Cyber Security and Internet of Things in Addressing its Challenges", International Journal of Recent Technology and Engineering, ISSN: 2277-3878,Volume 8, Issue 4, November 2019.

22. K.Vanitha, C.N.Vanitha, M.Mohamed Musthafa, S.Malathy, "Efficient Semantic Interrogation Scheme over Cryptographic Data in Cloud" IEEE Xplore Digital Library, DOI:10.1109/ICICT48043.2020.9112383, June 2020.

23. Dr.Vanitha C.N, Malathy.S "Optimizing wireless sensor networks path selection using Resource levelling technique in transmitting endscopy biomedical data", IEEE Xplore Digital Library, DOI: 10.1088/1757-899X/1055/1/012071.

24. Lalitha, K., Kumar, D. R., Poongodi, C., & Arumugam, J. (2021). Healthcare Internet of Things–The Role of Communication Tools and Technologies. In Blockchain, Internet of Things, and Artificial Intelligence (pp. 331-348). Chapman and Hall/CRC.

25. Dhiviya, S., Malathy, S., & Kumar, D. R. (2018). Internet of Things (IoT) Elements, Trends and Applications. Journal of Computational and Theoretical Nanoscience, 15(5), 1639–1643.

26. umar, D. R., Krishna, T. A., & Wahi, A. (2018). Health Monitoring Framework for in Time Recognition of Pulmonary Embolism Using Internet of Things. Journal of Computational and Theoretical Nanoscience, 15(5), 1598–1602. https://doi.org/10.1166/jctn.2018.7347

27. Jeyaselvi, M., Dhanaraj, R.K., Sathya, M. et al. A highly secured intrusion detection system for IoT using EXPSO-STFA feature selection for LAANN to detect attacks. Cluster Comput (2022). https://doi.org/10.1007/s10586-022-03607-1

28. Soumya Ranjan Jena, Raju Shanmugam, Rajesh Kumar Dhanaraj, Kavita Saini Recent Advances and Future Research Directions in Edge Cloud Framework. (2019). International Journal of Engineering and Advanced Technology, 9(2), 439–444. https://doi.org/10.35940/ijeat.b3090.129219

29. Rajesh Kumar D, & ManjupPriya S. (2013, December). Cloud based M-Healthcare emergency using SPOC. 2013 Fifth International Conference on Advanced Computing (ICoAC). 2013 Fifth International Conference on Advanced Computing (ICoAC). https://doi.org/10.1109/icoac.2013.6921965

30. Dhanaraj, R. K., Rajkumar, K., & Hariharan, U. (2020). Enterprise IoT Modeling: Supervised, Unsupervised, and Reinforcement Learning. In Business Intelligence for Enterprise Internet of Things (pp. 55–79). Springer International Publishing. https://doi.org/10.1007/978-3-030-44407-5_3, https://doi.org/10.1166/jctn.2018.7354

6

Exploration of Assorted Modernizations in Forecasting Renewable Energy Using Low Power Wireless Technologies for IoTSG

Logeswaran K.[1]*, Suresh P.[2], Ponselvakumar A.P.[1], Savitha S.[1], Sentamilselvan K.[3] and Adhithyaa N.[1]

[1]Kongu Engineering College, Perundurai, Erode, Tamil Nadu, India
[2]School of Computer Science and Engineering, Vellore Institute of Technology, Vellore, Tamil Nadu, India
[3]Sir Isaac Newton College of Engineering and Technology, Nagapattinam, Tamil Nadu, India

Abstract

The path between power plant and user is called as the electric grid. Electric grid consist of step-up, step-down transformer and several other components. Conventional grid is designed on "supply flow demand". Smart Grid is designed on idea that "demand follows supply". By leveraging the concept of cognitive modeling and Interne of Things (IoT), smartness can be enabled in traditional electric grid which gives the way for Smart Grid (SG). Smart Grid provides better ways of integrating electricity from wind, solar and other non-renewable into the grid. Through IoT, every device in grid and user are connected to internet by using wired and wireless technologies. A wide variety of Smart Grid implementations, including advanced metering and demand response, can be enabled by wireless technology. However there are many daunting obstacles in the deployment of wireless technology to smart grids, such as trade-offs between wireless reach and power, high connectivity efficiency and restricted spectral resources. Seamless two-way connectivity is a core feature of the smart grid vision. Several structured wired and wireless networking systems are available for different smart grid applications. As wireless networking is increasing lately, large, metropolitan, local and personal area networks are able to provide

*Corresponding author: klogesbtech@gmail.com

P. Sanjeevikumar, Rajesh Kumar Dhanaraj, Malathy Sathyamoorthy, Jens Bo Holm-Nielsen and Balamurugan Balusamy (eds.) *Smart Grids and Internet of Things: An Energy Perspective*, (157–192) © 2023 Scrivener Publishing LLC

streamlined technologies. Furthermore, wireless solutions offer major advantages over wired technology, such as low installation costs, quick rollout and mobility, but still more suited for remote applications. Researchers have shown considerable interest in possibilities for modernization of the activity of electric networks provided by ICT (Information and Communication Technologies). This is possible by decarburization and tracking and regulation by advanced networking standards. The integration of electrical and telecommunications technology is very important in this respect. Different standards of wireless connectivity viz WiMAX, Zig Bee, Wi-Fi, GSM, GPRS, UMTS, etc., can be used to build Smart Grid Network and expand connectivity through the distributed infrastructure.

This chapter seeks to examine many of the current upgrades in the use of low power wireless technology since many remotely installed wireless technology systems deplete the battery and make certain IoT device with battery power unfeasible or unpractical. In this section, the issues of integration and mitigation of renewables into the smart grid will be discussed. Due to the changeable output nature, the electrical power supply and distribution domains produce challenges in voltage and frequency fluctuations. A number of tactics will be described in order to address these problems, which include optimization, forecasting and new monitoring approaches.

Keywords: Low power wireless technology, smart grid, IoT, renewable energy, hydro energy, geothermal energy, nuclear energy, wind energy

6.1   Introduction to the Chapter

6.1.1   Fossil Fuels and Conventional Grid

Fossil fuels is a term used to describe a collection of energies which were built over the carboniferous period, about a few thousand millions years ago, from ancient plants and organisms. Fossil fuels are considered non-renewable natural resources such as coal, oil, and natural gas as they take millions of years to form, which ensures that once resources are used, they can not be filled up in human existence. Fossil fuels formed from organic matter in the geological deposit underneath the surface of the Earth over hundreds of millions of years. The decomposition organism was tapped into rocks and sediment during the carboniferous period and subject to pressure and warmth. This culminated in the fossil fuels we use today as energy rich hydrocarbons. For power, fossil fuels can be burned, or refined as heat or transport fuel. Various forms of fossil fuels formed during decomposition, depending on the combination of organic matter, temperature, time, and pressure. Three main types of coal, oil and natural gas fossil fuels exist. Coal is produced by the sun, pressure, and heat of ferns, plants and trees. Oil consists of small organisms such as zoological plankton and algae, in which pressure causes the decomposition of more complex organic matter. Natural gas is produced only when subjected to higher heat and pressure, which further decomposes and transforms it into gas.

Energy sources are searched for fossil fuels because of their high density of energy. They are the most powerful sources in the world. There are many uses for fossil fuels from the generation of electricity to transportation of gasoline. They can also be used in the production of a number of popular plastics and cosmetics products, including some medicines. These tools have driven and continue to drive industrialization throughout history.

Depending on the geographical location, fossil fuels may be plentiful, inexpensive, and in some cases scarce and costly. Therefore, because of lack of geopolitical problems, these highly useful resources are allocated naturally. The gradual decline of fossil fuel reserves that are most available for this purpose has forced companies to build more difficult or non-conventional reserves. This also involves increased safety and environmental risks and higher costs. However, fossil fuel is a greenhouse gas that releases carbon dioxide, a contributing climate change. As the world's primary source of oil, fossil fuels generate much of the global GHG emissions from human resources. Over the last 50 years, global greenhouse gas (GHG) emissions have almost doubled, with our agricultural, forestry, industrialization, transportation, and economic growth growing. Fossil fuels, for example coal, natural gas and oil contribute 57% of all anthropogenic CO_2 emissions and 35% of all the anthropogenic ones, make a significant contribution to GHG emissions. Moreover, both the environment and human health are at risk in their processing.

The main components of power grids include synchronous equipment, energy transformers, transmission lines, transmission substations, distribution lines, distribution substations, load formats, and the traditional electricity grid. They are located far from the demand area, and electricity is transmitted over long power lines. In the 1890s, with every decade of technological development, our current grid was designed and improved. There are now over 9,200 units with a generation output of over 1 million megawatts connecting to over 300,000 kilometers of power lines. Although the grid is recognized as a technical marvel, we extend it to its potential.

6.1.2   Renewable Energy and Smart Grid

Renewable energy comes from the sources of natural filling and never running; hydro, solar, wind, biomass and geothermal sources are common sources. Renewable energy in the world is on the rise, and the secret to fighting climate change will be this sustainable energy source. Fossil fuels account for more than 80.0% of the total energy produced by human beings. Renewables are, however, the world's fastest-growing energy sources.

Renewable energy has many benefits

- Climate change can be combated when no direct greenhouse gas emissions are produced. The only pollution they emit is that which comes from production, installation, operation and maintenance. The emissions are indirect. But they are even minimal.
- Renewable energy will minimize emissions, thereby reducing health threats. No emissions of air pollution and geothermal and biomass systems are significantly lower than non-renewable sources for wind, solar and hydro systems.
- Renewable energy sources are efficient since renewable energy sources are renewable and will never run out. Once renewable installations have been installed, their cost is relatively low and the fuel is also free because the price of renewable energy tends to be constant over time.

Downside of Renewable energy

- Strom generation on an equal scale is difficult for renewable energy sources as fossil fuels
- Building wind farmland and dams will damage wilderness and ecological patterns and damage
- Strom and wind are intermittent and produce power only when the sun shines or wind blows. Batteries for subsequent use can store excess energy. However, it is also expensive.

While renewable energy is a challenge, it is also an eco-friendly alternative to greenhouse gas emissions and fossil fuel pollution, and as technological progress makes renewables more affordable, available and efficient. We will be able to reach an end to climate change.

We need a new type of infrastructure to manage, in order to simplify and handle the growing complexities and needs of the electricity of the twenty-first century, the fundamental basis of digital and informatics equipment and technologies. In other words, the grid is smart with computer technology, which enables two-way contact between the enterprise and its customers and senses. Smart grid is made from commands, computers, robots and state-of-the-art technology and equipment, with the exception of a remote grid to meet our constantly changing demands. The smart grid is like internet.

   Need for Smart Grid

- To satisfy the increasing demand of electricity due to growing population
- To minimize the transmission and distribution loss
- Inclusion of the sources of renewable energy in the scheme to reduce fossil fuel reliance and free energy from emissions
- To step up a dual communication channel between utility and consumer
- To make fault detection, isolation and restoration easier and convenient
- For advance metering infrastructure
- For Distribution Grid Management
- For energy storage
- Due to non-replenishing nature of fossil fuels, energy cost increases rapidly which increases the demand for renewable energy management with smart grid
- Emissions of greenhouse gases from fossil fuels trigger earth pollution, increasing renewable energy innovation and the intelligent network

This chapter provide elaboration of possible architecture of smart gird that can actively participate in managing vast renewable energy sources and customer. In Section 6.3, the of role of IoT in brining smartness to conventional power grid is explained. Section 6.4, brings together various renewable energy resources (RES) and how this RES will as key technology for smart grid. Section 6.5 discuss about various Low power wireless Technologies for IoTSG.

6.2   Intangible Architecture of Smart Grid (SG)

Any smart grid architecture will broadly include the seven core components for its operation. Seven components includes bulk energy generators, transmission systems, distribution, customers, markets, operations and service providers. Bulk energy generators are the source of energy from which energy is produced. This generators may be fossil fuels or renewable energy sources. The main goal of this energy generators produces bulk quantity of power by means of energy. The generated energy is then transformed to the transmission network and then distribution network and then the customers. Service providers are the certain organizations which basically provides services to the generation systems, transmission systems, distribution systems and also to the customers. Markets are the participants, they will participate for trading of the energy power. Figure 6.1 shows the model view of processes involved in smart grid model.

The end user who uses energy is customers. Customer domain boundaries are usually regarded as the energy service interface and utility meter (ESI). The ESI offers a protected Utility-to-Consumer gui. The customer domain can be segmented into domain, business and industrial subdomains. Determining and gateway must be configured for every kind of customer domain. For any type of smart grid, communication network is essential to have data flow between different components of smart grid. The main responsibility of ESI is to communicate with advanced metering infrastructure or internet. This ESI communication is established through

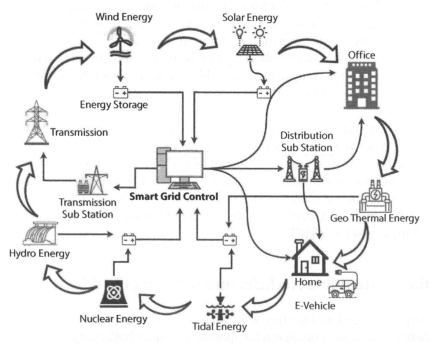

Figure 6.1 Model view of processes involved in smart grid model.

any type of communication network, which is within customer's premises. At first Micro generations is a part of customer domain that includes all distributed generations such as battery stored power. Next, Building and home automation is a another part of customer domain which controls various power related functions happening inside buildings of smart grid. Industrial automation is the another part of customer domain which controls various industrial process.

The market domain refers to the method of trade of the purchase and sale of grid properties. In the business sector, there are many challenges. Firstly, price segmentation and DER signals for every consumer subsection. Secondly, aggregators' capacities have to be broadened, helping small DER companies to become involved in the industry. Thirdly, the maintenance of interoperability between the different smart gird equipment, including generations, transmissions, delivery and customer facilities. Fourthly, utility retail and wholesale management and regulation. Market fields include different sub-domains, including DER aggregate, market management, company, wholesale, trading and retailing. Service providers, transmission, clients', processes, distributions and bulk generators are also accessed to these elements.

Service provider as the name implies offers several amenities to all the components involved in the smart grid. Numerous business processes involved in customer domain, distributor domain and power system producer are managed and controlled by service providers. The business processes range from home energy generation, energy management, customer billing management and customer profile management. The major challenge for service providers is to balance the environment, standards and power infrastructure interfaces of consumer demand. The areas covered by service providers are components such as installation, building management, home administration, evolving service, customer management and billing. The consumer, business and operational areas also interact with all of these service provider components. The smart grid domain is very large. The smooth running of the power grid is done by the operating domain participants. The operational domain components include maintenance and development, financing, supply chain logistics, assets, safety management, communication networks, meter reading and monitoring, planning and planning of operations and extensions [1]. All of these operating domain components include coordination between markets, service providers, customers, distribution, transmission and network operations. The operating domain provides continuous power supply by overcoming the obstacle caused by environmental considerations.

Bulk generation domain helps in generating energy in terms of power in huge quantity. The main source for this bulk generations may come from fossil fuels and renewable energy. Electricity generation is the electricity generation process based on a variety of sources of energy, ranging from chemical combustion to nuclear fission, water, wings, solar, radiation and geothermal heating. Mass Domain Generation is electrically linked to transmission domain and shares business, transmission and operational communication interfaces. Mainly rehabilitation of greenhouse-emission control, integration of renewable power sources, and the storage and management of energy from intermittent energy sources for future usage are necessary in order to achieve a bulk generation. Generation domain communicates with transmission, markets and operations. Also, the bulk generations should also maintain balance between power demand and power generated by controlling the frequency of power.

Power generated from various power sources are transmitted to end user customer through multiple substations of Transmission domain by scaling down the power voltage. Regional Transmission Operator (RTO) controls operations of this transmission network. RTO will ensure that supply demand chain is properly distributed in the transmission network so that frequency and voltage will be stable. Domain of operations: support and additional energy resources acquired by market domain are planned and delivered finally to the distribution networks and finally to the customer domain through the transmission domain.

6.3   Internet of Things (IoT)

The Internet of Things and IoT influences our way of life from our reactions to our behavior. IoT is a network of linked objects, and in our situation, the Internet of things is called these objects. IoT refers to the set of all devices capable of connecting, gathering data and exchanging information. That is why Internet of Things is called (IoT). Basically, these things or objects are equipped with sensors. We have device that collects data from its environment using sensors and actuators, and these data are sent to internet where the processing of data can happen. There are many devices that can be included in this example which includes smart phones, smart watches, smart tv, refrigerators, washing machines, Air Conditioners, cars, homes, medical equipment and many. These sensors have many software and hardware which combine together to achieve single or multiple purpose. In recent days, over 50 billion devices are connected to the web. With these many devices generate lot of data whose size may range from megabytes to petabytes. By using data science on these data, better capability can be derived in each and every field by making better decisions. In Figure 6.2, various layer involved in IoT framework was depicted.

Smart Health care is having major impact due to IoT. Smart health care is all about wellbeing to the best where we can use the hardware and software available to probably let the doctors to know about current health conditions, current well being and what not even if they are not physically present with each patient. All needs to be done is having these devices at hand and ensure that you have active internet connection and we will have the access to the entire world of smart healthcare.

Next impact of IoT is on convenience and automation. With respect to IoT you can change all mundane task done by humans and basically make everything smart and convenient for people. This ensures that each workforce will put in the time and effort to the task that are more productive and more qualitative and at the end of the day which drive more insights to business. Enabling this smartness at wearable technologies, buildings, cities, home and in every domain will increases the quality of human life. Thus, IoT is that the absolute endless hunt for making things smart [2].

Farming has been one of the industries that has stayed with us since the beginning of the human civilization itself. Now is the correct time to

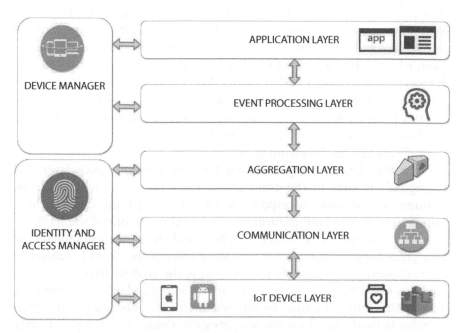

Figure 6.2 Different layers of IoT.

improve upon our traditional methods and shifting to modern farming to provide food for our ever-growing population. Smart technologies has definitely helped us to increase the productivity through new devices like smart tractor and analysis devices that will help us to get the better data analysis of soil, climate conditions, and plant conditions.

Manufacturing industry has already taken this IoT with open arms. It already has automation replacing many manual jobs. IoT will not only increases the interactivity but also boost efficiency and production as well. In education industry, better methods to teach children are already being implemented in conjunction with IoT. Hence having IoT will not only be beneficial to us individually, but also be beneficial to us as a society.

IoT works on a five main components such as hardware, software, internet, security and mobile. Hardware consists of the all of the sensors, actuators and everything which form the actual devices is the part of the sensing layer. Software contains the custom code and programming concepts which helps the hardware to talk to the internet.

Internet was used by the software to provide the pathway for communication through protocol layer. Security ensures that strong security protocol is used to protect the data which traverse around the internet. For ultimate control, a computer or mobile can be used. Both computers and mobile phones are outfitted with purpose specific applications (Google Play, Apple music, What's App etc), dashboard, and the controlling entity to go on make changes used or IoT devices and everything else. Layered architecture of IoT includes four layers. The first layer is sensing or device layer, which is basically the fin part of IoT. This layer includes embedded devices that has sensors and actuators that collects data from its environment based on specific functions such as temperature sensors, atmospheric sensors, pressure sensors, light sensors and etc. These devices will collect the data and give it embedded devices. Next layer is the aggregation layer. It simply groups the data from various sensors.

Once the data is being collected through sensing device layer and aggregated, it goes to the connectivity layer or communication layer. Communication layer is responsible for traversing these data to cloud using internet. This communication is made through one of the methods like Wi-Fi, Bluetooth, cellular, RFID, NFC and etc. Now comes the role of data processing layer, once the data once reaches the cloud is subject to the real essence of the whole process that is the analysis part of the data. Based on the different types of data being collected and other assumptions, various algorithms are used to get meaningful insights and pattern, then decision is made based on the insights gain. Once this hard part is over the result of the decision is conveyed to intended thing or IoT device. User

Interface (UI) or Application Layer is the top most layer that all of us will actually see. Using this layer end user will interact with the whole IoT platform. It is a front-end design to all backend process, which includes the previous layers.

In the internet rush era everyone wants to get into the internet today right so be it or attaining new information be it into using your internet as a marketplace or as a entertainment place, gathering new information, reading something, learning, mastering in technical skills.

6.4   Renewable Energy Source (RES)- Key Technology for SG

6.4.1   Renewable Energy: Basic Concepts and Readiness

Experts and the public increasingly focus on renewable energy (RE). In absolute and relative terms, RES studies have risen in recent years. RES fulfils a crucial duty by addressing depletion of fossil fuels and global warming. Fossil fuels, nuclear resources and renewable resources are the three main sources of energy. RES such as solar power, wind power, biomass, geothermal and hydropower regenerate energy, making it particularly beneficial to combat energy emergencies. Renewable energy resources are considered to be renewable energy resources, and are of crucial importance given their environmentally favorable presence. Domestic energy demands may be covered with the possibility of zero or near nil emissions of air pollution and energy services by RES [3]. RES can satisfy the energy requirements. A graphical depiction of several energy sources and their contribution to the creation of power is given in Figure 6.3. Data from the International Energy Association were acquired for Figure 6.3 (IEA).

There are various types of energy sources that include chemical, nuclear, mechanical storage, gravitational, sound, and electrical. Energy sources which are easily substituted by default and which can be used indefinitely i.e. over time, regardless of how often we use them. Solar, wind, hydro, biomass and geothermal oil. energy, energy. We don't have to use them carefully, since they are limitless and are continually supplemented by natural products such as wood, fruit, and vegetables. Wind turbines and solar panels are being substituted for prices all over the world. In the coming decades we expect a fast increase in the proportion of energy produced by sun and wind. Fossil fuel is goodbye to the rising expectations. Two-thirds of our world's energy is expected to be sourced from renewable sources. The change in energy will have numerous economic, political and human

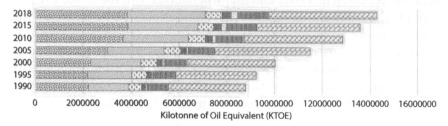

Figure 6.3 Total energy supply (TES) by source.

life consequences. We've been used to buildings with solar panels on the roof over recent years, and electric vehicles no longer are the exceptions. Everyone knows that we are going to a completely different planet. In future decades we will continue to grow our share of renewable energy and step closer to the end of coal, oil and gas. However, this transition from fossil fuels to renewables will also lead to dramatic changes beyond the energy sector. By the middle of 2050 we will see two-thirds of global electricity generated by renewable energy sources and the remainder of world electricity is projected to be powered by wind and solar power from two renewable sources. Rapid growth in the renewable energy sector is increasing worldwide. Previous studies of potential energy routes reveals that increased energy supply, air quality and energy efficiency can technically be achieved simultaneously while preventing harmful climate change. Indeed, many alternate combinations of capital, technologies and policies are found to achieve these goals [4].

Evaluation of readiness for renewable energy is a useful method to find holes that impede the use of the RET for developing countries, like GCC, and to recognize strengths and disadvantages of the RET development in the countries. The International Renewable Energy Agency (IRENA) defines the assessment and measures required to further enhance these conditions of the implementation and ongoing operation of a country's renewable energy facilities. The evaluation is carried out on the main requirements of Ret production and deployment in a country. IRENA describes readiness as 'the best choice for stakeholders to deploy renewables, taking all economic, social and environmental requirements into account.' It assesses 'actual national readiness, from national energy strategies and policies through to construction, operation and maintenance (O&M) across the project life cycle, and reduced capacities in all these aspects.' They assess the situation of the project. RE-readiness at the domestic level indicates that the country realizes that renewable energies are required and that renewable energy projects can be introduced and supported. This report defines the RE-readiness as the level of development of the infrastructure, institutions and human capital factor of a county which affects the attractiveness of investments in renewable energy projects, and which contributes to the reliability of RETs in their sustainable use. This study provides a framework for RE readiness, which can set a baseline for comparing countries and evaluating future progress.

6.4.2   Natural Sources of Renewable Energy

Renewable energy is a critical component of energy supply, capable of improving energy systems, balancing supply, and demand discrepancies, and safeguarding the environment. According to the International Renewable Energy Agency, renewable energy must account for two-thirds of all provided power worldwide by 2050. Figure 6.4 shows the graphical representation of % of renewable energy generated from each source. For Figure 6.4, data was collected from IEA. In recent years, there has been widespread attention to the production of renewable energy. Promoting renewable energy production and use has become an international consensus and concerted effort [5]. Figure 6.5 shows the various natural sources of renewable energy.

- **Solar Energy**
Sun's energy provides heat and light but may also be transformed into electricity. Photovoltaic solar technology is one (PV). In recent days PV panels have been apparent in many areas, but their performance and production

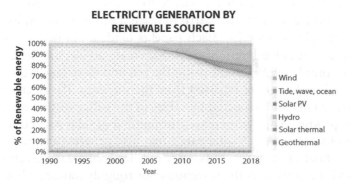

Figure 6.4 Electricity generation by renewable source.

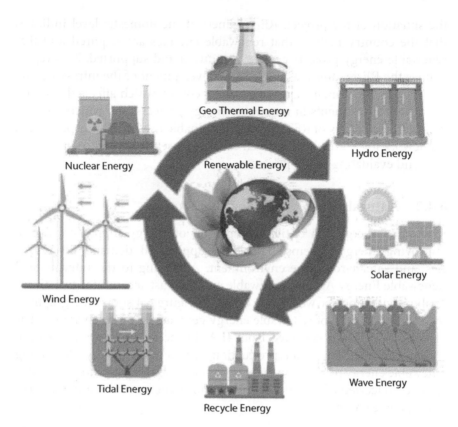

Figure 6.5 Natural sources of renewable energy.

have lately been significantly enhanced. Every hour for a complete year, adequate solar energy reaches the earth. Sunlight is made up of tiny energy packets called photons. They emanate from the sun and go roughly 93 million kilometers across the Earth to reach a semiconductor. Everything happens at light velocity [6]. Each panel is made up of multiple separate, positive, and negative layers of cells that create an electric field. It works like an accumulator. The photons hit the cell and electrons in the material of the semiconductor are released from their energy. The electron creates an electrical current connected by cables to the cell's positive and negative side. The produced power increases the number of solar panel cells and the number of solar panels. A solar range may also generate a large amount of power for host or business. This array of solar roof creates electricity in a house and the array over the warehouse for roughly thousand houses. The power is pure. No rubbish, no moving components, no noise or fossil-fuel water or energy generation are required. The power can be positioned in the middle of the night and can be connected to the gross.

- **Wind Energy**

Wind farms have been built in recent days to produce electricity to meet agriculture needs. These ancient windmills precede the generation of new, modern electricity generating wind turbines. The same wind used to pump bovine water turns giant wind turbines into electricity cities and households. Hot wilderness and high mountains are the perfect location for winds. The wind turbines today are much more complex than the old grassland. But both concepts harness the energy of the wind. The blade functions like an aircraft wing. Wind turbine blade. Both the sides of the blade move by blowing air. For the shape of the blade, the air pressure on one side of the blade is unevenly higher and on the other hand lower. This spins the blade and causes the blade to rotate around the middle of the turbine with an uneven pressure. The meteorological wing is attached to the machine to keep the turbine windy and catch the greatest energy. The blades are now connected to a rotator, which turns 18 turns a minute, so that electricity is not produced by itself. Thus, the rotating shaft rotates a range of rotations up to 1800 revolutions per minute. The generator will start generating electricity at this speed. The wind turbines are big, making the atmosphere windier. More wind means more power, of course. Larger turbines can more effectively harness wind power. The blades will flip in a circle in the sky that is longer in diameter than a football. Even a small wind farm may produce sufficient power to fulfil the requirements. The turbines will catch the wind not just on ground. Both the oceans and the large lakes provide a reliable and consistent wind source for electricity. With wind energy, growing further, offshore development can boost domestic energy products significantly, especially in the coastal regions.

- **Nuclear Energy**

The way fossil-fueled power plants produce electricity is close to nuclear energy production. Clean and healthy electricity is provided by nuclear power plants. Generation of coal, nuclear, and natural gas plants in most power stations This steam transforms the turbine which connects to the electromagnetic generator into a steam, some sort of energy is used for heating water. The generator generates power. The model is identical. There is an important distinction between nuclear power plants and other power plants. A chain response of splitting atoms releases heat in nuclear power plants. This reaction occurs in a reactor. All reactors have the highest priority design, construction and operation with protection. The nuclear power plant is one of the safest in the world, as it offers many redundant layers of protection systems and processes starting in the reactor core. With uranium pellets inside the nuclear reactor metal, fuel assemblies are arranged in a pack. The bundles are dipped into water in a pressurized vessel and the boiling water reactor pressure reactor is the two most common types of nuclear reactor. The heat generated by split atoms in a boiling water reactor causes the water to boil the steam generating the turbine. The steam is then turned back into liquid water and transferred to the centre of the reactor. After boiling the water reactor pressurised water reactors(PWR) were built and worked somewhat differently. In PWR, the reactor tank water is under pressure to prevent boiling, even though the temperature is very high. Water flows through thousands of small pipes in steam generators of PWR, and the heat in the pipes transforms the water into steam, driving the turbine then. The turbine drives the electricity generator in turn. Nuclear power stations will ensure that clean, healthy and stable energy continues to be generated. In order to quickly shutdown and stop the fusion process, reactors are cooled down and heat removed, and radiation barriers are created, preventing them from escape into the atmosphere. A new protection system is installed. The world's most powerful electricity source is nuclear power plant.

- **Geothermal Energy**

The heat emitted from deeper below the earth's surface generates geothermal energy. It can be used for clean electricity generation. The heat from the surface of the earth warms up water which is fast into the reservoirs of the land. In some areas when water gets hot, it can spread like steam or warm water through the earth's surface. This occurs normally when the earth's crust is meeting and shifting. The field where warm water followed close to the surface used to take advantage of geothermal energy. But we will take advantage of these natural renewable energy opportunities even further as geothermal technologies move forward. Engineers have established multiple methods to generating energy in the field from geothermal wells. The most popular form of geothermal technology today is the dry steamer geothermal power plant. Underground steam flows to a turbine to power the electricity generator. A flash steam power plant was another geothermal technology. A pump has moved hot fluid to a surface tank where it refreshes. When the fluid cools down, it becomes rapidly vaporized or flashy. The vapor then drives the generator and drives the turbine. Binary cycle geothermal plant is the next form of technology. It uses the second fluid called a heat transfer fluid in an enormous heat exchanger, two kinds of fluid from underground heat. The other fluid boils much lower than the first, so that at a lower temperature it flashes into the vapor. When the second fluid flashes, it rotates a generator engine. This smooth renewable energy source has significant environmental benefits all round the clock: low emissions, small physical footprint and negligible environmental effects. Few byproducts can also come in underground reinjections. Geothermal energy can also contribute to the recycling of wastewater. Some plants generate solid waste, but solid waste may have minerals that can be removed and distributed to reduce the costs of these energy sources.

- **Hydro Energy**

For thousands of years people have collected energy in flowing water. Today, they still have powerful tools to produce smooth, renewable, and affordable power. Energy is exploited and converted from flowing water to electricity called hydro or hydropower. Water flows from higher to lower heights, and a hydro-power system uses turbines and generators to turn this movement into power. Around 7% of our electricity is provided by hydroelectricity and is the largest renewable energy source. Water is a renewable source of hydropower. Water evaporates back to the earth as precipitation in the clouds and recycles. The water cycle recharges continuously and can be used along the way to generate electricity. Basically, it is possible to produce electricity by hydropower technologies. Dams built to store water in a reservoir are referred to as a rubble. When the water is released from these reservoirs, a turbine flows and turns a power generator. Another technology is known as diversion. It transforms part of a fluvial into a turbine and power supply system through a canal or pipe. It uses the river's natural flow and does not normally require a large dam. The next technology is called hydropower pumped storage that operates as a large battery. To charge the battery, during times of low energy consumption, water is returned to a reservoir during the night when the use of less equipment is reduced. Then, when people need more power during the day, electricity can be generated from the water. New technologies are improving the environmental performance of hydropower. Research has been undertaken to reduce the detrimental repercussions on fish and their natural habits and fish ladders. Hydropower has a wealth of history and is today a vital, efficient, and sustainable source of clean energy. It will be much more effective and will have higher production capacity using emerging technology.

6.4.3   Major Issues in Following RES to SG

You may still find huge engineering problems to finish the transition into an energy source, which is grounded on renewables by the center of the century. Innovation has historically been and can remain to be relaxing in the driving seat of this change. You will find 2 vital following steps to allow this: (i) for all those apps where technology treatments are present, the key following step is usually to enabling frameworks are required to scale up the deployment of theirs, together with (ii) for applications whereby treatments are right now also at the first phase of theirs of commercialization and don't really exist, the next thing is fostering technology development, together with enabling policy, financial and social measures, to quickly take the emerging pure solutions on the industry.

Even though many revolutionary solutions exist on a laboratory or maybe pilot scale, up scaling of economically viable robust fixes is typically still a struggle. Governments have a crucial role to play in the first stages of this changeover as these remedies struggle to achieve descend as well as scale on the learning cost curve. Moreover, the innovation problem goes beyond conventional federal electricity R&D. The sectors with probably the lowest improvement in in novation for decarburization, like big business in addition to freight transport as well as aviation, are those where correct policy rewards as well as long-range perspectives are missing [sixty one]. This particular challenge can't be ad dressed by increased R&D expense alone. Innovation likewise involves a fundamental rethink of manufacturing processes as well as power technologies necessary for the power transition [4].

While a profitable transformation is discovered to be technologically feasible, it is going to require the fast arrival of policies and essential political changes toward serious and coordinated efforts to incorporate worldwide concerns, like climate change, into national and local policy priorities (like pollution and wellness, energy access, along with energy security). An incorporated policy design will therefore be required to be able to determine economical win win remedies which can deliver on several goals at the same time. Farm land, electricity as well as water are among our most valuable resources, though the way & extent to which they're exploited plays a role in cli mate shift. Meanwhile, the devices which supply these materials are themselves extremely susceptible to changes in climate. Effective resource management is thus of great value, each for mitigation and for adaptation reasons. The absence of integration in policy making leads and resource assessments to inefficient use and inconsistent tactics of resources. A alternative view of climate, land use, electricity and water methods are able to make it possible to treat several of these shortcomings [4].

The alternative indicators for influencing factors are analyzed in order to predict renewable energy trends in each area according to the factor substitution process [5].

- **Economic factors**

Renewable energy production is linked from a country's economic prosperity. It is the main driver behind renewable energy sources development.

Given the connection between renewable energy and two causes (GDP per capita), renewable energy production and consumption is, to some extent, a result of per capita economic incomes and renewable energy development. The production of renewable energy is closely bound up with financing, on the other hand. Investment financing supports economic growth, is resistant to financial risks from renewable energy growth, increases the desire of investors to participate in renews, helps them explore the possibilities for developing renewable energies and enables sustained renewable energy generation development.

- **Technical elements Renewable**

The provision of competitive, cost efficient and sustainable energy supplies requires renewable technology. Promoting renewable energy technology would reduce development and maintenance costs, boost energy dependability, applicability and efficiency to encourage renewable energy production. New energy utilization capacity, power generating capability and research and development capabilities are the factors affecting technical advancement. Capacity for R&D is an important factor in generating renewable energy. The most commonly-used forms in the field of generating renewable energy are hydroelectric and solar photovoltaic electricity. The production cost of both are therefore used as a substitute measure in this analysis. The poor R&D capability would lead to low renewable energy usage and high development costs, hampering renewable energy generation applications. The degree of social awareness influences public and financial decisions. Knowledge of green energy advantages would make it easier for the public to undertake the initiatives on renewable energy.

- **Policy elements Policy**

Political aspects pertain largely to rules and laws relating to the production of renewable energy and to the implementation in one nation or region of energy generating. They have a huge impact and the driving force for this development on the future trend for the expansion of renewable energy in a country. The Government should take active measures to promote the health of renewable energy sources, to develop the framework for renewable energy policies continually, and to contribute substantially to the sustainable energy system for the long-term health of renewable energy sources. Increasing and attracting investment through grid subsidies and renewables tariffs, on the one hand. Investment earnings clarification. In most countries across the world, initiatives for the speeding up of the production and use of renewable energies have been good and helpful. Macroeconomic goals, government legitimacy and suggestions on renewable energy generation are the key indicators. A bigger strategy roadmap for renewables and renewables projects is the Renewable Energy Development Plan [7].

6.4.4   Integration of RES with SG

The Smart Grid Conception is an addition of the electricity infrastructure that will meet subsequent specifications, also called the Future Grid or Evolving Grid. This requires the application of electronic technologies and the expert communication processes to convert the electrical system's generation, transmission and supply components. In order to produce an integrated and distributed advanced power supply network, the smart grid uses bidi reactionary input and power [8].

Due to direct electric power utilisation by motors, movement can be generated cheaper and more efficiently and spread in the field in future. Excluding aircraft and other modes of transport which cannot receive energy from the electricity grid, and vehicles that need specific power and independence, such as ambulances, fire engines and police vehicles, for the future the transport of electricity is primarily powered by (1) on board battery power, (2) electric power grid, and, (3) electric hydrogen or methane to fuel cell or electric battery. Catenary networks such as light rail, subway, commuter rail and trolleybus provide public transit using systems linked to the grid. These are the most energy-efficient transport systems, where consumption is roughly 3,5, 4, 4,8, and 4,8 kW h/100 kilometers. GCVs are more effective than Battery-Electric Vehicles and should be a first choice in the future transport planning process (up to 95 per cent of GCVs compared to 80 per cent for BGVs). If there is a wider power grid for truck, bus or automobile (from the catenary to the earth), the only way to change the lanes and the "last miles" to the destination is to use the online battery power. This helps the batteries to be reduced as they can be recharged during road travel, where there is external power [9].

Optimization algorithms include rewording to accommodate changes in parameters related to smart grids and prosumers as well as real-time seasonal changes which are often not modelled by optimization [10]. ML is one approach for addressing parameter differences, such as the shift in demands for renewable energy production and environmental and seasonal drifts. Developing an Energy Management Model (EMM) ML algorithm is an appropriate choice since it minimizes the EMM's complexity by developing a single qualified model for prediction of the pervasive parameters of the EMM for multiple scenarios. With multiple formulations and data measurements such as renewable energy generation intermittent, plug and play facility, prosumer activities and complex power system formulation both in online and offline mode, ML algorithms are capable of developing a Shared Energy Management System (EMM) for the mutual trade of smart grid and EDs. A Gaussian Process Regression (GPR) is incorporated with the ML algorithm in order to create a trustworthy understanding of latent correlations between response parameters and input covariates [11].

In energy systems with a high proportion of VRE, juggling energy output and requirement is a major challenge, because insecurity of supply and demand contributes to time differences. IoT systems provide flexibility in meeting demand and production, reducing the complexities of VRE implementation, which contribute to higher renewable energy integration and lower emissions of GHGs. Moreover, with the use of IoT a more efficient energy use can be accomplished through the use of machine learning algorithms to achieve an optimum balance between the various technologies of supply and demand [12].

6.4.5   SG Renewable Energy Management Facilitated by IoT

An intelligent grid is a power grid using automated networking techniques to monitor and control the generation, transmission and delivery of electricity and developments in the local age. In a traditional power grid, energy usage patterns remain unexplained, resulting in wasted energy and money. This problem is severely pronounced in the developed world, where there is a big difference between demand and supply and frequent power outages and cargo shedding. Smart grids employ demand side management (DSM) to adjust power savings, by using many mechanisms including discounts and awareness-raising, to adjust consumption energy requirements. The smart grid DSM would use advanced technologies, including internet of things (IoT) and cloud and/or fog computing focused on intelligent energy management systems in the future (EMS) [8].

[8] show the EMS platform, specification, deployment and tests for the IoT architecture and cloud-based architecture to be applied in a load profile that is available both for users and for users. An IoT-and cloud-based architectural framework is designed for energy-efficient calculation and control. In real time, consumer energy usage data are gathered and transmitted to a cloud service via a smartphone device or web application [13]. The computer is built on a WeMos D1 Mini development board and mounted on a PCB. The setting is checked in Google Firebase, a Google load charts cloud platform. The computer tracks the current and the voltage of electrical equipment and transmits these data in a household or a building to existing Wi-Fi.

Rising renewable energy levels as well as reducing the environmental effects of energy usage can be used by IoT to improve energy efficiency. For the sensing and transmission of real-time data, IoT uses sensors and communications technology which enables quick and optimal calculations. In addition, IoT can move from a focused, intelligent, and integrated energy environment to a dispersed energy market [14]. This is a precondition for rollout, combined and optimised for many smaller users, by aggregating and optimising the needs of the local, renewable energies such as the wind and solar system. IoT-based devices, cameras and networking technologies automated, integrated, and monitored. Wide data gathering and the application of advanced algorithms in real time data analytics can enable users and devices track energy usage patterns effectively and at a variety of scales [12].

The 5G networks should create a larger scale on which the Fourth Industrial Revolution can take place. It provides a convergence of broadband, sensing, and knowledge that is leading to greater social and industrial change. The Internet of Things (IoT) will be moved to modern wireless networks and potential electricity markets, which will give the services and customers greater value. In history, 5G is pursuing a trend towards developing the need across the energy paradigm amongst public networking in wireless modes. Bringing 5G networks in the intelligent grid, along with automation and intelligent control, will create new business models on the utility side. The 5G and intelligent grids architecture opens up a variety of transmission and delivery properties. Multiple domains are involved both on consumer and utility level in the 5G slicing layers. New energy and users are created by the diversification of resources and challenge the balancing of loads. The other key feature in the architecture is on-demand implementation, which analyses the network functions based on service needs. In addition, 5G network cutting offers low latency insurance end-to-end network. Before introducing an efficient energy system in future, the safety issues involved in developing an efficient communication system within a smart grid are important to address. It's imperative that engineers and researchers respond to rising security threars in order to create a secure, advanced measuring infrastructure in smart grids. The physical layer security approach is a security technique which can be applied in smart grids. Efficient main protection technologies for smart grids [15] are public infrastructures, hashing and reliable computers. Various stack layer of IoT involved in processing the data is depicted in Figure 6.6.

The Smart Building business is undoubtedly going a long way to exploiting wireless technology and is mostly focusing on the application of the IoT perspective [16]. The variability and difference in quantities of both software and hardware in the extended solutions depart with the principles of IoT that need regular, consistent design to provide optimum performance. Intelligent building power management system based on IoT. A semantical framework is specially proposed for the standardized

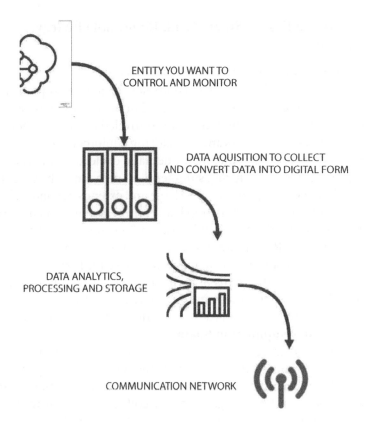

ENTITY YOU WANT TO
CONTROL AND MONITOR

DATA AQUISITION TO COLLECT
AND CONVERT DATA INTO DIGITAL FORM

DATA ANALYTICS,
PROCESSING AND STORAGE

COMMUNICATION NETWORK

Figure 6.6 IoT stack.

and uniform modelling of all things that form the context and relations and attributes of Smart Buildings. This particular semantic modelling aims for an alternate and practical technique that will answer many of Smart Building's current challenges and enhance decision-making and knowledge rationale [17].

The layered Smart Grid provides a starting tool to ease brand new energy and requirements policies implementation. The ZigBee technology implementation evaluation strategy just for the Smart Grid is presented [18]. ZigBee modules utilized in the area tests have been constructed taking in account probably the most desired characteristics of the ZigBee process for SG assets control: the capability to produce the information network mesh, the self healing, protection and also uniquely the particular module set up as well as positioning, constantly taking in consideration the requirements as well as issues of every SG participant installation environments [19].

6.4.6   Case Studies on Smart Grid: Renewable Energy Perception

- **Agriculture using Smart grid in California**

Smart Grid Project web to wireless controller for irrigation pumps for an agricultural demand response program in California (USA). In smart grid agriculture project, Irrigation pumps are controlled in wireless mode using wireless sensors, smart meters and monitoring equipment. Smart grid agriculture project focuses on reducing the demand of electricity to the average of 18 megawatts per event during summer peak demands. The potential for agricultural demand response may be large and extends beyond California. This project runs based on irrigation load control system, which represents around 60 megawatt of interruptible load on 300 pumps. Irrigation pumps are taped using PEAR program. Electric system summer peak demand can be managed by irrigation load management system. Farmer's web portal enables them to track the status of their land's irrigation pumps. Irrigation load control system equipment given to farmers at free of cost and also offers cash incentives as a reward of reducing electricity demand.

- **Smart grid development in Spain**

The Spanish innovative foundation of electrical frameworks FutuRed was made to coordinate the entirety of the customers engaged with the power area behind a bunch of shared objectives. FutuRed unites smart grid framework users; utilities, organizations, colleges, research foundations, associations, and policy implementation – with a sum of 127 elements as individuals. This to characterize and advance systems at the public level to permit the acknowledgment of a further developed force organization – one equipped for reacting to the difficulties of things to come in the future.

The Spanish electrical network stage was made to cultivate the innovative advancement of the Spanish power transmission and dispersion frameworks to advance mechanical authority, reasonable turn of events, and the expanded seriousness required for future development and flexibility.

Key features:

- Work together with organizations in the Spanish power area to grow new items and administrations dependent on innovation and advancement for the new electrical stockpile situation.
- Help out the appropriate associations in the improvement of Spain's electrical administrative structure, which advances and encourages the agreeable improvement of the electrical framework.

- Fortify collaboration in R&D among electric organizations and their administration and hardware providers, particularly SMEs, research focuses, and colleges.
- Work together with friendly specialists and organizations on preparing plans and the spreading of good practices for normal and feasible utilization of electrical force.

The improvement of the smart grid in Spain will require speculation of €10,200 million throughout the following 10 years to produce characteristic advantages of somewhere in the multiples of 2 or 3.5 times the venture. The introduction of modern communication technologies allows the integration of new applications into the electronic system, improves the quality of the whole system, supports sustainable economic growth, and enhances global leadership in the Spanish technology sector.In particular, the network is automatic. More efficient integration of energy distribution and greater customer participation with the system. Easy generation distribution management. And the integration of new agents such as storage and electric vehicles is complete.

6.5   Low Power Wireless Technologies for IoTSG

6.5.1   Role of IoT in SG

The smart grid (SG) is the integration of the traditional power grid of the 20th century of the modern 21st telecoms and information technology. This integration allows effective use of capital in order to maximize energy consumption, installing and managing distributed energy sources and the sharing of produced electricity. Via various wireless and wired networking protocols, for example wireless protocols, intelligent grid users connect in two ways. In both ways, networking protocols such as the Zigbee, Lease cable, wi-max, WIFI, Homeplug, power-line carrier, fibers, LE and GPRS can be applied to this link. Various software packages, such as Customer Information Systems (CIS), GIS, Outage Management System (OMS), Distribution Management System (DMSS), and the data acquisition and monitoring system are updated and further developed to suit existing operation, grid maintenance and administration (SCADA). Figure 6.7 shows the different SG-specific IoT technologies.

SGs are complex networks for the generation, transmission, distribution, calculation, and billing of energy consumption operated by electrical energy systems to operate integrated by computational intelligence and

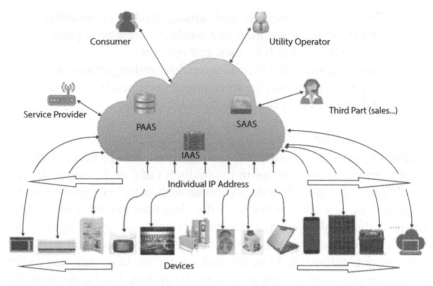

Figure 6.7 IoT technologies for SG.

network communication [20]. An SG is responsible for managing and overseeing essential infrastructures. Essential infrastructures are made up of systems and properties that are vital for a nation (virtual or physical). Their unavailability or loss may therefore have a high effect on a country's security and economic aspect.

6.5.2   Innovations in Low Power Wireless Technologies

Industry 4.0 is a concept specifically correlated with the so-called Fourth Industrial Revolution. This latest revolution, made possible by the availability of low-cost sensors and reliable wireless communications, is associated with an increasingly widespread use of data processing, computational technology data analysis, and new fully digitized and integrated materials, components and systems. The Industry 4.0 paradigm includes solutions for: optimizing production processes, promoting industrial automation processes and promoting business collaboration through advanced distributed planning techniques, and information technology interoperability [21].

Developing new infrastructure of communication with the current ones Smart grids can be better fitted with wireless technology. This offers advanced technology in which extra time and expense can be avoided. This will allow modern wireless networking technology to be upgraded to future smart grid communication systems. In the last four decades, the development of communications technology has become an unavoidable part of all modes of application and is heading into a new era of technology.

The smart grid of today covers a wide range of technologies, including: electricity generation (distributed generation sources, renewable energy), Dissemination and transmission (load management, demand response), Intelligent metering (residential, commercial and industrial) and Vehicles powered by electricity (charging stations). For several years, the breakthrough has aided utilities and energy consumers in the development of effective, highly stable smart grid solutions. Embedded Wireless Modules and Wireless Embedded SIMs are designed to be highly reliable, ruggedized, and cost-effective, with low power consumption. They're easy to set up, programme, and stable, and they're scalable from 2G to 4G. To minimise device complexity and save board space, the embedded modules portfolio includes built-in application processors, modems, and optional GNSS. As a result, open-source Linux-based platforms are available, making it easier and faster to build IoT applications for smart grids [22].

Intelligent Gateways, Management Tools, and Services for Rugged Environments: Innovation networking solutions needed in intelligent gateways, management tools, and services for rugged environments where reliability and security are critical [23]. They allow energy suppliers to manage facilities, instrumentation, and other equipment in smart grid applications by providing continuous connectivity, location-based services, and remote monitoring. cloud services make it easy to securely store, retrieve, analyse, and incorporate data to create new value in smart grid applications. With over-the-air monitoring and updates of cellular M2M systems, they can reduce time-to-market, reduce risk, and lower deployment and maintenance costs. With innovation in the smart grid environment, the following results gained Unparalleled energy industry expertise, Simple integration and deployment, Secure and rugged products, and Faster time-to-market [24].

6.5.3   Wireless Communication Technologies for IoTSG

The sensors may be considered as the material world's sensory organs for the raw input, transmission, analysis and feedback including heat, power, lighting, energy, sound and signal. In order to identify the status of electricity grid systems, awareness information may be transmitted and coordinated via ICTs [25]. The ICT may be categorized into two groups that depend on the spread: communication technologies with a short range and communication technology with a long range. IP-based internet, 2g/3g public mobile telephony network, power line carrier, Long Terminal

Evolution Timeline Division (TD-LTE) 4G network, OPLC, power data network wireless and satellite communication network all accomplish long-term communication [26].

- **Bluetooth 5.0**

Bluetooth is a technology that is 20 years old. The initial data transmission version was launched in 1994 for the digital modem environment. Currently, this technology is one of the foundations of the Internet of Things (IoT) and a long-term target that allows for constant communication among technological devices to impact and enhance performance. Bluetooth is a wireless technology that permits the connection of two or more devices utilizing radio waves.

The new Standard Bluetooth is simply called Bluetooth 5. The new specification is simply known as Bluetooth5 in contrast to existing iterations of the Bluetooth standard, which was implemented as X.0 and followed by improvements (e.g. 4.1 and 4.2). Bluetooth 5's classic edition is identical to previous ones, with BLE version improving the most. According to the requirements of the SIG, hardware boards can support three Bluetooth connections. The Bluetooth 5 at 2 Mb/s was launched as the latest high-speed link. In this case, the PHY layer speed is 2 Mb/s. Bluetooth 5 Coded is a modern Bluetooth 5 communication type. A significant aspect is the increase in data transfer speed. Bluetooth 5 supports a maximum speed of 2 Mb/s, compared to 1 Mb/s for Bluetooth 4.x. As a result, future wearable systems can synchronize twice as quickly as existing ones. The current Bluetooth data transfer speed is adequate for most applications. Speed isn't a major consideration in many IoT applications. This is particularly valid for non-streaming use cases.

The increased range and velocity might lead to higher energy usage. Due to innovative design, such as the way the signal is modified and progress in frequency spectrum use, Bluetooth 5 consumes fewer energy resources. It can really require twice as much power in the best case situation as the previous Bluetooth version. Doubles the energy usage when the speed of a wired link [27].

The objective of the study was to compare Bluetooth 5 to Bluetooth 4.2 and IEEE 802.15.4. The results were compared. Bluetooth 5 nRF52840 Nordic Semiconductor model boards in scenarios for test beds were utilized. These boards have a 64-MHz ARM Cortex-M4F processor, and a Bluetooth 5 protocol stack. Prototyping boards fitted with a Microchip PIC24FJ256GB108 microcontroller [28] and an MRF24J40MB radio frequency transceiver, both from Microchip Technology, have been used to implement IEEE 802.15.4.

- **ZigBee**

ZigBee is a low-power, low-rate, short-range wireless network technology built on the IEEE Standard 802.15.4 in many application categories such as industrial control, home management, healthcare, building automation, consumer electronics, remote control, etc. It is used for wireless metre reading, power distribution, electric parameter calculation and other applications in the electricity automation sector [29]. Precise control of the performance of power systems ensures the reliability and productivity of all these applications.

In order to achieve self-heal, interaction, compatibility, integration, optimization and security capability on the existing electrical network smart grid, combined the newest sensor technology, network technology, networking technology, emerging generation technologies, and electrical energy systems. In terms of grid architecture, network security monitoring, service and maintenance, data storage, security enforcement, parameters estimation and user engagement ZigBee can fully take advantage of its technical advantages. ZigBee can be used for knowledge and data aggregation with highly available power grid. The following are the features of smart grid in zigbee Low power, Low rate, Short delay, Self-organization, Large scale, High-security.

The Smart Grid allows the full convergence of configuration and control of electricity generation, transmission, supply, storage and consumption and will make the power grid a high voltage, two-way, real-time, interactive collaborative information network, hybrid energy network. Both markets, businesses and service providers constitute an interconnected network that is closely connected to each other and to the above four elements. Electrical interfaces, but also safe communications interfaces connect the formation of energy, transmission, distribution and use. Both these electrical and networking interfaces may, because of distributed power generation, be bidirectional in the smart grid. In the generation, storage, delivery and utilization fields, ZigBee technology will provide precise and reliable surveillance of data for effective smart grid operation. Both these protocols can be bi-directional in the Smart Grid due to the distributed power generation. In order to provide accurate and efficient data tracking for a successful Smart Grid operation, ZigBee technologies can be implemented in the generation, storage, distribution and consumption industries [30].

- **6LoWPAN**

Since IEEE adopted the Standard 802.15.4 for low-data connectivity between low-energy devices in 2003, there have been low-energy wireless sensor networks [31]. The Tmote Sky, one of the world's most common Wireless Sensor platforms, was created by Moteiv with UC Berkeley.

However, the IP layer was not used at the time on these platforms. RFC 4919 and RFC 4944, which are estimated to number millions, will be the first to tackle the problem of assigning the IP addresses of these devices. It was evident that IPv6 was required to build a true internet component of the Internet of Things with 667 000 addresses available to each square nm of Earth's surface. The 6LoWPAN Basic Specifications for RFC 6282 were published in September 2011. RFC 6775 presented the update of the 6LoWPAN neighbor discovery mechanism.

The Tmote Sky motes are the 6LoWPAN low-power wireless sensors utilised in this system. They are one of the cheapest wireless sensors on the market, making an ideal test ground for sophisticated IPv6 address assignment. The units have an 8 MHz microcontroller, a RAM 10 KB, a 48 KB ROM, an external MB flash memory and an IEEE 802.15.4 compliant TI CC2420. ContikiOS 2.7 was used on these platforms to establish a test network using Tmote sky to establish a tunnel interface with tunslip6 on a Raspberry pi using the Contiki RPL-Border-Router example.

The Raspberry Pi we used was the Debian Wheezy 512MB RAM model B. The eth0 interface of Raspberry Pi was linked to the Virginia Tech network supporting IPv4 and native IPv6. Virginia Tech, on the other hand, has no routable IPv6 subnetwork. The software Hurricane Electric has been used to delegate /48 subnetworks to tunnelbroker.net. Then we developed an interface in the Raspberry Pi called he-ipv6, which ends a tunnel with 6in4s. The 6in4 tunnel offers the prefix /64 outside of the 2002 network compared to 6to4 tunnel::0/16, a fixed tunnel endpoint and a much more robust and troubleshooting connection [32].

6.5.4   Case Studies on Low Power Wireless Technologies Used in IoTSG

The Industrial Revolution has four phases. During the first revolution, new energy sources were utilised in power machines. The major building feature at the time was innovation in the Mass Carbon Mining and Steam Plant. A huge development in the iron and steel sector, often known as the mass industry and energy generation, characterized the Second Industrial Revolution. During this era several enormous factories have been set up with assembly lines and new businesses developed.

Supervisory and optimum power production, T&D grids and end use Smart Grids are the most effective ICT technology accessible. A intelligent grid creates a multi-directional information flow by connecting multiple intelligent metres, allowing sensors to be optimized and energy efficiently distributed. Smart grid deployments can be illustrated or taken as a whole, particularly in sub-sectors of the energy system such as energy storage, housing or transport.

For recharging batteries into regular networks power lines and an AC/DC converter. In a clever grid using inductive charging technology, the batteries may wirelessly be charged. The data gathered from an IoT network, such as mobile telephones or electric car charging, would consider external users as energy consumption trends. The nearest recharge station allows the object/automobile to be charged in due course. Another advantage is that IoT needs improved management and monitoring of battery-powered devices to deliver greater power.

The Wireless Battery Charge Station closest to you allocates the correct time and charges the device. Another benefit of IoT is that it may improve the control and the tracking of battery-powered vehicles to alter the energy distribution and ensure the power supply [33]. The unnecessary use of energy would be considerably reduced. The device/vehicle will then be assigned to the required time slot at the nearest wireless battery charging station, and it will be charged. Another advantage of IoT is that it allows for easier monitoring and tracking of battery-powered vehicles, allowing for better energy delivery and, second, ensuring that these vehicles have access to electricity. As a result, there will be a substantial decrease in unnecessary energy consumption.

Smart grid warnings operators via smart devices before an urgent problem occurs with the collaboration of different sectors. For example, continuous monitoring may be done if demand for electricity increase the grid capacity. Since real-time details are received, officials will take various tactics and redirect energy usage to a moment when demand is forecast to decrease. In certain places the prices for volatile energy rates is called smart (or dynamic). Power and real-time (RTP) costs are higher for some time [12].

- **Activities to standardize IoT-assisted SG systems**

Standardization initiatives are essential for the realistic implementation of technology. Although attempts are being made to standardize IoT and SG systems at a single stage, it is still necessary to work together to standardize IoT-aided SG systems. In the following pages we take the standardization of IoT, SG and IoT-assisted SG structures into account [34]. A number of normalization efforts are underway in the space of IoT. Include a very thorough debate on standardization practices by IoT and the various standardization bodies. The oneM2M standard is a widespread M2M and IoT standard. SG has a range of global standardization efforts.

The IoT-supported SG system is a dynamic system that requires various communication technologies to meet the system's different requirements. In this case standardization IoT-assisted SG network framework ensures that interoperability between protocols, workflows and messages is feasible in contrast with traditional telecom standardization. Therefore, a consensus must not be based on a common communication technology for an IoT-assisted SG unit, but rather on the usage and understanding of message and interface to ensure the proper integration of the various technologies and requirements [35, 36].

6.6   Conclusion

Researchers warn that their natural appeasement concerns and GHG pollution pre-vailed threats prevent their dependence on fossil fuels. Oil peaks and industry contests against solar and wind power capacity are expected to trigger the end of fossil fuels. As exploration costs increase, fossil fuels are becoming more expensive and renewables less expensive as production costs decrease. However, there is a real concern about sporadic renews that cannot substitute 100% fossil fuels as a simple load. This article relies first on the architecture of the SG and its important. It then explains the integrating RES to SG and major challenges involved in it with case study. This article will tell about the construction of a smart, stable, safe power grid and the needs and challenges of developing SG applications. Future potential analysis about Low power wireless Technologies for IoTSG.

References

1. M. Mirz *et al.*, "A Cosimulation Architecture for Power System, Communication, and Market in the Smart Grid," *Complexity*, vol. 2018, 2018, doi: 10.1155/2018/7154031.
2. M. Diyan, B. Nathali Silva, J. Han, Z. B. Cao, and K. Han, "Intelligent Internet of Things gateway supporting heterogeneous energy data management and processing," *Trans. Emerg. Telecommun. Technol.*, no. February, pp. 1–15, 2020, doi: 10.1002/ett.3919.
3. A. Qazi *et al.*, "Towards Sustainable Energy: A Systematic Review of Renewable Energy Sources, Technologies, and Public Opinions," *IEEE Access*, vol. 7, pp. 63837–63851, 2019, doi: 10.1109/ACCESS.2019.2906402.
4. D. Gielen, F. Boshell, D. Saygin, M. D. Bazilian, N. Wagner, and R. Gorini, "The role of renewable energy in the global energy transformation,"

Energy Strateg. Rev., vol. 24, no. June 2018, pp. 38–50, 2019, doi: 10.1016/j.esr.2019.01.006.

5. X. Xu, Z. Wei, Q. Ji, C. Wang, and G. Gao, "Global renewable energy development: Influencing factors, trend predictions and countermeasures," *Resour. Policy*, vol. 63, no. August, 2019, doi: 10.1016/j.resourpol.2019.101470.

6. A. Ahmed Abdulkadir and F. Al-Turjman, "Smart-grid and solar energy harvesting in the IoT era: An overview," *Concurr. Comput.*, vol. 33, no. 4, pp. 1–10, 2021, doi: 10.1002/cpe.4896.

7. K. Kimani, V. Oduol, and K. Langat, "Cyber security challenges for IoT-based smart grid networks," *Int. J. Crit. Infrastruct. Prot.*, vol. 25, pp. 36–49, 2019, doi: 10.1016/j.ijcip.2019.01.001.

8. S. A. Hashmi, C. F. Ali, and S. Zafar, "Internet of things and cloud computing-based energy management system for demand side management in smart grid," *Int. J. Energy Res.*, vol. 45, no. 1, pp. 1007–1022, 2021, doi: 10.1002/er.6141.

9. A. García-Olivares, J. Solé, and O. Osychenko, "Transportation in a 100% renewable energy system," *Energy Convers. Manag.*, vol. 158, no. August 2017, pp. 266–285, 2018, doi: 10.1016/j.enconman.2017.12.053.

10. D. Kolokotsa *et al.*, "On the integration of the energy storage in smart grids: Technologies and applications," *Energy Storage*, vol. 1, no. 1, p. e50, 2019, doi: 10.1002/est2.50.

11. W. Ahmed *et al.*, "Machine learning based energy management model for smart grid and renewable energy districts," *IEEE Access*, vol. 8, pp. 185059–185078, 2020, doi: 10.1109/ACCESS.2020.3029943.

12. N. H. Motlagh, M. Mohammadrezaei, J. Hunt, and B. Zakeri, "Internet of things (IoT) and the energy sector," *Energies*, vol. 13, no. 2, pp. 1–27, 2020, doi: 10.3390/en13020494.

13. R. W. R. de Souza, L. R. Moreira, J. J. P. C. Rodrigues, R. R. Moreira, and V. H. C. de Albuquerque, "Deploying wireless sensor networks–based smart grid for smart meters monitoring and control," *Int. J. Commun. Syst.*, vol. 31, no. 10, pp. 1–13, 2018, doi: 10.1002/dac.3557.

14. H. Shahinzadeh, J. Moradi, G. B. Gharehpetian, H. Nafisi, and M. Abedi, "Internet of Energy (IoE) in Smart Power Systems," *2019 IEEE 5th Conf. Knowl. Based Eng. Innov. KBEI 2019*, pp. 627–636, 2019, doi: 10.1109/KBEI.2019.8735086.

15. T. Dragičević, P. Siano, S. R. Prabaharan, and others, "Future generation 5G wireless networks for smart grid: a comprehensive review," *Energies*, vol. 12, no. 11, p. 2140, 2019.

16. Y. Liu, C. Yang, L. Jiang, S. Xie, and Y. Zhang, "Intelligent Edge Computing for IoT-Based Energy Management in Smart Cities," *IEEE Netw.*, vol. 33, no. 2, pp. 111–117, 2019, doi: 10.1109/MNET.2019.1800254.

17. V. Marinakis and H. Doukas, "An advanced IoT-based system for intelligent energy management in buildings," *Sensors (Switzerland)*, vol. 18, no. 2, 2018, doi: 10.3390/s18020610.

18. R. Zafar, A. Mahmood, S. Razzaq, W. Ali, U. Naeem, and K. Shehzad, "Prosumer based energy management and sharing in smart grid," *Renew. Sustain. Energy Rev.*, vol. 82, no. July 2017, pp. 1675–1684, 2018, doi: 10.1016/j.rser.2017.07.018.

19. N. C. Batista, R. Melício, and V. M. F. Mendes, "Layered Smart Grid architecture approach and field tests by ZigBee technology," *Energy Convers. Manag.*, vol. 88, pp. 49–59, 2014, doi: 10.1016/j.enconman.2014.08.020.

20. D. B. Avancini, J. J. P. C. Rodrigues, R. A. L. Rabêlo, A. K. Das, S. Kozlov, and P. Solic, "A new IoT-based smart energy meter for smart grids," *Int. J. Energy Res.*, no. December 2019, pp. 1–14, 2020, doi: 10.1002/er.5177.

21. V. Abreu, A. O. Santin, E. K. Viegas, and V. V. V. Cogo, "Identity and Access Management for IoT in Smart Grid," in *Advances in Intelligent Systems and Computing*, Apr. 2020, vol. 1151 AISC, pp. 1215–1226, doi: 10.1007/978-3-030-44041-1_104.

22. Q. M. Qadir, T. A. Rashid, N. K. Al-Salihi, B. Ismael, A. A. Kist, and Z. Zhang, "Low power wide area networks: A survey of enabling technologies, applications and interoperability needs," *IEEE Access*, vol. 6, pp. 77454–77473, 2018, doi: 10.1109/ACCESS.2018.2883151.

23. Q. Ou, Y. Zhen, X. Li, Y. Zhang, and L. Zeng, "Application of internet of things in smart grid power transmission," in *Proceedings - 2012 3rd FTRA International Conference on Mobile, Ubiquitous, and Intelligent Computing, MUSIC 2012*, 2012, pp. 96–100, doi: 10.1109/MUSIC.2012.24.

24. M. Faheem *et al.*, "Smart grid communication and information technologies in the perspective of Industry 4.0: Opportunities and challenges," *Comput. Sci. Rev.*, vol. 30, pp. 1–30, 2018, doi: 10.1016/j.cosrev.2018.08.001.

25. K. R. Anjana and R. S. Shaji, "A review on the features and technologies for energy efficiency of smart grid," *Int. J. Energy Res.*, vol. 42, no. 3, pp. 936–952, 2018, doi: 10.1002/er.3852.

26. A. Usman and S. H. Shami, "Evolution of communication technologies for smart grid applications," *Renewable and Sustainable Energy Reviews*, vol. 19. Pergamon, pp. 191–199, Mar. 01, 2013, doi: 10.1016/j.rser.2012.11.002.

27. M. Collotta, G. Pau, T. Talty, and O. K. Tonguz, "Bluetooth 5: A Concrete Step Forward toward the IoT," *IEEE Commun. Mag.*, vol. 56, no. 7, pp. 125–131, Jul. 2018, doi: 10.1109/MCOM.2018.1700053.

28. M. Pipattanasomporn, M. Kuzlu, W. Khamphanchai, A. Saha, K. Rathinavel, and S. Rahman, "BEMOSS: An agent platform to facilitate grid-interactive building operation with IoT devices," *Proc. 2015 IEEE Innov. Smart Grid Technol. - Asia, ISGT ASIA 2015*, pp. 1–6, 2016, doi: 10.1109/ISGT-Asia.2015.7387018.

29. H. Al Haj Hassan, A. Pelov, and L. Nuaymi, "Integrating cellular networks, smart grid, and renewable energy: Analysis, architecture, and challenges," *IEEE Access*, vol. 3, pp. 2755–2770, Dec. 2015, doi: 10.1109/ACCESS.2015.2507781.

30. Q. Zhang, Y. Sun, and Z. Cui, "Application and analysis of ZigBee technology for Smart Grid," in *Proceedings of ICCIA 2010 - 2010 International Conference on Computer and Information Application*, 2010, pp. 171–174, doi: 10.1109/ICCIA.2010.6141563.

31. M. Sherburne, R. Marchany, and J. Tront, "Implementing Moving Target IPv6 Defense to secure 6LoWPAN in the internet of things and smart grid," in *ACM International Conference Proceeding Series*, 2014, pp. 37–40, doi: 10.1145/2602087.2602107.

32. C. W. Lu, S. C. Li, and Q. Wu, "Interconnecting ZigBee and 6LoWPAN wireless sensor networks for smart grid applications," in *Proceedings of the International Conference on Sensing Technology, ICST*, 2011, pp. 267–272, doi: 10.1109/ICSensT.2011.6136979.

33. K. Logeswaran, P. Suresh, A. P. Ponselvakumar, and S. Savitha, "A study on data driven technologies involved in the development of viable anticipated smart cities," *Mater. Today Proc.*, no. xxxx, Feb. 2021, doi: 10.1016/j.matpr.2020.12.1067.

34. Chandraprabha, M., & Dhanaraj, R. K. (2020, November 5). Machine learning based Pedantic Analysis of Predictive Algorithms in Crop Yield Management. 2020 4th International Conference on Electronics, Communication and Aerospace Technology (ICECA).

35. Y. Saleem, N. Crespi, M. H. Rehmani, and R. Copeland, "Internet of Things-Aided Smart Grid: Technologies, Architectures, Applications, Prototypes, and Future Research Directions," *IEEE Access*, vol. 7, pp. 62962–63003, 2019, doi: 10.1109/ACCESS.2019.2913984.

36. K. Logeswaran, A.P. Ponselvakumar, V.Saranraj, S. Savitha. "Discovery of Potential High Utility Itemset from Uncertain Database using Multi Objective Discrete Differential Evolutionary Algorithm," 2022 International Conference on Computer Communication and Informatics (ICCCI), 2022, pp. 1-5, doi: 10.1109/ICCCI54379.2022.9740966.

30. Q. Zhang, J. Sun, and Z. Cui, "Application and analysis of ZigBee technology for Smart Grid," in Proceeding of CCCM 2010 - 2010 International Conference on Computer and Information Application, 2010, pp. 171-174, doi: 10.1109/ICCIA.2010.11833.

31. ... Stojkoska, R. Mladenov, and I. ... "Implementing a living ... Data Devices to realize ShdWPN ... in the Internet of things for smart grid ..." in ACM International C... Workshop ... 2014, pp. 45-50. doi: 10.1145/2660129.2660136.

32. C. ... Wu, D. ... Li, and G. ... "Mine Communication Sensor and ... WPAN wireless sensor networks for ... smart and applications," in Proceeding of the International Conference on ... Technology, 2013, pp. 267-272, doi: 10.1109/... Sept. ...

33. K. Kr... , R. ... , ... Papagionnaki, and S. Savikki, "A study on data driven technologies involved in the ... deployment of data ..." ... pred ... Chaos Aktive ... Inter ... Lett ... Vol. 462, doi: 10.1016/j.metho.2020.12.1022.

34. ... Chandran, Singh, O. ... , ... "... M... data ... ... Reduced ... adapt to ... better signal ... ..." in ... C... Proceeding ... Intern...al Conference on Electronics Communication and ... , ... , ... , 2018.

35. ... D... , K. ... , P. ... Ramon and H. ... ... , "... Bridge Added ... Grid ... Network ... Architecture ... ..." ... ... , 2019, doi: 10.1109/JSEN.2019.29123994.

36. S. ... , ... , ... , S. Savikki, "... Discovery of Parallel Task using license Reset ... Tree based on using High ... ... , 11th Inter... P... s ... , 2022, in ...

7

Effective Load Balance in IOTSG with Various Machine Learning Techniques

Thenmozhi K.[1]*, Pyingkodi M.[2] and Kanimozhi K.[3]

[1]Department of CS, Kristu Jayanti College Autonomous, Bengaluru, India
[2]Department of MCA, Kongu Engineering College, Perundurai, India
[3]Department of IT, Sri Krishna Adithya College of Arts and Science, Coimbatore, India

Abstract

In this chapter denotes the Internet of Things (IOT or IoT) incorporated with Smart Grid (SG) system, which can offer resourceful load balancing and meaningful data attainment technique with of cost worthy. Connection and communication is the central core of SG. Through the internet, the node or device can make a communication to other node or device in the system, which is said to be internet of things. In real world data growth become Unsaturated that is handled by the variety of technologies. The data source like geographical data, social data, market data, power system data, weather data, and medical data, and so on. Massive volume of data analysis from SG increase complexity so these data information effectively tackle with machine learning technology integrated with IoT and SG. One of the elementary foundations of machine learning is data mining. It can use together the more accurate data information. It is more helpful to achieve better results in machine learning technique. The passage of the electric part towards smart grids difficulty the ceaseless growth of machine learning techniques since their execution can cordially incorporate all the mechanism used which endowment consistency in smart electric systems as well as assurance a service of quality, efficiency, reliability, and stability. The huge volume of data can distribute via internet, and establishes the machine learning technique followed preprocessing the data information using the smart gird to enhance the accuracy and security and reduce the storage and save the power.

*Corresponding author: thenmegu@gmail.com; thenmozhi@kristujayanti.com

P. Sanjeevikumar, Rajesh Kumar Dhanaraj, Malathy Sathyamoorthy, Jens Bo Holm-Nielsen and Balamurugan Balusamy (eds.) Smart Grids and Internet of Things: An Energy Perspective, (193–206) © 2023 Scrivener Publishing LLC

Keywords: Internet of Things, load balance, smart grid, big data, machine learning

I. Introduction

This chapter enhance the recent technological up gradation place an important role in IoT (Internet of Things). It means a thing which has to be connected with the internet or network (smart technology). In the real world, overgrowth of data is a difficult process to maintain the information of data to give solution for particular problem. A wireless or wired sensor network shows an important place in IoT, which is to perform to assemble and transfer the data in real time using various sensors and technology. IoT provides various applications. Smart grid is one of the important IoT applications.

Smart grids are electrically connected with grid and board which show solution digitally. Nowadays smart grid applied throwaway in smart cities, electronic device, architecture, agriculture, home appliance, shopping market, power plant, energy generation, etc.

Machine learning is a subset of Artificial intelligence (AI) which is concentrate to make applications that understand a data in meaningful and improve the results accuracy with minimum time of execution. This technique suitable for all type of data such as text (sequential) statistical data, numerical data, and categorical data and so on. Nowadays, machine learning is all around the world to solve the problems with accurate and efficient outcome for specific decision-making process. Smart devices and AI are entered in digital world such as search in web, recognize the audio, video, voice, face, eye, structure of the part and etc. It rolls up on robots in wearable technology, medical environment, agricultural area, data analytics, space data, internet of things and images in all the fields [1].

Big data is an emerging field in world wide. In real world application the data will overgrowth, need to manage the overgrowth of data using various applications. The relationship between big data and IoT tends to grouping huge volume of object or data and the IoT finds to execute the data analytics using some simulation tools to support real world applications for real time decision making.

Load balancing refers to the techniques involved in the effective distribution of network load and management of network traffic among servers from server pool. Load balanced between client and server device, communication, network transformation available for every application without traffic among the data. Load balance maintains the execution time and space management. It performs various tasks like distributing the client request or efficiently loading the network among various servers. Such tasks are completed to guarantee to provide high availability and reliability in networks by sending request to servers through online. The load balance provides various benefits like

- ➢ Scalable
- ➢ Redundancy
- ➢ Flexibility
- ➢ Efficient
- ➢ Reduce the execution time
- ➢ Manage the space
- ➢ Reduce network traffic
- ➢ Fast data transfer and so on.

Load balancing is one of important part in data manipulation. Besides the load balance among the device is not done efficiently, the data transfer also should not be done effectively. Load balanced across servers, mutable configuration among the servers, balanced across hardware and software, balance in Open System Interconnection (OSI) layers and so on. Different types of methodologies used in this load balance like cloud, Domain Name System (DNS), global server, hybrid, OSI layers, round robin, Service Socket Layer (SSL), network, etc. SG with IoT integrates with various technologies place a vital role to improve the load balance among the servers.

II. IoT in Big Data

Big data is a most emerging field in world wide. Big data handles huge volume of informative data. The data collected from various sources, which is comes from living organism, nature, environment, social impacts etc. It analyzes various types of data such as discrete, continuous, nominal, and ordinal and so on. The IBM popularized four V's concepts like volume, variety, velocity, and veracity. Volume is referring to huge amount of data from different sources. Variety refers to various types of data like numeric, categorical, sequence or text, audio, video, clips and so on. Velocity refers to speed of the data generation and processing, and veracity refers to calculate the accuracy of particular processing data item [2].

IoT is a sequence of stream that incorporate on big data for analyzing the data in various manner. The giant set of associated with sensor, device, network and other 'things' which is related to the IoT. This can use for various fields like agriculture to develop smart machineries especially arduino sensor (UNO), medical to develop smart machine measurements like remote health monitor, workshops used tracking sensor, and banking sector related to IoT to transfer money and so on.

IoT facilitates big data, which required analytics, and it enhances the processes for more IoT device. The incorporation of IoT and big data was used to develop diffident task and process in device sectors. The combining these two areas such as big data and IoT make enormous development in future generation.

The fruition of IoT makes living so much easier. IoT helps users manage their smart gadgets and have trouble-shooting solutions. Numerous IoT functions like smart cities, that are mechanized, and offer purchaser goods like wearable, gadgets are on hand. IoT is truly the association of devices that surround sensors, software, electronics, and connectivity. It permits these belongings to bond, interrelate and switch over the data [3]. Recent days, IoT enter a step foot in everything from home appliance, farm, hospitals, transportation etc.

Big IoT analytics processed with types, methods and technologies. The huge amount of data processed by device, sensors like temperature, digital device monitor, social media and various applications like health care, different software applications, which is applicable for various type of data like structured, semi structured and unstructured data [4].

The relational architecture of intelligent network for analyzing the applications of IoT are shown in Figure 7.1.

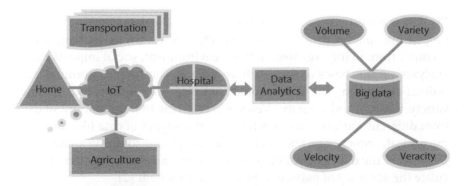

Figure 7.1 Relationship between IoT and big data.

III. IoT in Machine Learning

Machine learning integrate with IoT to enhance various application [5, 6]. There are four basic phases for structure a machine learning model. These are naturally achieved by data experts employed narrowly with the commercial experts for whom the application is actuality established.

Step 1: Choice and make a training data set
Training data set is a statistics data set descript the data in machine learning model that will swallowing the problem. In such case, these training data is labeled based on the features, which comes under the classification model in data mining. Classification otherwise called as supervised learning; it means can able to predict the data meaning (knowing data). These types of learning represent the label data, the results can compare and verify using this label data. For example, choose the data for discase identification, in which the data set contains a number of attributes and rows, one attribute must be labeled as normal data or diseased data. It prepares the needs like randomized, check the imbalances among the data. This data can classify into two subset one is called training subset which is used to train the application and another one is called evaluation subset which is used to evaluate the results using testing.

Step 2: Select a method to run on the training data set
Each and every method has sets of processing data based on the type of data that is labeled or unlabeled. If data is unlabeled it can follow the clustering techniques otherwise it can proceed with classification techniques. Here list out the few machine algorithms used for labeled data such as regression techniques, decision tree, and instance-based algorithm.
   Regression techniques: It is the linear combination of features which is used to realize the relationship among the data. This technique used to forecast the rate of dependent variable and based on the rate of independent variable. Two different types of regression are available such as linear regression and logistic regression. In linear regression could be used for dependent binary variable and linear regression could be used to prediction based on independent binary variable. Support vector machine is one of the useful to classify the dependent variable.
   Decision tree: It could classify the data in tree structure manner which is classified based on some set of decision rule.

Instance based algorithms: Best example for this algorithm is K-Nearest Neighbor (KNN). It works like clustering that is, similar or nearest data is classified to member of particular groups that have similar attributes. Conversly, dissimilar is classified to another group based on K values. It can be grouped based on similar feature between the data or distance-based grouping.

The following algorithm used for unlabeled data such as clustering algorithm, association algorithm, and neural networks.

Clustering: Collections of similar data grouped into one cluster. The Main focus of clustering the similarities among the data in particular group. Clustering works without knowing the prior knowledge about data in groups. Clustering otherwise is classified as unsupervised learning, this type of leaning does not know about data knowledge.

Association algorithms: It can find the relationships and patterns among the data using if-then relationship called association rule. It is similar to data mining rule.

Neural Networks: the neural networks based on three different layers such as input layer, hidden layer, and output layer. In input layer, the data is given in this layer and the hidden layer, where the manipulation are performed for particular problem to get solution based on input data and the output layer, where assigned the value of conclusion based on input and hidden layer. A deep neural network refers a network with more than one hidden layer and produces the optimum results successively refines in previous layer.

Step 3: Train the algorithm to generate model

Training the procedure is a recursive process which includes consecutively variables over the process, linking the production with the outcomes it must have created, altering masses and favoritisms indoors the procedure that force produce a supplementary precise outcome, and successively the variables yet again till the process yields the accurate outcome furthermost of the period. The ensuing qualified, correct procedure is the machine learning prototypical—an imperative discrepancy to memorandum, because 'algorithm' and 'model' are erroneously used interchangeably, even by machine learning doyens.

Step 4: Consuming and enlightening the model

The last step is to usage the classical with novel data and, in the greatest case, for it to rally in accurateness and efficacy over time. Where the novel data originates from will be contingent on the problematic presence resolved. For instance, a machine learning model calculated to classify junk will consume email communications, while a machine learning model that ambitions an automaton vacuum cleaner will consume data resulting from practical communication with enthused equipment or newfangled substances in the area.

IV. Machine Learning Methods in IoT

This technique is applicable for different type of data sets like nominal, ordinal, discrete, continuous and so on. The main difference between machine learning and IoT is connection among the data set. Machine learning permit the businesses to quick respond from customers, clouds in various images, finding planet deep space etc. IoT is wireless devices interconnected to accessing done through the internet. The powerful data inter connected with IoT devices to get an optimum outcome from source environment. Various machine learning techniques used to solve human diseases also like spectral clustering and genetic algorithm [7, 8].

IoT used in number fields for successful and meaningful intelligent data processing. Besides, number of infrastructures provide like cloud, fog, edge and so on. The limitation of IoT application layer in open-source interconnection is transmitting or receiving the information is to be creating a powerful and meaningful IoT applications. Hence, IoT form data which is to be processed and analyzed for machine learning and point out the difficult challenges in upcoming intelligent solution in IoT environment. The data collected from various source and processed using IoT with smart grid for balancing the load with the support of machine learning techniques to get final information [9].

The data collected from various source and different type of data sets like medical data, educational data, and voter data. Final information received in 3 ways such as local grid, IoT, global grid. Local grid cluster the meaningful and similar data from source A , source B, and source C using clustering techniques. Second, internet of things carries the information from local grid to global grid. Local grid locally clusters the data based on data representative and global grid received the meaningful data and collect it from the IoT and local grid and get the final information for balancing the load. The load balanced based on local grid, global grid and internet of things. Figures 7.2 and 7.3 shows the workflow of machine learning with IoTSG and architecture of distributed clustering for heterogeneous data set.

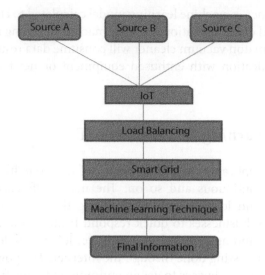

Figure 7.2 Workflow of machine learning with IoTSG.

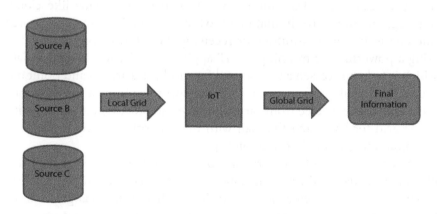

Figure 7.3 Distributed clustering architecture.

V. IoT with SG

Recent days, IoT mostly used in various fields like home appliance, vehicle, factories, colleges for administration, market, agriculture, cities, health care, device, shops, energy resource, storage, power plants (Thermal,

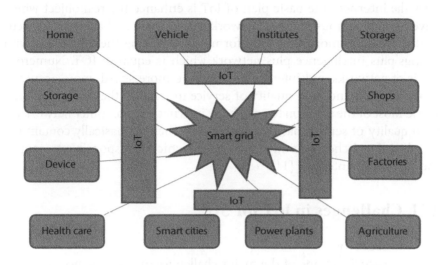

Figure 7.4 Internet of Things with smart grid.

nuclear, hydraulic, solar, wind, electric) and so on. The smart usage of Internet in real time applications are shown in Figure 7.4.

VI. Deep Learning with IoT

In recent years, the internet interconnected with the various device and objects representation. IoT increase the volume of information and the number of interconnections among the device to transform the information to knowledge in the culture [10]. The sensors are organized to screen one or more actions in an unattended atmosphere. A big amount of the occurrence information will be made over a period of time in IoT. Henceforth, the load balancing procedure is serious thoughts in the enterprise of IoT. Consequently, suggest a mediator Loadout that events grid load and procedure organizational formation by analysing a huge quantity of handler information and grid load, and applying Deep Learning's Deep Belief Network technique in directive to attain well-organized weight complementary in IoT. Similarly, we suggest an agent Stability bot that procedures a neural load forecast procedure created on Deep Learning's Q-learning technique and neural prior collective. It discourses the important purposes for future arrangement and pretend the effectiveness of planned arrangement using precise study.

IoT is a creation of wireless sensor networks, which has to be the capability of scanning the various applications across the network connectivity over the internet. The basic plan of IoT is enhance the real object which have tip into various sensors, network connectivity and actuator to accumulate the data among them. IoT formula describes as the connection with Things plus intelligence plus network which is equal to IOT. Numerous fields of networks and internet required the more speed, more accuracy, more security, and high quality of service to transfer the data across network. Most of the solution to enrich the internet and computer network for high quality of service has been enhanced. The data basically contain the number of switches, gateways and routers which is responsible to control the subroutine interface [11].

VII. Challenges in IoT for SG

❖ **Security**
  Security is one of the major challenges in maintenance and execution of IoT with smart grid networks. The security issues in IOTSG is classified as follows, lack of awareness and user understanding, security issues in device update, lack of fitness trackers, device located in remote location, botnet attacks, device record user information, etc.

❖ **Load balance**
  Need to balance the load for avoid the network traffic among data transfer. Bandwidth, capacity of repository, speed of the process, regulation among the network, compatibility in device update is difficult task in load balance.

❖ **Reduce network traffic**
  The traffic management will endure an evolution in IoT compliant to avoid the network traffic. IoT is an interconnection among the device and services which permit a data flow freely cross the intermediation.

❖ **Fast data transfer**
  Fast data transfer is one of the tools for fast upload the data from single machine to various machines. The data cluster and data accessing process also consider the fast transfer which is avoid the storing the data in silent.

VIII. IoT Applications for SG

In previous days, efficiently sharing the large amount of information is crucial task. Data losing, Security, load balances were considered as major issues in data sharing. Nowadays, Due to the technological growth, the digitalization issues, load balance and security issues can be overcome by easily. It can be done by transient the information which contain huge number of functions in machine by wireless sensor directly connected to the internet which has been processed from any remote places using remote sensors. It Suitable for controlled through the internet which connected to all the loads for proper operation and should follow constrain to share the information from one machine to other.

Application of IoT in smart control: There are number of applications of IoT in power, like,

- ❖ **Smart grid**
  It is one of the frameworks for IoT, which is to be used to accessing the data in remote monitor. It will manage everything from traffic signs, congestion among traffic, lighting, road traffic signals, road tracking, traffic warning, parking place, weather and so son.
- ❖ **Distribution switching**
  Distributed switching integrates with IOT relay in network. Number of distributed queues switches linked for data transfer without network traffic. It's mainly avoided the load balancing difficulty among device, meanwhile each and every device allocate and process the load using various distributed switching.
- ❖ **Power management**
  Battery power management is vital for all devices and sensors. Every sensors and device run over the power management. Wired and wireless both the devices used power, which one give better results with low power consumption that device and sensors consider as best device.
- ❖ **Renewable energy**
  In IOT infrastructure helps to control the renewable energy and done it effectively. IOT users can tie up with their solar panels, smart roof, harvesters based on rainwater, and so on. Every user can control the job of their electrical devices with help of concern mobile applications.
  Network sharing like LAN, MAN, WAN and so on.
  It gives an important space in sharing data among network. The data transfer done in two ways such that wireless and wired based on the distance between the device the

network type will be decided to transfer the data or information from one device to another device.

IX. Application of IoT in Various Domain

❖ **Smart device**

IOT devices are the part of hardware such that sensors, gadgets, appliances, and machine which programmed for certain applications or software to transfer the data over the internet or other networks. There is different type of IOT devices are used like laptop, fit bit, Bluetooth, alexa, smart phones, personal computers, mini computes, digital device, and so on.

❖ **Smart shop**

IOT make changes in human lives with sophisticated for linking everyday things together. The RFID (Radio-Frequency Identification) tags or labels detected through radio waves, meanwhile attached with every product for easy shopping.

❖ **Smart cook**

It means connecting Bluetooth technologies import into the kitchen so appliances can interconnect with each other, control the application, deliver the better taste and optimum result and carries the secrets needed to cook at home.

❖ **Smart vehicle**

The users can keep track or monitor the vehicle for fixing the sensor in vehicle, which is to protect from thefts, managing remote accessing, avoid accidents using tracking system, monitor continuously and control remotely.

❖ **Smart home**

IoT automation is have a capability to control the home appliance by electronically and internet. Home security through camera, switch on or off the home appliance through the remote sensors, and so on.

❖ **Smart stocks**

IOTSG stocks the computer and smart gadgets are not only connecting with the internet device. Everyday things like lights, TVs, washing machine, AC, Fan and main appliance even the door bells also have a connectivity with internet. It consumes the devices, manage software platforms, manage cloud computing services, etc.

❖ **Smart medical**
  Timely treatment in hospitalization is major role for different medical condition. Lot of health monitoring equipment used through the IOT sensors. It offers to enable doctor for understanding each person keep on monitoring the health condition of patients through the smart medicine.

❖ **Smart utilities and Smart business**
  IOT is overgrowing web devices ranged from smart gadgets to sensor manufacturing robots which are interconnected through the internet. In day today life facilitates the data can send receive the data or object through smart business.

❖ **Smart industrial automation**
  IOT helps to generate new technologies to solve problems, enhance the development and operation through DevOps tools and increase the productivity to improve the business which make an impact on industrial automation and it makes us to use the tablets computers, smart phones, cloud storage, distributed access, visualized patterns and so on.

❖ **Smart aircraft and smart warfare**
  It enables the functions in airline and airplane manufactures to monitor and control the planes in critical situations when aircraft is flight and this information is sent and receive through the satellite. The data being collected by aircraft smart device, network reliable, robust, scalable infrastructure is needed. Smart warfare based on ecosystem in smart devices can able to monitor the warfare.

X. Conclusion

Load balancing is a difficult task in real world application. Various technologies available for balance bot like machine learning, deep learning, data mining, artificial intelligent, data analytics, Neural networks, Genetic algorithms and so on. Main issues in load balance is affect the effectiveness and efficiency of algorithm, increase the space complexity and time complexity of algorithm, lacking to get optimum results for specific problems. To overcome these issues, need to maintain balance bot of load which is integrate with IoT for getting optimum solution for the problem. IoT receive the information from source data and transform the meaningful information to final result integrates with various techniques and devices which effectively balance the load across the network.

References

1. S.M. Mohammad, R. Mohammadreza, B. Mohammadamin, A. Peyman, B. Payam, and P.S. Amit, *Machine learning for internet of things data analysis: a survey*, Digital Communications and Networks, Vol. 4, No.3, p.161-175, 2018.
2. Y Qiang, D.Mianziong, and Z. Qingchen, *IoT Big Data Analytics*, wireless communications and mobile computing, 2019.
3. M. Pankaj and M Megha, *Internet of Things (IoT) and Big Data: A Review*, International Journal of Management Technology and Engineering, Vol. 8, p.5001-5007, 2018.
4. M. Mohsen, N. Fariza, G.Abdullah, K.Ahmad, A.Ibrahim, and H. Targio, *Big IoT analytics processed with types, methods and technologies*, Journal & magazines, IEEE access, Vol. 5, 2018.
5. Website: https://www.ibm.com/cloud/learn/machine-learning.
6. A. Erwin, A. Adnan, B. Zubair, and Z. Sherali, *Machine learning and data analytics for the IoT*, Neural Computing and Applications, Vol. 32, p. 16205–16233, 2020.
7. K. Thenmozhi, N. V. Karthikeyani, S. Shanthi and M. Pyingkodi, *Distributed ICSA Clustering Approach for Large Scale Protein Sequences and Cancer Diagnosis*, Asian pacific journal of Cancer Prevention, Vol. 19, No. 11, p. 3105-3109,2018.
8. K. Thenmozhi, N.V. Karthikeyani and S. Shanthi, *Distributed Fuzzy Estimate Spectral Clustering for Cancer Detection with Protein Sequence and Structural Motifs*, Asian pacific journal of Cancer Prevention, Vol. 19, No. 7, 1935–1940, 2018.
9. K. Hye-Young and K. Jong-Min, *A load balancing scheme based on deep-learning in IoT*, Cluster Computing, Vol. 20, p.873–878, 2017.
10. A.S. Nadia, Al-Jamali, S. Hamed, and Al-Raweshidy, *Intelligent Traffic Management and Load Balance Based on Spike ISDN-IoT*, IEEE Systems Journal, p.1-12, 2019.
11. P. Vijayapriya, G. Sreedip, and M. Kowsalya, *Internet of Things (IOT) Application for Smart Grid*, International Journal of Pure and Applied Mathematics, Vol. 118, No.18, p. 4107-4120, 2020.

8

Fault and Delay Tolerant IoT Smart Grid

K. Sangeetha and P. Vishnu Raja

*Department of Computer Science and Engineering, Kongu Engineering College,
Perundurai, India*

Abstract

Conventional electric networks are extended turned into Smart Grids (SGs) to report concerns such as unidirectional data flow, energy waste, rising energy request, dependability, and safety in the present power organization. Smart Grids, which include power generation, transmission, delivery, and usage systems, allow for bidirectional energy flow amongst facility sources as well as customers. SGs use a variety of instruments for grid observing, analysis, and control, which are widely arranged at power plants, distribution centers, and customers' homes. As a result, a Smart Grid necessitates device connectivity, automation, and tracking. The Internet of Things is used to accomplish this task. By combining IoT equipment and delivering the necessary data, IoT aids Smart Grid systems in supporting various network tasks during the generation, communication, distribution, and intake of energy. This chapter provides a thorough inspection of IoT assisted Smart Grid systems, including designs, applications, and energy efficiency and security. It also identifies unresolved questions, problems, and areas for further study.

Keywords: Internet of Things (IoT), smart grid (SG), delay tolerant network (DTN), architecture, energy efficiency, security, applications

8.1 Introduction

DTNs (Delay Tolerant Networks) are a type of network architecture that addresses the problem of intermittent network connectivity. Delay Tolerant Networks (DTN) is portable networks that might or might not

Corresponding author: sangeetha_k.cse@kongu.edu

P. Sanjeevikumar, Rajesh Kumar Dhanaraj, Malathy Sathyamoorthy, Jens Bo Holm-Nielsen
and Balamurugan Balusamy (eds.) Smart Grids and Internet of Things: An Energy Perspective,
(207–234) © 2023 Scrivener Publishing LLC

have a continuous path from end to end. DTN differs from standard Ad hoc Networks in its properties. As a result, if a communication is released in transitional node during communication, it can be saved and transmitted once the intermediate node rejoins the network [16, 24].

The Internet of Things (IoT) is expanding its application sectors (industry 4.0, eHealth, smart cities, and so on). The Internet of Things (IoT) has become one of the utmost widely used technologies. Things are diverse, with limited memory and processing power. Because traditional based existing security mechanisms are not appropriate for IoT devices, the deployment of the IoT system poses security and privacy issues. Meanwhile, limited computational, storage, and energy limits of smart things continue to pose communication issues for IoT. The usage of a Delay Tolerant Network (DTN) as a communication platform in the Internet of Things appears promising, but further research is needed. As a result, more open information and data arrangements must be established then used. Some of the system's primary issues include management and regulation of the composed and managed statistics, in addition to the data supplied (IoT). DTN networks can be used to resolve this. In reality, DTN can help improve IoT by more efficiently regulating systems and enabling behavior. The variability of the kinds of kit used in the DTN network [7] has an important impact on the distribution rate and delivery delay limitations in the context of IoT [6]. These performance indicators are also heavily influenced by the routing technique. The novel technologies can all employ distinct DTN directing protocols, which has a significant impact on network connection. As a result, establishing a novel consistent and ascendable DTN protocol is a big undertaking. Furthermore, the terminals may be heterogeneous and scaled up, with varying computational and storage capacities. Furthermore, the communication terminals' resources (in terms of energy) may be restricted. The routing of data is one of the IoT's problems [27].

Smart grid technologies are self-contained systems that can swiftly solve faults in an available system, reducing the workforce and ensuring that all customers have access to sustainable, dependable, safe, and high-quality power. Associations of preliminary research for the next step in smart grid applications will benefit authorities in the long run by assisting in the establishment of standards that are compatible with all applications, allowing all smart grid applications to be coordinated under the same authority.

Unlike the traditional central generation model, the contemporary "Smart Grid" permits two-way communication energy movements and transitive energy. Because of the abundance of information presently accessible, these features are conceivable. Traditional monitoring and control systems struggle to cope with the growing complexity and dynamic of smart grids, prompting business and research to look towards dispersed device and computing results for the grid. To confirm mobility, the majority of these reorganized, actual, implanted computing systems should be established on open software solicitation boards that follow business ethics and procedures. In comparison to traditional power grids, smart grids have integrated many progressive technologies, such as information detecting and regulator, data gathering and observing, into customary power grids, allowing for more well-organized and consistent power distribution from power generation, communication, and supply to customer depletion, as well as support for renewable energy [3, 4].

8.1.1 The Structures of the Intelligent Network

The Intelligent Network encompasses all existing along with planned solutions to the difficulties of power delivery. There are multiple challenging classifications and no arrangement on a universal definition due to the wide range of elements. Nonetheless, one probable classification is provided. The types can be divided into four modules: operational competence, energy efficiency, Flexibility in network topology and Reliability [55].

8.1.1.1 Operational Competence

The smart grid improves operational competence by integrating dispersed Distributed Energy Resources generation (DER). Each user has the ability to generate energy from renewable resources. There is a shift from a model with one manufacturer and numerous consumers to one with several manufacturers and customers. Then, utilizing the Supervisory Control and Data Acquisition (SCADA) system, it enables distant checking and diagnostics by assimilating devices located crosswise the net. These instruments provide fast feedback on electrical flow and usage. Nonetheless, it enhances community service power dependability, operational routine and total production [53].

8.1.1.2 Energy Efficiency

By optimizing power flows, the smart grid aids to decrease fatalities on the energy broadcast and circulation system. It helps you to see the state of your network in real time, predict events, and make better decisions.

8.1.1.3   Flexibility in Network Topology

Next-generation broadcast and delivery organization will be improved able to lever bidirectional energy currents, permitting for dispersed generation such as photovoltaic boards on construction tops, as well as charging to/from electric car and supplementary bases.

Customary grids were built for unidirectional electrical flow, but if a resident sub-network produces extra power than it consumes, the inverse movement might pose a safety and dependability risk [9, 11].

8.1.1.4   Reliability

The smart grid takes usage of skills like public approximation [17], which increase problem discovery and let the network to self-heal without the need for human involvement. This will result in a more stable electrical supply as well as a lower susceptibility to natural catastrophes or assault.

Although the smart grid is marketed as having various paths, the previous grid had several paths as well. The radial approach was used to build the first electrical lines in the grid; later, connectivity was ensured by different pathways, referred to as a network structure [5, 14].

8.1.2   Need for Smart Grid

The comparison between traditional grid and smart grid is given in the below Table 8.1 from which the need for the smart grid can be observed.

Table 8.1 Traditional grid vs. smart grid (intelligent network).

Criteria	Traditional network	Intelligent network
Metering	Electromechanical, solid state	Digital/Microprocessor
Communication	Unidirectional	Combines bi-directional message
Customer Interaction	Limited	Extensive
Generation	Central	Centralized and Circulated generation
Power Flow Control	Restricted safety, supervision and management organization	WAMPAC, Accustomed security

(Continued)

Table 8.1 Traditional grid vs. smart grid (intelligent network). (*Continued*)

Criteria	Traditional network	Intelligent network
Monitoring	No Technique	Automatic
Restoration	Physical	Automatic
Operation and Maintenance	Physical	Check system from distance login system
Control	Partial management scheme	Persistent management scheme
Reliability	Assessed prone to breakdown as well as cascading outages	Analytical: pro-active real time protection and islanding
Topology	Radial	Network

8.1.3   Motivation for Enabling Delay Tolerant IoT

The relationship between DTN features and IoT limitations is quite strong. The necessity of adopting delay tolerance techniques for IoT applications is demonstrated in Figure 8.2 and prior work by [17]. This dependence makes it easy to see how to modify DTN clarifications by improving specific performance indicators while also taking into account IoT concerns. Most IoT applications, as stated in [17], consist of a great numeral of networked items.

Since result, bulky volume of information transferred is an issue, as the application must analyze all of the essential data from the atmosphere. Perceptibly, the massive amount of information presents a greater test for DTN style in terms of improving distribution proportion and information economy. The two key DTN features addressed by scalability in the IoT are delivery delay and network analysis work. In the IoT and DTN designs, resource management is also a restriction. To build effective and optimum DTN systems, take into account the restricted power supply and memory buffer in tiny object [10, 30].

8.1.4   IoT-Enabled Smart Grid

In comparison to a traditional power grid, the SG share technology across the entire energy chain via extensive arrangement of various types of sensing, actuating, and extra entrenched equipment, as well as the usage of smart meters, smart utilizations, entirely of which share computing and communication capabilities. The employment of common message procedures, namely the TCP/IP stack, has made the Internet worldwide ubiquitous. Regardless of their access technique, any two computers located anywhere in the globe may readily communicate end-to-end. The Internet of Things (IoT) expands the reachability of the Hyperspace to everything with the intention of interaction and be addressed individually, using established message procedures. This addresses the large quantity of devices/objects organized arranged over the Smart Grid, as well as critical necessity for physical time connection with them using standardized message procedures.

Assume a country's SG includes 20 million smart meters, as well as 50 million devices also actuators to screen the entire power grid infrastructure. It will be fascinating for the SG's worker to be able to distantly monitor and adjust smart meters and sensors/actuators – independent of producer– as well as obtain data on the last mile grid's position. It will be interesting for energy suppliers to obtain remote energy usage from SMs in order to correctly charge consumers and identify efforts at interfering with the SMs. Final-users will also be interested in getting latest prices in order to better control their use, as well as receiving early warnings about planned disconnections. Obviously, IP-based message procedures (unless it is impossible or inappropriate), as well as public communication infrastructures, will greatly benefit all of these bidirectional end-to-end communications and transportations, making them more scalable and lowering associated costs.

8.2　Architecture

A numeral of designs is existing on behalf of IoT-supported Smart Grid structure. It is surveyed by way of such designs in this segment, and their arrangement is characterized in Figure 8.1. There are numerous details wherefore orientation design for IoT is a respect able item:

- IoT equipment is intrinsically linked – they require a method to engage with them, which is often hampered by firewalls, Network Address Translation (NAT), and other roadblocks.
- Here are now billions of these plans in use, and the figure is rapidly increasing; design for scalability is required. Furthermore, because these devices often interact 24 hours a day, a Highly-Available (HA) strategy that allows distribution crossways information centers is required for Disaster Recovery (DR).
- Because the equipment might not have User Interfaces and are clearly intended for "daily" use, support for automated and controlled upgrades, in addition to the ability to remotely organize these procedures, is required.

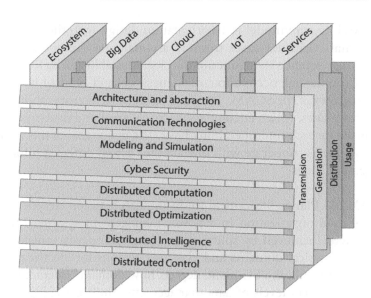

Figure 8.1 IoT enabled smart grid technology.

- Personal data is frequently collected and analyzed via IoT devices. A model for managing IoT device identities and access control, as well as the data they broadcast and consume, is a must.

The goal is to deliver a design that provisions combination amongst organizations and plans. The overall requirements of IoT supported Intelligent Network architecture as in Figure 8.2 is given below

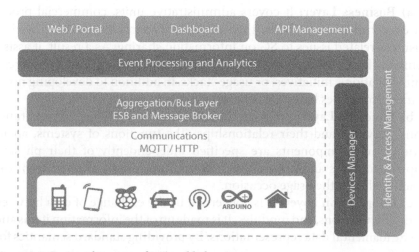

Figure 8.2 Basic architecture of IoT enabled system.

The Architecture model is an orientation design with the goal of illustrating Smart Grid use cases from an architectural standpoint. It is the result of the reference style functioning cluster established by EU Mandate M/490. Commercial, occupation, data, message, and element layers make up the majority of the SGAM. These are referred as interoperability layers. Smart grid planes, which encompass electrical areas and data organization areas, make up each interoperability layer. The major goal of this ideal is to show how are as cooperate with one another across different information management zones.

1) SGAM SG Planes: It's critical to distinguish between electrical procedure and data organization in a power management system. This separation may be achieved by splitting the electrical energy transformation cables into physical domains and classified regions for electrical process control. As a result, the SG plane depicts how domains interact with one another at different levels of data management. The areas are: generation, broadcast, delivery, and distributed energy resources (DER). End users and electrical producers are both included in the customer premises. Operations are divided into hierarchical zones for the administration of electrical processes.

2) SGAM Interoperability Layers: For easier display in addition to manipulation of the architectural standard, the SGAM is separated into five interoperability levels. The respite of this segment explores into every layer of interoperability.

   a) Business Layer: It covers administrative units, commercial procedures, commercial abilities, then supervisory circumstances, as well as business-related issues to SG on information sharing. As a result, it assists company leaders in making decisions about novel or current commercial representations, initiatives, or usage stacks, in addition to developing novel market prototypes based on supervisory requirements.

   b) Function Layer: From an architectural standpoint, it depicts functions, services, and their relationships. The functions of systems, applications, and components are specified independently of their physical implementations and actors. The functions are mostly derived from the functionality of the usage occasion.

   c) Information Layer: It is concerned by the exchange of data between facilities, functions, and modules. It is made up of the information items and the fundamental data representations. By providing standard semantics for services and occupations via message channels, the fundamental information representations and information objects enable interoperable information sharing.

d) Message Layer: It defines the techniques and procedures for interoperable data interchange among modules (such as the fundamental facility, purpose, or use case) and information representations or data entities.

e) Component Layer: It is responsible for the physical delivery of altogether SG machineries, including solicitations, actors, equipment, devices, message organization, and servers. Through information items and communication protocols, they communicate with one another.

8.3 Opportunities and Challenges in Delay Tolerant Network for the Internet of Things

8.3.1 Design Goals

The succeeding scheme goals are to be attained for the IoT enabled Smart Grid:

a) **Privacy-preserving:** For starters, even if an external attacker, A may eavesdrop on communication channels, he or she cannot reveal users' confidential practice statistics. Second, although if A can install certain untraceable virus, it still won't be able to access users' personal information. Third, any player in the authentic challenger exemplary cannot deduce relevant information around built-up customers' secrecy by listening in on and studying all contributions, in-between message streams, and yields that are not their individual. Finally, A is unable to properly execute a differential attack in order to get the privacy of a single user.

b) **Fault Tolerance:** Even in the face of failing meters, the system can nevertheless effectively and efficiently gather data from working meters.

c) **Computation Efficiency:** The suggested protocol's compute efficiency should be high enough to accommodate the data aggregation of thousands or millions of residential users.

Errors that can rise at diverse layers of the scheme can be characterized in this manner:

1. **Equipment edge error:** The errors happen while a manual scheme does not role correctly.
2. **Transmission error:** The errors happen as message stations and are triggered by physical connection failures, kernel failures, or when nodule goes dejected before converts remote.
3. **Device error:** As a Module raises hardware exclusion, such as a subdivision problem, the kernel generates a sign that is delivered to the Actor to which the Module belongs, resulting in a sign created by the core and sent to the Actor to which the Module belongs.
4. **Core error:** The errors be produced through a defect in the Module cipher before admission destruction that reasons an unsuccessful scheme appeal.
5. **Performer error:** The errors happen when the performer procedure break downs or when the Module code raises an exception that is recognized at the Actor level. Resource Management Faults are a subset of Actor Faults that occur when a module requests more resources than it has been allocated.
6. **Structure error:** The errors are originated as faults in the basic structure program.
7. **Rational error:** The errors are originated as faults in the industry reasoning of the Module system.

1) Poor Ecological situations and Inhibited Equipment: Hyperspace-assisted Smart Grid schemes work in a variety of situations, including those that are extremely harsh, such as power transmission line monitoring. As a result, it's critical to think about requirements for hybrid communication systems' durability, availability, compatibility, and signaling coverage in harsh environments [15]. Auto recovery and auto association IoT solutions should also be explored. When a collection of IoT devices fails, for example, the self-healing capability should choose another path by the dependability of IoT-assisted Smart Grid systems is safe. The restricted devices that are employed are also one of the constraints of IoT-aided SG systems. These gadgets may remain resistant to the elements, but they lack memory and computing capacity, limiting their capacity to perform local tasks. Because such devices have such a lengthy lifespan (up to ten years), backward compatibility is still a concern.

2) Energy Acquisition: Many IoT end strategies and devices are powered by batteries in IoT-assisted Smart Grid schemes. For instance, numerous devices, video cameras, and support nodes put on broad cast posts and broad cast ranks, which are generally powered by batteries, are used to monitor power transmission lines online. As a result, obtaining energy for these devices' power usage is a significant challenge in implementing IoT technology in Smart Grid [8]. Effective energy storing bases for IoT devices, as well as energy producing procedures paired with energy collecting via energy adaptation, must be created for this purpose [18]. At normal usage, the modern generation of sets can already previous ten years. However, there are still limits to the amount of power that may be used at the scheme.

3) Ecologically Harmless Devices: Under certain Smart Grid applications, including as power production, transmission, and distribution substations, IoT devices are installed outside and in harsh electromagnetic circumstances.

4) Communication Networks: In favor of the communication along with cooperation of Internet of Things strategies in Internet of Things-aided Smart Grid schemes, data and message nets are critical. Based on the transmission range [15], statistics and message nets may be categorized into binary basic groups: large range and small variety message nets. Extended-distance data broadcast is accomplished concluded a wide-area communication network. Bluetooth, Zigbee (IEEE 802.15.4), and Ultra-Wideband (UWB) are utilized in short-range communication networks. Extended-distance data broadcast is accomplished by Internet Protocol-based Internet, PLC, 2G/3G mobile networks, LTE, and satellite networks in a wide-area communication network. Bluetooth, Zigbee (IEEE 802.15.4), and Ultra-Wideband (UWB) are all examples of short-range communication networks. Wireless sensor nodes in IoT-assisted Smart Grid schemes, for example, have less control, less speed, and inadequate space capabilities, as well as storage and processing restrictions. As a result, in this circumstance, ZigBee is an acceptable communication network. The reliability and speed of connection become increasingly important as IoT-assisted Smart Grid applications evolve since just informational amenities and appliance scheduling to automatic power organization and mission-critical power source. The IoT-assisted SG systems use a hybrid mix of message system at a variety of phases of the similar activity, which is unusual in other industries. This communication line passes via numerous 'legs,' including devices to the limited association, intermediate nodes, core systems, and may be the storage, all of which use various protocols. This means that, despite dispersed connection phases and different network providers, more complex implementations of IoT-assisted Smart Grid schemes must be guaranteed of reliable net provision.

5) Information Fusion: The practice of merging statistics from different bases is known as data fusion. In IoT-assisted Smart Grid schemes, IoT devices occur to be stock restricted, with restricted mobile lifetime, computation, bandwidth, and storing capacities. Since a result, it is inefficient for IoT strategies to communicate all information to an entrance during the data collecting practice, as this would take a substantial amount of energy and bandwidth. Information synthesis technologies shall exist which are used to screen and combine individual meaningful statistics from many IoT strategies, which will improve data gathering competence and save energy and bandwidth [15]. Techniques for recognizing important information, such as smart combination, are a novel subject that resolve likely have an influence on IoT-assisted SG systems.

6) Interoperability and Integration of Devices: The capacity of binary or extra varied nets to communicate information and use that information in a shared purpose is characterized as interoperability [58]. The Internet of Things-assisted Smart Grid system is made up as variety of IoT devices and gateways that varies in terms of their features, operation, and resources as well as the message masses and protocols they use. The absence of method compatibility and integration is a significant stumbling block to the development of IoT-assisted SG systems. In favor of the expansion of Internet of Things supported Intelligent Network scheme one viable approach described in [1] is to transform proprietary protocol networks into IP based networks. The SG will be able to profit as of the smooth combination of different kind of system/plans in order to achieve interoperability as a result of this. Furthermore, future IoT devices should support a variety of message procedure and standards that function on various regularities and permit diverse designs to connect with one another. Interoperability concerns must also be distinguished at several layers, such as message level, the corporal level, and the request level. For tackling interoperability in Internet of Things-aided Smart Grid systems, a comprehensive method to facilities, strategies, and standards must be taken [8].

7) Announcement Interoperability: Smart Grid links a wide quantity of control generators, power sharing system, and end users. All component of these schemes necessitates a message medium, which is autonomous of the corporeal media, as glowing as manufacturers and device types. Multiple communication protocols and standards should coexist in the announcement structural design of Internet of Things-aided Smart Grid systems. [34, 49] show an example of such an announcement style. Cellular wireless technology is able to be employed to attach intelligent meters to the central system. Many regularities command recommend intelligent meters have also underlined the relevance and requirement for dependability for message structures, smart measuring plans, and systems.

8) Cross-domain Interprocedurability: The IoT is made up as variety of strategies, message conventions, in addition to requests. As a result, inter-procedures may be a significant difficulty inside the Internet of Things. While Internet of Things is combined through Smart Grid, Internet of Things assisted Smart Grid schemes confront the issue of interoperability, which is an inherent problem with IoT. Smart Grid is made up of several systems and sub-systems. As a result, IoT-assisted Smart Grid systems must deal with two different sorts of mediate area inter-procedures concerns. The primary need is mixed area compatibility connecting every SG scheme and mediate scheme.

9) Massive Information Management: The combination of IoT knowledge with Smart Grid originates at the price of more recurrent dispensation and storage of massive amounts of statistics, putting a greater strain on IoT message nets. Power utilization, consumer weight order, superior metering report, control line failures, and so on are examples of this type of data. Using great bandwidth and statistics speeds, such as those provided by LTE, improves capacity to carry such statistics while causing bottlenecks away. As a result, utility companies should build systems with greater capabilities for efficiently storing, managing, and processing the acquired data [17].

8.4   Energy Efficient IoT Enabled Smart Grid

Energy is currently produced mostly by big, centralized energy plants using Nonrenewable Energy Sources (NRESs). The utilization of central energy units results in energy fatalities and environmental deterioration throughout electricity broadcast. Because energy is generated near to where it is used, an elevated diffusion of renewable power foundation into energy network decreases the ecological disaster and energy depletion. The advent of Distributed Energy Resources is another answer to centralized energy generating (DERs). By switching from NRES to RES, DER boosts total charge investments for the client, allowing customers to regulate their electricity, and minimizes gas emissions [51].

In a LEED gold-certified green office building, a modest pattern for smart energy connecting just one user was created. It connected electrical items in binary different sites: a flat and a workplace in a structure [52]. The goal of this example was to allow a user to regulate and accomplish applications in dual places dynamically. Afterward noticing deviations in the worker's site, the prototype allows the server to initiate the energy strategy controller development by rotating electrical utilizations ON or OFF in the double places. Users may easily establish and manage their individual power strategy during actual instance, ensuring that the vitality ingestion is equal to their real usage. While this modest pattern has one user and two regulator strategies, the system may easily be scaled up to allow several users to operate their devices at various places at the same time.

8.5　Security in DTN IoT Smart Grid

There are several types of networks in the IoT, including dispersed, pervasive, grid, and vehicle networks. Sensors deployed in the patient physique to monitor in dangerous disorder, watching gas leaks in smart kitchens, farm fields, smart vehicle parking, and smart conveyance, and tracing products particulars in stock sequence systems employing sensors in the supply chain. The sensors are resource-constrained strategies linked across heterogeneous networks through wired or wireless connections. IoT networks have varying levels of security, privacy, and vulnerability to hackers [2, 19].

8.5.1　Safety Problems

When a Hyperspace scheme is used, the Internet of Things-assisted Smart Grid will face numerous safety disputes:

1. **Impersonation/Identity Spoofing:** Using the identity of a valid item, this attack attempts to communicate on its behalf in an unlawful manner. An attacker might impersonate the identity of a smart meter to trick it into paying for its energy usage.
2. **Eavesdropping:** Because IoT-based SG objects/devices connect utilizing communal announcement arrangement, an attacker can simply get rights to the data they transmit. An attacker can quickly figure out how much energy a home uses.
3. **Data tampering:** An attacker can alter communicated information, such as energetic pricing supplied before peak periods, to make them the lowest prices possible. As a result, homes may increase their consumption slightly than decrease it, resulting in an overburdened control system.
4. **Authorization and Control Access issues:** Because many strategy, since hybrid meters or area organized devices as

well as actuators within division substations, can be monitored and configured remotely, an invader or enraged worker can aim to increase illegal admission and influence them, causing material damage (for example, modifiers) or power outages.

5. **Privacy issue:** In private homes, smart meters and smart equipment might reveal additional to power use. Their delicate data might compromise classified operators by revealing information about their routines, whether they are at home or away, if they are on vacation, and so on [44].

6. **Compromising and Malicious code:** The Smart Grid's computing and message capabilities make them vulnerable to physical or remote compromise. Furthermore, because they run several kind of software, they might exist infected with a variety of kind of software or mischievous policy in direction to regulate and operate them. Furthermore, mass-deployed goods containing restricted electronics are typically resistant, creating physical compromise a simple process [33].

7. **Availability and DoS issues:** This is difficult toward marking accessibility of resources in the traditional power grid, particularly at a greater level. In the Smart Grid, technology will be combined even into critical power grid assets, allowing them to be targeted and rendered partially or completely unavailable, culminating in a DoS assault. Furthermore, given that the majority of strategies are IP-supported and do not run copyrighted protocols, an experienced Internet attacker will have an easier time.

8. **Cyber-attack:** The Smart Grid may be thought of as the world's biggest Cyber-Physical-System (CPS), with tangible schemes on behalf of the SG's physical possessions and ICT systems controlling/managing physical things. Currently, a cyber-attack may affect physical resources [60].

8.5.2 Safety Works for the Internet of Things-Based Intelligent Network

The key safety facilities that should be considered for the Internet of Things-based Smart Grid:

1. **Certification:** The capacities in the direction of verify and confirm identification of some collaborating scheme within

the Smart Grid. On behalf of example, in order to notice the appropriate consumer, the energy provider must authenticate each smart meter.

2. **Data Integrity:** Guarantees that (received) data were not altered in an illegal way. For example, smart meters want to certify the reliability of a software update, in addition to source origin.

3. **Confidentiality:** Certifies that information (stored or transmitted) is reachable only to the envisioned receivers. For instance, end-users' depletion want to be recognized by the Smart Grid's worker and the energy supplier simply.

4. **User's Privacy:** Guarantees that any information related to the consumer could not be acquired devoid of its clear support, and will be used only for the intended purposes. For instance, energy ingestion information used for billing couldn't be used for other reasons

5. **Authorization and Control Access:** Assumes that a genuine object/person has been granted the appropriate permissions to access certain assets or is permitted to do certain activities. To execute physical arrangement on a smart meter, for example, an on-the-field agent need permission and access control privileges.

8.5.3   Security Standards for the Smart Grid

The implementation of the smart grid network has been described by several standardization groups. The smart grid design has been specified by the American organization National International Standard Technology (NIST).

8.5.3.1   The Design Offered by NIST

The fundamental design for intelligent network is presented by NIST. Delivery, communication, consumer, fairs, processes, and service provider are the seven areas of this architecture. as shown in Figure 8.3 [42].

8.5.3.2   The Design Planned by IEEE

All customers produce power by renewable things. The additional power is controlled through the customer; surplus energy organization is dispersed. Assumed the difficulty of the organization task, the IEEE offered design

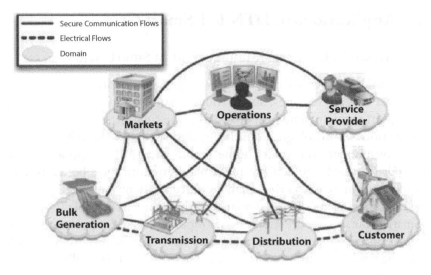

Figure 8.3 NIST architecture.

grounded on NIST's, and then created a novel arena called DER, which provides for the centralized management of energy surpluses created. IEEE has also offered recommendations for thoughtful and essential intelligent network procedural activity as in Figure 8.4.

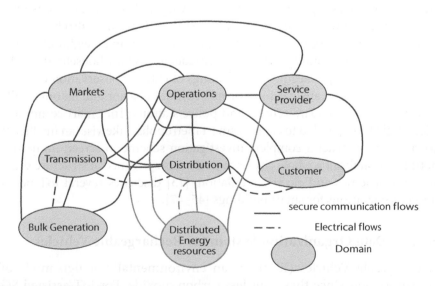

Figure 8.4 IEEE architecture.

8.6   Applications of DTN IoT Smart Grid

8.6.1   Household Energy Management in Smart Grids

IoT technology benefits smart homes and products including smart TVs, home-based safety schemes, smart fridges, laundry mechanisms, fire discovery, light regulator, and heat observing. The smart house has device and actuator nodes for ecological observing, and sending data to house's controller component. The smart home is thus a critical component of the Smart Grid in order to achieve real-time communication between users and the grid, increase service quality and capacity of integrated grid services, and meet users' energy demands as efficiently as possible [64].

Smart home services are widely used to optimise everyday power use. Users can, for example, put on boilers or air conditioners earlier inward household to like their selected atmosphere without having to wait. Surveillance data is also used by the control unit to sense distrustful activity and alert employers to proceed with relevant action. Altogether of these features are only possible because to the Internet of Things. This scheme acts as a power management system and manages energy based on energetic rating. As a result, it avoids using household appliances during uttermost periods. The Android submission is created that allows users to retrieve their data remotely. Furthermore, by integrating Reed Solomon Codes for fault discovery and improvement, [32] developed a characteristic for smart home security improvements. In smart homes, the IoT is used to operate smart appliances, multi-meter reading, electric ingesting data, capacity observing and device, and consumer communication with smart equipment. IoT knowledge may also be used by NANs, which can connect a number of smart houses in a neighborhood to build a smart community [12]. As a consequence, smart households in the smooth public might segment the findings of exterior observation cameras in order to identify any calamity or mistrustful behavior and automatically notify the relevant spare centers and police stations. The smart communal idea might be expanded to create a smart metropolis. Likewise, an intelligent town may construct a complete investigation scheme to screen numerous actions throughout a whole city or even a country. Aimed at structure organization schemes and electric regulation, [13] discusses several IoT needs and considerations for smart buildings [45–47].

8.6.2   Data Organization System for Rechargeable Vehicles

Rechargeable Vehicles (RVs) are an environmentally benign mode of transportation since they emit less carbon dioxide. For IoT-assisted SG systems, this is an intriguing possibility. An electric quantity system, indicting tools, and an observing scheme make up an electric vehicle charging scheme. The electric source scheme is in charge of electricity output and administration [56]. The charging equipment comprises both AC and DC chargers for charging and discharging electric vehicles. AC chargers are commonly used in the house and provide sluggish charging. Rapid RV charging necessitates the use of DC chargers, which are commonly found at open indicting locations [50]. Together kinds of mounts come with an advertising feature. The charging scheme and its security are monitored in actual spell by the monitoring system. The Internet of Things (IoT) shows a key part in this observing scheme, offering an information management system that combines various charging system components [28]. For example, IoT technology allows electric source and actual observing schemes to direct data to an organization structure, which then sends the data to a control station, allowing for the appropriate steps to be made [29].

8.6.3   Advanced Metering Infrastructure (AMI)

Conventionally, power ingesting data is physically gathered on-site at predetermined times. Inevitably, the technique resulted in inaccuracies in terms of accuracy and timeliness. Using community or reserved message networks, IoT allows AMI [15] or distant meter interpretation schemes grounded on Wireless Sensor Network. Some of the important essential roles of the Smart Grid is the WSN scheme, which collects high-reliability real-time electricity consumption data, processes it, and therefore provides real-time observing, figures, and energy utilization investigation. Intelligent meters are improved also computerized varieties of standard electric meters used outside of the house. One of the most essential tasks of the SG is the AMI system, which collects and processes real-time electricity usage data, allowing for real-time observing, figures, and power usage exploration. AMI meters remain improved plus digitized forms of standard digital meters used outside the house. AMI meters, in addition to tracking power use, also transfer energy and pricing data from efficacy providers to user locations, facilitating two-way message over the Internet of Things [17]. As a result, users may alter their energy use depending on the energy and evaluating statistics obtained by AMI, and therefore protect cash. The relevance, competence, and correctness of the energy depletion statistics are critical features of this system. IoT technology might help consumers protect currency by altering their power practice behavior grounded on an examination of their electric use if they employ this system [41, 43].

8.6.4   Energy Organization

Energy organization is precise by way of the adjustment of consumers' energy feeding outlines in response to utility companies' different power costs [25, 26]. It is used to lower the customer's power tariff, the power grid's working costs, and energy fatalities, also to move request capacity from uttermost to peak. The energy ingestion needs of several household purposes are collected by IoT devices and transmitted to the home-based switch elements. Following that, the Smart Grid control unit plans household appliance energy use depending on the users' stated inclinations, lowering all end user power cost. At several levels of the SG, demand-side energy management may be implemented. It can, for example, be done at the consumer's house to protect their confidentiality. It may also be done at an advanced level to assistant both customers and utility corporations by providing a more efficient scheduling plan. Previously, patrolling of electricity generation, transmission, and distribution was mostly a human operation carried out at regular intervals. However, the quality and amount of patrols is not always as planned because of climatic situations and together social and ecological variables. Furthermore, electricity personnel typically find it difficult to patrol unattended substation equipment [61–63].

8.6.5   Transmission Tower Protection

Broadcast post security is a WAN application of IoT-assisted Smart Grid schemes established to safeguard broadcast posts from physical loss caused through robbery of works, regular calamities, improper construction, and the growth of trees underneath the grounds [59]. The most common causes of transmission tower damage are burglary and intentional destruction by individuals. Usual calamities such as cyclones, tough storms, and universal heating effects have the potential to bring transmission towers down. The risks of working near high-voltage transmission towers are commonly overlooked by construction companies. They use a lot of heavy construction equipment, which not only puts their workers in risk, but also has the potential to damage transmission cables and towers. Such contractors may fail to notify the proper power broadcast sectors, making it difficult for power broadcast workers to examine and observe entire power broadcast services, perhaps placing transmission towers at risk [36, 48].

Furthermore, because of their physical location, certain transmission towers are difficult to access. As a result, the quality of patrols cannot be guaranteed. The patrolling time fluctuates between 1 and 10 weeks, implying inadequate surveillance and increased security threats. While some technology is put on broadcast posts to observe theft and other possible damage, the precision and stability of this technology is still lacking [57]. IoT expertise can enable distant observing in tackling these safety issues with the use of WSNs. Various sensors in the IoT-assisted transmission tower safety system produce early alerts of risks to high-voltage transmission towers, allowing for swift actions. Vibration sensors, secure bolts, an inclined sensor, and an audiovisual camera are among the sensors. A WSN [54] is formed by these devices and the sink node. The sensors notice any danger and communicate warning sign to the coordinator device. The base node gets the sign of threat from the coordinator device. The sink node obtains the signs after the devices, turns them to information, and delivers it over Internet or another community or reserved message net to moni toring station [31].

8.6.6   Online Monitoring of Power Broadcast Lines

Some of the greatest essential IoT uses in the Smart Grid, particularly for calamity protection and modification, is online monitoring of electricity transmission lines [37, 39]. Natural catastrophes in recent years have emphasized the issues of high voltage electricity transmission lines in terms of security, dependability, and stability. High-voltage transmission line monitoring has always been done by hand. Actual operational checking of electricity broadcast lines is now possible thanks to sensors that measure electrode galloping, gust vibration, electrode temperature, minicomputer meteorology, and ice. There are two aspects to this innovative online power transmission line monitoring system. The devices are put on the control broadcast outlines among broadcast posts in first segment to monitor the status of the lines. Devices are mounted on transmission towers in the second stage to screen their statuses and environmental conditions. The Internet of Things allows electricity transmission line sensors and transmission tower sensors to communicate [35, 38, 40].

8.7   Conclusion

The Intelligent network is the grid of the prospect, which tackles the conventional control system's concerns of unidirectional information flow, energy waste, rising energy consumption, dependability and security. The Internet of Things (IoT) enables networking wherever and at some period. It assists Smart Grid by issuing smart strategies or Internet of Things plans for grid observing, examination, then control, in addition to communication, computerization, and tracing. This results in an IoT-assisted SG organization that cares and enhances numerous network operations in the power generating sector. A complete assessment of IoT-assisted SG systems is offered in this chapter, as well as a number of concerns that need to be solved.

To begin with, here are numerous principles for IoT and SG, but there is a lack of regulations for the IoT-assisted SG scheme as an entire. As a result, it's critical to consider the regulation of IoT-assisted SG systems. Second, relatively little effort has been finished on the uses of IoT-assisted SG organizations from the standpoint of uses. For an improved understanding of IoT-aided SG schemes, it is necessary to consider the rapid evolution of all applications. Third, from the standpoint of architectures, the present designs place a strong emphasis on general covered design and HAN designs. Layered designs are generalist designs that don't include many key features of Smart Grid and organizations. As a result, a new standard design for IoT-assisted Smart Grid systems is required, with these precise factors taken into account. Fourth, there are few published prototypes for IoT-assisted SG organizations. Furthermore, there are no readily available open source test beds or simulation tools to allow for the testing and performance assessment of IoT assisted SG systems. Both of these features of prototyping must be taken into account. In conclusion, IoT assisted SG systems combine two developing and promising worlds: IoT and SG. There has already been a lot of progress in the field of IoT aided SG systems, as we saw in this chapter, then here is still a lot further to be done aimed at a improved and more full implementation of Internet of Things-aided Smart Grid systems.

References

1. Fadi Al-Turjman, Mohammad Abujubbeh, "IoT-enabled smart grid via SM: An overview" Future Generation Computer Systems, Elsevier Journal 2019.
2. Security Issues and Challenges for the IoT-based Smart Grid Chakib BEKARA, Proceedings of International Workshop on Communicating Objects and Machine to Machine for Mission- Critical Applications
3. S. E. Collier, "The emerging Enernet: Convergence of the Smart Grid with the Internet of Things," in IEEE Industry Applications Magazine, vol. 2, 2017, pp. 12–16.

4. R. Deng, Z. Yang, M.-Y. Chow, and J. Chen, "A Survey on Demand Response in Smart Grids: Mathematical Models and Approaches," IEEE Transactions on Industrial Informatics, vol. 11, no. 3, pp. 570–582, 2015.

5. S. Temel, V. C. Gungor, and T. Kocak, "Routing Protocol Design Guidelines for Smart Grid Environments," Computer Networks, vol. 60, pp. 160–170, 2014.

6. R. Ma, H.-H. Chen, Y.-R. Huang, and W. Meng, "Smart Grid Communication: Its Challenges and Opportunities," IEEE Transactions on Smart Grid, vol. 4, no. 1, pp. 36–46, 2013.

7. W. Wang, Y. Xu, and M. Khanna, "A Survey on the Communication Architectures in Smart Grid," Computer Networks, vol. 55, no. 15, pp. 3604–3629, 2011.

8. E. Yaacoub and A. Abu-Dayya, "Automatic Meter Reading in the Smart Grid using Contention Based Random Access over the Free Cellular Spectrum," Computer Networks, vol. 59, pp. 171–183, 2014.

9. M. Yigit, V. C. Gungor, and S. Baktir, "Cloud Computing for Smart Grid Applications," Computer Networks, vol. 70, pp. 312–329, 2014.

10. H. Sun, A. Nallanathan, B. Tan, J. S. Thompson, J. Jiang, and H. V. Poor, "Relaying Technologies for Smart Grid communications," IEEE Wireless Communications, vol. 19, no. 6, pp. 52–59, 2012.

11. S. Bush, "Network Theory and Smart Grid Distribution Automation,"IEEE Journal on Selected Areas in Communications, vol. 32, no. 7, pp.1451–1459, 2014.

12. C. Wang, X. Li, Y. Liu, and H. Wang, "The Research on Development Direction and Points in IoT in China Power Grid," in International Conference on Information Science, Electronics and Electrical Engineering (ISEEE), vol. 1, 2014, pp. 245–248.

13. X. Chen, L. Sun, H. Zhu, Y. Zhen, and H. Chen, "Application of Internet of Things in Power-Line Monitoring," in International Conference on Cyber-Enabled Distributed Computing and Knowledge Discovery (CyberC), 2012, pp. 423–426.

14. W. Meng, R. Ma, and H.-H. Chen, "Smart Grid Neighborhood Area Networks: A Survey," IEEE Network, vol. 28, no. 1, pp. 24–32, 2014.

15. Smart Grid News, "Smart Grid 101: The Internet of Things and the Smart Grid (Part 1)," 12 November 2013, accessed: January 2016. [Online]. Available: http://www.smartgridnews.com/story/smart-grid 101-internet-things-and-smart-grid-part-1/2013-11-12

16. EAI International Conference on Smart Grid and Internet of Things (SGIoT). [Online]. Available: http://sgiot.org

17. Z. M. Fadlullah, A.-S. K. Pathan, and K. Singh, "Smart Grid Internet of Things," Mobile Networks and Applications, pp. 1–2, 2017.

18. F. Al-Turjman and M. Abujubbeh, "IoT-enabled Smart Grid via SM: An Overview," Future Generation Computer Systems, In Press, 2019.

19. Gupta, A. Anpalagan, G. H. Carvalho, L. Guan, and I. Woungang, "Prevailing and Emerging Cyber Threats and Security Practices in IoTenabled Smart Grids: A Survey," Journal of Network and Computer Applications, vol. 132, p. 1, 2019.

20. G. De La Torre Parra, P. Rad, and K.-K. R. Choo, "Implementation of Deep Packet Inspection in Smart Grids and Industrial Internet of Things: Challenges and Opportunities," Journal of Network and Computer Applications, vol. 135, pp. 32–46, 2019.

21. G. Bedi, G. K. Venayagamoorthy, R. Singh, R. R. Brooks, and K.-C.Wang, "Review of Internet of Things (IoT) in Electric Power and Energy Systems," IEEE Internet of Things Journal, vol. 5, no. 2, pp. 847–870, 2018.

22. S. S. Reka and T. Dragicevic, "Future Effectual Role of Energy Delivery:A Comprehensive Review of Internet of Things and Smart Grid," Renewable and Sustainable Energy Reviews, vol. 91, pp. 90–108, 2018.

23. K. Sohraby, D. Minoli, B. Occhiogrosso, and W. Wang, "A Review of Wireless and Satellite-Based M2M/IoT Services in Support of Smart Grids," Mobile Networks and Applications, pp. 1–15, 2017.

24. S. Jain, N. Kumar, A. Paventhan, V. K. Chinnaiyan, V. Arnachalam,and M. Pradish, "Survey on Smart Grid Technologies-Smart Metering, IoT and EMS," in Students' Conference on Electrical, Electronics and Computer Science (SCEECS), 2014, pp. 1–6.

25. Al-Ali and R. Aburukba, "Role of Internet of Things in the Smart Grid Technology," Journal of Computer and Communications, vol. 3, no. 05, p. 229, 2015.

26. S. K. Viswanath, C. Yuen, W. Tushar, W.-T. Li, C.-K. Wen, K. Hu, C. Chen, and X. Liu, "System Design of the Internet of Things for Residential Smart Grid," IEEE Wireless Communications, vol. 23, no. 5, pp. 90–98, 2016.

27. Q. Yang, "Internet of Things Application in Smart Grid: A Brief Overview of Challenges, Opportunities, and Future Trends," in Smart Power Distribution Systems. Elsevier, 2019, pp. 267–283.

28. Al-Fuqaha, M. Guizani, M. Mohammadi, M. Aledhari, and M. Ayyash, "Internet of Things: A Survey on Enabling Technologies, Protocols and Applications," IEEE Communications Surveys & Tutorials, 2015.

29. E. Borgia, "The Internet of Things Vision: Key Features, Applications and Open Issues," Computer Communications, vol. 54, pp. 1–31, 2014.

30. Mashal, O. Alsaryrah, T.-Y. Chung, C.-Z. Yang, W.-H. Kuo, and D. P. Agrawal, "Choices for Interaction with Things on Internet and Underlying Issues," Ad Hoc Networks, vol. 28, pp. 68–90, 2015.

31. M. Nitti, V. Pilloni, G. Colistra, and L. Atzori, "The Virtual Object as a Major Element of the Internet of Things: a Survey," IEEE Communications Surveys & Tutorials, 2015.

32. Granjal, E. Monteiro, and J. Silva, "Security for the Internet of Things: A Survey of Existing Protocols and Open Research Issues," IEEE Communications Surveys & Tutorials, vol. 17, no. 3, pp. 1294– 1312, 2015.

33. Granjal, E. Monteiro, and J. S. Silva, "Security in the Integration of Low-Power Wireless Sensor Networks with the Internet: A Survey," Ad Hoc Networks, vol. 24, pp. 264–287, 2015.
34. S. Sicari, A. Rizzardi, L. Grieco, and A. Coen-Porisini, "Security,Privacy and Trust in Internet of Things: The Road Ahead," Computer Networks, vol. 76, pp. 146–164, 2015.
35. Botta, W. de Donato, V. Persico, and A. Pescape, "Integration of Cloud Computing and Internet of Things: A survey," Future Generation Computer Systems, 2015.
36. Atzori, A. Iera, G. Morabito, and M. Nitti, "The Social Internet of Things (SIoT)–When Social Networks Meet the Internet of Things: Concept, Architecture and Network Characterization," Computer Networks, vol. 56, no. 16, pp. 3594–3608, 2012.
37. M. Ortiz, D. Hussein, S. Park, S. N. Han, and N. Crespi, "The Cluster Between Internet of Things and Social Networks: Review and Research Challenges," IEEE Internet of Things Journal, vol. 1, no. 3, pp. 206–215, 2014.
38. K. Sood, S. Yu, and Y. Xiang, "Software Defined Wireless Networking Opportunities and Challenges for Internet of Things: A Review," IEEE Internet of Things Journal, vol. 3, no. 4, pp. 453–463, 2016.
39. C.-W. Tsai, C.-F. Lai, M.-C. Chiang, and L. T. Yang, "Data Mining for Internet of Things: A Survey," IEEE Communications Surveys & Tutorials, vol. 16, no. 1, pp. 77–97, 2014.
40. Mehaseb, Y. Gadallah, A. Elhamy, and H. El-Hennawy, "Classification of LTE Uplink Scheduling Techniques: An M2M Perspective,"IEEE Communications Surveys & Tutorials, vol. 18, no. 2, pp. 1310–1335, 2016.
41. Perera, A. Zaslavsky, P. Christen, and D. Georgakopoulos, "Context Aware Computing for the Internet of Things: A Survey," IEEE Communications Surveys & Tutorials, vol. 16, no. 1, pp. 414–454, 2014.
42. R. Palattella, N. Accettura, X. Vilajosana, T. Watteyne, L. A. Grieco,G. Boggia, and M. Dohler, "Standardized Protocol Stack for the Internet of (important) Things," IEEE Communications Surveys & Tutorials, vol. 15, no. 3, pp. 1389–1406, 2013.
43. Aijaz and A. H. Aghvami, "Cognitive Machine-to-Machine Communications for Internet-of-Things: A Protocol Stack Perspective," IEEE Internet of Things Journal, vol. 2, no. 2, pp. 103–112, 2015.
44. S. L. Keoh, S. S. Kumar, and H. Tschofenig, "Securing the Internet of Things: A Standardization Perspective," IEEE Internet of Things Journal, vol. 1, no. 3, pp. 265–275, 2014.
45. E. Commission. Standardization Mandate to European Standardisation Organisations (ESOs) to support European Smart Grid deployment. Last accessed: May 2018. [Online]. Available: ftp://ftp.cencenelec.eu/ CENELEC/ Smart grid/M490.pdf
46. Kumar, D. R., Krishna, T. A., & Wahi, A. (2018). Health Monitoring Framework for in Time Recognition of Pulmonary Embolism Using Internet

of Things. Journal of Computational and Theoretical Nanoscience, 15(5), 1598–1602.

47. Smart grids - European Standardisation. Last accessed: May 2018.[Online]. Available:https://www.cenelec.eu/aboutcenelec/whatwedo/technologysectors/ smartgrids.html

48. K. H. Chang, "Interoperable Nan standards: a path to cost-effective smart grid solutions," IEEE Wireless Communications, vol. 20, no. 3, pp. 4–5, 2013.

49. H. Wang, Y. Qian, and H. Sharif, "Multimedia communications over cognitive radio networks for smart grid applications," IEEE Wireless Communications, vol. 20, no. 4, pp. 125–132, 2013.

50. E. Commission. Standardization Mandate to CEN, CENELEC and ETSI Concerning the Charging of Electric Vehicles. Last accessed: March 2019. [Online]. Available: ftp://ftp.cen.eu/CEN/Sectors/List/Transport/ Automobile/ElectricVehiclesMandate.pdf

51. "Smart Meters Co-ordination Group (SM-CG)," Interim response report to M/441, 2009.

52. Y. Zhen, X. Li, Y. Zhang, L. Zeng, Q. Ou, and X. Yin, "Transmission Tower Protection System based on Internet of Things in Smart Grid," in 7th IEEE International Conference on Computer Science & Education (ICCSE), 2012, pp. 863–867.

53. X. Chen, J. Liu, X. Li, L. Sun, and Y. Zhen, "Integration of IoT with Smart Grid," in International Conference on Communication Technology and Application (ICCTA), 2011, pp. 723–726.

54. F. K. Santoso and N. C. Vun, "Securing IoT for smart home system," in IEEE International Symposium on Consumer Electronics (ISCE). IEEE, 2015, pp. 1–2.

55. M. Jaradat, M. Jarrah, A. Bousselham, Y. Jararweh, and M. Al-Ayyoub, "The Internet of Energy: Smart Sensor Networks and Big Data Management for Smart Grid," Procedia Computer Science, vol. 56, pp. 592–597, 2015.

56. X. Li, R. Lu, X. Liang, X. Shen, J. Chen, and X. Lin, "SmartCommunity: An Internet of Things Application," IEEE Communications Magazine, vol. 49, no. 11, pp. 68–75, 2011.

57. L. Yu, T. Jiang, Y. Cao, and Q. Qi, "Carbon-aware Energy Cost Minimization for Distributed Internet Data Centers in Smart Microgrids," IEEE Internet of Things Journal, vol. 1, no. 3, pp. 255–264, 2014.

58. Dhiviya, S., Malathy, S., & Kumar, D. R. (2018). Internet of Things (IoT) Elements, Trends and Applications. Journal of Computational and Theoretical Nanoscience, 15(5), 1639–1643.

59. V. Balijepalli, V. Pradhan, S. Khaparde, and R. Shereef, "Review of Demand Response under Smart Grid Paradigm," in IEEE PES Innovative Smart Grid Technologies (ISGT), 2011, pp. 236–243.

60. Y. Kong, "Wireless neighborhood area networks with QoS support for demand response in smart grid," IEEE Transactions on Smart Grid, 2016.

61. Siano, "Demand Response and Smart Grids-A Survey," Renewable and Sustainable Energy Reviews, vol. 30, pp. 461–478, 2014.

62. M. Jaradat, M. Jarrah, Y. Jararweh, M. Al-Ayyoub, and A. Bousselham,"Integration of Renewable Energy in Demand-side Management forHome Appliances," in International Renewable and Sustainable Energy Conference (IRSEC), 2014, pp. 571–576.

63. S. Mohanty, B. N. Panda, and B. S. Pattnaik, "Implementation of a Web of Things based Smart Grid to Remotely Monitor and Control Renewable Energy Sources," in Students' Conference on Electrical,Electronics and Computer Science (SCEECS), 2014, pp. 1–5.

64. M. Khan, N. B. Silva, and H. Kijun, "Internet of Things based Energy Aware Smart Home Control System," IEEE Access, 2016.

Significance of Block Chain in IoTSG - A Prominent and Reliable Solution

S. Vinothkumar*, S. Varadhaganapathy, R. Shanthakumari
and M. Ramalingam

*Department of Information Technology, Kongu Engineering College, Perundurai,
Erode, Tamil Nadu, India*

Abstract

IoT is the highest degree of predominantly growing technology in the world recently. IoT technology exists now using a larger number of digital devices or nodes in the network and the technologies that are related to IoT are rapidly grown in research as well as in industries. Nowadays the centralized IoT environments complete monetary communications and are forwarded to IoT platform providers. Privacy and secrecy problems are predictable for unauthorized or un-legitimate IoT platform suppliers. To overcome the problem a hybrid blockchain is used composed of a decentralized and encrypted to that has the leger and account information hidden in its framework. In the proposed plan, the provider of the Internet of things platform doesn't play a proxy function, the nodes of IoT can confidentially and proficiently communicate a accredit with other network nodes. Blockchain's secure end-to-end functionality allows to include features of transparency and consistency in IoT communications. Also, an agreement of distributed-blockchain, give an accredit-sharing element to IoT clients in the vitality and profitability market. To give this element, present a nearby square structure for the administration of the executives in the credit-sharing gathering. An interconnection position, called the scaffold, is familiar with disconnecting distributed exchanges of IoT customers and connecting the concept of blockchain to another sub-network blockchain (s) in a mixture scheme to safeguard the protection of IoT customers and avoid any data spillage to the basic blockchain. Finally, the expansion is subjected to a k-namelessness guarantee. Mixed-Bridge was used to model the vitality use case scenario in order to assess the efficiency of the required hybrid

Corresponding author: vinoth21787@gmail.com

P. Sanjeevikumar, Rajesh Kumar Dhanaraj, Malathy Sathyamoorthy, Jens Bo Holm-Nielsen
and Balamurugan Balusamy (eds.) Smart Grids and Internet of Things: An Energy Perspective,
(235–272) © 2023 Scrivener Publishing LLC

blockchain-based charging. The pretend findings illustrate that with a justifiable degree of data loss, consumption of memory, CPU and may protect user privacy.

Keywords: Blockchain, accredit-sharing, Internet of Things (IoT), secrecy-protective

9.1   Introduction

Decentralised, diverse, and distributed energy networks are becoming more popular. More energy is produced and used locally in microgrids as a result of the number of renewable sources are increased (e.g., lunar or energy of wind) and dispersed applications of energy or power resources (DER), transforming conventional centralised energy supply systems [2]. Using monitoring and tracking telecommunication techniques, an innovative situation developed in a smart grid network to efficiently engage energy or power resources (e.g., alive customer) in the generation of power and utilize. The purpose of blockchain platforms is to give a decentralised resolution for energy transactions are going to be monitored securely [3, 4]. Using a blockchain, the smart grid activities of customers will be protected and documented into unchallengeable, open and tamper-evidence smart networks [5]. Conventionally, the connection between power suppliers and customers there has been a one-sided energy market. Consumers use the grid's electricity and pay the provider's bills, and the cycle repeats. This conventional relationship shifts the trend towards DERs. Customers with top of the house solar systems, for example, require mutual power contracts to the suppliers. Furthermore, neighbour-to-neighbour energy transfers are applicable choice, making the power association more complex and each and every side. As a consequence, when linked to the public grid, excess solar power will be fed into the network or traded to neighbours in small networks. Customer privacy is considered a major problem in the implementation of this scenario, same to ethical or stability, due to the each and every sided relationship in the smart network [6]. In the Internet-of-Things higher number of various devices are who support modern energy grids in a nimble grid (IoT). IoT systems collect data in the smart grid to demonstrate whether more power is required or whether there is an opportunity to sell surplus energy to neighbours [7]. The facility of structure to oversees billing and indicting actions are more important feature to boost the number of various structures that have emerged as a result from introduction for these type of applications in the power and service industry.

Clearly and the single point of defeat, the intruder knows where, including a malicious insider, can target and compromise the trusted IoT platform provider [9, 10]. In addition, the privacy of IoT users may be compromised by an untrusted provider of IoT platforms with basic monitoring capabilities. Furthermore, since there is a lack of trust in providing standards in the IoT ecosystem, a reliability framework is needed. More data would be exchanged as IoT devices become more integrated and this could threaten the privacy of users [8]. IoT network providers typically serve as intermediaries to offer general services, that is policy enforcement, authorization control, charging contrivance and billing. The disadvantages of a first point of lost e and the consequences of centralised control, combined with the danger of communication of information change, can pose privacy, trust, and confidentiality problems for IoT customers in an unauthenticated grid.

As a result, the abilities of successful payment and billing are required to address the authentication and secrecy problems in each and every side of energy associations in the IoT power industry. The financial sector is expected to benefit from blockchain technology's impressive capabilities in the areas of trust, expense, flexibility, and reliability. We'll focus at how the technology is based on blockchain going to be used to provide payment and charges functions to the IoT energy industry in this paper. Mixed-Bridge, a blockchain hybrid architecture based on the IoT service layer, is being implemented. Using blockchain-based invoice and payments features are design IoT service layer blockchain concept allows us to incorporate a compatible network that can be used in a variety of IoT domains.

This entails a smart network, which is the made up of the number of IoT providers from various vendors. A hybrid blockchain is consist Hy-Bridge and subnetworks. The hybrid blockchain is developed to protect the secrecy of IoT consumer and provide the safe billing and charging the workflow of communication; that is, there is no tracking of user-to-user energy transactions. The secrecy of the users of IoT is safeguarded by differentiating the communications. The energy network and microgrid are combined in this hybrid frameworks. The link is created between the foremost blockchain and its sub-divided networks at the end. Now the IoT consumer able to exchange the power service with users are available in the networks by using Hy-new Bridge's credit sharing feature.

Since the microgrid is operated by a blockchain subnetwork, P2P energy transactions of IoT users can be privately exchanged in the microgrid. A k-anonymity network of IoT users exists within the credit-distributing category. The Users of IoT has been programmed, and they can use the shared energy service anonymously while also monitoring their devices of IoT activities in the blockchain sub network [11]. To handle the credit-sharing community's P2P exchanges, a neighbourhood node will be installed in the microgrid's subnetwork. There is an additionally header named Header of Credit in the nearby node [12] that allows IoT nodes to be permitted and a credit-sharing plan to be executed. Furthermore, before being submitted to the main grid as a standardised dataset, the private data of IoT users in the microgrid utilisation dataset is anonymized and masked. As a result, the detailed information of power consumption and P2P communications in the microgrid does not leak to the smart networks upper-layer of organisations, which may aid in user identification and profiling. To establish the possibility of the planned framework, since a smart structure with a top of building solar power collection arrangements. Solar energy is exchanged between a lease through a local peer-to-peer energy network, or microgrid (e.g., IoT users). In connection to the rooftop solar power system, the structures or homes use the public power grid as a supplementary source of energy. The solar energy plant is believed can be owned in service corporation, as well as the manager of rental homes purchases all of the solar energy and exchanges it to the residents through the power system. Mixed-Bridge establishes trusting relationships with several sided of parties with the chief of rental properties, IoT customers that are in the home, IoT network supplier, and solar power facility supplier.

This article's key contributions are as follows:

In the Invoices and payments network to the energy market, the proposed Mixed-Bridge to keep the privacy of IoT users in an energy market for billing and charging network. The bridge which is an interconnection location is implemented in this hybrid blockchain to connect the main blockchain to its subnetworks. To prevent user profiling and user recognition, the bridge handles the transactions in two separate blockchains. At this end, the bridge offers anonymization protection to maintain the privacy and also it can isolate all of the microgrids P2P energy communication of IoT users. Maintaining a credit distribution party's P2P communication in the microgrid, the secondary header is designed in the concept of a restricted segment. The payment header is used to allow computers and facilitate credit-sharing policies and conducted a laboratory experiment like simulation to determine the lack of privacy of mixed-Bridge to examine the performance of executed hybrid blockchain-enabled IoT architecture. The loss of data can analyse by adopting k-anonymity. Finally, we calculated Hy-usage Bridges of resources (memory and CPU) to handle power utilization communications.

The rest of the research article is structured as appeared. The difficulties and the essential for trustworthy communications in a unauthorized network to be identify in Section 9.2. An associated study is introduced in

Section 9.3. In Section 9.4, Explains an overview of present privacy security for the K-anonymity and blockchains. The introductions of Hybrid-Bridge are explained in Section 9.5 and some Hybrid-Bridge use cases that are added in the Segment 9.6. In Segment 9.7, Hybrid-bridge functions and and communications are outlined. Section 9.8 analyzes various security features of Blockchain encription, and efficiency. Lastly, in Section 9.9, includes our inferences and address upcoming work.

9.2 Trustful Difficulties with Monetary Communications for IoT Forum

Generally, the IoT ecosystem is three layers of division: the IoT consumer layer, platform layer, and the business layer. The physical elements are (e.g., IoT devices, Entry Point of Network (gateways), and network cables used for connection) are available in the User layer of IoT, the layer of the platform which is includes implements for all the facets of IoT providers, including information stream implements, flow proceedings, storage of information, and outside connections. The firm layer consists of service management advancements as well as a range of business applications. An IoT network provider, as shown in Figure 9.1, has agreements with unauthorized facility suppliers in the layer of enterprise and performs the role of disbursement contributor for both users of IoT and service contributor. Any questions and answer among a service facilitator and a user of IoT has conventionally to go among the platform provider. As a result, the platform render will collect debt and payment details among the relevant accounts [13]. The failure of a single point is possible because of the infrastructure control authority of an IoT platform render. Any errors could disrupt the authentication and payment processes, putting the entire system's operation and security at risk [10]. How does a unauthorized party (example, an attacker or intruder) detect the data is incorrect if they compromise a platform provider and modify some transaction? Account holders must have faith in the provider IoT platform. There are problems if more number and united platforms of IoT exists and therefore the facility or service supplier and the IoT consumers are recorded at totally various IoT platforms suppliers [13].

In most monetary transactions, the parties are believed to be suspicious of each other and to be curious adversaries. This contributes to the conditions that must be met in order for transactions to be trusted. Without jeopardising their privacy, the parties concerned should be intelligent to

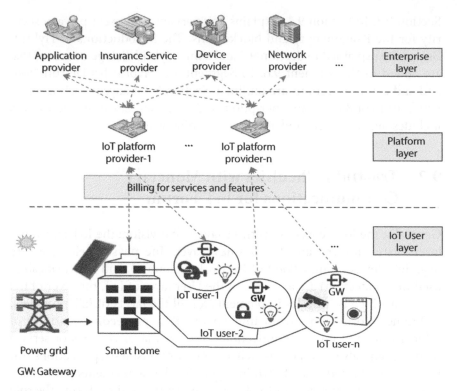

Figure 9.1 Monetary association in energy of Internet-of-Things (IoT) and service market.

a disagreement and demonstrate the debting and expenses to a monetary service. For a trustful monetary communication in a less-than-complete-trusted network, the following basic conditions must be met:

Accountability
In an accountable information exchange, both actors are aware of how their decisions will be carried out and who is to blame if a transaction fails due to a system flaw [14]. Furthermore, in the event of a successful or unsuccessful transaction, the parties may demonstrate the transaction's performance.

Reliability
In general, financial statement information is trustworthy if the monetary transactions should be authenticated, inspected, and validated for the person who is concerned, using impartial proof. In further

words, enhancing internal control functions over financial transactions will improve efficiency [15].

Privacy-protection

Financial institution information on communication and history of payments has traditionally acted as the basis for most financial choice models (e.g., credit assessment or scoring) [16]. A major factor influencing users' privacy issues is the readiness of past information and personal information across the number of financial communications. Private information from previous transactions cannot be used in any way in the privacy-preserving financial prototype, which contributes to user recognition and profiling.

Efficiency

Efficiency refers to making the same amount of effect with less capital. The effectiveness of a financial model is improved by growing the outcome with comparable amounts of the present capital [17]. The efficiency of data exchange is improved by information compatibility (on a syntactic or conceptual basis) among various financial systems. An efficient financial framework for an IoT ecosystem should enable interoperability between the number of platforms, allowing various IoT applications to communicate one another [18].

Although transparency ensures that the billing and claimed payment are both verifiable, reliability establishes a simulated link among the communicating parties. In the current scenario, the unauthorized entity and IoT customers will enter into a direct financial arrangement with no involvement from the IoT platform provider. Invoices and payments functions can offer reliable and effective services. The current-time and from beginning to end properties, in this view, help to add critical consistency and trustworthiness to Invoices and payments functions for customers and facility providers.

In some financial transactions the payments do not necessitates that identify the principals [13]. The authentication of the communicating parties is protected by extending such property to other purposes. For example, since we have no connection to the people who has actual identities involved in an Invoices and payments scheme, and also include an anonymousness function its preserves the secrecy. Because of this decoupling, service providers are unable to decide if a particular customer used their service. The capability of a invoice and payments scheme to operate with various infrastructures without conflict is determined by its efficiency property. An effective billing and charging system for an IoT ecosystem should allow for interoperability between different platforms. In contrast to centralised systems, all of the above conditions must be met in decentralised a consumer person-to-person transaction without use of a central regulatory authority or intermediaries. Any transaction between users can be validated by the blockchain in this scenario.

9.3   Privacy in Blockchain Related Work

The applications that are based privacy-focused blockchain has attracted a lot of interest in the ground power transaction IoT network. Due to distributed nature of blockchain, users are vulnerable to privacy attacks because transaction data is accessible in the public ledger. The hacker attempts to connect certain case to the user's personal information in a linking attack [19, 20]. The interloper endeavours to describe secret insights concerning a gathering of peoples and keeps track of their communications for a set of specified periods. To deal with this crisis, numerous security techniques have been suggested to dissociate clients' unidentified personalities in the particular exchanges, forestalling endeavours to interface executing parties dependent on information in the blockchain [21, 22].

To offer anonymous types of assistance, ephemeral pseudonyms (model, ephemeral wallets in Bitcoin [23]) are utilized. Generally, they're made to make it hard for a connecting assailant to associate the different exchanges in the record [10, 21]. Clients in such frameworks create the addresses for each and every transaction made, send a new response indiscriminately [10, 20, 24, 25]. Every transaction is given another id (which fills in as a key) in the solution proposed in [20]. In [25], every user makes many unidentified and grants his energy utilization information under different unidentified try not to interface the unidentified and the consumer by coordinating the power utilization and the user's practices. In spite of these pseudonym solutions, the connecting assaults' fruitful heuristics investigation has uncovered the probability of user re-distinguishing proof. Meiklejohn et al. [26] to categorise Cryptocurrency members and their contact details, researchers used an aggregating heuristic that focused on change addresses to cluster addresses with a similar consumer. Moreover, in requirement point of the view, Pseudonym solutions are not suitable for financial communications due to long-term authentication and the high computational load placed on IoT users.

Besides, to ensure the privacy of the user, energy utilization information is muddled [27–29]. For user profiling, the semantics of energy use might be utilized. By covering the points of interest of energy use, Abidin *et al.* [27] made an attempted to ensure a user's confidentiality. The power utilization of power providers figures just last month usage bill per user, not each time slot's individual metering data, by accumulating the personal information of the power utilization recorded in the shrewd meters [27]. Sun *et al.* [28] to meet the residential electricity demand, mechanical equipment and power units were used. They recommended utilizing domestic power storage units like to decreased or remove the load-hiding dependency on locally rechargeable batteries, use Renewable energy sources and HVAC (heating, ventilation, and air conditioning) devices. To obscure the energy utilization/generation data, a middle person job among the service supplier/aggregator and the users is utilized. Azar *et al.* [29] suggested to utilizing the simulated power source to haggle with the aggregator for the benefit of community prosumers, where no private data about the prosumers was traded. Notwithstanding the exchange, reliability issues may represent an issue for consumers who buy goods and services and the undermined provider in this methodology. In Mixed-Bridge, the problem of trust by utilizing the consumer-to-consumer sub-network blockchain in which who are all communicated the energy communications are managed and confirmed by the community peoples. The propose mixed bridge's reliability can be checked by implementing a worthy arrangement in the subnetwork blockchain since it is the people of the group of credit sharing members and give the reports of energy utilization to the primary blockchain.

Off-chain interaction solutions take care of the blockchain's security issue by executing several peer-to-peer communications among the two large gatherings peoples without having to write them to the blockchain. The on/off-chain is a system that allows you to switch things on and off that permits just the on-chain strategy to be conveyed onto the blockchain. This sets aside the blockchain's cash while additionally hiding the confidential details engaged with off-chain transactions [10, 30]. To minimise transaction costs and address privacy issues, The payment channel was extended by Khalil *et al.* [32] in that a group of users uses a payment channel in an organization. These subnetworks, similar to payment networks, permit instalments to be made among parties who aren't linked to a payment channel at the same time. In spite of the advantages of the off-chain method as far as keeping up security and bringing down transaction charges (for instance, Bitcoin), Small channel transmission capability, The cost of opening and closing networks, as well as data protection in financial transactions routing, both are disadvantages [31, 33]. Hy-Bridge stays away from the previously mentioned disadvantages by isolating transactions into two well defined blockchains with various purposes.

9.4   Initial Preparations

9.4.1   Blockchain Overview

A distributed database Blockchain is used to monitors the nuances in a chain of computerized occasions or a public record of all transactions that have been finished and traded among the members [34]. The public and private blockchain systems are the two primary kinds of blockchain frameworks. In the first type of blockchain which is public block chain, any node can enter and exit the network at any time without access control, but in the personal or private blockchain, nodes are authenticated and permitted by using an access control mechanism. Subsequently, in a private blockchain, every node's personality is known by different nodes [35] only verified nodes can see and take part in activities on a private blockchain. A blended blockchain consolidates the advantages of the two personal or private and public blockchains, showing the advantages of the two while having an agreement mechanism oversaw by known, favoured servers. The hybrid blockchain is just halfway decentralized since the duplicates of the blockchain are just circulated among the endorsed participants [36].

As shown in Figure 9.2, In the Blockchain every component is consist of a header and a table of interactions. Each header is fully filled with the secured hash value of the preceding block, the present time or timestamp, the random number, the hash function of the relative quantity of contact in the block, and the value of the hash of the system after managing the block. The timestamp is also called as the current time, and the preceding hash of the preceding block is in the header, that muddle cost that focuses to the preceding block. The present period shows that an information needed to exist at the hour of recording to be added in the hash value [23]. Nonce is nothing but it is a 4-byte number at random that guarantees the hash value figuring is unique and forestalls repetitive assaults. The blockchain technology has two integrity security systems to recognize any unapproved data altering. Initially, the Merkle tree is the root of all the communications in the networks ensures the chain's worldwide states [35]. Any state moves that results in new root hash value, just as the expansion of another transaction. A block's hash value is the block's hash once it has been processed. Second, the past of the block is secured by a chain-like

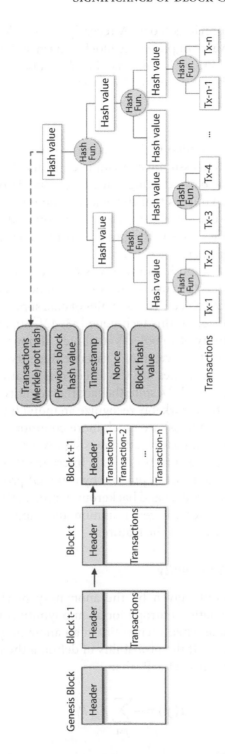

Figure 9.2 Blockchain structure.

association with the previous block. A recently affixed block, as found in Figure 9.2, holds the value of preceding block of hash and made the blocks permanently attached [35, 37]. This linked hash can be traced back to the very first block, which was generated by a miner.

9.4.2   k-Anonymity

k-anonymity is recommended by Samarati and Sweeney [38]. The possibility of inside the system assurance to avoid being linked to other publicly available data in order to avoid being detected by associative assaults. The affirmation of k-Anonymity is that the objective item is unclear from the other k 1 objects in a cluster of k objects with a similitude [39–41]. Since unidentified objects are visible with a probability of 1/k [38], the bigger the value k, the more prominent the privacy.

The basic thought behind k-anonymity is to shroud data among comparable anonymous objects to break the association between the identified identity and the dataset's object. The activities of data suppression and value generalization are utilized in this technique [38, 42]. Suppression implies erasing any or the entirety of an object's attributes, although generalisation entails replacing one distinct value of a variable. Identity, quasi-identifier (QI), and affectability attributes are the three sorts of attributes that can be found in a dataset record. Despite the fact that identity attributes (like name) can be utilized to remarkably recognize an individual, QI identifiers (such as gender or zip address) are much more common and can be used to identify people. The compassion attributes signify a person's private and delicate subtleties (e.g., an infection) [42]. Inference threats identify an object in the confidentiality set in practise by using QI properties that can be correlated with external data and background information [43]. By concealing the original dataset, the generalisation and suppression processes made anonymity sets and alter the features.

9.4.2.1   Degree of Anonymity

The degree of anonymity given by the anonymity mechanism can be measured using information entropy for an anonymity community. H(y) shows the entropy value when each entity in an anonymity model of Y is considered as data point. If the probability of defining the jth individual in a k-member confidentiality set is P_j, then

$$H(y) = -\sum_{j=1}^{k} p_j(P_j) \qquad (9.1)$$

When all of the k individuals in a k-anonymity set share this very same 1/k probability measure to be known, the maximum entropy, H_M, is achieved:

$$H_M = log_2(k) \tag{9.2}$$

The ability of unauthorized person is to obtain information through an assault on this confidentiality collection can be written as follows:

$$\frac{H_M - H(y)}{H_M} \tag{9.3}$$

By sharing by HM [41], the data is normalised. As a result, Diaz et al. [44] described the anonymity degree as surveys:

$$d = 1 - \frac{H_M - H(y)}{H_M} = \frac{II(y)}{H_M} \tag{9.4}$$

The confidentiality value of d, which is a number between 0 ($0 \leq d \leq 1$) represents the encrypting level of the confidentiality model. An anonymity framework has the smallest rate of the confidentiality grade (d = 0). If a member in the confidentiality set seems to be recognised with a proportion of p = 1, when the systems have the highest rate of the degree of anonymity (d = 1) if all of the people use similar chance of presence recognised (p = 1/k), the system has the extreme value of the confidentiality rate (d = 1).

9.4.2.2   Data Forfeiture

The processes of deleting and generalising result in some knowledge as a result of asymmetric encryption, there is a loss. Developers can quantify the loss of information by contrasting the masked information to the source information. The less data that is lost, the more similar the particulars are [45]. The performance degradation associated with the map f, depending on the Shannon entropy, the probable database map f: Y—-Z with the measures of probability p and q, respectively, for the databases of Y and Z, is defined as inequality among the entropy values in the recorded and real databases [46].

$$H(p) - H(q) \tag{9.5}$$

The information loss of data anonymization refers to how closely the disguised database and generalised characteristics resemble the unique ones. The non-uniform entropy (NE) can be used to calculate in an asymmetric encryption process, data loss implemented by the hiding database D to D [45, 47]:

$$NE = -\sum_{i=1}^{n} P_\gamma (Di|Di) \qquad (9.6)$$

9.5   In the IoT Power and Service Markets, Reliable Transactions and Billing

Hybrid-Bridge is a subnet-based mixture of blockchain. For protected payment and charging transactions, the suggested engineering includes a key blockchain (MaBC), just as at least one subnetwork blockchains (SuBCs) for P2P energy exchanges in microgrids among IoT end users. Designers presumed that every IoT network have the number of IoT nodes linked to various substances in various layers via a gateway. In this model, we considered two sorts of transactions: Device to Device (U2U) and user to-device (U2S) transactions. The Device-to-Device U2U occurred between one user's IoT gadgets or between various users' IoT gadgets. invoicing and charging transactions were completed between IoT users and elements in the upper layers through U2S transactions Figure 9.3 depicts typical mixture blockchain for the IoT power and utility marketplace. In the engineering, designers imagined the control group system in individually IoT system, which could be certain gadget or a section of the entry point. We discovered an entry point to be the control community for comfort. It worked as a miner, handling both approaching and outgoing transactions. To put it another way, the entry point was a blockchain device that assembled transactions into a block, which was then attached to that same chain. It is used personal data stockpiling and dealt with everything, including authentication, authorization, genesis transaction creation, and key management. IoT device may discuss straightforwardly with each other in a local network or through a gateway with an outside.

Since Mixed-Bridge is a service-based framework, A blockchain is created among IoT nodes (the property administrator) and the user when another service is accessed, the service provider(s), and an IoT network supplier. Every customer is known by a distinct customer id, which fills in as their asymmetric and doesn't have any association with their actual

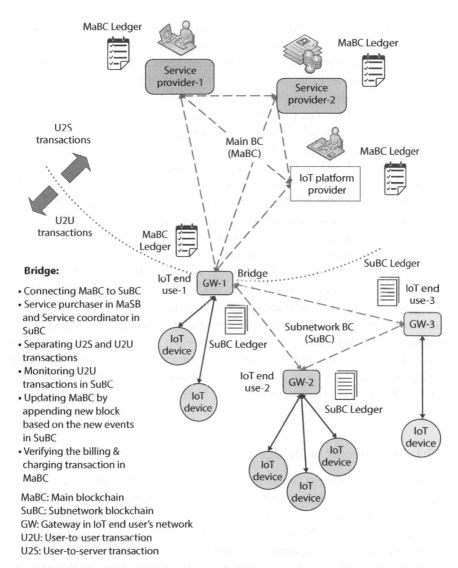

Figure 9.3 A primary blockchain for payment and billing payments and subnetwork blockchains for peer-to-peer transactions make up the proposed mixed blockchain.

character. At the point when an IoT client buys another service, the provider creates a beginning transaction. Any service-related transactions, for example, credit buys, use, redesigning, charging, and invoicing, are pressed into the block subsequent to being checked by a miner. More service provider can enter the blockchain relying upon the kind of service, for example, roaming. On the off chance that a supplier can offer a service notwithstanding those offered by the local area, they can enter the block-chain and a copy is automatically recorded on the ledger of the blockchain. Service level arrangements (SLAs) between service providers are needed for this situation to build up service strategies. When a device enrols in the service provider, Mixed-Bridge forms an SLA among all these custom-ers from the platform or platforms. An approaches service provider B for credit. If an SLA exists for these transactions, a U2U transaction is gener-ated. SuBC(s) exchange the transaction first, and afterward a U2S trans-action is engendered to MaBC supplier classes. In the wake of checking in the MaBC, the access authorization is given, and the client gets a credit access grant transaction. To identify any pernicious or duping conduct, the credit sum and use are followed in both the MaBC and SuBC block-chains. IoT service providers in the microgrid create a SuBC for their peer-to-peer energy exchange, such as sharing excess energy with neighbours or gaining access to a shared credit. Service providers fabricate a nearby personal blockchain and concede to how to exchange their IoT gadgets' energy transactions. Contingent upon their topographical area, associa-tions between IoT clients might be immediate associations between IoT gadgets or through an IoT platform provider. The cryptographic keys needed by the IoT gateways are divided among them. Here, we present the bridge, an interconnection area that interfaces the MaBC and the SuBC(s). That bridge is the entry point for an IoT user who has acquired a facility and is reselling to further customers.

9.5.1   Connector or Bridge

In the proposed hybrid breed blockchain, the property owner acts as an interface by buying energy services and reselling them to various clients in a credit-sharing network. A bridge client is one who is a member of both the MaBC and the SuBC(s) at the same time. In the MaBC, the bridge is a distribution service customer, as well as a distributor and service coor-dinator in the SuBC(s). As an anonymizer, the bridge protects the privacy of IoT clients by isolating transactions inside the subnetwork from those outside. To achieve this, the bridge utilizes k-anonymity and performs generalisation and data suppression anonymization cycles to eradicate any connects to the end handlers' characters. Thus, the upper layer entities in MaBC can't follow P2P energy transaction between IoT devices. In view of the exercises of users in the SuBC, the bridge creates the comparing transaction and affixs them to the MaBC. These transactions don't have any personal data about the operator (e.g., IOT operator and addition-ally IoT node) because of data anonymization. At the point when other communications in MaBC, for example, upgrading the service or invoice and payments, the bridge produces a U2U transaction, which refreshes the local subnetwork.

9.5.2 Group of Credit-Sharing

To add another function, we develop the way that the principals' identification is not needed to pay for the infrastructure [13]. Users of the Internet of Things will form a credit-sharing network and provide access to their services. Others locally approach the passwords, Interoperability, protection characteristics, or special access to a service purchased via an IoT user profile are all scenarios of utilities that can be bought via an IoT user profile. The gathering individuals may control the contact situations (e.g., IoT gadget type, entree period, and length). To create a credit-sharing group, IoT clients basically need to enter a SuBC and disseminate a record to follow credit use. Individuals from the gathering stick to such guidelines or laws, track the enlisted service state, and control the credits as result. The principles will be controlled by the arrangements that IoT clients have made with each other, just as the current status of these agreements. By means of the SuBC, a savvy contract performs checking. This model could be utilized for savvy driving help, shared energy moves, electric vehicle charging, and mobile wallet services, in addition to other things. A keen high-rise apartment, for instance, could have a solar array, a Tesla Powerpack, and an enormous solar-warmed boiling water tank, which are all possessed by the building's proprietor. During off-top hours, when energy costs were least, the batteries and high temp water tank(s) will be recharging from the power system. P2P energy transaction empowers individuals from the credit community to get to the power bought in the property owner's name. The microgrid's power is divided between the individuals' IoT gadgets. A U2U transaction is utilized to screen all utilization in the SuBC. The bridge, then again, who bought the service, exchanges the significant actions in MaBC with the upper layer elements through a U2S transaction. All exercises identified with the bought service are covered by U2S transactions, including access events, offering new functionality, downloading, invoice and payments.

9.5.3 Local Block

SuBC uses domestic blocks to handle U2U transactions. A block header as well as a credit header are both present in every local block. The credit header has been used to favour users and ensure compliance with the economic sharing protocol. It has five boundaries, as demonstrated in Figure 9.4. The PC that plays out the transaction is alluded to as the device management (DMG). This boundary is utilized as the Device-id for local devices to separate the IoT nodes who have permission to use the service. The privacy (SEC) region contains the For access to services, security factors are taken into consideration, like Authorization protection and authentication. The concurred policies required for credit management are put away in the credit management function (CMF) parameter. These policies oversee service access, length, number, and need for IoT clients. The credit trigger function (CTF) parameter measures and shows the complete amount of credits exhausted. When the cutoff point (THR) value is reached, access to the service is limited to predefined highest - priority IoT devices.

The gateway makes a beginning transaction to associate another IoT device to each IoT client network and offers a key with this device. As per the entrance control list, a shared session key is transferred to nodes that are qualified for utilize an exchanged service. An IoT purchaser presents IoT gadgets are permitted to utilize the exchanged service and sets the policies. Access is directed by the policies settled upon by the IoT clients. These agreements portray the access time, length, and utilization limits per unit.

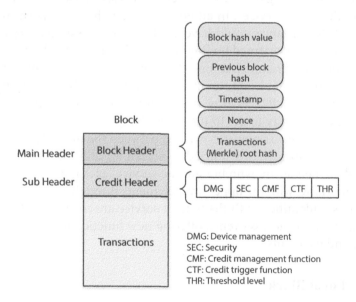

Figure 9.4 SuBC's local schematic view for U2U interactions.

9.6 Potential Applications and Use Cases

Mixed Bridge is a general-purpose service layer engineering with an assortment of applications that can profit by its functionality. In this part, we'll go through three diverse Mixed-Bridge applications.

9.6.1 Utilities and Energy

In the IoT energy and utility industry, Mixed-Bridge will give transaction protection and availability for authorization, smart meter control, and power utilization. The U2U transaction in the local blocks of the SuBC mean microgrid events and P2P power transactions. DMG shows the IoT gadgets that approach solar power in the local block (SuBC), and The CMF region exhibits the access requirements. To gain access to these facilities, a Proposed scheme sends a power access request. The level of access is deter mined by the DMG's complexities [1]. The smart metre at each IoT client's location estimates energy use, and the CTF arena is adjusted through the IoT client's entry point. The minute the extreme level is reached, the IoT gateway disables power entree, as indicated via the THR region. The bridge disperses the power service utilization to different elements in the MaBC by adding another block. Accordingly, the SuBC disperses P2P energy transactions, while the MaBC disperse billing and charging transactions.

9.6.2 Charging of Electric Vehicles

Electric vehicles (EVs) are giving the savvy grid new viewpoints on power utilization [50]. Vehicle-to-grid (V2G) information presents new trust and privacy issues, presenting new difficulties in smart grid assortment and the management. Electric vehicle charging (EVC) is another zone where IoT and blockchain innovation can exist together. For pole charging EVs, numerous applications for smart contracts and machine-to-machine (M2M) associations have been created. EVC applications incorporate way traffic question, self-sufficient charging, station determination, billing, and automatic payment. Block charge [51], for instance, is a charging that is based on the block chain, verification, and Electric vehicle billing system. Billing and payments are dealt with automatically by Block charge, because of the utilization of a cryptographic money (Ethereum blockchain).

With our credit-sharing functionality, we can offer another service for EVC applications. When a paid advance of time/post-paid electric vehicle amount is exchanged, a SuBC is formed a credit-sharing group that would give a secure and hidden transaction grid, a Mixed blockchain technology is established. In the mixed configuration, the connection links the MaBC and the SuBC too is in charge of payment and charging exchanges. Also, k-anonymity is maintained in the SuBC, wherever Ev charging exchange acclaim and the MaBC manages payment and billing services. Based on our executed credit-sharing functionality, EVChain [33] is a responsible and dependable answer for the EVC business, saving the privacy of EV proprietors.

9.6.3   Credit Transfer

Mobile wallets are normal web-based business, bill payment, and other monetary transaction service offered by telecommunication companies or non-banking foundations. Clients and service providers like them since they have pervasive payment option, online vouchers and discounts, and location-based service, just as help different payment sourcing structures [52]. Mobile wallets are secured from security dangers by adding a few layers of authentication. Utilizing blockchain innovation to address issues of confidence and security of digital wallet service is a smart thought. A client-to-client credit move service empowers a client to move assets from their wallet to different clients on the equivalent or various network. Transfers are normally centralised and overseen by the service provider. For credit transfer, mixture-Bridge may give a decentralized and distributed design. In this structure, a client imparts credit to those in the SuBC and sets up the policies that should be followed. The SuBC directs the balance, consumption conditions, (for example, time and threshold levels), and need. The MaBC circulates transaction that bring about balance notifications or credit charging among the bridge and the service supplier. For this situation, Mixture-Bridges helps with eliminating the wallet service provider central function, permitting customers to safely impart credit to different users in the community of credit-sharing.

9.7   Proposed Work Execution

As already specified, Generally the local energy sources are solar energy devices that are located in the top roof of the building and created the use case power environments. The solar energy is simulated to be given by a service originator with the manager of the property reselling it the renders by using the microgrid. The renders are the users of IoT, they are using the group of credit sharing to get the energy the connector node is used to connects MaBC and the SuBC was built by the user. The SuBC is added to the bridge node but reflects the energy usage and P2P energy exchanges in the group of credit distribution as specified through U2U communications in the MaBC. In this implementation the process of miner and mining method was not inserted. Since the main objective is to provide trustworthy communications and the encrypted ledger. As a result, the development of the credit sharing community. The establishment of U2U and U2S contact, network encryption, connection, inspecting, and registry entry processes in each of these blockchains were implemented in this application. In addition, most blockchains' data anonymizing, linking, and upgrading bridge features were developed and evaluated.

9.7.1   Creating the Group of Energy Sharing

The bridge is used to connects the SuBC and the MaBC at the same time to share the energy and form a group of credit sharing that is shown in Figure 9.3. To start this group, first initiate the header of the credit in the local block. Now the IoT nodes who all are permitted to register in DMG field. The field of the SEC consist of any needed keys, the present negotiated policy and total power is showed by the CMF and the THR specify the energy threshold level. The genesis block of SuBC has information of THR, CMF and CTF. In the case study of mixed bridge, the smart house of the occupants is the bridge that is used to connect the MaBC to the SuBC.

9.7.2   Handling of Transaction

The procedures for getting control in a credit-sharing network and also the management of payment and billing transfers, are depicted in Figure 9.5. To begin, an entry point receives an access permission from an IoT device, requesting power usage permission. To assess the IoT device's eligibility and offer authorization, the entry point evaluates the credit header. Following that, the gateway groups these authenticate transactions into a recent block and modifies the CTF field's credit amount to reflect the new credit amount. At the end, the recent block is added to the SuBC and made available to all other nodes. The gateway tests the CMF's policies for access conditions before allocating the key and sharing it with the device. Providing the assigned key is valid, the service is available.

Figure 9.5 gives the step by step to gaining the access of energy in the group of credit sharing and the way of the invoice and payments transactions First, the devices in IoT network sends a gaining request to gateway and asked for authorization to use the energy. The entry point or Gateway

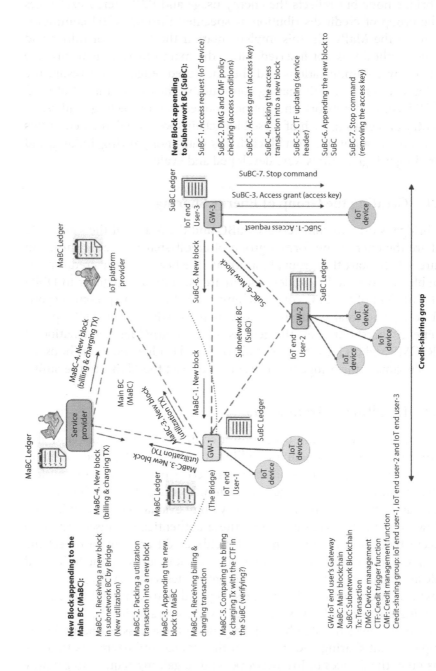

New Block appending to the Main BC (MaBC):

MaBC-1. Receiving a new block in subnetwork BC by Bridge (New utilization)

MaBC-2. Packing a utilization transaction into a new block

MaBC-3. Appending the new block to MaBC

MaBC-4. Receiving billing & charging transaction

MaBC-5. Comparing the billing & charging Tx with the CTF in the SuBC (verifying?)

GW: IoT end user's Gateway
MaBC: Main blockchain
SuBC: Subnetwork Blockchain
Tx: Transaction
DMG: Device management
CTF: Credit trigger function
CMF: Credit management function
Credit-sharing group: IoT end user-1, IoT end user-2 and IoT end user-3

New Block appending to Subnetwork BC (SuBC):

SuBC-1. Access request (IoT device)

SuBC-2. DMG and CMF policy checking (access conditions)

SuBC-3. Access grant (access key)

SuBC-4. Packing the access transaction into a new block

SuBC-5. CTF updating (service header)

SuBC-6. Appending the new block to SuBC

SuBC-7. Stop command (removing the access key)

Figure 9.5 Handling of exchanges SuBC-x represents transaction improvement in SuBC; MaBC-x represents transaction improvements in MaBC.

verifying the header of the credit to validate the IoT devices acceptance and give the permission depends on the parameter of DMG. The gateway may reject the request or gives the permission by allocate the access key, prior to the key allocation. The Gateway examines the polices of CMF'S based on the access conditions (Example, period, time of access) and then the gateway communicate the key with the IoT devices. The facility is authenticated based on the validity of the allocated key. After that, these details of access transaction packed by the gateway and transfer to the new block and store the new information in the header of new block by modify the cash which is specified in CTF field. At last, the new block is supplementary in to the SuBC and communicated with other nodes. Personal block chain device required to take part in the general agreement [55]. In SuBC the new block is added and has to be examined and authenticated by all the users of IoT. The consumption of power that leads to establish the P2P power communications and adding the new User to User block (U2U) in the SuBC. As in Figure 9.6. The bridge is removed anonymity the energy

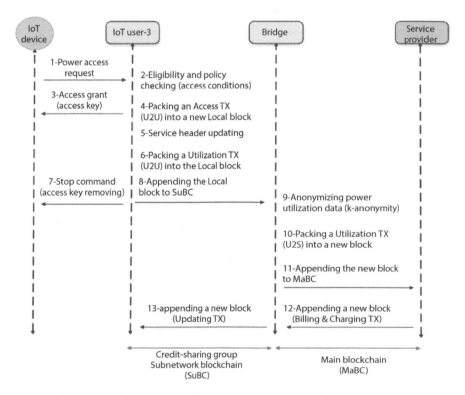

Figure 9.6 Access of power and handling the transaction utilization.

feeding information and provides a transaction of U2S is going to be added in to the MaBC by identifying a local block in the SuBC.

In the SuBC, the updated new service usage is readily available for the bridge, by getting an invoice and payment transactions. The bridge can authenticate and gives the confirmation to the issued bill.

The block which are formed in the situation exposed in Figure 9.5 is given in Figure 9.7. The credit title fields display the details about the group of credit sharing. Such as IoT devices that is enrolled in DMG, contracts used, consumption of power and already defined cut off. The next U2U block has two P2P energy a that specify the origin and the last node of the energy usage by an IoT nodes. The quantity of energy usage by an IoT nodes is displayed in the credit header field of CFT fields. At the same time by adding a U2U block to SuBC the bridge is used to add the U2S block into the MaBC to display the usage of power. The detailed information

Subnetwork Blockchain (SuBC)

```
Your action: "15"
U2U Block<DMG: ('01', '02', '03', '10', '11', '20', '21'
, '30'), CMF: Policy-1, CTF: 0, THR: 500, hash: 761c971a
810028aae40adf35616863dadf9467a2c43b3a40bdd551456ef01eb9
, prev_hash: None, txactions: [Txaction<hash: 1da14c27c5
b66e3b8ebd4659064e84063502da9a088ebbf0326ac144f6908c26,
prev_hash: None, data: Initialization>], time: 154724926
5.64>
- - - - - - - - - - - - - - - -
U2U Block<DMG: ('01', '02', '03', '10', '11', '20', '21'
, '30'), CMF: Policy-1, CTF: 13, THR: 500, hash: 62da2730
9136351b1bf9f6a1ceffe444184eb1391c94716a91f94b0e5f3805e3
, prev_hash: 761c971a810028aae40adf35616863dadf9467a2c43
b3a40bdd551456ef01eb9, txactions: [Txaction<hash: 6800f0
fe84b7a654ed2b41043622f75392088f0c32519da1ca6d7f6608dd27
00, prev_hash: None, data: IoT02-AccessGrant-0>, Txactio
n<hash: 5117798ca502ccff48aac6c56bc7aef44651c54e09007bf9
debe73082830476d, prev_hash: 6800f0fe84b7a654ed2b4104362
2f75392088f0c32519da1ca6d7f6608dd2700, data: IoT02-Acces
sEnd-13>], time: 1547249329.45>
- - - - - - - - - - - - - - - -
()
Your action: "4"
```

Main Blockchain (MaBC)

```
U2S Block<hash: 82af8fe93cd1fe23612d150c6a0182f81a486e7d
61b206b76b69c6032a70382c, prev_hash: None, txactions: [T
xaction<hash: 6787a1f9bc3ce4314fd8ac50ac535ca6cd7c17a4ef
d74d6ed35ff7c9672829ab, prev_hash: None, data: Total usa
ge is: 0>], time: 1547249265.64>
- - - - - - - - - - - - - - - -
U2S Block<hash: 763f958003797575edb2d85db709316d5543e3f8
fe0d0af417ef98d1c44a75d3, prev_hash: 82af8fe93cd1fe23612
d150c6a0182f81a486e7d61b206b76b69c6032a70382c, txactions
: [Txaction<hash: 7835d5a885062d2f7bae1e80e9334e65765976
3eb9ef0b8a1fa02867303422c3, prev_hash: None, data: Total
usage is: 13>], time: 1547249329.45>
- - - - - - - - - - - - - - - -
()
Your action:
```

Figure 9.7 SuBC and MaBC all have power consumption exchanges.

about the removed anonymity process are specified and examined in the forthcoming segment.

9.8   Investigation of Secrecy and Trustworthy

The hacker wants to connect certain truths to the user's authentication in a linking attack [19, 20]. The intruder attempts to characterise confidential details about a group of people and keeps track of their transactions over period of time. The k-anonymity solution is used for to fix the privacy concerns in the credit-distribution cluster to hide the real characteristics of IOT handlers in the consumption of power group of information. The mixed-trustworthiness Bridge's and secrecy protection features are discussed in this segment.

9.8.1   Trustworthy

Because of the blockchain's decentralised nature, the IoT network provider's intermediary role in the making of rules and billing providers can be eliminated. This is also providing a trustworthy plan for invoice and payments services in an open , but encrypted grid with this functionality and the communications are distributed logged and authenticable. The trustful monetary transactions among IoT users and service providers are addressed by the transparency and reliability criteria to this trustworthy end-to-end feature [53].

The IoT user activities in the neighbourhood are kept private in the Hy-Bridge. Because the bridge's distinction between the transactions of User to User (U2U) and User to subnetwork, the specifics the activities of IoT device is protected from any unauthorised person. In a nutshell, the bridge hides local purchases from upper-layer organisations and keeps the CMF up to date by buying new credits. In terms of trustworthiness, the bridge can identify financial fraud and falsification due to blockchain technology. The bridge will check the provided bill by obtaining an invoice and payments transaction in MaBC, the SuBC consist of the bridge is accessible by using the revised service usage.

The shared service in the SuBC, on the other hand, is only authenticated IoT nodes in the credit-sharing network have access. The party does not have access to the other local transactions. As a result, an IoT user's other behaviours are not infringing on their privacy. All SuBC members are closely monitored and all access to the exchanged service is controlled by agreed-upon regulations. The personal blockchain grid is SuBC, so access to the private ledger is restricted to its registered members [54]. The credit, usage, and access policies are all accessible information. Every access to credit (for example, consumption of energy) causes an CTF should be modified in the credit header, which SuBC members must verify. Each person of the credit-sharing group will be monitored with recovery choices via the credit header in the local block in the event of fraud or malicious conduct. To punish a cheating participant, proper strategies can be conveyed and delegated.

9.8.2   Privacy-Protection

The activities of IoT users to hide with the power transactions in the microgrid by distinguishing the P2P Power exchanging the SuBC's transactions involving invoices and payments within the MaBC. The energy information uses by the microgrid's Internet of Things consumers is recorded in a table for the credit-sharing group. This information is accessible in the SuBC as P2P power communications. The first Table 9.1 depicts a day's worth of IoT computer power usage in a microgrid. This microgrid is made up of four IoT users who link to the smart building's subnetwork power grid. For each power use, this table contains information about the identity of the users (IoT-user), identity of the device (IoT-dvc), the number of the user's building unit (Unit), The amount of power used (Usage), the type of IoT unit (IoT-type), and the time and length (Time/Duration).

To protect IoT handlers' secrecy, the bridge encrypts the energy consumption list in the credit- - distribution system and establishes a new table to be distributed with system cluster associations in the MaBC. In reality, the latest table's information of power consumption is a version that has been altered of the microgrid's primary table. The MaBC's U2S contracts give you access to the information in this table. Table 9.2 shows the power usage statistics in the facility communal and is a confidential interpretation of the data in Table 9.1. Table 9.2 demonstrates a four-anonymity view of Table 9.1 based on the assumption that the quantity of IOT users in the keen construction is accessible to system group associates (e.g., service provider) through exterior data.

The generalisation and suppression processes anonymize the data in Table 9.2. The Identity characteristics of IoT users and component figures are generalised into the id of the user and report in these processes. This feature is disabled in the new table since IoT system identity is linked to the IoT user's identity. The other attributes remain unchanged and include details about a customer who has enrolled power id consumption. The sensitivity characteristics is the last quality (IoT-type), which displays subtle

Table 9.1 Data on energy consumption in the credit-distribution group (SuBC).

Time/ duration	Consumer	IoT-device	Address	Utilization (W-hr)	IoT-type
17:30/10	C-3	21	211	300	Water Heater
18:00/10	C-2	15	102	150	Television
19:10/30	C-1	14	302	60	Lights
19:40/10	C-3	12	211	90	Mixer grinder
19:35/10	C-3	32	211	400	Television
20:20/30	C-2	42	102	500	Home appliance
20:50/20	C-2	32	102	110	Lights
21:20/20	C-1	21	302	130	Television
21:40/20	C-1	15	302	130	Home appliances
22:00/30	C-3	11	211	50	Lights
22:30/30	C-2	11	102	60	Home Appliances
21:30/30	C-3	22	211	60	Television

information, and the remaining attributes in this 4-anonymity package are QI parameters for each document. IoT users have no private info, and all usage data is bound to the system id required at the time-of-facility purchase. As a result, the secrecy of IoT users protected because the bridge in the service community hides their activities.

9.8.2.1   Degree of Confidentiality

The degree of anonymity introduced in Section 9.4 is used to assess the level of anonymity offered by our solution. Assumed that, the intruder is aware of the number of IoT users in the microgrid based on side information. Identifying the connection, it could be possible to deduce it from the relationship among an IOT user and his or her IoT devices that are listed with another service. The attacker has no knowledge of the IoT users'

Table 9.2 Data on power usage in the service community that has been anonymized (MaBC).

Time/duration	Consumer	Address	Usage (W-hr)	IoT-type
17:30/10	C-11	211	300	Water Heater
18:00/10	C-11	102	150	Television
19:10/30	C-11	302	60	Lights
19:40/10	C-11	211	90	Mixer grinder
19:35/10	C-11	211	400	Television
20:20/30	C-11	102	500	Home appliance
20:50/20	C-11	102	110	Lights
21:20/20	C-11	302	130	Television
21:40/20	C-11	302	130	Home appliances
22:00/30	C-11	211	50	Lights
22:30/30	C-11	102	60	Home Appliances
21:30/30	C-11	211	60	Television

identities, and in the privacy table, there is no relationship among IoT users and applications.

Based on Second Table information, In the best anonymized case, in which the intruder is unable to connection an IoT device form to a particular user, the probability of recognizing an IoT client are 1/4. The provided confidentiality set's confidentiality degree is equal to the following:

$$d = \frac{H(y)}{H_N} = -\sum_{k=1}^{8} WP_j^W P_j \qquad (9.8)$$

Table 9.2 shows how the names of IoT users and devices are hidden to obtain the highest level of anonymity (d = 1). If the attacker identifies an IoT user based on the vulnerability feature in the table (IoT device type), the confidentiality set is reduced to a 3-anonymity set, and the intruder has a p = 1/3 chance of discovering other users. Figure 9.8 depicts the slope

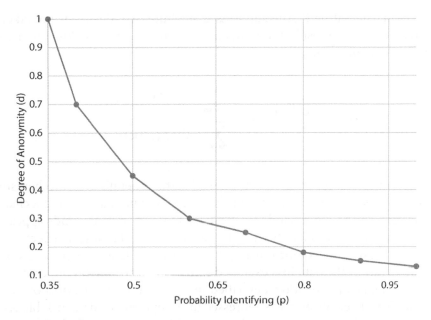

Figure 9.8 Anonymity degree curve for anonymity set in Table 9.2.

of the confidentiality stage for the confidentiality set measured in Table 9.2. The confidentiality set has the smallest degree of privacy (d = 0) if a user exploits side details from the IQ and sensitivity features to classify IoT users in a linking assault. The relationship between both the IoT user and the IoT devices can be established using a connecting attack and profiling the recipient's presence schedule in the facility.

9.8.2.2 Data Forfeiture

To maintain anonymity the energy ingesting information in Tables 9.1 and 9.2, the two factors of customer and report stand simplified. Additionally, the IoT-device parameter is disabled to prevent any link from being used to identify IoT customers as credit-distribution. The data loss caused through the generalisation is quantified using the non-uniform entropy presented in Segment 4.

$$P_a[d_k \mid e_k] = \left[\frac{\sum_{J=1}^{10} W(L(D(k) = d_k))}{\sum_{J=1}^{10} W(L(D(k) = e_k))} \right]$$

When calculating P_a, the suppressed attribute (IoT-device) is not taken into account. As a result, for all documents, the information loss imposed by the generalisation is equal to:

$$NE = -\sum_{k=1}^{18} W \, log_2 \frac{\sum_{J=1}^{10} (L(D(k) = d_k)}{\sum_{J=1}^{10} W(L(D(k) = e_k)} = 0$$

As a result, in our anonymization model, the generalisation mechanism does not result in any loss of data. In the unencrypted list, hiding a characteristic, on the other hand, results in data loss. Despite its crude appearance, the suppression is highly useful in practise because it effectively masks data without compromising the properties of irrelevant information [48]. To ration the data loss executed through repression, developers used the KL departure equation described in Segment 4. The features of IoT-device have been absolutely suppressed to anonymize the data in Table 9.1. As a result, there is no knowledge about this attribute in Table 9.2. As a result, the knowledge loss is equal to:

$$D_{Lk}(m(y)\|n(y)) = \sum_{j=1}^{18} W \, m(y_i) log_2^W m(y_i) - n(y_i)$$

Since the IoT-type is no longer present in Table 9.2, log2q(x) is no longer measurable, and the attribute data is lost. As a consequence, Table 9.1 summarizes that the likelihood of the IoT-device elements equals this suppression's information loss. This implication gratifies the idea of data loss, as seen by the Shannon entropy in Equation (9.5) and loss of knowledge caused by conquest is as follows [49]:

$$|D_{Lk}(m(y) \| n(y)| = H(m)$$

Table 9.2: Information lost whenever the IoT-device parameter is suppressed 2 is almost 3 bits for the power consumption example shown in Table 9.1. While attribute suppression invariably results in information loss, the data utility of anonymized information is unaffected. Table 9.2's knowledge has the same data usefulness as Table 9.1's Because the Usage (W-hr) and Blockchain attributes haven't changed.

9.8.3   Evaluation of Results

To deliver a practical comparison, developers measured Hy-resource Structure's (storage and CPU) utilisation and evaluated it to a normal blockchain reminiscence and CPU usage. In addition, developers compared the processing times in both blockchains for inserting and verifying blocks. In the same energy consumption situation, Figures 9.9 and 9.10

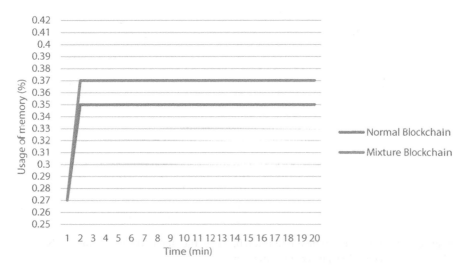

Figure 9.9 Memory percentages in Mixed-Bridge and the regular blockchain.

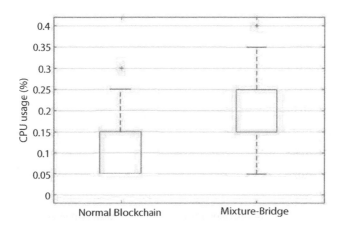

Figure 9.10 Percentages of CPU used by Mixed-Bridge and the regular blockchain.

display the memory and Storage percentages used by Hybrid-Bridge and the conventional blockchain. The period dealing out for block addition and block verifying operations in the regular blockchain and the Hybrid-Bridge are shown in Figures 9.11 and 9.12.

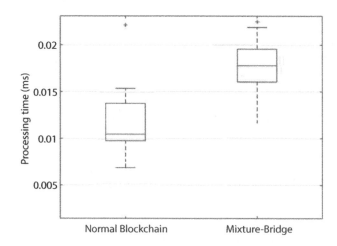

Figure 9.11 Dealing out time for addition blocks to the standard blockchain and the Hy-Bridge based on IoT power consumption.

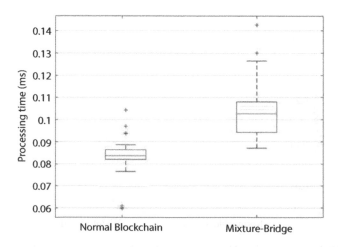

Figure 9.12 Dealing out period for block collateral in a traditional blockchain and a Hy-Bridge founded on IOT power feeding.

9.9 Conclusion

In this paper, we have proposed a Mixed-Bridge, a new innovative block chain-based structure for ensured trustful transactions for financial applications in the field of IoT and efficacy markets. Hy-Bridge is a mechanism of hybrid blockchain that makes use of subnetworks of local networks to divide separate IoT users of P2P transactions. The network with least trust level also will offer accountable and reliable transactions in this architecture. The primary feature of blockchain i.e., accountability and reliability offer security to IoT participants. The transactions which involve billing and charging can be easily proven. Any fraudulence and financial abuse will be easily prevented by the blockchain technology.

In the proposed Mixed blockchain architecture, the bridge location is added to isolate P2P transactions and this will manage and control the IoT users' activities. In case of user that involves in credit- sharing feature, k-anonymity feature will be used for protecting the IoT users privacy. This feature of users of IoT provides access to a shared service anonymously. As a conclusion of this, the used bridge anonymizes the details of IoT Users P2P Transactions energy in the microgrid. This ensures that private information of the microgrid is not leaked to the main power grid.

To manage the P2P communications of credit sharing party in the subnetwork blockchain, the key idea of a localized block with more than normal to additional header is implemented. The service layer of the architecture in the service layer provides the address of the efficiency requirement. The IoT User may use the credit sharing facility of IoT devices connected. In comparing with traditional blockchain, the better improvement is observed in terms of Mixed Bridge imposes aggregate memory and CPU. In the future, the proposed algorithm may be used in real world scenarios and incorporate the blockchain technology to provide the realistic feedback.

References

1. Mahdi Daghmehchi Firoozjaei, Ali Ghorbani, Hyoungshick Kim and JaeSeung Song, Hy-Bridge: A Hybrid Blockchain for Privacy-Preserving and Trustful Energy Transactions in Internet-of-Things Platforms. 2020.
2. IRENA. Off-grid Renewable Energy Systems: Status and Methodological Issues. 2015. Avaiable online: https: //www.irena.org/media/Files/IRENA/Agency/Publication/2015/IRENA_Off-grid_Renewable_Systems_WP_2015.pdf.

3. Lopez, C.; Sargolzaei, A.; Santana, H.; Huerta, C. Smart Grid Cyber Security: An Overview of Threats and Countermeasures. J. Energy Power Eng. 2015, 9, 632–647.

4. Islam, S.N.; Mahmud, M.; Oo, A. Impact of optimal false data injection attacks on local energy trading in a residential microgrid. ICT Express 2018, 4, 30–34. [CrossRef]

5. Andonia, M.; Robu, V.; Flynn, D.; Abram, S.; Geach, D.; Jenkins, D.; McCallum, P.; Peacock, A. Blockchain technology in the energy sector: A systematic review of challenges and opportunities. Renew. Sustain. Energy Rev. 2019, 100, 143–174. [CrossRef]

6. Cavoukian, A. Privacy by Design: Achieving the Gold Standard in Data Protection for the Smart Grid; Office of the Information and Privacy Commissioner of Ontario: Toronto, ON, Canada, 2010.

7. Park, L.; Lee, S.; Chang, H. A Sustainable Home Energy Prosumer-Chain Methodology with Energy Tags over the Blockchain. Sustainability 2018, 10, 658. [CrossRef]

8. Jia, B.; Zhou, T.; Li, W.; Liu, Z.; Zhang, J. A Blockchain-Based Location Privacy Protection Incentive Mechanism in Crowd Sensing Networks. Sensors 2018, 18, 3894. [CrossRef]

9. Chaudhary, R.; Jindal, A.; Aujla, G.S.; Aggarwal, S.; Kumar, N.; Choo, K.K.R. BEST: Blockchain-based Secure Energy Trading in SDN-enabled Intelligent Transportation System. Comput. Secur. 2019, doi:10.1016/j.cose.2019.05.006. [CrossRef]

10. Wang, N.; Zhou, X.; Lu, X.; Guan, Z.; Wu, L.; Du, X.; Guizani, M. When energy trading meets blockchain in electrical power system: The state of the art. Appl. Sci. 2019, 9, 1561. [CrossRef]

11. Liu, B.; Zhou, W.; Zhu, T.; Gao, L.; Xiang, Y. Location Privacy and Its Applications: A Systematic Study. IEEE Access 2018, 6, 17606–17624. [CrossRef]

12. Mashima, D.; Serikova, A.; Cheng, Y.; Chen, B. Towards quantitative evaluation of privacy protection schemes for electricity usage data sharing. ICT Express 2018, 4, 35–41. [CrossRef]

13. Bohli, J.; Dietrich, A.; Petrlic, R.; Sorge, C. A Comparison of Payment Schemes for the IoT. In Open Identity Summit 2017; Fritsch, L., Roßnagel, H., Hühnlein, D., Eds.; Gesellschaft für Informatik: Bonn, Germany, 2017; pp. 181–186.

14. Weber, R. Accountability in the Internet of Things. Comput. Law Secur. Rev. 2011, 27, 133–138. [CrossRef]

15. Abdullah, Z.; Almsafir, M.; Al-Smadi, A. Transparency and reliability in financial statement: Do they exist? Evidence from Malaysia. Open J. Account. 2015, 4, 29. [CrossRef]

16. Board, F.S. Artificial Intelligence and Machine Learning in Financial Services. 2017. Available online:http://www.fsb.org/2017/11/artificialintelligence-and-machine-learning-in-financial service/Sensors 2020, 20, 928 24 of 25.

17. Rajesh Kumar, D., & Shanmugam, A. (2017). A Hyper Heuristic Localization Based Cloned Node Detection Technique Using GSA Based Simulated Annealing in Sensor Networks. In Cognitive Computing for Big Data Systems Over IoT (pp. 307–335). Springer International Publishing. https://doi.org/10.1007/978-3-319-70688-7_13

18. Wu, C.; Lin, F.; Wang, C.; Chang, N. OneM2M-based IoT protocol integration. In Proceedings of the 2017 IEEE Conference on Standards for Communications and Networking (CSCN), Helsinki, Finland, 18–21 September 2017; pp. 252–257.

19. Matte, C.; Achara, J.; Cunche, M. Short: Device-to-Identity Linking Attack Using Targeted Wi-Fi Geolocation Spoofing. In WiSec '15: Proceedings of the 8th ACM Conference on Security & Privacy in Wireless and Mobile Networks; ACM: New York, NY, USA, 2015; doi:10.1145/2766498.2766521.

20. Dorri, A.; Steger, M.; Kanhere, S.S.; Jurdak, R. BlockChain: A Distributed Solution to Automotive Security and Privacy. IEEE Commun. Mag. 2017, 55, 119–125. [CrossRef]

21. Henry, R.; Herzberg, A.; Kate, A. Blockchain Access Privacy: Challenges and Directions. IEEE Secur. Priv. 2018, 16, 38–45.

22. Zimba, A.; Wang, Z.; Chen, H. Multi-stage crypto ransomware attacks: A new emerging cyber threat to critical infrastructure and industrial control systems. ICT Express 2018, 4, 14–18. [CrossRef]

23. Soumya Ranjan Jena, Raju Shanmugam, Rajesh Kumar Dhanaraj, Kavita Saini Recent Advances and Future Research Directions in Edge Cloud Framework. (2019). International Journal of Engineering and Advanced Technology, 9(2), 439–444.

24. Laszka, A.; Dubey, A.; Walker, M.; Schmidt, D. Providing Privacy, Safety, and Security in IoT-Based Transactive Energy Systems using Distributed Ledgers. In Proceedings of the Seventh International Conference on the Internet of Things, Linz, Austria, 22–25 October 2017; p. 13.

25. Guan, Z.; Si, G.; Zhang, X.; Wu, L.; Guizani, N.; Du, X.; Ma, Y. Privacy-Preserving and Efficient Aggregation Based on Blockchain for Power Grid Communications in Smart Communities. IEEE Commun. Mag. 2018, 56, 82–88.

26. Meiklejohn, S.; Pomarole, M.; Jordan, G.; Levchenko, K.; McCoy, D.; Voelker, G.; Savage, S. A Fistful of Bitcoins: Characterizing Payments Among Men with No Names. In IMC '13: Proceedings of the 2013 Conference on Internet Measurement Conference; ACM: New York, NY, USA, 2013; pp. 127–140.

27. Abidin, A.; Aly, A.; Cleemput, S.; Mustafa, M. Secure and Privacy-Friendly Local Electricity Trading and Billing in Smart Grid. arXiv 2018, arXiv:1801.08354.

28. Sun, Y.; Lampe, L.; Wong, V. Smart Meter Privacy: Exploiting the Potential of Household Energy Storage Units. IEEE Internet Things J. 2017, 5, 69–78.

29. Azar, A.; Nazaripouya, H.; Khaki, B.; Chu, C.; Gadh, R.; Jacobsen, R. A Non-Cooperative Framework for Coordinating a Neighborhood of istributed Prosumers. IEEE Trans. Ind. Inform. 2019, 15, 2523–2534.

30. Li, C.; Palanisamy, B.; Xu, R. Scalable and Privacy-preserving Design of On/Off-chain Smart Contracts. arXiv 2019, arXiv:1902.06359.
31. Erdin, E.; Cebe, M.; Akkaya, K.; Solak, S.; Bulut, E.; Uluagac, S. Building a Private Bitcoin-based Payment Network among Electric Vehicles and Charging Stations. In Proceedings of the 2018 IEEE International Conference on Internet of Things (iThings) and IEEE Green Computing and Communications (GreenCom) and IEEE Cyber, Physical and Social Computing (CPSCom) and IEEE Smart Data (SmartData), Halifax, NS, Canada, 30 July–3 August 2018; pp. 1609–1615.
32. Khalil, R.; Gervais, A. Revive: Rebalancing off-blockchain payment networks. In Proceedings of the 2017 ACM SIGSAC Conference on Computer and Communications Security; ACM: New York, NY, USA, 2017; pp. 439–453.
33. Daghmehchi Firoozjaei, M.; Ghorbani, A.; Kim, H.; Song, J. EVChain: A Blockchain-based Credit Sharing in Electric Vehicles Charging. In Proceedings of the 17th International Conference on Privacy, Security and Trust Conference, Fredericton, NB, Canada, 26–28 August 2019; pp. 247–251.
34. Crosby, M.; Nachiappan, N.; Pattanayak, P.; Verma, S.; Kalyanaraman, V. BlockChain Technology; Technical Report; Sutardja Center for Entrepreneurship & Technology: Berkeley, CA, USA, 2015.
35. Dinh, T.; Liu, R.; Zhang, M.; Chen, G.; Ooi, B.; Wang, J. Untangling Blockchain: A Data Processing View of Blockchain Systems. IEEE Trans. Knowl. Data Eng. 2018, 30, 1366–1385.
36. Sultan, K.; Ruhi, U.; Lakhani, R. Conceptualizing Blockchains: Characteristics & Applications. arXiv 2018, arXiv:1806.03693.
37. Christidis, K.; Devetsikiotis, M. Blockchains and Smart Contracts for the Internet of Things. IEEE Access 2016, 4, 2292–2303. Sensors 2020, 20, 928.
38. Samarati, P.; Sweeney, L. Generalizing Data to Provide Anonymity when Disclosing Information. In PODS '98: Proceedings of the Seventeenth ACM SIGACT-SIGMOD-SIGART Symposium on Principles of Database Systems; ACM: New York, NY, USA, 1998; doi:10.1145/275487.275508.
39. Machanavajjhala, A.; Gehrke, J.; Kifer, D.; Venkitasubramaniam, M. l-Diversity: Privacy Beyond k-Anonymity. In Proceedings of the 22nd International Conference on Data Engineering, Atlanta, GA, USA, 3–7 April 2006.
40. Xiangmin, R.; Jing, Y.; Jianpei, Z.; Kechao, W. An Improved RSLK-Anonymity Algorithm for Privacy Protection of Data Stream. Int. J. Adv. Comput. Technol. 2012, 4, 218–225.
41. Daghmehchi Firoozjaei, M.; Yu, J.; Choi, H.; Kim, H. Privacy-preserving nearest neighbor queries using geographical features of cellular networks. Comput. Commun. 2017, 98, 11–19.
42. AboHossein, A.; Darwish, N.; Hefny, H. Multiple-Published Tables Privacy-Preserving Data Mining: A Survey for Multiple-Published Tables Techniques. Int. J. Adv. Comput. Sci. Appl. 2015, 6, 80–85.

43. Sweeney, L. k-anonymity: A model for protecting privacy. Int. J. Uncertain. Fuzziness Knowl. Based Syst. 2002, 10, 557–570.

44. Diaz, C.; Seys, S.; Claessens, J.; Preneel, B. Towards measuring anonymity. In PET'02: Proceedings of the 2nd International Conference on Privacy Enhancing Technologies; Springer-Verlag: Berlin/Heidelberg, Germany, 2003; pp. 54–68.

45. Issa, R. Satisfying K-Anonymity: New Algorithm and Empirical Evaluation. Master's Thesis, Carleton University, Ottawa, ON, Canada, 2009.

46. Baez, J.; Fritz, T.; Leinster, T. A Characterization of Entropy in Terms of Information Loss. Entropy 2011, 13, 1945–1957.

47. Croft, W.; Shi, W.; Sack, J.; Corriveau, J. A Novel Geographic Partitioning System for Anonymizing Health Care Data. 2015. Available online: http://xxx.lanl.gov/abs/1505.06939 (accessed on 7 March 2019).

48. Li, J.; Liu, J.; Baig, M.; Wong, R. Information Based Data Anonymization for Classification Utility. Data Knowl. Eng. 2011, 70, 1030–1045. [CrossRef]

49. Perez-Cruz, F. Kullback-Leibler Divergence Estimation of Continuous Distributions. In Proceedings of the 2008 IEEE International Symposium on Information Theory, Toronto, ON, Canada, 6–11 July 2008.

50. Tan, S.; De, D.; Song, W.; Yang, J.; Das, S. Survey of Security Advances in Smart Grid: A Data Driven Approach. IEEE Commun. Surv. Tutor. 2017, 19, 397–422.

51. BlockCharge - EV Charging via the Ethereum BlockChain. 2016. Avaiable online: https://cryptofr.com/ topic/2565/blockcharge-ev-charging-via-the-ethereum-blockchain.

52. Christl, M. The Final Countdown - Breakthrough of Mobile Wallets. PCM. Paym. Cards Netw. 2017, 3, 4–6.

53. Vinothkumar, S., Varadhaganapathy, S., Shanthakumari, R., An improvement in password protection overriding trade-off between security and usability, International Journal of Scientific and Technology Research, 2020, 9(2), pp. 3313–3318.

54. Digital Wallet to Make Payments Faster, Easier and Secure. 2016. Avaiable online: https://www.commsmea.com/16436-etisalat-launches-digital-wallet-to-make-payments-fastereasier-and-secure.

55. Martino, W. Mining and Private Blockchains don't Mix. 2016. Available online: http://kadena.io/blog/ MiningInPrivate.html.

10

IoTSG in Maintenance Management

T.C. Kalaiselvi[1*] and C.N. Vanitha[2]

¹Kongu Engineering College, Perundurai, Erode, Tamil Nadu, India
*²Department of Computer Science and Engineering, Kongu Engineering College,
Perundurai, Erode, Tamil Nadu, India*

Abstract

In our today internet world the next step advancement is Internet of Things (IoT). In Internet of Things (IoT) any physical thing or object having the computation and communication capabilities to be ideally integrated at different levels and it could be connected to the internet. Smart cities, smart grid, smart transportation, smart grid, and smart environment have recently emerged with Internet of Things (IoT). Smart Grid (SG) is one of the most important applications of IoT. In data communication network, Smart Grid (SG) is merged with the power grid to collect the data and it inspect the data. It is obtained from waveguides, Transponders, Receivers and uplink, downlinks. To digitalizes the physical movements and actions of human and machine predictive measurement was used. It strongly depends on Internet of Things (IoT), which allows person-to-person, person-to-system and system-to-system connections for human understanding. To reach the maturity stage of predictive maintenance there are several issues to be addressed for widespread application. To reach the maturity level, IoT permits data science capabilities, for advanced digitalization, which is supporting decision making to optimally act on the physical systems. The chapter explains a global point of view of the current predictive maintenance issues. The final aim is to provide a deeper understanding of the limitations and strengths of the effective maintenance paradigm and also provide the deeper understanding of the challenges and opportunities of this better for effective maintenance paradigm that is finished by the in depth analysis researchand analysis of the scientific and technical literature. For better development and classification of IoT-enabled predictive maintenance some main research issues to be addressed in industry. IoT architectures

---

Corresponding author: kalaiselvi@kongu.ac.in

P. Sanjeevikumar, Rajesh Kumar Dhanaraj, Malathy Sathyamoorthy, Jens Bo Holm-Nielsen
and Balamurugan Balusamy (eds.) Smart Grids and Internet of Things: An Energy Perspective,
(273–318) © 2023 Scrivener Publishing LLC

in Smart Grid, needs for victimization IoT in SG, IoT applications and services in SG, and challenges and future work are discussed.

Keywords: Internet of Things, smart grid, predictive maintenance, infrastructure, data science capabilities

10.1   Introduction to the Chapter

Conventionally, the two most maintenance management technologies is reactive or preventive. Reactive maintenance is an unsuccessful method in which servicing procedures are carried out after the element failure. Preventive maintenance focused on time related approach that carries out maintenance after a certain date. The advantages and vulnerabilities in all approaches are. Reactive maintenance can save money in the short term, but in the long term it can lead to greater cost of repair and longer downtime. Preventive maintenance results in improved efficiency, but it can be more costly because the maintenance is done before it is actually needed.

In order to achieve both high reliability and reduced price, a predictive maintenance approach should be introduced. Predictive maintenance is condition-related and maintenance only takes place as needed by the element. Predictive maintenance often allows the maintainer to be prepared for a malfunction until the failure is making predictions that one component fails. A highly stable enterprise can provide an efficient and cost-effective maintenance schedule with the introduction of predictive maintenance.

Background

Maintenance is a big part of any business and can constitute 15 to 60 percent of the operating expense, depending on the sector. Industries in the United States are spending over $200 billion annually on maintenance. Latest surveys revealed the need for better maintenance. Free and unnecessary repairs accounts for about 33 % per cent of maintenance costs.

Successful predictive maintenance presents several benefits, including reduced maintenance rates, improved availability, and strengthened protection feels. To gain these advantages, new methods and procedures are used in predictive maintenance. Training and training in the execution of a predictive maintenance plan are all important here. If repair staff and then other customers would not suitably qualified in the unrelated predictive maintenance techniques, there would be little proof of cost savings and efficiency.

A center for predictive maintenance has developed IoT-based techniques to create a demonstration which can be used for predictive maintenance training and informing users. In different areas, such as general mechanical systems, oil and petrochemicals and water treatment, this approach can be applied. While these industries require different mainte-nance requirements and procedures, the same IoT maintenance predictive methodology may be employed.

IoT- Internet of Things

The IoT defined as a network of connected objects or things via the internet. This objects can interconnect and convey independently of their physical position with each other [1]. These objects are integrated with sensors to track the state of the object into the maintenance environment. The IoT has grown in success with service over the years. This gives users a method for linking and gathering data from all components and devices under man-agement. The data is processed and evaluated in real time for meaningful connections to be identified and extracted in the data. The data obtained can also be compared by historical data against past trends. In addition to the IoT frame, the physical modules and systems are often associated with each user during maintenance. This implies, to know its status, a customer does not have to physically be with the asset. They have actual dashboards and alerts about the details that a person needs [2].

IoT has modified the way in which users think about knowledge. A huge amount of data is obtained from the sensor network in real time, if an IoT architecture is implemented. There are many useful insights and good rela-tions in knowledge gathered from the modules and systems, but there also are certain challenges. One problem is how IoT data can be handled and extracted. Information can be stored locally in the past, but capacity and performance limits have been achieved by this method. Cloud storage can be used for the fast storage, monitoring and review of IoT data [3].

In addition to doing this directly on your computer, cloud computing uses a network of webservers to store, monitor and analyze information. This configuration enables resource sharing such as computer resources and storage over a server network with a large capacity for storage and pro-cessing. As Figure 10.1.1 shows, the cloud infrastructure can be broken up into separate regions, including cloud computing. Databases for the data captured and stored are required for the Cloud computing. Cloud appli-cations provide user-accessible programs. This incorporates data analysis, diagnostic and prediction models, generated reports and task orders, and information-containing real-time dashboards. The network configuration is the cloud computing. An individual can use right passwords anywhere for data and programs stored in the cloud. There is the bonus that reports and data can be displayed from any computer since the devices are not installed in your area locally but in the cloud [4].

The topic of IoT data collection and retrieval is addressed by cloud storage, but the challenge of understanding it is not fixed. Here comes the

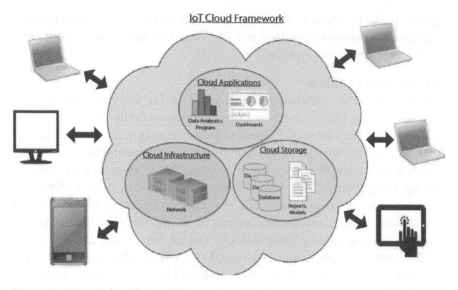

Figure 10.1.1 IoT cloud framework.

study field for Big Data Analytics. Big data is a concept used to categorize vast volumes of data sets for patterns, trends and connections. Significant quantities of information are related and generated by maintenance [5]. Historical or current evidence can have a direct effect on the status of a component or device (real-time). Past offers logistical detail from maintenance records and will also provide consumers with experience and skills. Historical knowledge also encompasses recently acquired sensor data. Present information requires the retrieval of sensor data. Other sources of information, such as weather or environmental factors, can also be obtained that can impact the state of a device or device. Data and information from professional handbooks and publications are also useful. In order to extract helpful information on any of these results, sophisticated processing techniques for big data will be required [6].

10.2   IoT in Smart Grid

The smart grid is necessary for the growth, the International Energy Agency (IEA) says, of a secure, cleaner and sustainable future. The intelligent grid is an IoT-controlled device for remotely tracking and automating everything from illumination, traffic signals, travel pollution, car parks, road warning and early detection, including the incidence of power inflows, as well as lighting and traffic signals. Intelligent meters, distribution automation, substation systems, transformers, sensors, applications and more are found in enterprises and homes in the Smart Grid [7].

Today, developments in the Smart Grid all allow IoT energy storage technology efficient and currently lacking. Via double-way communication between embedded systems and devices that sense and satisfy customer needs, the IoT Smart Grid is made simpler. This innovations ensure high efficiency and minimal cost of an intelligent grid than the present power system [8].

Advantages of IoT Monitoring and Regulation-Smart Grid
Present power grids are not designed to survive large electricity consumption and information transfer to billions worldwide. The smart grid can track energy shortages and infrastructure failures, reduce power disruptions and power supply to people in need more quickly.

These are just few of the benefits that IoT smart grid technology can offer:

A. Smarter Energy Use
By using and storing data, Smart Grid systems can help reduce power consumption and costs. Intelligent lighting would be suitable for tracking the uses of different locations, for example by using intelligent urban technologies, adapting quickly to circumstances such as rain or fog, modifying efficiency to suit daylight hours and traffic patterns and effectively detecting and restoring light outages. User may use software while working or on holiday to adjust the temperature of their home thermostats in consumer applications [9].

B. Cleaner Energy Use
Smart grid infrastructure has lower battery loads, a carbon saving technology that reduces the peak load on the feeders. The U.S. Energy Department already integrates renewable infrastructure into its IoT smart management for more effective solutions. Integrated wind turbines, solar panels, microgrid systems and feeder systems may take advantage of all levels of the delivery chain.

C. Minimal Costs
Today, as reported by the Department of Energy has stated, power outages and breaks costs of US people minimum 150 billion dollars annually to set rates at about 500 dollars per person. The older networks are unable to meet increasing requirements as the global population continues to increase. Smart grids are designed to reduce costs, by way of intelligent energy IoT control and source substitution where a power outage can be detected [10].

D. Transportation and Parking Improvement
Smart sensors of IoT gather data in real time and relay details to drivers and police. This would potentially relieve the traffic jams, and bring preferable

parking spaces and caution to drivers of traffic collisions, and make it easy to pay for road and parking meters automatically. IoT will also charge electric vehicles wirelessly in the upcoming years.

E. Waste and water management services

In its waste and water disposal methods, smarter cities enhance performance and minimize costs. Stock tracking and theft/loss prevention can be supported in real-time by IoT Applications. The cloud-focused monitoring and traffic control would improve time and programming for lorries. Advanced power analysis may gather water flow, force, humidity and more in order to help customers track changes in use. Timers and devices from the utilities will aid with waste management and waste reduction [11].

F. Developing countries Energy Enhancing

The International Energy Agency (IEA) study explains how intelligent grids can be used to deliver power to sparsely inhabited areas by moving from fast and one-off pathways to electrification (eg. household electrification by battery) into Municipal grids that could then be connected with national and regional grids. Such grids would be vital to introduce modern electricity infrastructures in developed countries that start to witness the effects of overflowing populations. New innovations are the perfect way to accomplish economic growth.

G. Greater Insight into Regional Issues

Optimized solutions for intelligent cities offer a clearer description of metropolitan issues. Imagine a clever grid set in a dry climate to cope with localized drought or wildfires. Likewise, adaptive fog lights for towns in the northeast of America, but unsuccessful elsewhere, would be fine. The working life in countless metropolitan populations can be transformed by personalized technology and enhanced data collection [12].

This are just some of the many benefits that IoT's intelligent grid systems offer. When entirely combined, smart grid infrastructure could change the method we live, interact and connect with the planet around us.

10.2.1   Uses and Facilities in SG

IoT could activate Smart grid technologies (SG). Robust IoT detecting and processing capability will boost the SG skills such as detection, alertness, consciousness, recovery plans and reliability. The incorporation of IoT and SG will significantly facilitate the development of intelligent models, indicators and detectors, data and communication devices. For the purpose of achieving effective data transmission and resource levelling in wired and wireless infrastructures [15], IoT can be used in different parts of SG as follows,

1. IoT may be used in power generation for the purpose of monitoring electricity generation from different types of power stations, greenhouse emissions, conservation of energy, energy consumption, and predicting customer demand.
2. The IoT can be used for the acquisition, delivery, monitoring and safe usage of electricity, power grids, substations and poles, and for equipment retention and operation.
3. In smart meters, IoT could be used on the customer side to calculate various kind of specifications, smart power usage, connectivity among numerous networks, electric vehicle charging and discharge, energy efficiency management and power demand.

Innovative Smart Grid Technologies
Smart grid operations rely on a wide range of technology and infrastructure solutions. IoT-based and data technology-based smart grids are prevalent and involve many significant components:

- **Smart sensors and meters:** These are the very basic elements of a smart grid that allow the user to monitor energy usage. Sensors continuously generate and report status data in smart appliances to enable monitoring and control. Smart meters collect data on energy usage and show a complete picture of household energy use, including loads and approximate costs.
- **Automated distribution:** Real-time data is used by advanced distribution systems to automatically adapt to load changes, detect blackouts and correct distribution of power to allow both safety and economic savings. This is the section where automation and self-management are implemented by the smart grid using IoT.
- **Charging stations and smart storage:** Power storage and charging stations play an important role in the smart grid concept. In cases of outages or injuries, these technologies not only allow households to safely go off-grid. They also represent the rising demand for autonomous, renewable residential systems.

The principal scenarios for the IoT implementation are as follows:

1. **High reliability AMI**: AMI is an essential feature in SG. In AMI, IoT is used for data collection, SG anomaly calculation, knowledge exchange between intelligent metering systems, energy efficiency tracking and delivery of power, and user consumption behavior analyses.
2. **Smart home**: A smart home can support consumers and Smart Grid, enhance Smart Grid facilities, satisfy advertising request, enhance Quality of Service, monitor smart homes, read smart meter energy consumption data and track green energy.
3. **Transmission line monitoring**: Transmission lines can be tracked by using wireless broadband networking systems to identify and avoid fault problems.
4. **Assistant management system for electric vehicles (EV)**: A charging station, an EV and a control center are EV supportive governance systems. Consumers can check their parking information using GPS at local charging stations. The Global Positioning System (GPS) can spontaneously guide drivers to the most adaptable charging station. Car batteries, charging devices, charging stations and optimization tools are handled by the monitoring center.

10.2.2   Architectures in SG

The utilization of IoT in smart grids enables information to be exchanged between all grid components. The IoT has a vital role to play in the introduction of smart cities and smart grids. Smart energy management is also possible via IoT. The IoT exploits powerful sensing capabilities and greater smart meter networking functionality. In large scale settings, the usage patterns can be understood and can be used for energy and billing optimization. In the implementation of these networks, the privacy and protection variables in the IoT-based smart grids have many challenges. Security and privacy is the big challenge. In large scale settings, the usage patterns can be understood and can be used for energy and billing optimization. In the implementation of these networks, the privacy and protection variables in the IoT-based smart grids have many challenges. Security and privacy is the big challenge. It is important to resolve various passive attacks such as message content release and traffic analysis and active attacks such as denial of

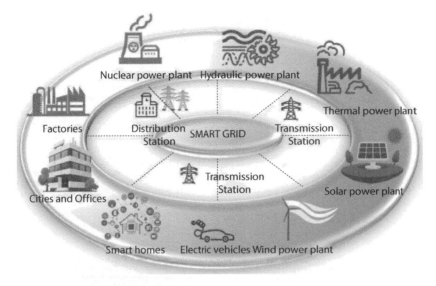

Figure 10.2.1 Architecture of smart grid.

service, jamming, false data injection (FDI) and masquerade. Firewalls and encryption methods will be considered for this reason. Several researchers are investigating the Flocking-based model, alert systems, Jamming Attack Detection Based on Estimate (JADE), Cryptographic Keys [14], Real-Time False Data Injection Detection, Minimizing Message Delay under Jamming Conditions, Aggregated Key Encryption, Intrusion Detection and other solutions.

A Smart Grid is conceptualized as a mix of infrastructure for electrical networks and communication. A Smart Grid architecture as in Figure 10.2.1 is an energy network that can coordinate the activities of all users linked to it intelligently, generators, customers and others who do both, in order to provide reliable, economical and stable electricity supplies efficiently as depicted in Figure 10.2.2.

Smart Grid Architecture

   i. Conceptual model
   ii. Electrical network
   iii. Communication network

i. Conceptual model

The computational model of SG illustrates the general architecture and implementations of electric grid networks. It helps to give the system an

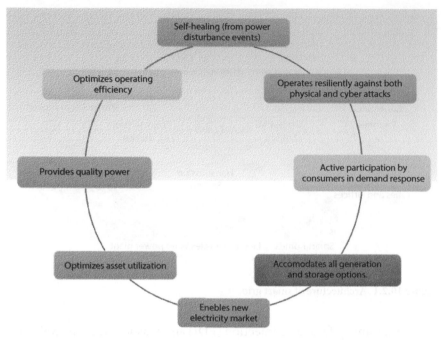

Figure 10.2.2 Features smart grid.

unavoidable viewpoint that several partners will perceive. The design model is refreshed for each System correction, which was originally introduced in the 2010 publication of the first NIST Smart Grid Interoperability Framework. The SG Conceptual Model (CM) upgrade which is documented is illustrated in Figure 10.2.3 was shown. It affects the enormous expansions of the numbers and kinds conveyed power assets (DERs) utilized all through grid, expanding significance, automation of distribution systems, distribution systems are providers of job services.

In the updated conceptual model, the central concepts remain relatively similar to previous models. Secondly, the roles and responsibilities of equipment and actors in the electrical grid are part their sphere of implementation. For this reason, we understand that depending on the nature or domain of the grid in which this equipment is used the appropriate functionalities are likely to differ. In the same way, the advantages of facilities, services or behavior can be varied compared to domain and other circumstances. Alternatively when difficulty has been increased, Conceptual Models (CM) reinforces the contrast between the increasing complexity of the information sharing needed to work with the grid and the very simplistic transfers of physical energy which is currently the network. With

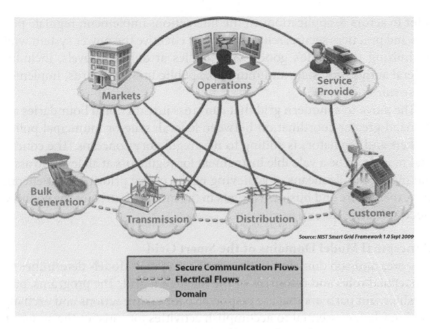

Figure 10.2.3 Conceptual model of smart grid framework.

the diversification of energies across the system and grid dynamics become less certain, power generation or consumption still depends on very few basic physical connections. In the other hand, network transmission and data complexity burst, as individuals leverage the abundance of low-cost power electronics, sensors and microchips, which were once solely close to physically large generating systems to support grid operations through small-scale, organizing and scattering system conduct. Information flows are spreading everywhere along the grid, whether to extend high voltage device synchronization or to extend the life of established distribution networks (1). The NIST Smart Grid Technical Model high-level assumptions have proved stable over time, but the grid is still increasingly shifting. The CM to its variants were upgrades to affect the several improvements with the system, exploring the associated effect on system interoperability requirements.

The high-level conceptual trend in Figure 10.2.3 is only useful in investigating, even with these shifts, the electric and contact flows between grid domains. In the fields of the grid, much change is made, which makes us more aware of the connections between infrastructure, communications and interoperability.

The CM is built upon a legal and legislative system that governs several aspects of the electric grid. Throughout the framework, the regulations refer to actors & applications to the interactions implement, regulate policies and practices secure, reliable and cost effective the power system while optimizing the public's goods. Any bodies at different levels, including federal authorities, state and municipal public utilities boards, implement these rules.

The move to a modern grid that can cross jurisdictional boundaries and demand greater coordination between federal, state or municipal policymakers and regulators is adding to new regulatory concerns. The conceptual model can be a valuable instrument for regulators at all levels to assess the most possible means of achieving public policy priorities that encourage expenditure and business targets in the modernization of the country's electric energy system.

Conceptual Model Domains of the Smart Grid

Any area and sub domain - within the Conceptual Model- determines the conceptual roles and resources of the intelligent grid. The programs, partnerships and partners that are responsible for taking actions and exchanging knowledge essential to accomplish activities for satisfies the system to achieve the goals such as, demand response and customer support, distributed generation aggregation and failure management. One or more roles execute services within a domain. Home automation, Distributed Energy Resources (DER) and consumer demand responses will, for example, be a solution to load control and condition adaptation across regions.

Seven NIST SM CM domains is discussed in Table 10.2.1.

ii. Electrical Network
  a. Production Domain
  b. Transmission Domain
  c. Distribution Domain

a. Production Domain
A combination of nuclear, solar, coal, wind or hydroelectric power plants

1. **Scale Shift** - Generation has altered the domain name like distributed energy resources to recognize explicitly the expanded variety in grid resources scale and use.
2. **Diversity in technology** - The number and types of developments in the generation of US assets have expanded.
3. **Physical location** – The distributed energy resources domain generation is expanded such that the symbols of massive technology are closest to the domain and the distribution

Table 10.2.1 Conceptual model of SG.

S. no.	Domain	Services and roles in the domain
1	Customer	End-users electricity Power usage can be created, stored & handled. There are historically three market classes, each with their own subsection: domestic, residential and manufacturing.
2	Markets	Coordinator and members on the energy consumption markets also other economic processes have been used to encourage action & maximize scheme outcomes.
3	Service Provider	Electrical and benefit customers service provided by organizations.
4	Operations	Electricity Movement Managers
5	Generation Including distributed sources of energy	The electricity producers. It can also store energy for future supplies. This field encompasses conventional sources of energy production and distribution. 'Generation' involves conventional larger-scale technology, typically connected at the conceptual stage with the transmission grid, like traditional thermal generation, large-scale hydro and sustainable utility networks, usually related to the transmission line. Distributed sources of energy is connected to the consumer, delivery and renewable resources consolidated by network operators producing, storing and demand responses.
6	Transmission	High-voltage power transmitters for long distances. It can be store & produce fuel.
7	Distribution	The power supplies from and to the customers. Store & produce power, too.

and user realms are visually identical to smaller or more compact techniques.

4. **Customer involvement** - One of the many resource strategies available in the distributed energy resources domain requires client services, including generation or demand management.

b. Transmission Domain
Operating centers and the substations are managed by large number of network, a high number of power lines deliver the electricity to the distribution domain.

c. Distribution Domain
The combination of complex network topologies provides electricity for use in suburban areas, rural farms, urban areas, and industrial areas.

1. **Expanding position** - In order to represent the increasing roles of distribution systems for optimizing the grid function, the distribution domain has to be extended also positioned more centrally within the conceptual model.
2. **Improved sensing** - To improve state awareness, sense the distribution systems is necessary, a prerequisite for optimizing grid operation.
3. **Controllability and knowledge** - The increasing availability and use of real-time data for intelligent control of distribution grids is described by computer servers.
4. **New actors** - As historically demonstrated by the current link between infrastructure authorities and power suppliers, distribution operators, service providers and other players in the province are gradually supplying network grid equipment and services.
5. **Consumer domain distributed processes** – Monitoring and automation are available on the grid edge, as described by the device display that is mirrored on the Operations Domain, with active grid energy management possible.
6. **Diversification of consumers** - Consumer domain to be upgraded to serve many kinds of energy network customers, from mixtures to industry and campuses.

iii. Communication Network
Communication networks for smart grid systems use a broad variety of wired, wireless and hybrid communication technologies.

a. Home Area Network (HAN)
b. Neighborhood Area Network (NAN)
c. Field Area Network (FAN)
d. Wide Area Network (WAN)

a. Home Area Network (HAN)
1. Network for Customer Domain

2. Covers smart devices and appliances in the home.
3. IED sends data readings to AMI applications via HAN with home smart meters or residential gateways.
4. The home energy management system (HEMS) that enables consumers to has the household power consumption in real time is an important component of HAN.
5. When introduced in business/buildings or industrial areas, BAN and IAN networks apply to parallel HAN networks.
6. Wireless Engineering-ZigBee, 6LowPan

b. Neighborhood Area Network (NAN)
1. Domain Network delivery
2. Smart Meters mesh
3. NAN links the access point for AMI applications to smart meters in the client domain and various gateways in the delivery domain.
4. Data collection from smart meters for monitoring and control is the main purpose of this network.
5. Wireless-ZigBee, 6LowPan, 3G and 4G, WiMAX, LTE. -PLC and Ethernet Wired

c. Field Area Network (FAN)
1. Network of distribution domains.
2. Power line sensors, breaker controls, voltage regulators, capacitor bank controllers, transformers, data collectors, etc. are included in the FAN.
3. These are used for automated response when any anomalies and failures are observed.
4. Enable mobile workers to use their laptops, tablets, or portable devices to access field devices.
5. Wireless - WiMAX, LTE, 3G and 4G and wired - PLC and Ethernet could be used for FAN

d. Wide Area Network (WAN)
1. Affords smart grid & main power system communications networks.
2. It has two types of backhaul and core network networks.
3. The link between substations and utility systems is given by the core network.
4. Link the NAN network to the core network using the backhaul network.
5. WiMAX, 4G, and PLC these are the variety of technologies used could be used in WAN networks. MPLS virtual technologies also used for core network.

10.3   IoT in the Generation Level, Transmission Level, Distribution Level

I. IoT in the generation level

Using local control gadgets, the administration of generating resources used to be managed. For remote control, the machine operator has minimal controllability and various tasks should be done by submitting instructions or guidance to a local operator. Similarly, the operation of power system capital is getting more modern than ever as a result of certain factors. Real-time monitoring for generation from an IoT-oriented control center is shown in Figure 10.3.1. Initially, in power systems, the perforation of environmentally friendly power resources, an enormous source of vulnerability, has increased. In the future, the inevitability of electric vehicles would have an boundless use that consequences on the generation of power systems planning. Third, as demand response services, the presence of loads is rising, which is extremely equal to the unpredictable periodic electricity rates. The rate of energy is often associated with several things, such as the nature of the power market and the rapid price of petrol. In addition, in the future, request-side medium or small-scale distributed generation (DG) may have a wide pervasiveness, denoted as Virtual Power Plant sources (VPPs). Furthermore, making grid constraints, the operator must assign with such a high degree of instability and irregularity that can lead to the imposing of load discharging or reduction in certain cases. To avoid such steps and to maintain the protection, solidity, accuracy and affordability of the power system, IoT technology will make it easier to manage troubles and challenges. In IoT-related smart grids, it is possible to track all oscillations and

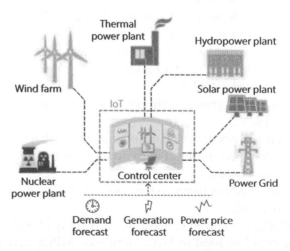

Figure 10.3.1 Real-time monitoring for generation from an IoT-oriented control center.

generations on demand sides and supply sides perpetually and reliably, and the operator would be able to provide more detailed grid control. The incorporation of a few renewable energy resources is tackled by IoT technologies at the generation level in order to boost the efficiency of the generation sector and preserve the dynamic and static protection of the power system. Moreover, energy storage services can be used to correct mismatches created by different sources of instability that IoT infrastructures can affect. The IoT has so far concentrated largely on the demand side, with lack of observation paid to the supply side. Due to a higher degree of manageable and recognizable, the implementation of IoT at this level will lead to another stage of efficiency and performance, which gives considerable gain to power systems.

A. Renewable sources of energy

1) Wind energy
In view of performance and size, wind technologies are developing quickly. For the wind energy region, energy specialists have aggressive pioneering execution targets. The inherent intermittency of these resources is the principal challenge facing the production of wind energy (2). Therefore, if the wind units meet the demand with a broad perforation, various mismatch will endanger the system's safety. The real-time method schedules the rest of the power system so that fluctuations are rewarded without sharp ramp levels. Furthermore, closer coordination with the supply of storing energy can only be accomplished if data between energy storage and wind units are exchanged real-time.

Furthermore, wind farm keepers are able to execute exact predictive maintenance planning, which avoid enormous losses, with the IoT technologies as well as ICT framework. This can be achieved by machine learning and data mining techniques. The Leveled Cost of Energy (LCoE) index for wind resources can, for instance, be minimized by the on-time preservation, which indicates the net current value of a turbine cost over its durability. In using wind energy, IoT is needed to automatically capture and evaluate data relevant to wind turbines and wind farms. There are currently two problems that need to be faced including the obstacles to the transmission period for offshore wind turbines and minimal bandwidth for information to remote areas. So the analyzing process (like closing down the turbine to deter the cascade devastation) can be made quicker or optimized if the crucial information can be gathered and monitored in real time. The use of IoT systems for wind farm design and service as well as the construction and management of turbines in the wind-farm sector underlines the need for more robust solutions for cost-beneficial, stable and healthy framework systems.

2) Solar energy

Following the oil blockage of 1973 and the energy collapse of 1979, greater recognition was devoted to exploiting non-fossil sources of energy. Climate change and environmental problems 25 have meant that renewable energies must perforate the world's energy demand more effectively. Solar power has the greatest impact on renewable energy source. This source is therefore considered to be a major participant to long term clean power grids. Solar energy relates to sunlight and heat radiants and can be exploited through the inclusion of photovoltaic (PV) techniques that are constantly changing. PVs may be sparsely configured in distributed (decentralized), concentrated solar power (CSP) systems.

The solar cells (PV arrays), insulation, controls, assembly mechanism and inventors are ultimately made of a PV system. These items can be provided with a storage battery pack (battery bank). Current PV systems admire more effective solar energy extraction technology such as the MPPT controller, GPS photovoltaic detector, solar radiation sensor systems, anemometer and several other mission items. These are often fitted with current PV systems. Unlike traditional solar photovoltaic systems, the photovoltaic concentrator (CPV) comes with optically adjustable and curved lens that allow irradiance to be centered on a small and extremely effective solar panel. In addition, in order to increase the performance, a cooling system normally is built into CPVs. CPV and CSP are ideally suitable for high-medium-irradiation areas (like Sunbelt area in the United States or Golden Banana area in Europe). Efficient photovoltaic systems could be utilized for end-user distributions, like rooftop or building maintenance solar output, since the profitability per kW is appropriately lower. The grid instead of the standalone are presently a large contributor of PV modules. PV modules' output power focuses largely on room temperature and ferocity of direct sun emission. It is interesting that shade and debris, which can induce a dramatic decline in power output, can significantly improve the act of the PV module. Moreover, the performance of the PV module worsens at extreme temperature. The MPPT system flips the screen squarely to the sun, even when it is slightly dark, to the darkest portion of the sky. The existence of a storage device is important that when required, the solar power will be collected and storage will provide the stored energy if necessary.

The strength of the solar radiation varies and relies greatly on the climatic conditions. The generation is therefore not feasible at a consistent rate. This impacts obliquely the working of other parts of the system such as battery charging and voltage converters. Moreover, environmental factors (like cloud and rain), debris storage, snow upon this PV system and the adverse effect on the sediment of the exterior cover (e.g. hydrophobic) cause the PV module to fail partly or fail part-of-the-growth. Based on the belief that photovoltaic installations have either been next to a roofing photovoltaic device or as far off as a solar power plant in the desert, it is very hard for people to keep track of all photovoltaic panels to avoid any errors and failures, as regular trips to the photovoltaic plant are required and operating data logs are kept. It consumes a long time to cope with these human shortcomings which is not easy to comprehend. Consequently, it is important to configure a persistent real-time surveillance system with PV modules, to track the PV module specifications and store necessary info in a cloud-based system. The info stored should used to help understand the act of the PV systems and the reasons for its inefficiency. The use of IoT technology thus helps problems to be solved and upkeep on schedule.

B. Thermal generation

Thermal energy sources are actually an integral feature of all energy schemes. These kinds of units mean that the grid service is efficient and robust. Consequently, owing to environmental considerations, it is attempted in forthcoming energy plants to replace nuclear thermal power stations with renewable energy. Their productivity and poor versatility are still working. Gas-fired systems are currently also known as pricey generators. These problems mean that, relative with other sections of the electricity grid including renewables, supply or the demand sector, IoT is possibly least implemented in this segment. In two ways, IoT may nevertheless play a significant role. One is that it should be specifically displayed in the central service and control center, the output status of the generators, the condition of transformers and tap-changers together with the power inserted at every unit. The IoT infrastructure thus makes it easier to view those information in real time. In comparison, the traditional steam power stations have a number of components and objects. Every power plant technician with improved IoT-based sensors must effectively detect and monitor each person's condition to perform preventive maintenance planning, which exacerbates the possibility of unexpected failures.

III. Level of transmission in IoT

The link among the generation and the distribution stage is the transmission stage. This stage is a vital component of power grids to maintain a stable demand supply. In two ways, it is essential to incorporate IoT into transmission stages. One is the IoT's role in improving congestion control, and the other is the effect of IoT on system safety maintenance. In order to notify handler of the electrical status of lines including loss perturbations the IoT provided intelligent electronic devices (IEDs) can be mounted in the transmissions field. Phasor Measurement Units (PMU), for time coincidence, will sense the degree, inclination of the current and voltage at a certain point of the line. It may also discern the frequency. A commercial edition of PMU will record measures of approx. 30-60 readings/sec with greater spatial resolutions. This allows engineers of the power system to evaluate complex situations in the power system. With conventional SCADA, a calculation of every 2 or 4 sec is not feasible at such a quick and precise stage. In conjunction with defensive relays, the wide-range defense systems can be deployed using PMU. The development of non-GPS sample period synchronization with nano PMUs can provide 120 samples/sec that help to avoid severe power outages. PMUs will give data that shows high accuracy active and reactive power across the line, improving device visibility. This refers to wise and preventive control mechanisms and techniques. Real-time power flow management via the lines helps the controller to manually handle pressure in cramped power sources or locally clogged areas, notably in crises and uncertainties. The operator will thus be improved in survivability. Overhead lines are also prone to natural hazards. High winds and extreme snow conditions lead to roaring and glazing lines causing the use of uneven pulling power on lines that can lean towers. These factors weaken overhead lines that raise the operating risk. Moreover, the transmitting infrastructure is spread through a large region in which servicing and control are distant and complicated. IoT will minimize the harm caused by these natural events. Highly developed sensor nodes mounted on the tower conductor of the line must have sufficient data. The data will be transmit the sync node computer and then transmitted by an optical fiber framework or wireless transmission to the centralized monitoring centre. Sync node variance sensor, weather forecasting sensors, wind velocity sensor, driver acceleration sensor, sag and current discharge sensor are the IoT gadgets which can be integrated into transmission system. These systems can help improve the control of the car, insulations and towers in real-time.

IV. Level of distribution in IoT

The smart power grid should be fitted with IoT technology at all crucial points in the distribution system Different layers of integration of IoT in distribution level shown in Figure 10.3.2. AMIs are often the first step in the installation, from a customer perspective, of an intelligent delivery grid. One of the most important components of AMI systems is the communication system. It offers the two-way connections among servers and data collection companies, counters, clients and receiver companies. They are reliable and stable. In terms of local requirements and expenditure budget,

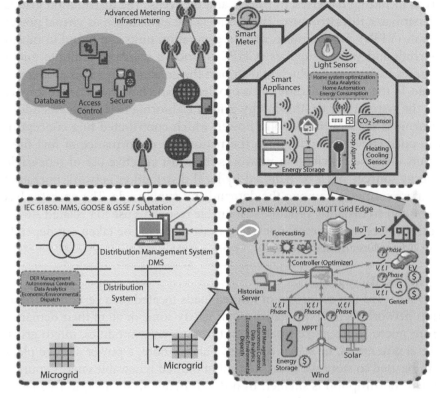

Figure 10.3.2 Different layers of integration of IoT in distribution level.

this connectivity infrastructure can be applied differently. Incorporating IoT in the level of distribution has practical advantages, such as the ability to enforce rapid response services, the authority to enact self-healing mechanisms, energy-consuming issues on minimal voltage transmission lines, and on-line control on the customer pattern of use. Moreover, data obtained from both feeders and busses should be digitized and exchanged by nearby ICT networks, in order to allow the dealer to track and visualize the distribution grid rigorously. In addition, the self - repairing mechanism has been one of the main delivery grid configurations to improve grid reliability in the years to come. Self-repairing mechanisms must be applied as soon as feasible in the real time to recover the necessary and required capabilities.

A. Active distribution networks of IoT
Effective distribution network means a distribution grid of medium-sized or small-sized distributed energy resources (DER) like diesel generating units, coal, wind and solar power plants, small turbines and then storage

areas including batteries, flywheels and fuel cells. The distribution grid is a distributer infrastructure. These outlets are also known as virtual power plants (VPPs). Furthermore, certain generation units can found in mixed warmth and power supplies (CHP). In such a scenario, multiple micro sources are included, which may impact the greater-scale generation time-table. In the coming decades, this problem would have much more impact on the system. For eg, the energy grid of California is facing tremendous enormous perforation of solar power, which contributed to a concept of the duck curve. In addition to the reasonable performance of fuel-fired assets in those distribution networks the most effective use of renewable energy sources must be handled by local distribution network operators that are connected among the demand and supply side. The operator has to be able to instantly produce sustainable resources use IoT related AMIs, and the necessary control operation must manually be taken out depending on predetermined setups.

B. IoT in Microgrid

A micro grid is a collection of limited loads located on a certain distribution network feeding mechanism that satisfy some or all of their demands from micro sources like small wind turbines, solar modules, micro grids, diesel generators, or steam turbines. Furthermore, a power storage plant can be used to store the excess output of limited renewable energy sources when consumption is smaller. In order to maintain micro grid frequency reliability, battery units have been the greater common form of storage for such applications. In certain cases, though, fuel cell, micro CAES and fly-wheel modules would be used. The micro-grid architecture may have a sep-arated framework (out-grid or stand-alone), particularly in rural areas, or a separated structure (in the main grids). Linked mode is often referred to as integrated, and separated mode is also referred to as autonomous mode, off-grid or separated mode. In partnership with an upstream network, the micro grid will sell excess internal energy for those grids. As hybrid plans are several experiments, the collaborative operation and collection of micro sources and plants is proposed. In addition, several researchers are also presenting the model of integrated micro grids for minimizing dependency on the main grid. However, there are three problems in today's micro grids which seem to be the reliability of the micro grid, its power quality and its protection. The addition of IoT will lead to addressing these concerns, resulting in the increased proliferation of the microgrid plan that the power system dealer seek.

The micro grid electricity control must be carried out independently of the central grid. The upstream grid seems to have no micro-sources power or controllability. The micro grid operator should carry out predictions with unknown micro sources. An internal storage system must correct the generated imbalances. However, provided that such networks have minimal capability for sustainability, unscheduled load shedding or sudden cut-offs must be enforced by the controller of the micro-grid. Moreover, whether two or several micro grids are related, mutual stability may be compromised due to abnormality of size. Any extreme disequilibrium in one will therefore endanger the protection of others. In this respect, in order to satisfy the needs without interference, real-time frequency and tensile stability control systems must be used. This includes the use of the internet ecosystem that benefits from IoT infrastructure (3). Info among all sensors should be obtained to notify the monitoring equipment of the real-time status of important parameters. The data has to be analyzed through the cloud server, and in accordance with the preset instructions, the correct action has to be decided.

To summarize, the data corresponding to all interior micro grid parts and micro sources should be transmitted to the upstream power grid by applying the IoT system, which is currently not achieved. This allows the main grid controller to track micro sources and components in the micro-grid (maneuverability). Moreover, the micro grid controller can exploit sustainable power and benefit further by coordinating the storage device effectively with the sources of supply. In addition, IoT-related technologies allow the operator to retain integrated micro grid safety.

10.4   Challenges and Future Research Directions in SG

Therefore, in order to fulfill the technical goals of using Internet of Things in SG, the upcoming research indicators must overcome certain problems, such as IoT systems in a wide variety of potentially challenging conditions (e.g. hot and cold temperatures, elevated voltages, electrical wave exposure, operating water) and meet the demands in these circumstances. IoT devices and sensors are working with several operating systems on batteries (i.e., multiple sensors for tracking transmission lines) to use or develop sufficient strategies to collect electricity. In order to transfer data from smart meter data to medium-size framework, we have many communication networks in various sections of SG and IoT devices should therefore support the required communication standards.

As IoT devices in SG have restricted resources and capacities like the batteries, computing capacity, storage, or bandwidth, data mixing techniques need to be used for compressing and consolidating usable data, so that bandwidth is used efficiently and used in the process of data collection and SG cannot meet the requirements set out before ie., maximum allowable delay. You must also minimize latency, look for the optimum number of gateways and IoT modules, optimize the network architecture and minimize the number of links between each gateway. Since intelligent grids have separate gateways and IoT products, the interoperability between the two is very important for the information exchange.

The use of an IP-based network is one approach for interoperability. Another solution is that IoT systems have to accept a range of protocols and architectures for communication. Similar sensors, including sensor and smart meter, monitor and gather information on smart grids, generate big data and enclosures which can use a lot of electricity and other resources. intelligent grids must be built to store and process this massive volume of data obtained effectively.

There are several different standards on IoT devices, but there are no unified standards on IoT devices that can result in IoT devices' stability, reliability and interoperability problems within SG. Normalization efforts must then be combined. We can use the extremely insecure Internet for tracking and managing IoT devices in SG. Attackers will exploit data measured by smart sensors and meter, causing a lot of financial loss. We should therefore create stable IoT connectivity in the intelligent smart grid, taking into account the IoT devices' resource constraints and establishing those safeguards.

For instance, IoT devices having computational and storage limits. Therefore, security solutions should be developed or enforced to allow IoT devices to operate them. Data obtained from smart meters may be derived from such usage behaviors (i.e., acceptable protocols for protection activities such as confidence management, authorization, approval, integrity-inventive data (inter-IoT devices operated by various parties, i.e. consumers and utilities) retained secrecy and identity spoofing identified.

10.5   Components for Predictive Management

In general, Maintenance strategies are classified into two major groups: Corrective Maintenance and Preventive Maintenance. The CM runs the components until failure; replacement or reconstruction is then carried out. Instead, proactive maintenance covers all steps to maintain a component in such circumstances by systemically testing, predicting, and avoiding incipient failures. Preventive methods can also therefore be subdivided into three subsets: Scheduled Maintenance (SM), where activities are carried out over a pre-fixed level, Condition-Based Maintenance (CBM), which involves status control to detect early-stage issues, and performance monitoring until the extent of deterioration is reached, and PdM, a progression to CBM: Element deterioration is expected in the future and Remaining Useful Life (RUL) is projected in the future. One tenting misunderstanding is that PdM is now the right maintenance policy inside the Industry 4.0 model. It's not that way. The potential for management in Industry 4.0 lies instead in the capacity to assess the optimum control for each parts considering its device specifics, i.e. relevant protection and environment rules, quality requirements, market significance, structural and logical features, etc. And in 1970's, Reliability-Centered Maintenance (RCM) was introduced to tackle the problem of choosing the good maintenance technique for each part of a unit. RCM is currently developed for the various business sectors with the availability of specialized CMMS backed by a wide variety of progress events. RCM's principal concept is to focus maintenance activities on protection and company asset parts, and apply the most efficient maintenance solution to them, as a result of evaluating their performance. In doing so, RCM is based on a flowchart of judgment, which first challenges the feasibility to track and establish a specified threshold for the element in order to preserve the element, i.e. a physical vector that indicates how the element degrades, in order to prevent a loss with significant repercussions. In the event of an actual response, CBM may be considered theoretically feasible; otherwise, the judgment flowchart continues with certain queries about the element's performance to validate its application; If this is still not true, the part will eventually collapse, and appropriate management will be compensated. The argument for RCM applies to Industry 4.0, but with certain important constraints:

1.) As in training of Industry 4.0, the whole first RCM query upon on choice of situation tracking of the usefulness of CBM may be deceptive: while the CBM may be feasible in the event of a positive reaction to the query, a negative response would not actually lead to an abandonment of CBM. Indeed, PHM methods were developed for the detectives of early losses on the basis of numerous signals that did not specifically quantify the state of this component such as Principal Component Analysis (PCA), Auto-Associative Kernel regression (AAKR) and Self Organizing Maps (SOM). In particular, PHM's techniques for removal and sorting (e.g. wavelet transformation) can distinguish combinations of characteristics from possible signals which could be inferred by CBM, even though they do not explicitly quantify the element degradation condition.

2.) PdM will not join the maintenance allocation analysis flowchart. If the first RCM query on CBM is answered favorably, it doesn't mean exactly that PdM is possible too, since CBM tracking cannot have the details necessary for PdM.

3.) CBM and PdM need expenditure expenses for equipment, tools, skills etc, which are to be compensated by the advantages that they will provide. The cost-efficacy of maintenance process should be recognized. From this it seems that RCM actually applies to the context of Industry 4.0: explicitly and solid ideas of defining those elements that the proper repair decision is taken by PdM are required for selection.

10.6   Data Management and Infrastructure of IoT for Predictive Management

A significant misconception in Industry 4.0 is that greater volumes of the information collected and hence more broad-based IoT networks often contribute to finer PdM performance. That's not the case because the acquisition, handling, management and review of data requires cost changes as the volumes of information rises.

Internet of Things (IoT) is a versatile and worldwide networking infrastructure, that defines, separately and self-configures "Things"—subsystems and actual physical and virtual entities. "Things" are to connect with and engage with the surroundings through the interchange of sensing data and respond to activities that regulate the physical universe. The objective to be accomplished by IoT is the development of a standardized forum to create mutual apps and services which exploit the combined strength of the current capital through each "Things." At just the center of such tools are the abundance of data that could be made accessible by combining real-time and permanence repository data. This data can enable new, uncommon and originative applications and value added resources to be applied and is an invaluable resource of pattern analysis and planned opportunities. To do this, it is also important to provide a robust data storage system created and stored by entities inside the IoT.

Data management is a general term that refers to the architectures, policies and processes for better management of the system's data lifecycle requires. Data management can serve as a layer in the sense of IoT in between entities and systems that generate the data and the apps that use data for analytical and services reasons. The systems may be organized together into subsystems or subspaces of separate administration and interior hierarchical management. Based on the extent of privacy required by the subsystem operators, the purpose and information given by such subsystems shall be open to the IoT network.

IoT Data Management

The collection, processing and modification of simple data objects, databases and archives is performed through conventional data management systems. Data processing systems should review information on the Internet in the sense of IoT, by ensuring offline survey collection, logging and inspection services. This extends the idea of data management from offline storage, question and transaction management to dual online storage/communication. In order to better understand IoT data management, we identify the data lifecycle inside IoT first and explain the energy usage profile in each step.

IoT Data Lifecycle

The data life cycle in an IoT system, as seen in Figure 10.6.1, goes from the manufacturing of data to collection, conversion, unforced filtering and preprocessing and eventually to storage and archiving. The search and analysis are the final points that trigger (demand) and absorb the output of data, but the manufacturing of data is "pushed" to IoT consumption

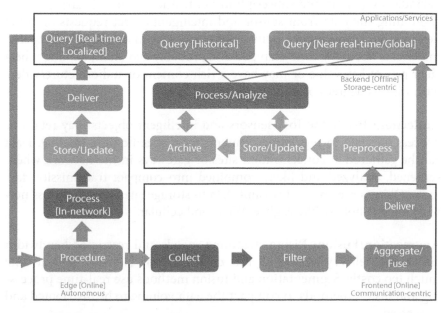

Figure 10.6.1 IoT data lifecycle and data management.

resources. Online, interaction services are regarded for output, compilation, processing, filtering, and other fundamental querying and initial processing functions. The offline include extensive preprocessing, durable archiving, and in-depth analysis.

Storage functioning tend to provide data with perpetual upgrade on a durable basis, whereas archiving applies to read only data. Since in-networking data for real-time and constrained services can be generated, processed in certain IoT systems that do not have to further disseminate this data to concentrated points in the system, "edges," which incorporate all processing and storage parts may exist as stand-alones. Each aspect of the lifecycle of IoT data is discussed in the following subsections (4).

Querying: Data-indepth systems use the searching method for obtaining and recovering data as their central process. Inside IoT, a question may be made to either demand the collectability of real-time data for the reason of temporary tracking or to gain any view of the data contained in the device. The first instance is common if a data request is requested for (mostly located) real time. In the second instance the data is more increasingly global and then the trends and patterns are studied extensively.

Production: Data collection includes detecting and transmission of data from 'Things' in the IoT system and disclosing these data to entities from periodically (e.g. in the subscription/notification concept), disrupting or submitting the data from sensor and intelligent object requests onto the network into convergence points and ultimately on database servers. The material is normally time-stamped and probably geo-stamped, might be a clear pair of key value or may have a rich content of audio/picture/video, with various degrees of difficulty between them.

Collection: Inside the IoT, sensors and intelligent objects may retain or process the data to regulating elements for a specific time interval. Data can be gathered at concentration sites or gateways in the network where screened, analyzed and likely combined into compact transmission formats. Objects are able to transmit data to storage sites using wireless networking technology like Zigbee, Wi-Fi and cellular.

Aggregation/Fusion: Rising streaming speeds and restricted bandwidth also make delivery among all raw data from the Network in real time much too costly. Segmentation and fusion methods use real-time processing and fusion methods to compact the data volume to be distributed and processed.

Delivery: When the data is cleared, analyzed and ultimately served in the IoT both at the points of focus or independent virtual units, the outcome of such processes which need to be forwarded as final answers to the device or for storage and thorough review. The delivery to perpetual data stores is based on wired or wireless network communications.

Preprocessing: Data from IoT sources with multiple configurations and structures can come from various sources. It could be important to preprocess data for handling lost data, eliminating redundancies and combining data from multiple sources into a single scheme before storing them. This preprocessing is known as data cleaning in data mining. The incorporation of the scheme does not mean that all data is brutally incorporated in a predetermined relation format, but also implies a much more abstract description of a standard approach to data without having to personalize access to the data format for every source. In this step, IoT necessary data may add chances at various levels of the schema in order to cope with ambiguity which may arise in the data or even with the confidence lost in data sources.

Storage/Update-Archive: The effective data collection and management as well as the continuing upgrading of the data with up to date info is handled during this process. Archiving denotes to the durable offline storing of data not necessary immediately for the continuing activities of the system. The core aspect of unified storage is the use of storage systems that fit into different varieties of data and data storage frequency. Relational database management systems are a common option for data management into such a table scheme with predefined links and documentation for later retrieval performance. NoSQL's core value stories became common as large-data management storage solutions without dependency on relational schemes and strict criteria for accuracy characteristic of relational database systems. Stocking for automated IoT systems might be decentralized if data is stored for objects created, and the device is not forwarded. Even so, the storage space remains small relative to the consolidated storage model considering the restricted capacity of these items.

Processing/Analysis: In order to learn about historical information and forecast potential patterns and to identify data failure that could cause additional investigation or intervention, it is important to continue the recovery and review operations undertaken and retained and archived data. Prior to practical service, task-specific preprocessing can be required to sort and clean data. If an IoT subsystem is separate and does not need permanent data storage, but retains processing and storage within the network, in-network processing might be carried out in order to respond to real-time or locally processed requests.

In Figure 10.6.1, data flow might follow one of the three ways: the way for automated systems inside the IoT, from query to output, to in-network processing and then distribution; the way that begins from production and begins to gather & filter/aggregate/fuse and concludes with transmitting data to enable queries and at last, the road to aggregation expands output further and covers pre-processing, preservation and archiving of permanent data and comprehensive treatment and review. With respect to the life cycle mentioned above, we illustrate in this corresponding section, the require for data management technologies that transcend the existing capabilities of conventional data management.

There are also problems that must be tackled in upcoming research directions to reach technological targets in the implementation of IoT in SG. As IoT devices should run in various areas with brutal conditions, they must also meet specifications such as durability or usability.

In certain applications, battery-operated IoT systems and sensors are used or equipped to use appropriate power harvest approaches. In various parts of SG, we have multiple communication networks, so the IoT devices can hold up required protocols of communication such that data can be transmitted from smart meters into the centralized system and assured.

Since IoT equipment in Smart Grid have restricted capacities, like batteries, computing power, space or bandwidth, it is therefore important to use the data fusion methods to compact and combine usable data to allow the use of energy, bandwidth and data collection very effective.

Delay and failure of packages are key elements for the productivity of intelligent girds. As clogging causes delay and failure of the packet, it diminishes device performance, and SG cannot fulfill default conditions such as maximal bearable delay. Thus, delays must be eliminated, networking architecture streamlined by discovering an excellent amount of gateways and devices of IoT and the amount of links to a gateway must be decreased.

As the smart grid has a wide variety of various gateways and IoT modules, connectivity between these devices is critical to the information sharing. The need of IP-related networks is a strategy for connectivity. Another approach is for IoT devices to endorse multiple protocols and architectures of communication.

Sensors, intelligent meters, and other like instruments that calculate and gather data in a SG generate vast volumes of data capable of energy and other services and of creating a bottleneck. The smart grid must be built so that this massive volume of accumulated data can be saved and processed effectively.

There are several different specifications for IoT applications; however the SG does not have a single IoT standard. This could lead to problems with stability, usability and connectivity for SG IoT devices. Normative efforts must also be united.

We must use the extremely insecure Internet to track and manage IoT devices in SG, so that perpetrators can exploit data calculated by smart meters and sensors and bring a variety of economic loss. Consequently, by understanding resource constraints of IoT devices and deciding protection mechanisms for these devices, we could establish stable connectivity for IoT devices upon this SG. IoT devices, for instance, have processing and storage limits. Therefore, security measures must be designed or used in order that IoT devices can operate them. It is necessary to separate some information about customer preferences from the data obtained by smart meters and thus it should be assured that this personal data has not been used without the consent of customers. Furthermore, adequate protocols should be built for safety measures such as trust protection, verification, authorization, data security, privacy maintenance and identification spoofing.

10.6.1   PHM Algorithms for Predictive Management

A. PHM algorithms taxonomy

As described at literature, and with several effective implementations, a wide variety of identification, prognostic and predictive techniques have been proposed. PHM approaches can usually be classified into two major groups, but there are also hybrid strategies:

1.) Data-driven approaches, that use tracking of the element health conditions performance information. These are obtained in tests and/or on-the-field and could be used where the element procedure is not easy to grasp or the element is really complicated that it is extremely costly to create a correct physical model. The reference list is definitely incomplete, as it contains literature reviews on some groups of algorithms, considering the vast amount of works in this field. Please note that the constraints of class algorithms are poor in some situations.

2.) Model-related techniques used to approximate its healthy conditions and forecast its decay using physical model part models. The benefits of using these models are that it could be used with modules that lose information from irregular operating environments. Data models in such situations cannot either detect the component's pathological behavior, nor can they forecast the direction of failure. Conversely, physics related models for the simulation of component-impacting deterioration and the RUL estimation can be established. These prototypes are at the base of Digital Twins as in the era of industry 4.0. However, physics simulations cannot often be established because they are very expensive and, thus, the consequences of environmental factors are also not entirely taken into consideration and depend on factors that are difficult to predict. Note that the prototypes of IoT-enabled PdM based on IoT data really aren't important.

B. Challenges

This is maintained by a proactive research and business loop, whereas research solutions strive to include industry with resources to develop as industry poses new research challenges. Despite usable PHM algorithms, businesses that wish to profit through Industry 4.0 also have to pay for PdM's capital costs for purchasing the necessary resources, technologies and expertise. This drawback is considered to be important at the outset of the growth of PdM if there is a shortage or scarcity of real evidence regarding normal and irregular behaviors, and where new technologies lack knowledge of activity. This can lead businesses to a loss of interest in PdM investments. The real challenge is to combine cost models with the flexible and stable frame working for directing PdM development in a structured and reasonable decision making framework: this should make it possible to update and adapt PHM algorithms based on the expertise, details, and data required in increments with the evolution from design to service that continually evolves, owing to component and sensor degradation, repair, updated component and system architecture, and improvements to environmental and operating conditions. These changes in machine behavior, commonly known as concept drifts or functions in a Evolving Environment (EE), threaten the implementation of PHM algorithms. In EDP, transition learning and gradual methods of learning have recently been discussed. The latter applies to the estimation of sample labeling from a destination domain, with labelled samples deriving out of the source domain and unlabeled samples deriving out of the target domain themselves. A cautious revision of the algorithms for this adjustment of the domain, which explains similar problems. This contribute primarily to computational and theoretical pressures and minimize analyst awareness of the particular usage of concern frequently needed to depart from several potential alternatives for appropriate reform. Iterative concepts and ideas can be broken between passive and aggressive approaches. Any time new data batches are available, the former adapts the empirical model. The labelling time series and iterative process retraining are important, and this is not always feasible. Only where a paradigm drift happens will successful methods cause the models to be adapted. Usually, the following groups are classified:

1.) Sequential evaluated methods that evaluate newly obtained signals again and again until it is slightly higher than the likelihood of future observation below different distribution than under the initial distribution.
2.) Database drift identification methods for the delivery of crude information from two different time windows: stable time series operating window and sliding frame containing the latest acquired information.
3.) Drift detection methods related to the success of learners are based on the development of a classifier and their error rate variations.

The drawbacks to introducing active techniques in PHM are simultaneous and autonomous tasks related to idea drift identification, data tagging and analytical model updating. This involves the use of various algorithms that use the same data stored in the time series data set for various reasons and at various times. In conclusion, it is possible to monitor the progress and efficiency of the PHM system and to enhance its adjustable characteristic of the techniques and the algorithms. Even so, computing and analytical burdens are required. The concern is how the production of PHM solutions can be streamlined, and thus quicker and easier.

10.6.2 Decision Making with Predictive Management

The knowledge on the RUL of the devices is used for PdM under various viewpoints until the PHM techniques has been established and verified for their results. PHM algorithms outlook is given in Table 10.6.1. The subsequent three are considered: security, enterprise and Operation and Maintenance (O&M).

A. Decision making for security
Predictive aspects will conceptually have a major effect on safety as they permit tracking of the risk of loss of sections, thus avoiding PdM failures (5).

Table I. PHM algorithms outlook.

Algorithm	Explanation	Advantages	Disadvantages
Markov Models (MM) including: 1. Hidden Markov Models (HMM); 2. Semi-Markov Models (SMM); 3. Hidden SMM	The Markov model follows a series of states representing partial reduction from new to failing. Transformation possibilities between provinces depend not on the way to progress but on the current situation and time to stay in the current state. HMM thinks that corruption is not directly visible.	1. Acceptable when discrete states can describe degradation; 2. Simple to interpret and even non-expert experts can clearly understand; 3. A sound literature can be dependent on.	1. Can be totally more cost and a great amount of simulations are necessary; 2. Require the deterioration status description and the transformation status likelihood estimation.
Artificial Neural Networks (ANN), including: 1. Convolutional NN; 2. Extreme Learning Machines (ELM); 3. Radial Basis Networks (RBN); 4. Recurrent Neural Networks (RNN);	ANNs consist of computing elements called neurons, which communicate with the input, secret and output layers through numerically weighted ties. Data from the training is used to construct regression models by changing the	Provides excellent functional mapping between input and output data points in many real PHM instances.	1. ANN demands vast volumes of training data to represent the true spectrum of data and variability; 2. Performance often depends on the user's ability to define the optimal environment (i.e. number

(Continued)

Table I. PHM algorithms outlook. (*Continued*)

Algorithm	Explanation	Advantages	Disadvantages
5. Echo State Networks (ESN); 6. Auto-Encoders; 7. Self Organizing Maps (SOM); 8. Long Short Term memory (LSTM);	weights of neuron links to minimize network errors. The educated ANN processes the new data and determines the predicted effects. The RNNs and their specialized variants (ESN, LSTM, etc.) are ANNs with input links to the previous layer from the hidden layer or from the Output layer. Those connections provide the ANN with the ability to accommodate the time dependence between the inputs and outputs. Auto-encoders are ANNs used in an unattended manner to learn effective data coding.		of neurons, layers, feature activation, etc.); 3. The service and preparation methods are black boxes since it is impossible to grasp the structures constructed, except qualitative models; 4. ANN can be reluctant to converge during the exercise

(*Continued*)

Table I. PHM algorithms outlook. (*Continued*)

Algorithm	Explanation	Advantages	Disadvantages
Statistical techniques, including: 1. Principal Components Analysis; 2. Regression Models (Linear, Logistic, etc.);	It relies on both the Bayesian framework and the frequents framework to provide a probabilistic interpretation of the results.	1. Rigorous theoretical background; 2. Confusion regarding the calculation of parameters.	1. Many data for frequent approaches are required; 2. Bayesian methods can be computationally expensive.
Instance-Based methods, including: 1. Fuzzy Similarity; 2. K-Nearest Neighbors; 3. Kernel Machines (e.g., Support Vector Machines, Relevance Vector Machines, Gaussian Fields, Auto Associative Kernel Regression);	On the basis of the data stored as a training sample, they measure the distance or similarity with the current training instances while they estimate the importance of a new iteration.	1. Small and large data sets are effective; 2. Can provide real-time analysis and ensure high generalization efficiency; 3. Can handle machine modeling that is not linear and complicated; 4. Models are specifically generated from their own training cases.	1. The tuning of parameters has a huge effect on performance; 2. Heavy use of memory to store all training events; 3. Over fitting hazard.

While a number of literature knowledge is documented on potential applications of PdM to security scenarios, there is still a lack of a formal modeling methodology quantifying PdM's benefit to security and security requirements still require several improvement measures needed in order for PDM development to evolve enough to be used in security circumstances. To improve this modeling approach, one should draw on the framework that formally establishes relationships between PDM supporting PHM algorithms and the possibility of a failure. This enables the specified threshold of a variety of success indicators to be established that maintain the optimal safety standard with acceptable margins relevant to uncertainty. In the other side, PHM can be combined with operators' behavior and automated control systems, in the hierarchical probabilistic risk analysis (PRA) models to combine dynamic forecasts and unreliability. A first effort is proposed that does not, nevertheless, take into consideration the dynamic existence of the forecasts. The capacity to model the effect of safety forecasts also enables reliability assignment schemes to be balanced by PdM deployments and consistency. Finally, for the writers of the best expertise, the effect of IoT on safety-critical applications remains to be a discovery field.

B. Decision making for enterprise

The indirect effect of the assumptions is a large part of the importance of PdM. The advantage of PdM for wind turbines, for example, could not only be generated from the resulting growth, but rather from better logistics for triggered maintenance. In production facilities, economic advantages of PdM can be obtained from warehouse management and can be assisted by RUL expertise. Time-efficiency saving has to be minimized. PdM's industry, sector, includes marketing chance to provide drivers with the driver's present and restful wellbeing, by using this convincing technology. until there is a loss. Opportunities of sales are given by seminar facilities: the after-sales team can advise on scheduling a special arrangement at the reception desk for a very quick action. Discount on spare parts. In comparison, this increases customer satisfaction. Further gains are extracted from the agency's tracking and are the means of enhancing reclassification of agent stock plans and the distribution of after-sales expenditures to distributors, depending on their sales efficiency.

C. Decision making for Operation & Maintenance

The PdM research needs to take resource management decisions and must take the effect of maintenance on infrastructure, security, budgets and so on into account, in order to take full advantage of the prediction power.

A systematic maintenance of the asset is also called rigid maintenance. In order to provide optimum options for the administration of maintenance at the asset level, different asset maintenance programs are combined. For instance, while predictive maintenance can suggest revision of application fixtures, a prescriptive approach can also advise the decision making that the duration for malfunction to the planned maintenance window can be increased if device steps are slowed down, and if the expected production needs will have to be satisfied. Prescriptive processes should be 'cognitive' in order to do this, which means focusing on sophisticated technologies at the crossroads of data analytics, artificial intelligence and interpretation.

10.7   Research Challenges in the Maintenance of Internet of Things

The reality is the IoT software and the examples mentioned is very fascinating, offering smart devices with all, but the IoT definition is difficult to incorporate in terms of expense (6). The presumption that a huge amount of entities would provide the technology at a minimal cost. IoT confronts several other challenges as well, for example:

A. Scalability: IoT seems to have a major idea that things collaborate in an open world, than the traditional Internet devices. Thus, the fundamental functionality, such as collaboration and service discovery ought to operate in small and large-scale contexts equally effectively. In order to achieve effective operation for optimization, the IoT needs a fresh function and process.

B. Self-organization: Smart things must not be administered as systems which need their customers to personalize and adjust to unique circumstances. Mobile objects, frequently used only intermittently, have to randomly attach to be able to arrange and set up in their own convenient manner.

C. Data capacity: Certain network implementation examples include rare connectivity and the information-gathering of sensor networks, or the formulation of infrastructure and large-scale networks, gathers a tremendous amount of data on servers. Furthermore, emerging technology for stocking, processing and administration, this phenomenon entails massive data, which includes multiple operating mechanisms.

D. Data interpretation: The local meaning defined by sensors has to be understood as correctly as possible to help the users of intelligent things. In order to allow service providers to draw any generalizable assumptions on the perceived sensors data, the fragmented data that will be produced.

E. Interoperability: The Internet provides numerous data, retrieval and communication possibilities for each category of intelligent objects. Various intelligent objects will also be prone to various factors such as supply of resources and bandwidth requirements for communications. Common norms are needed to promote contact and collaboration between such entities.

F. Software rigidity: In order to handle and maintain intelligent objects, further detailed software architecture would be required on the network and context servers. This is because smart object computing systems, like traditional embedded devices, had to deal with limited resources.

G. Privacy and security issues: Other standards of the Internet of Things will be essential in regard to the security and safety facets of the Internet, including in the area of data secrecy, accuracy and continuity of communication parties and message credibility. Any services must be reached or the contact with other IoT goods must be stopped, and smart business concerns need to be shielded from the public scrutiny of competitions.

H. Fault forbearance: Entities in IoT are much more versatile and portable than software and unanticipated change. Organizing a stable and trusting internet of things will require several layers of reliability and the ability to respond to changing situations instantly.

I. Power Supply: Objects normally go around without being powered, so their cleverness must be powered by an autonomous source of energy. Then while passive RFID transmitters would not require a source of energy of their own, they do have very minimal features and communications. Former low energy processors and connectivity units for embedded devices with substantially lower energy function are expected. Energy savings is not only a consideration in the design of hardware and systems, but in software like implementing protocol stacks, in which any single byte of communication must explain its presence.

J. Wireless Communications: Ever-powered wireless technology, such as GSM, UMTS, Wi-Fi and Bluetooth are much less suitable; more current

WPAN protocols such as Zig Bee and other already in the process, will consume far less bandwidth, but they do utilize notably low power.

Related Future Technologies of Internet of Things
Numerous emerging developments connected to IoT to demonstrate the convergence of wired/wireless control, connectivity and IT techniques that link several sub-systems and stuff that work expertly under a single network.

A. Cloud Computing

The Cloud and Internet of Things have been changing rapidly and independently (7). Both environments are somewhat dissimilar from one another but their attributes are also augmented by IoT, particularly, in order to remunerate for its technical shortcomings, for example space, refining and communications, by nearly infinite space and power of the cloud. Cloud is able to provide an efficient result for IoT service handling and configuration and also developing software and services that take advantage of the knowledge they create. By widening its range to cover real-world matters in a much more complex and dispersed way and to include new applications in a wide range of real-world contexts, cloud will gain through IoT. In many ways, cloud will provide the intermediary layer between items and apps that masks the complexities and flexibility required to execute them. In this way, new problems are created, in particular in a cloud-based system or fog cloud, through the collection, analysis, and transfer of information. Additionally, fast configuration and incorporation of new items, Cloud allows IoT application to allow data storage and data analysis, while at the same time retaining minimal development costs and complicated data processing costs. Cloud seems to be the most suitable and cost effective approach for handling IoT-produced data and provides additional data collection, collaboration and sharing possibilities with external parties. When entered in the cloud, information can be viewed as homogeneous by means of very well APIs, secured with superior protection and accessible directly from anywhere.

B. Big Data

The exponential growth of the networks means that in physical areas, the numerous gadgets and sensors within the networks are growing incrementally, that would change the data conveying networks, services, technologies in different domains. Desires for next year indicate that about 50 billion gadgets in the various field of smart grids, intellective housing, medical treatment, robotics, travel, infrastructure and environmental observation would produce vast quantities of the information from multiple technologies and services. The corresponding technology and methods that permit incorporation of modern world information and services into the present information networking techniques are also defined underneath the term Internet of Things. There is already an increasing amount of data on the network and the internet. Approximately 2.5 quintillion bytes of data are produced each day, and an approximate 90% of data generated today over the last 2 years. Gathered data from sensors can be processed and converted into actual data for us to achieve a deeper view of our physical environment and produce more value for resources. Such sensory data as data from prediction and steady power use on intelligent grids, analyzed data on contamination, climate and clogging, sensory data captured to provide enhanced traffic regulation and control, and data obtained by sensory tools to provide better health care facilities to track and evaluate health signals. Additionally, social media info and real environment findings and measurements submitted by the users can provide a great deal of information (Big Data). The incorporation of IoT of data from different physical, cyber and communication tools helps software and services to be built that can take into integrate circumstances and context perception and produce smarter applications and improved services in strategic planning processes. Furthermore, machine accessible and comprehensible data descriptions, problems relating to integrations, automation and information analytics would involve common data interpretation and data representation structures for large quantities of distributed and mixed IoT data.

C. Distributed Computing

For the same computing reason, the distributed computing employs sets of computers for tasks. Distributed computation has many similar problems with parallel and competitive computing, as all three fall within the realm of scientific computing. A significant range of scalable information technologies, along with domestic appliances virtualization, service-oriented infrastructure and stand-alone and computer technology, have now contributed to cloud computing. IoT of distributed information technologies reflects a future where the Internet expands to real-life objects. Real objects are not isolated from the digital universe but can be controlled remotely and serve as physical approach values to internet resource.

D. Fog Computing

Fog computing is synonymous with cloud edge computing. Unlike cloud, fog platforms are represented at the edge of the network as dense computer architectures. Features such as minimal delay, location recognition and use of cellular networking are allegedly included. Although edge computing can only mean analyzes of devices on or near the edge of the network, a fog enumerating architecture can analyze anything between the middle of your network and the edge. IoT will most definitely be enabled by carbon computing, where the enumerating, storing, managing and networking capacity of data center, server, edge devices like access points or routers will occur everywhere in the network, edge appliances such as a computer or in sensors.

E. Security and Privacy

Since IoT apps are capable of accessing various technical domains and participation in various ownership plans, a confidence mechanism is required to allow device users to be assured that they can indeed rely on information and resources that are shared. The assurance system must be able to interact with people and machines as consumers, since it must transfer confidence to humans and must be sufficiently stable to be used in devices without a negation of service. In areas such as dedicated public key infrastructures (PKI), development would be necessary to build assurance mechanisms that deal with that requirement. Dedicated key management frame work are used to make the use of minimal interactions and processing scheme to encrypt trust, in keeping with the resource-restricted existence of several IoT devices.

IoT applications need metadata database consistency that can be used to test their IoT data responsibility. A new way of measuring trust in individuals, devices and data is needed for IoT-related systems. Among the most widely used ways of negotiating the trust requires two parties to agree the minimal trust level necessary to enable access to a facility or bit of data immediately, according to a sequence of trust policies. IoT uses approaches to deter untrustworthy data abuses by testing the mechanism to make such information correctly used in compliance with a predefined protocol after the granting of access to data.

Recently, the IoT has become a core component of internet smart devices, and is increasingly necessary to ensuring sufficient security for the IoT infrastructure. A wide-ranging device and IoT-based facilities are increasingly vulnerable to attack disruptions or identity stealing. Many sophisticated protection methods in many fields will have to ensure that IoT is protected from threats, fraud and several other safety problems, including Disk operating System attacks, hacked nodes and malware code hacking threats. As IoT is vulnerable to these attacks, complex procedures and mechanisms will have to be enforced to assure travel, electricity and urban infrastructure is not disabled or weakened.

In order to support the different authorizations and templates that are needed by the customer, the IoT includes a range of access control and related accounting systems. New dedicated systems need to be built because of the heterogeneity and variability of devices/gateways which require access control. Without the aid of human intervention, IoT must perform nearly all modes of action itself, similar to AI. A self-controlled IoT requires new techniques and methods including, for example, machine learning. In IoT-related systems, cryptographic methods are often very necessary to allow data security means to be accessed and exchanged without other parties needing to control information contents. These technologies are possible candidates for creating such methods like homomorphic and discoverable encryption.

10.8 Summary

The internet of things (IoT) is a phenomenon that is going to have a major influence on the planet. Some people appear to be doubtful of this theory and whether it would influence society adversely or positively. This is very valuable and can be used to support and enrich people's lives worldwide [13]. Humans can be more protected, as they are capable of tracking and safeguarding their life and food patterns from intruders. It would also support corporations all over the nation by the quality of their plans and goods. The benefits of the IoT certainly outweigh the drawbacks and the IoT would have a beneficial effect on the planet. IoT is a massive and diverse multi-national internet-enabled business network system for web services. The Smart Grid would be one of IoT's major applications (SG). SG is an interconnected data exchange network that gathers and analyzes data from transmission, distribution and consumer using the energy grid. All is about IoT and SG, and their relation. Certain IoT architectures in SG, IoT technologies and IoT facilities and specifications in SG, and problems and future work are described. Predictive maintenance would be one of industry 4.0's more practical applications. It permits the collection of statistical data from computers and diligent systems management. It uses a description and realistic examples to illustrate how maintenance is predictive. This revolutionary idea should be motivated and looked at every day in order to better our lives.

References

1. Kumar, D. R., Krishna, T. A., & Wahi, A. (2018). Health Monitoring Framework for in Time Recognition of Pulmonary Embolism Using Internet

of Things. Journal of Computational and Theoretical Nanoscience, 15(5), 1598–1602.

2. Al - omar, B., Al – Ali, A.R., Ahmed, R., Landolsi, T. Role of Information and communication technologies in the smart grid, Journal of Emerging trends in computing and information science, Vol.3, p.707-716, 2012.

3. Ramakrishnan, V., Chenniappan, P., Dhanaraj, R. K., Hsu, C. H., Xiao, Y., & Al-Turjman, F. (2021). Bootstrap aggregative mean shift clustering for big data anti-pattern detection analytics in 5G/6G communication networks. *Computers & Electrical Engineering*, 95, 107380.

4. Gungor, V.C., Sahin, D., Kocak, T., Ergut, S., Buccella, C., Cocati, C. and Hancke, G.P.A., survey on smart grid potential Applications and Communication requirements, IEEE transacting on Industrial Informations, Vol.9, p.28-42,2013.

5. Kumar, R. N., Chandran, V., Valarmathi, R. S., & Kumar, D. R. (2018). Bitstream Compression for High Speed Embedded Systems Using Separated Split Look Up Tables (LUTs). Journal of Computational and Theoretical Nanoscience, 15(5), 1719–1727.

6. Krishnasamy, L., Ramasamy, T., Dhanaraj, R., & Chinnasamy, P. (2021). A geodesic deployment and radial shaped clustering (RSC) algorithm with statistical aggregation in sensor networks. Turkish Journal of Electrical Engineering & Computer Sciences, 29(3).

7. A.R.Al-Ali, RanfatAburukha, Role of Internet of Things in the Smart grid technology, vol.3, p.229-233,2015.

8. PallaviSethi, Smruthi R. Sarangi, Internet of Things: Architecture , Protocols and Applications, Journal of Electrical and Computer Engineering ,2017.

9. Nickkadanvar, Energy Management: The Internet of Things changes everything, Embedded computing design, 2019.

10. Dhiviya, S., Malathy, S., & Kumar, D. R. (2018). Internet of Things (IoT) Elements, Trends and Applications. Journal of Computational and Theoretical Nanoscience, 15(5), 1639–1643.

11. AlfredoVaccaro, Ahmed F.Zobar, PrabhakarKarthikeyanShanmugam, Research Trends and Challenges in Smart grid, University of Sannio,Benevento,2020.

12. Faheem, M., Shah, S.B.H., Butt, R.A., Raza, B., Anwar, M., Ashraf, M.W., Ngadi, M.A. and Gungor, V.C., Smart grid communication and information technologies in the perspective of Industry 4.0: Opportunities and challenges. Computer Science Review, 30, pp.1-30, 2018

13. S.Malathy, Dr.C.N.Vanitha, "Secure Integration of Cyber Security and Internet of Things in Addressing its Challenges", International Journal of Recent Technology and Engineering, ISSN: 2277-3878,Volume 8, Issue 4, November 2019.

14. K.Vanitha, C.N.Vanitha, M.Mohamed Musthafa, S.Malathy, "Efficient Semantic Interrogation Scheme over Cryptographic Data in Cloud" IEEE Xplore Digital Library, DOI:10.1109/ICICT48043.2020.9112383, June 2020.

15. Dr.Vanitha C.N, Malathy.S "Optimizing wireless sensor networks path selection using Resource levelling technique in transmitting endscopy biomedical data", IEEE Xplore Digital Library, DOI: 10.1088/1757-899X/1055/1/012071.

11

Intelligent Home Appliance Energy Monitoring with IoT

**S. Tamilselvan[1], D. Deepa[1]*, C. Poongodi[1], P. Thangavel[2]
and Sarumathi Murali[3]**

*[1]Bannari Amman Institute of Technology, Sathyamangalam, India
[2]Kongu Engineering College, Perundurai, India
[3]University of Sydney, NSW, Australia*

Abstract

Energy monitoring for home appliances is an emerging requirement for better consumption and preservation of energy. Ample studies have focused on smart home applications through the Internet of Things (IoT) technology. Over 94 percent of automations are done on this smart home application worldwide. This mechanism extends an ample range of research spots to enhance smart home energy monitoring. Furthermore, the added intelligence to the smart home greatly reduces the burden of decision making and monitoring the home appliances based on various operating conditions. The Home appliance control makes life comfortable for everyone. By controlling the heating and cooling applications, 64% of the energy may be saved. Since these devices are connected to the centralized IoT controller, that is programmed to monitor the energy consumption and give periodic notifications on energy consumption. Also, any abrupt changes in energy consumption will be immediately notified and decision may be taken accordingly. Monitoring the energy consumption of home appliance is done with IoT based controllers and the sensors. A dedicated app is created to update the status of all the electrical items. End nodes are connected to the gateway by using the connectivity protocols like Bluetooth Low Energy (BLE), Wi-Fi or RF technology, and the data from the sensors are uploaded into the cloud via the communication protocols like The Hypertext Transfer Protocol, Constrained Application Protocol and The Message Queuing Telemetry Transport.

In recent times, home automation may be of security based, Lifestyle and Convenience based, Smart living based, Smart lighting based and Climate

---

*Corresponding author: ddeepa@bitsathy.ac.in

P. Sanjeevikumar, Rajesh Kumar Dhanaraj, Malathy Sathyamoorthy, Jens Bo Holm-Nielsen
and Balamurugan Balusamy (eds.) *Smart Grids and Internet of Things: An Energy Perspective*,
(319–338) © 2023 Scrivener Publishing LLC

controlling based automation. This work adds an additional feature with the existing techniques like turning off light through a customized app when not in use and
adjusting the light brightness according to the climate and bedtime there by reducing electricity usage. Next major energy savings can be done through pathway light.
The lights will be turned on in the roads and home only when an object or person
is detected. It greatly reduces the consumption rate above 70%. When compared to
the existing automations, this proposed method will monitor and notify 24x7 the
unwanted changes or abrupt consumption of energy. So this method could reduce
the energy consumption by 65% to 78% in the faulty system and 48% on the normal systems. For monitoring the energy GUI featured clouds could be the best
choice, because anyone can easily understand without much technical knowledge.
This system can be applied in buildings, floors and rooms for electrical equipment
monitoring and control. Also the same can be used in schools, colleges, shopping
malls, showrooms, offices, etc., where the control of electricity usage is required.

Keywords: Internet of Things, energy monitoring, energy consumption, sensors
and controllers

11.1   Introduction

Intelligent Home Appliance Energy Monitoring with IoT will lead the world
in future. The reason behind this statement is that, nowadays in the busy
schedule of human life it is very difficult to monitor or control the usage of
home appliances. Sometimes people forget to switch off the appliance for
the entire day without their knowledge. This leads to more consumption
of energy and waste of energy. No one will be able to utilize this wasted
energy and in turn would be able to meet the energy deficiency. The impact
of this will reflect on the electricity bill and it is difficult to exactly find
where the system went wrong. A smart solution for the above mentioned
problem is Intelligent Home Appliance Energy Monitoring (IHAEM) with
IoT as this will help to warn before the energy utilization reaches the above
average level and the people may take necessary decisions. It provides a
tracking mechanism to visualise the energy consumption details ranging
from minutes to years. For example, if many lights and fans in home are left
ON, then this IHAEM will give an alert signal to turn them OFF and also
it controls the appliances from handheld mobile devices.

11.2   Survey on Energy Monitoring

IoT is an innovative communication and network concept developed,
and various research have been made to know the IoT based energy

monitoring. To further emphasize, the electrical energy requirement will increase for both the commercial and residential applications by 2025 [1]. To satisfy this rising demand, smart grids (SGs) may be involved in either of the two programs: Power plants may be installed for generation and Demand Response programs may be involved for managing the energy generated [2]. In-home Plugin Hybrid Electric Vehicles (PHEVs) will be used by end users for storing energy when it is generated in the daytime and usage of energy in night-time for the benefit, from the expense what they have spent. The authors in References [3 to 10] have reported may smart grid systems for home automation and energy management techniques. Fortino [11] proposed an architecture named as multi-layered agent-based architecture to design, develop and implement smart objects based on the scenario required through a Jadex agents-based middleware. This design considered devices from sensitive to active, from minimumto huge size, and from independent to dependent. Gubbi [12] presented an idea for cloud based IoT. This paper discusses the key technologies and innovations made using the concept of IoT. Atzori [13] analyzed, import ant requirements arising from the work that combines social networking concepts into the cloud based IoT. Cirani [14] proposed a work of measurable and configuring architecture for large-scale IoT. This will offer independent services and resource discovery mechanisms without human involvement and as smart systems. This paper deals with both limited and comprehensive service.

Various issues on energy problems are addressed on a ZigBee-based HEMS that, is discussed in the field of consumer electronics [15–17]. The methods proposed utilizes IEEE 802.15.4 standard for various types of wireless networks and implementation. In the works [18, 19] the framework for multiplatform domain based on House Area network, wireless sensor and actuator networks for enabling efficient and effective building management was proposed. [8] presented a system to gather energy consumption which is mandatory and requirement from household appliances. Based on the cost function model the work in [20] has been proposed with a scattered home energy management framework.

Hu and Li [21] proposed and implemented a smart HEMS with the functions of sensors, communication devices, and deep learning methodologies. In the paper [22] a solution for DR for residential users is proposed and implemented.

Considering the cost and power consumption, the ZigBee wireless communication technology has been adopted in the PV systems. In the paper [23] a performance measuring system is proposed for distributed solar panels. [24] presented a three-level monitoring which is for systems, string and module schemes for fault diagnosis of PV systems. In the paper [25] HEMS integrated with a PV system has been designed. It deals with the energy organization system which gets the data from the PV system and home appliances and is used to control the system with the generated solar energy.

In the works proposed in the papers [26–29] various energy management studies has need varied out and RTPS DR programs are used in these methods based on the performance it is identified that the complexity is more.

11.3 Internet of Things System Architecture

The Internet of Things architecture shown in Figure 11.1 consists of IoT End node sensors, controller, Gateway, Cloud and the Remote Access Machine.

The IoT End Node: The IoT End Node has the IoT controller, Sensors and actuators.

Gateway: Gateways provide the connectivity to the IoT End Node to exchange data with cloud using any communication protocols. Here the connectivity protocols include Wi-Fi, ZigBee, Bluetooth or any other RF

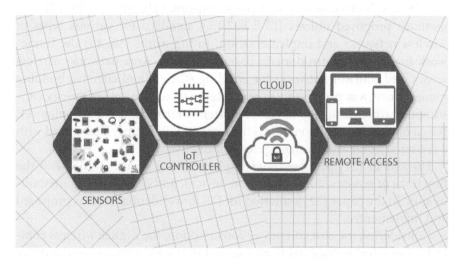

Figure 11.1 IoT system architecture.

technology. Whereas the communication protocols such as MQTT, HTTP, XAMPP, CoAP or other can be used.

Cloud: This will store the sensor data received from the IoT End Nodes and Sends the data to be processed by the remote machine.

Remote Access Machine: Remote Access Machine on the other hand will use any processer based system to analyse the data and send controlling information back into the IoT End Node.

Connectivity Protocol: Wi-Fi
It offers the energy monitoring within accessible distance and if it is connected to the internet, then accessible from anywhere. Bluetooth connectivity is a better alternative but not that much efficient like Wi-Fi.

Architectures can have 3 or 5 layers. In three layer modes application layer, network layer and Perception layers are the most essential blocks available.

11.4 Proposed Energy Monitoring System with IoT

Measurement Techniques:
Current sensor is used to measure the current for a fixed voltage to the appliances and the energy consumption is calculated from the current and voltage over a period of time.

Installation Compatibility:
In order to implement this IHAEM system, there is no need to modify the entire electrical wiring setup in the home. Just an extra controller along with the relays could be added to the existing wiring connections and could be automated easily.

Manual and Automated mode:
While controlling the home appliances, this system offers to work both in manual and automated mode. In automated mode, the predefined programs will take care of turning ON and turning OFF of the appliances based on the situation. But, if the customer likes to operate the electrical appliances manually, then they could choose the manual mode also. So it won't affect the normal working procedure available in the home.

Solar panel Monitoring:
The additional feature of this IHAEM system is that it also incorporates the solar energy for balanced usage. If the solar energy is sufficient, then it switches to the solar panel instead of EB supply. Hence better cost and energy savings can be achieved.

Avoids power failure:
Since the individual components health status is measured frequently, the unexpected power failures and components breaking could be avoided using this method. It informs about the malfunctioning well in advance and prompts to repair or replace the particular components then and there.

11.5   Energy Management Structure (Proposed)

The energy management structure is explained here. The IoT based Sharing System Operators (SSO) convey the Stipulated Response (SR) programs like Pricing System in terms of Time (PSiTT), Future Pricing System (FPS) and Concurrent Pricing System (CPS) are simulate to achieve the power management of housing units by using the Stipulated Response (SR) signal received. The housing units are provided with the Smart refrigerators, Smart TV, Wireless Home area Network (WHAN), Smart Energy Meter, Smart Lighting and more. The proposed system schematic view is shown in Figure 11.2.

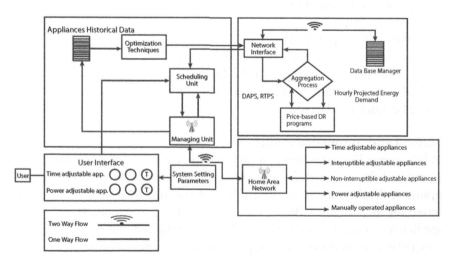

Figure 11.2 IoT energy management framework. Source: https://www.ncbi.nlm.nih.gov/pmc/articles/PMC7313710/figure/sensors-20-03155-f002/

11.6   Implementation of the System

11.6.1   Implementation of IoT Board

Figure 11.3 shows the hardware implementation of the proposed Lightweight Photovoltaic System (LPS). The LPS has a power controller unit. If any AC appliances need to be operated, then the DC power from LPS will be converted by the inverter.

The Energy Monitoring & Controlling Unit (EMCU) will have a sensors & actuators along with the IoT Controllers. These controllers were connected with the gateway using anyone connectivity protocols (Just to provide an internet service to the things). Using the communication protocols the gateway connected to the cloud and communicates with the database. These two units were knows as Communication Units (CU). The data stored in the cloud will be analysed using Personal Computer (PC) or by handheld devices like mobile phone via app. This unit is called as Analysis Unit (AU).

11.6.2   Software Implementation

✓ Cloud

The MySql database could be created in virtual machine to log the sensor details and status information and the same can be accessed from virtual location using PHP code. We have paid clouds like AWS, IBM, Google cloud and more to provide these services from the scratch or GUI with monthly payment basis.

If you design a basic demo model, then a built in GUI based cloud services like Adafruit, Thingspeak, Firebase, Blynk and more can be used. The only restriction is the

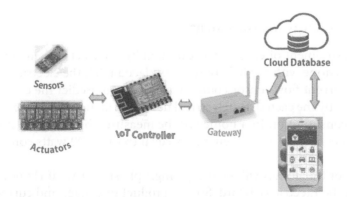

Figure 11.3 Hardware implementation of proposed system.

number of hits per minute (30 hits per minute). The duration in which the data retained in the cloud will be limited to couple of weeks (maximum of 30 days).

✓ Analytics tools
The data stored in the cloud will be analysed either in cloud or using a PC or mobile phone app. Various app service provides like Android Studio, Flutter or MIT app inventor used to design the app based on the user needs. The outcome of the analysis report will be in the form of graphs and charts which displays the energy consumption details &decision making like to turn a device ON or OFF.

11.7   Smart Home Automation Forecasts

The functionality of the IHAEM is shown in the Figure 11.4. The functions of IoT controller are

1. Energy Measurement
2. Irregularity Detection
3. Finding the problems with the device
4. Periodically updating the status in the cloud
5. Indicating the house owner about the issues
6. Suggesting for the remedial actions

IHAEM is a methodology cum device to monitor the energy consumption in a smart home and saves the energy being wasted in various applications using artificial intelligence added in the IoT controller.

11.7.1   Energy Measurement

The measurement of energy consumption by the electrical and electronic devices is done with the help of sensors placed in all the electrical devices. Simple current flow sensor could be sufficient to predict the current consumption by the each of the electrical devices in an hour basis. Because, the energy consumption in a home will be measured by using the unit kWh (kilo-watts hour). 1 unit of energy is equal to the 1000 watts consumed in an hour.

Most of the homes will be using single phase 230 V, 50 Hz power supplyfrom the Electricity Board. So, the product of voltage and current gives the power in watts. Here the voltage is fixed to 230V and if we measure the

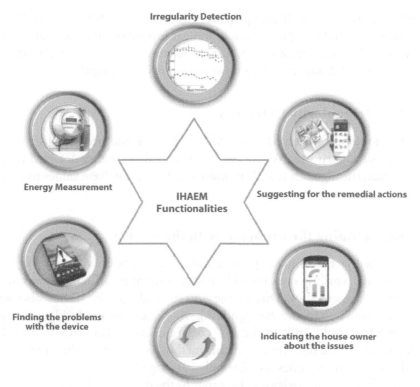

Figure 11.4 Functionalities of the IHAEM.

current alone using current sensor, then the energy consumption can be found easily.

11.7.2 Periodically Updating the Status in the Cloud

The measured energy consumption details will be updated into the cloud using any IoT controllers. By using the connectivity protocols like Bluetooth Low Energy (BLE), Wi-Fi or RF technology, end nodes are connected to the gateway and via the communication protocols like HTTP, XAMPP, CoAP and MQTT the sensor data are uploaded into the cloud. In recent days Wi-Fi, MQTT and API based updating is followed.

The clouds like Amazon Web Services (AWS), Google Cloud Database can be customized using algorithms. Free clouds will serve the same with restricted amount of hits. The hit in the cloud refers to the data uploading or reading into the cloud database. Free clouds may have customized but limited channel usage. It also provides Graphical User Interface (GUI) for the better visibility of the data in graphical format or chart format. In the case of paid cloud, we can even customize from the scratch or we can use the existing GUI interfacing to show the energy consumption.

11.7.3   Irregularity Detection

In the cloud, the received data will be cleaned and analysed using the intelligence algorithms. Whenever there is an abnormality detected in the cloud data, the algorithm will compare it with the database values to check for the issues.

11.7.4   Finding the Problems with the Device

Device used as the home appliance may perform poor with aging or due to the faulty working conditions like short circuiting which may result in the heavy current flow. Due to the current leakage, the device also will consume more than the average level. This could be easily identified by setting a threshold limit in the IoT controller itself. This could avoid the delay in taking the decision. Also, this method is known as edge computing method. Such techniques are also called as Edge IoT.

Apart from the above issues, there may be the problems like; the device will be working during off hours (when not needed). For example, the night lamps may glow even in the day time. Refrigerator may run without any items in it. TVs may run without any people. So many issues will come if these devices work beyond the limited time and energy is always wasted due to these issues. So to have low energy consumption, an IHAEM system is to be implemented.

For an example,
- ✓ The corridor lights may turn on only when it detects people.
- ✓ Private room light may be used if and only if there is an occupant.
- ✓ Air-conditions may run with the people availability.
- ✓ Fans may run only if the temperature of the room is above the people temperature.

Also, overall energy consumptions could be informed to the consumers in a periodical interval of time. Also daily statistics will be informed to the consumers through dedicated app.

It also informs about the energy consumptions above the average level on daily basis.

11.7.5   Indicating the House Owner About the Issues

It acts like prepaid mobile phone. Initially the consumers can set a monthly amount and they get notifications based on their need (like hourly/daily/monthly/between billing cycles). Actually customer need not pay like prepaid bill. But the system will assume like that amount is recharged like prepaid mobile phone and gives alert like call history and amount utilised. So the customers can plan accordingly.

11.7.6   Suggestions for Remedial Actions

The following suggestions may be considered for remedial action for energy saving

- ✓ Use energy efficient appliances.
- ✓ Turnoff the light when not in use
- ✓ Unplugging the device when it is not going to be used for few or more days.
- ✓ Also cheese a right and good monitoring device to get updates periodically and that can take decision by its own.
- ✓ It recommends you to unplug the devices which are not in use for the long period of time
- ✓ So if we use the real time monitoring system (laptop/desktop) or mobile app, it alerts the unwanted energy consumption situation like refrigerator door open.
- ✓ IHAEM will also checks the internet about the latest low power devices available in the market to replace your old device when the power consumption is more than 20% (Can be adjusted based on our need)
- ✓ For example, if our home FAN consumes 600 kWh and if a product with 400 kWh is available in the market, then it suggests or notifies you to check for the replacement.

With the out dated and aged appliances, most of the electricity is being wasted every minute. For an example, a 10 years old refrigerator could use 1000 kWh of electricity per year, when compared to the energy saving refrigerator newly available in the market which consumes less than 500 kWh. This would save the energy consumption by 50% of what normally consumed. So you may imagine, if all the items were updated then it reduces our energy bill by 50% what we rare paying actually.

This IHAEM intelligent solution will give you suggestions to plan accordingly. Based on the need you may choose a plan which will be calculated based on the daily average consumption and number of appliances used. It also gives you an overview of how many hours that you can use a specific alliance within the billing periods.

11.8   Energy Reduction Based on IoT

11.8.1   House Energy Consumption (HEC) - Cost Saving

The test bed decides the range of pricing for this HEC. Network formed inside the house using the Bluetooth communication makes reliable communication with all the gateways. Depending on the number of rooms available and the size of the room inside the house, two or more gateways were needed.

Recently the Bluetooth Low Energy (BLE) makes reliable communication between 10m area with lowest energy consumption. This technique is also known as Bluetooth 4.0 and it may extend up to 100m. But depending on the physical arrangements and appearance of the room like (walls, types of floors, types materials used inside the rooms, Electronic items used inside and communication devices such as WiFi routers which produces the strong electromagnetic waves) and other environmental parameters, the maximum coverage area may be affected (usually decreases the coverage area). In such situations, the number of gateways required may be increased more than the usual count. Based on the previous experiences, it is suggested to use minimum two gateways in a room and minimum eight gateways with sockets connected to the Ethernet is required in the HAN test bed. In the absence of such sockets, installation of Ethernet would increase the cost. During hardware failure conditions, huge amount is required to replace the entire system and this cost will further increased in the case of large buildings.

11.9   Performance Evaluation

11.9.1   Data Analytics and Visualization

The data analysis is made based on the number of appliances in the home, their daily usage in hours, number of days the appliance is used, rated power of the appliance and total energy consumption by the appliance per month. There are devices and appliances that consume power even when

Table 11.1 Typical energy consumption of a home.

Home appliances	No of items	Average daily use (hrs)	No of days used	Rated power (w)	Total energy consumption in a month (kWh)
CFL bulb	2	05	30	0.018	0.01
Tube light	4	05	30	0.025	0.02
Energy saver light	2	05	30	0.015	0.00
LED TV	1	07	30	0.040	0.01
Iron box	1	02	08	1.500	0.02
Kettle	1	0.5	23	1.000	0.01
Hote plate	1	01	24	1.000	0.02
Refrigerator	1	10	30	0.250	0.08

Table 11.2 Hidden energy usage of household appliances.

Product	On (watts)	Off (watts)
Apple TV	21W	17W
Samsung Cable Box*	28W, Recording	26W, Not Recording
Apple MacBook Charger	Plugged In 28W Charging	27W, Fully Charged
Netgear Router*	4W	0W
Technicolor Cable Modem*	15W	0W
Vizio HDTV*	21W	1W
Game Console*	27W	23W, Plugged In
Cuisinart Toaster	876W	0W
Krups Coffee Maker	922W	3W

* Rarely turned OFF, almost always in use.

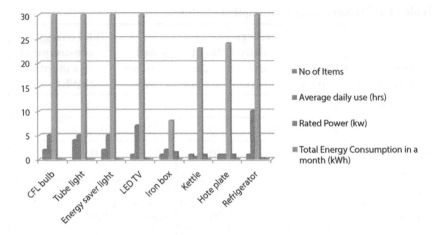

Figure 11.5 Typical energy consumption of a home. Source: https://www.aepenergy.com/wp-content/uploads/2017/07/final-chart.jpg

they are not turned on and few devices consume power when they are plugged. Therefore, in the analysis for energy consumption and methods of saving energy, the hidden energy usage of household appliances is also to be considered as shown in Tables 11.1 & 11.2. Figure 11.5 shows the typical energy consumption of a home.

11.10   Benefits for Different User Categories

The benefits of different user categories depend on the factors like Installation Compatibility, Wired or wireless communication (between gateway and End nodes), Accurate measurement of Voltage, Current and Power, energy theft identification and Reliability of the system. Hence these benefits are also to be considered in implementing an energy efficient smart home.

11.11   Results and Discussion with Benefits of User Categories

Data from the previous history
It gives access to the energy data from the past month or year. This will guide you to choose a plan for the forth coming months.

Live Energy monitoring
Can visualize all the appliances connected to the internet anytime at anywhere from the world.

Controlling appliances in Real time

All the connected appliances can be set or reset (Turned ON or OFF) easily anytime at anywhere from the world.

Virtual Assistance for energy monitoring

This IHAEM will act as virtual assistant for personalized monitoring and controlling appliances with its health details. It gives periodical notification about everything inside your home.

Complete Home Optimisation

Efficient home automation with added intelligence provides complete solution under one control.

Figure 11.6 IHAEM app sample view.

11.12   Summary

This method also provides a customized user interfacing via app to visualize all the energy related parameters and to control the appliances. The following are the highlighted features of the IHAEM app and the sample view is shown in Figure 11.6.

Features of IHAEM app:
   ✓ Daily consumption details
   ✓ GUI
   ✓ Chart based representation
   ✓ Billing details
   ✓ Reminder for paying the bills
   ✓ Alerts for abrupt consumption
   ✓ Current leakage notification
   ✓ Shows the details of each appliances separately
   ✓ Overall energy usage prediction
   ✓ Estimate the bill based on user suggestion
   ✓ No need of internet within 100 meters range
   ✓ Can control all appliances anywhere from the world
   ✓ User friendly menus
   ✓ Customised settings
   ✓ Available in Local language
   ✓ Supports all android and IOS mobile platforms
   ✓ Supports all OS (Windows, Linux, MAC etc)
   ✓ Available in hourly, daily, weekly, monthly and yearly views
   ✓ Live Energy monitoring
   ✓ Instant updates
   ✓ Downloading detailed Report of the energy consumptions ranging from minutes to years details
   ✓ Sets the ideal device to sleep mode
   ✓ Saves money in a better way than ever

References

1. Energy Reports. [(accessed on 10 February 2019)]; Available online: http://www.enerdata.net/enerdatauk/press-and-publication/energyfeatures/enerfuture-2007.php.

2. FERC Demand Response Compensation in Organized Wholesale Energy markets, FERC Docket RM101700. [(accessed on 18 March 2019)]; Available online: http://www.ferc.gov/eventcalender/files/20110315105757RM101700.pdf.

3. Hafeez G., Khan A.W., Judge M.A., Iqbal Z., Javaid N. International Conference on P2P, Parallel, Grid, Cloud, and Internet Computing. Springer; Cham, Switzerland: 2017. Optimal Residential Load Scheduling Under Utility and Rooftop PV units.

4. Chandraprabha, M., & Dhanaraj, R. K. (2020, November 5). Machine learning based Pedantic Analysis of Predictive Algorithms in Crop Yield Management. 2020 4th International Conference on Electronics, Communication and Aerospace Technology (ICECA).

5. Rastegar M., Fotuhi-Firuzabad M. Outage management in residential demand response programs. IEEE Trans. Smart Grid. 2014;6:1453–1462. doi: 10.1109/TSG.2014.2338794.

6. Fernandes F., Morais H., Vale Z., Ramos C. Dynamic load management in a smart home to participate in demand response events. Energy Build. 2014; 82:592–606. doi: 10.1016/j.enbuild.2014.07.067.

7. Ashfaq A., Jamil K. Real-time Load Scheduling and Storage Management for Solar Powered Network Connected EVs. IEEE Trans. Sustain. Energy. 2019 doi: 10.1109/TSTE.2019.2921024.

8. Aslam S., Khalid A., Javaid N. Towards efficient energy management in smart grids considering microgrids with day-ahead energy forecasting. Electr. Power Syst. Res. 2020;182:106232. doi: 10.1016/j.epsr.2020.106232.

9. Yousefi M., Hajizadeh A., Soltani M.N. A Comparison Study on Stochastic Modeling Methods for Home Energy Management System. IEEE Trans. Ind. Inform. 2019;15:4799–4808. doi: 10.1109/TII.2019.2908431.

10. Costanzo G.T., Zhu G., Anjos M.F., Savard G. A system architecture for autonomous demand-side load management in smart buildings. IEEE Trans. Smart Grid. 2012;3:2157–2165. doi: 10.1109/TSG.2012.2217358.

11. Al Essa M.J.M. Home energy management of thermostatically controlled loads and photovoltaic-battery systems. Energy. 2019;176:742–752. doi: 10.1016/j.energy.2019.04.041.

12. Pipattanasomporn M., Kuzlu M., Rahman S. An algorithm for intelligent home energy management and demand response analysis. IEEE Trans. Smart Grid. 2012;3:2166–2173. doi: 10.1109/TSG.2012.2201182.

13. Goncalves I., Gomes A., Antunes C.H. Optimizing the management of smart home energy resources under different power cost scenarios. Appl. Energy. 2019;242:351–363. doi: 10.1016/j.apenergy.2019.03.108.

14. Hernandez-Ocana B., Hernandez-Torruco J., Chavez-Bosquez O., Calva-Yanez M.B., Portilla-Flores E.A. Bacterial Foraging-Based Algorithm for Optimizing the Power Generation of an Isolated Microgrid. Appl. Sci. 2019;9:1261. doi: 10.3390/app9061261.

15. Xin J., Xiao C. Household Energy Demand Management Strategy Based on Operating Power by Genetic Algorithm. IEEE Access. 2019;7:96414–96423.
16. Zhuang Z., Lee W.C., Shin Y., Song K.B. An optimal power scheduling method for demand response in home energy management system. IEEE Trans. Smart Grid. 2013;4:1391–1400. doi: 10.1109/TSG.2013.2251018.
17. Ramakrishnan, V., Chenniappan, P., Dhanaraj, R. K., Hsu, C. H., Xiao, Y., & Al-Turjman, F. (2021). Bootstrap aggregative mean shift clustering for big data anti-pattern detection analytics in 5G/6G communication networks. *Computers & Electrical Engineering, 95,* 107380.
18. Nadeem J., Naseem M., Rasheed M.B., Mahmood D., Khan S.A., Alrajeh N., Iqbal Z. A new heuristically optimized Home Energy Management controller for smart grid. Sustain. Cities Soc. 2017;34:211–227.
19. Nadeem J., Hafeez G., Iqbal S., Alrajeh N., Alabed M.S., Guizani M. Energy efficient integration of renewable energy sources in the smart grid for demand side management. IEEE Access. 2018;6:77077–77096.
20. Kumar, R. N., Chandran, V., Valarmathi, R. S., & Kumar, D. R. (2018). Bitstream Compression for High Speed Embedded Systems Using Separated Split Look Up Tables (LUTs). Journal of Computational and Theoretical Nanoscience, 15(5), 1719–1727.
21. Qayyum F.A., Naeem M., Khwaja A.S., Anpalagan A., Guan L., Venkatesh B. Appliance scheduling optimization in smart home networks. IEEE Access. 2015;3:2176–2190. doi: 10.1109/ACCESS.2015.2496117.
22. Elham S., Jadid S. Optimal residential appliance scheduling under dynamic pricing scheme via HEMDAS. Energy Build. 2015;93:40–49.
23. Sereen A., Mancarella P., Mutale J. Automated demand response from home energy management system under dynamic pricing and power and comfort constraints. IEEE Trans. Smart Grid. 2015;6:1874–1883.
24. Ma J., Chen H.H., Song L., Li Y. Residential load scheduling in smart grid: A cost efficiency perspective. IEEE Trans. Smart Grid. 2015;7:771–784. doi: 10.1109/TSG.2015.2419818.
25. Jo H.-C., Kim S., Joo S. Smart heating and air conditioning scheduling method incorporating customer convenience for home energy management system. IEEE Trans. Consum. Electron. 2013;59:316–322. doi: 10.1109/TCE.2013.6531112.
26. Nagpal H., Staino A., Basu B. Automated Scheduling of Household Appliances Using Predictive Mixed Integer Programming. *Preprints.* 2019 doi: 10.20944/preprints201902.0256.v1.
27. Rahmani-Andebili M. Scheduling deferrable appliances and energy resources of a smart home applying multi-time scale stochastic model predictive control. *Sustain. Cities Soc.* 2017;32:338–347. doi: 10.1016/j.scs.2017.04.006.

28. Staino A., Nagpal H., Basu B. Cooperative optimization of building energy systems in an economic model predictive control framework. *Energy Build.* 2016;128:713–722. doi: 10.1016/j.enbuild.2016.07.009.

29. Moser A., Muschick D., Gölles M., Nageler P., Schranzhofer H., Mach T., Ribas C., Leusbrock I., Stark S., Lackner F., *et al.* A MILP-based modular energy management system for urban multi-energy systems: Performance and sensitivity analysis. *Appl. Energy.* 2020;261:114342. doi: 10.1016/j. apenergy.2019.114342.

12

Applications of IoTSG in Smart Industrial Monitoring Environments

Mohanasundaram T.[1]*, Vetrivel S.C.[2] and Krishnamoorthy V.[2]

*[1]Department of Management Studies, M S Ramaiah Institute of Technology,
Bengaluru, Karnataka, India
[2]School of Management Studies, Kongu Engineering College,
Erode, Tamil Nadu, India*

Abstract

The Internet of Things and Smart Grid (IoTSG) applications have a broader application in the industrial monitoring environment, including workflow automation, predictive maintenance, inventory monitoring, alerting in the event of any deviations, remote equipment management, quality control, supply chain optimization, and so on. Smart grid enhances transmission line operation and allow for speedier system restoration following a fault. It also helps to reduce power costs. In this chapter, the authors investigate the use of IoTSG in energy management, which is critical in every industrial unit. IoTSG is crucial in the monitoring, control, and conservation of energy in the industrial environment. The function and uses of IoTSG in the banking, automobile, and healthcare sectors are thoroughly examined in this chapter. Banking, as an industry, is critical to the economic stability of the country. IoT has a big impact on many aspects of the banking business, including customer relationship management, lending sanctioning, customer service, leasing finance automation, and so on. Similarly, the smart grid uses cutting-edge technologies to solve difficulties with energy systems in banks. Smart grids play an important role in reducing energy usage in banks by supplementing renewable energy and the green environment. The deployment of IoTSG in automobiles is critical. Better fleet and driver management, predictive maintenance, real-time vehicle telematics, and in-car infotainment are all made possible by IoT. IoT applications are also critical in linked autos and fleet management. With electric vehicles gaining popularity in recent years, the smart grid has the potential to

*Corresponding author: tmohansun@gmail.com

P. Sanjeevikumar, Rajesh Kumar Dhanaraj, Malathy Sathyamoorthy, Jens Bo Holm-Nielsen
and Balamurugan Balusamy (eds.) *Smart Grids and Internet of Things: An Energy Perspective,*
(339–364) © 2023 Scrivener Publishing LLC

revolutionise the face of the automobile industry. IoT enables healthcare professionals to be more watchful and engage with patients proactively. Data collected from IoT devices can help doctors and surgeons choose the optimal treatment plan for their patients. IoT devices equipped with sensors are utilised to determine the real-time position of medical equipment. The deployment of medical personnel at various sites may also be analysed in real-time. Smart microgrids may be used to successfully control hospital energy costs. IoTSG is a technology-enabled network that enables people to accomplish more with fewer resources. As all industries require better energy management, the scope of IoTSG is expected to go up in future as the new applications of these smart devices are expected to be explored continuously.

Keywords: IoT, smart grid, environment, industry, banking, automobile, healthcare

12.1   Introduction

The world has witnessed some sweeping changes in almost every sphere. Technological advancements played a predominant part in those massive revolutions. Internet of Things (IoT) empowers automation in each process of industrial function and it also brings operational efficiency in all sectors — supply chain and logistics, manufacturing, energy, banking and financial services, telecommunications, automobile, retail, hospitality etc. The Buzz word 'Internet of Things' denotes a structure of interconnected, internet-enabled objects that are capable to gather, collate and transfer data through a wireless network without interruption of human resource. The people, business and societal potentials are unbounded. Nowadays, business organizations are inspired by IoT and there are possibilities of higher income, falling operational costs and better efficiencies. Both inland and overseas business operations are guided by well-framed regulatory policies and necessary compliances. Availability of IoT instruments offers the data and insights essential to restructure and modernize the flow of work, predict patterns of use, process automation, accomplish compliance necessities, and effactually compete in a dynamic business environment. IoT helps to unlock efficiencies and productivity in an industrial province. There are numerous benefits of IoT for business enterprises viz., minimizes operating costs, offer valuable insights in decision areas, reduces downtime by enabling predictive maintenance for capital goods and equipment etc.

The application of IoT in energy management got distinct recognition from producers, governments and other stakeholders. IoT enabled energy management systems to contribute to a novel smart grid that promises astonishing energy and cost control, enhanced security and greater efficiency. As stated earlier, IoT based energy management has extensive use in the electricity supply chain network, right from generation of power to payment of electricity bills by users. IoT technology in the energy sectors offers benefits like – minimize the spending on energy consumption, reduce CO_2 emission, fulfils government norms, augments green energy, improve asset maintenance, automation of processes, detect and prevent malfunctions, avoids accidents and estimate demand effectively. A fundamental progress of the internet into a network of internet of objects has not only harvests information but also interacts with the physical world [1]. IoT helps in Smart lighting as IoT enabled systems can vigorously correct the regimes depending on the availability of daylight in changing circumstances and avoid unnecessary energy use. Today, IoT-based household solar systems provide free power to accomplish the energy requirements of households. IoT techniques also play a pivotal role in better maintenance and preventing machine downtimes apart from assisting the energy management system to collect, collate and analyse actual data on energy consumption. [2] studied the various applications of IoT in finance and analyzed the impact of digital trends and IoT on the procedural scheme of a traditional bank. IoT offers numerous benefits to different sectors that includes enhanced employee productivity, lesser human force, efficient business management, cost-effective solutions, better safety, in-depth analysis, improved customer service etc. On the other hand, IoT suffers from some limitations and challenges viz., capturing sensitive data brings concern about data security, IoT devices are exposed to hackers, over dependent on technology, job losses etc. The four-stage process of IoT mechanism is explained in Figure 12.1.

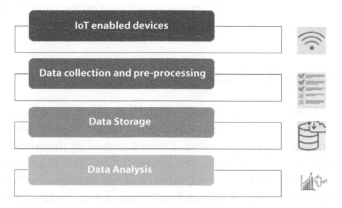

Figure 12.1 Four-stage process of IoT mechanism.

Another superlative technology that is making a pragmatic change in the dynamic industrial ecosystem is the emergence of the Smart Grid. The Smart Grid is an electricity network that integrates all users linked in the system to provide sustainable power with high quality and safety. The scope for new opportunities in various industries is abundant by making power grids smarter with energy intelligence. IoT solutions are used in smart grids for active adjustment to changes in the grid. For reliable and cost-effective grid operation, leveraging data through energy intelligence is vital. The way businesses are operated depends largely on sustainable energy supply. The energy sector's vital revolution comes through digitalization and decarbonization policies. Smart Grids are increasingly used in organizations because of their obvious benefits like enhanced power quality and cost-efficiency. Smart Grid provides necessary information and techniques to make decisions about energy use from the available alternatives and it also acts as a mainstay in innovative business models like smart city, electric vehicles etc. Over the years, the power grid has experienced numerous technological changes. In the contemporary phase, digitalization, and automation will make the enduring transformation process to continue at a faster pace.

The upsurge of innovative and smart devices along with the availability of massive data has already influenced most businesses. Among the sectors, Banking is one of the dynamic sectors where technology and automation in process improvement and security management keep coming. The effect of IoT and Smart Grid in the banking sector needs to be assessed in detail to understand how these technological systems had brought and expected to bring changes in the way the banking industry is functioning. Similarly, the application of IoT and Smart Grid in the Automobile industry is extensive. This chapter focuses on two emerging technologies – IoT and Smart Grid and their role in transforming two prominent industries across the globe viz., Banking and Automobile are explored.

12.2 Energy Management

The term "Energy Management," comprises planning and operational activities relating to energy production, energy consumption, energy distribution and storage of energy. Every resource in the world is scarce. Energy is the core for all productive activities, proper management of it is crucial for sustainable development and technological advancement. The principal objectives of energy management are; energy conservation, protecting the environment from the adversities of climate change, and cost minimization. The management of energy is significant in all business areas, more so for improved environmental conditions, efficient production and logistics. Smart Grid sensors enable smart energy management system and provide real-time energy optimization and facilitate new approaches for energy load management [3].

In simple words, energy management can be stated as the process of monitoring and minimizing the consumption of energy. The organizations are striving for controlling the energy cost by examining the pattern of prevailing energy usage. Enhancement in energy efficiency through benchmarking is the order of the day for all modern organizations. It is necessary for all business enterprises to integrate energy management into the organizational structure in order to achieve optimum usage of energy. Energy management is all about dealing with energy issues and finding the best possible solution to all energy matters. A consistent energy management system is required considering environmental concerns. For a commercial entity, energy management is a complex task involving, suitable technology, appropriate process and effective management. A detailed study on understanding the gap in energy management will go a long way in successfully managing energy in organizations. The standard steps to be followed in energy management has been formulated by Energy Star (a US-based Environmental Protection Agency). The first and foremost prominent step is the commitment to continuous improvement in energy efficiency. This requires strong top management support by framing a fitting energy management and environment policy by appointing a top-level executive who will be accountable for the implementation and continual of best energy management practises in the organization. The second step is about assessing the performance by comparing it with the industry benchmark. A quality circle comprising cross-functional team members should be formed for evaluating the performances and recognize the improvement prospects from various viewpoints. The third step involves setting a higher, but genuine goal to minimize the energy usage and prevailing pollution for attaining successful results. The fourth step in the process is to create an action plan which is proposed to serve as a framework to direct and monitor the methodical approach to achieve enhanced energy and environmental performance. The fifth step is about the successful implementation of the action plan by creating awareness and motivating the people involved in the process. The clear communication of action plan helps in achieving energy efficiency and environmental sustainability. Step six is about assessing the progress of the action taken in attaining energy efficiency. The last step in the formulation process is recognizing achievements. It is critical to maintaining a commitment to continuous

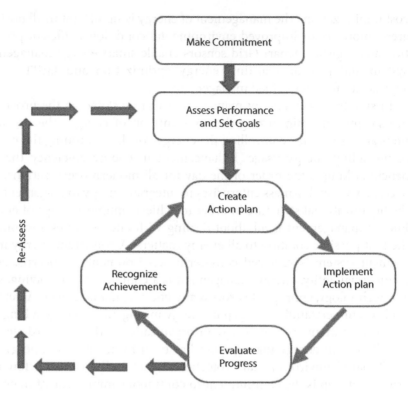

Figure 12.2 Steps in energy management. (Source: Energy Star, a US Environmental Protection Agency.)

improvement. Appreciating and celebrating achievements is required to sustain the momentum in achieving excellence in energy management and environmental safeguards. There are seven important steps to be followed which have been depicted in the Figure 12.2.

Energy management in this dynamic environment is more vital than ever for modern enterprises, as the corporates are looking forward to controlling their cost and energy, and draw the attention of the environmental conscious younger generation. Leading corporations in energy are aware of their social responsibility to create a pollution-free environment. However, it is unfortunate to note that several commercial entities do not have their own energy manager and also lacked automated solutions to implement energy management practices. Some of the major energy management advantages to corporate entities are; 1. It combats issues like climate change by reducing CO_2 emissions; 2. It saves funds through competitive procurement apart from purposefully reducing energy consumption; 3. It monitors and tracks the energy utility costs which in-turn helps in preparing the precise budget and gives a better understanding of operating costs; and 4. It minimizes the dependency on unstable energy supply chains. The well-planned and scientifically implemented energy management practices usually apply technology to enable strategic decisions. Real success in energy management can be achieved only by aligning energy management strategies with business and financial goals. Although many organizations are doing energy audits, such audits on their own can't do anything and they are just tools to address the necessity of energy efficiency. Implementing energy management in an organization is a decision about incurring capital expenditure at present versus the value of energy savings over the life of the project. The usage of renewable energy in the areas of transportation, generating electricity, and heating and cooling the air and water etc. are playing a significant role in energy efficiency and contributing 19.3% to human global energy consumption. The lesser the use of coal, natural gas, nuclear energy benefits society. The three important renewable energy sources are; Wind, solar and hydroelectricity.

In recent years, the emergence of advent technologies like the Internet of Things (IoT) and Smart Grid plays a pivotal role in energy efficiency. The IoT enabled system helps in automatic adjust to air circulation, temperature and lighting in an enterprise. Similarly, Smart Grid comprises numerous energy measures that help to transmit energy in the most desirable way. Although energy management is imperative in every industrial sector, in this study, we focus on two industries viz., Banking and Automobile. A well-planned and executed energy management practices can enhance the overall financial performance and the brand image of banks and financial institutions. Similarly, the automobile industry is one of the largest sectors which uses a large quantum of energy. This chapter mainly focuses on the application of IoT and Smart Grid on the energy management solutions in two prominent industries – Banking and Automobile.

12.3 Role of IoT and Smart Grid in the Banking Industry

The banking industry is the heart of all economic activities of a country. The banking industry facilitates capital formation, the supply of funds to industries and mobilization of capital. The banking sector has emerged as important drivers of economic growth. The banking sector has undergone significant development over the years. Indian banking sector consists of a mixture of public sector banks, private sector banks and foreign banks. The banking sector is a customer-oriented industry. High-quality service is indispensable for the growth of the bank. The banking customer has high bargaining power and has numerous investment alternative like Non-Banking Financial companies, mutual funds, Government securities. The banking sector has slowly shifted from a protected environment to a competitive environment. To sustain in the competitive environment, banks need to adopt the Internet of Things (IoT).

In the changing business scenario, innovation is considered key to the banking sector. Today, information technology-based innovation is the main driver for all business, the banking sector is no exception. IoT is the Interconnection of complex devices within the Internet infrastructure. The banking sector has experienced change on account of the digital revolution. Traditional Banks have started rethinking their way of operating their service in the digital era. Banks can use IoT application to collect data about their customer and analyse the same to predict customers' needs and requirement. This could help the bank to offer tailor-made products and services to the customer. In the banking sector, IoT is regarded as a big thing. Internet of things facilitates optimization of Banking Operation. Boosting productivity and reduction of costs. As a result of advancement in information technology, the number of devices connected with the internet also increasing. The increasing competition in the banking sector compelled the banks to opt application of the Internet of things in banking.

Smart Grid is swiftly turning into a bank for energy. The implementation of Smart Grid technologies will assist in improving the economies of operation for any sector which is also true in the banking industry. The pressing need for Smart Grid technologies was felt in India due to frequent power shortages in 2012. Since then, cooperation between different states and between the central government and states ensured the timely employment of Smart Grid technologies which in-turn augmented power supply in the country.

12.3.1   Application of IoT in the Banking Sector

IoT's use in various fields is growing at a faster pace and on a very large scale. We are progressively using technologies and devices that are linked to the internet in one or the other way. One of the main advantages of IoT is that it can be remotely monitored and controlled. Internet of things has been widely used in medicine, health care, smart cities, business and automobile Industries. FinTech can present a new service of tools and products for the promising businesses through the internet of services which provide ideas linked in internet [4]. The application of the Internet of things in banking Sector is well spread across different functions.

Figure 12.3 IoT applications for banking.

The changes brought in by the IoT in banking and finance was extensively studied [5]. Figure 12.3 explains the thurst areas in which IoT is sucessfully applied and yielding greater results.

12.3.1.1 Customer Relationship Management (CRM)

Of late Indian banks have adopted customer relationship strategies and technology to attract and retain existing customers. The IoT facilitates bank customers to use banking facility at any time and any place by using connected devices. These devices will generate data. The banking sector can analyse the data to obtain customer requirement and offer the right – products to the right customer at right time. IoT technologies bridge the gap between manger and customer in exchanging their communications. CRM systems in banks are gradually leveraging IoT devices to expand and enhance the front-end banking processes. IoT gives insight into different sections or operations of the banks by connecting the products and devices to the internet. IoT enables banks to optimize customer services and increases sales. With IoT, banks can realize new ways to connect with customers. The Bank can use the service data to formulate suitable services for the bank customer so as to retain the existing customer in the competitive era. IoT may facilitate bank officials to predict the amount of cash requirement at different locations of automated teller machine (ATM). Furthermore, IoT may facilitate the bank installation of ATM in certain places based on ATM user data. Real-time data about bank customer choice and preference of banking product obtained from IoT Landscape facilitate the banking officials to develop customer relationship strategy.

12.3.1.2   Loan Sanctions

Banks can use IoT is sanctioning Loan to business customer and farmers. With the help of IoT Banks can access and analyse the agricultural yield that allows the banks to estimate the crop loan value to the farmers. Furthermore, with information-based customer data obtained via IoT, the bank can estimate the Actual Loan requirements of the individual customer and corporate customers.

12.3.1.3   Customer Service

The banking sector can use IoT Technology to augment its range of services. IoT gives bank customer timely information. Device connectivity with the bank enables a customer to schedule an appointment with bank officials and they can redress their grievances. IoT has facilitated various banking operations like lending, know your customer (KYC) norms, working capital finance, trade finance etc.

12.3.1.4   Leasing Finance Automation

Real-time monitoring of depreciation of assets and assets usage could dispense data for pricing leased assets. This may help the banks to block the assets of the borrower in case of termination of the contract. The banks can carry-out customer segmentation analysis through IoT, to Identify the right customer and to design tailor-made products and services to the requirement of a specific customer. The Internet of Things (IoT) facilitates the banking sector to formulate pricing strategy for different services, predicting competitor's price and competitor bank promotion strategies. Furthermore, IoT helps the bank to build the value propositions of the services, based on service availing patterns, and design personalized communication between banks and customer regarding services.

12.3.1.5   Capacity Management

Internet of things will help the banking sector to optimize the opening of bank branches. By way of obtaining, processing and sharing the real-time customer database, the bank officials can predict the number of bank customers visiting the bank per day, and how much manpower is required to handle the customers at peak hours, peak season and the value of the transaction.

12.3.2   Application of Smart Grid in the Banking Sector

Smart Grid is becoming a new facet of the energy sector. It integrates several cutting-edge technologies to overcome the problems faced by conventional energy systems. Across the globe, banks are becoming progressively conscious of the necessity to increase their acquaintance to clean energy. ICICI Bank, a leading private sector bank in India has recorded a significant decline in energy consumption between the years 2015 and 2020. The energy performance index (EPI) of the bank has been brought down by 21.3 per cent during this period. Banks are making investments in Green building, energy-efficient equipment, renewable energy etc. Bureau of Energy Efficiency (BEE), a statutory body in energy management plays a significant role in bringing optimise the use of energy in banks and financial institutions. For banks, energy cost is 1/3rd of the total costs per bank branch[1]. The main energy consumption devices are; air-conditioning system, lighting system, work equipment, automation and security systems.

The establishment of a power diffusion mechanism with the help of Smart Grids to connect solar and wind plant to transmission grid would enable to use of renewable energy prospective in India. The prevailing grids are having limitations to accomplish the increasing demands of power consumption in addition to providing a stable and viable energy supply. These challenges in the energy sector pave to a convincing reason for adopting Smart Grid devices in India. The Smart Grids not just increase the efficacy of the grids in use, but also enable to meet the rising demand through demand response management system. The banks in India are started using smart grid solutions that employ communication and automation systems. The banks in India are using more smart buildings to minimize energy cost. Transforming the bank's retail branches into SMART branches embrace digitalization, which is the need of the hour for commercial banks in India. SMART branches are possible through IoT and Smart Grid-enabled technologies.

12.4   Role of IoT and Smart Grid in the Automobile Industry

Among the different recent revolutionary technological advances in the automobile industry, the two prominent technologies are IoT and Smart Grid. The industrial Internet of things (IIoT) sends data from systems that

---

[1]www.dexma.com.

monitor and control the physical world to data processing systems that cloud computing has shown to be important tools for meeting processing requirements [6]. This section of the chapter elaborates on how these two technologies are bringing innovation and development in the automobile sector, specifically in energy management.

12.4.1   Application of IoT in the Automobile Industry

In the manufacturing sector, the growth of the Automobile industry witnessed one of the largest in the world, having more than 72 million units per year. It is estimated that in the year 2017, the global turnover of the Automobile industry was more than $3 trillion. Which is astonishing data for the business industry. This adds to 3.65 per cent of GDP at the global level.

12.4.1.1   *What Exactly is the Internet of Things (IoT) Mean to the Automobile Sector?*

Many studies are available to access the impact of IoT on automotive sector. The effects of IoT, Big Data and other emerging technologies on the automotive industry was vastly discussed [7]. IoT as a disruptive technology has enabled interaction between cyber world and Physical world [8]. Millions of complex devices are connected through tangible devices like actuators, gateways, platform hubs, electronics and sensors. A wireless network connection is used to connect and interact with each other. Data is shared among the connected objects and things with each other. The system operates without human intervention. A study by Gartner stated that by the end of the year 2020, the potential of IoT can be estimated more than 20 billion IoT devices. Manufacturing companies first witnessed a hefty implementation of IoT to reduce production cost and accomplish autonomy. Further, the applications of IoT bowed towards more commercial and general usage.

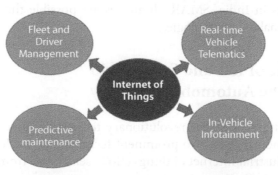

Figure 12.4 IoT for smart monitoring and control in automobile industry.

However, the Internet of Things brings the possibilities for the Automobile industry are really enormous. Figure 12.4 depicts the use of IoT for smart monitoring and control in automobile industry. IoT created a different way people interact with their vehicles, which the industry could see through the automobile revolution. IoT paves way for GPS system in cars and self-driven automation cars. It also helps the automobile firms to update the software system and respond to real-time maintenance issues by enabling a data communication system. It plays a massive role in preventing accidents.

12.4.1.2 Transportation and Logistics

The transportation industry received a great positive impact with a revolutionary change in the industrial pattern (i.e.) Industry 4.0 and further Internet of Things (IoT). The industry guidelines and market conditions mandated the transportation industry to perform better with limited resources. Cutthroat competition and demand for digital transformation become responsible for the implementation of IoT like technologies in optimizing business activities across the globe. This paved for efficient and effective transport management and enhances safety in travelling. For the past five years, (i.e.) since 2016, car sales ranging between 76 to 81 million units. Of course, due to COVID-19 the year 2020 faced a steep drop down in sales at the global level. Otherwise, also the Automobile industry could not make any breakthrough in recent past years. Because customers expect a car or a heavy vehicle not only a vehicle with four tyres and steering but they expect some innovative features and changes in their vehicle. Customers expect a high-tech vehicle with which they can able to get connected and interact also. Which paved an idea through the Internet of Things, which is one such upsetting technology which helps the Automobile sector to figure out a batch of next-generation vehicles. Carmakers got a new avenue through the advent of the Internet of Things and this is given a boost to the customers and buyers of automobile vehicles across the world. Internet of Things in the Automobile sector has become an important hot spot with multipurpose applications to fulfil the need of the day. The application of this IoT started from connected cars to fully automated transport system. In the global automobile market Internet of Things has made a great impact.

12.4.1.3 Connected Cars

The idea of cars connection through the wireless network is not new. A study by Gartner states that more than 250 million cars in the world would have been connected by the end of the year 2020. Cellular vehicle to everything

(CV2X) is the IoT network used to connect these cars. The CV2X network system used to connect smart transport systems with each other and also cars. Upsurge drivers' response time and high-speed data transmission facilitate superior vehicle communication between the connected cars. Depend upon the vehicle's connection with various objects, the CV2X base IoT network system is sub-divided into the following four categories:

a. *Vehicle to Network (V2N):* This network system is used to alert drivers regarding an accident on the road or about variation in weather conditions. It is being used by the weather forecast department in association with Intelligent Transport System (ITM). Through smart phones, vehicles can be connected. The vehicle music system and GPS of the car can be operated through voice commands by the drivers while driving.

b. *Vehicle to vehicle (V2V):* This connection used to share data with each other among cars that are in a proximate range. Vehicle speed, location, and dynamics related information shared among the cars. The V2V connection helps in accidents prevention and provide a way for emergency vehicles like ambulances and fire trucks to have ease of passage through traffic without any difficulty.

c. *Vehicle to infrastructure (V2I):* In this connection, the network of vehicles is associated with road infrastructures, which generally includes toll booths, traffic lights and lane markings. Long queues at toll booths or petrol pumps are being avoided and smooth traffic flow ensured through the facilitation of IoT through Vehicle to the infrastructure network.

d. *Vehicle to pedestrians (V2P):* Mobile application is used to operate this network and CV2X network can be accessed by a pedestrian also. This application can be used by a common man on the street to locate nearby taxis and to observe the estimated time of arrival for transits. The same is used by call Taxi Operators like Ola, Uber in India.

12.4.1.4   Fleet Management

A huge development has been perceived in the field of managing vehicle fleet in the automobile sector due to the implementation of IoT. Nowadays, vehicles especially Trucks integration is done with location tracking, weight measurement and numerous other sensors. A cloud application is used to store the bulk of gathered sensory data from a large fleet of trucks used with an IoT fleet management system. Processing of the collected data is processed completely through various analytics methods and conceptualized into a pictorial format. It is easy for the fleet operator to monitor the parameters associated with his fleet operation through this information in order to have total control and efficient operation of his fleet. IoT Solution provides a safe, cleaner and cost-effective fleet management for transport business operators.

IoT based fleet management system provides numerous benefits to the fleet managers. Real-time location monitoring of the fleet includes Truck, Trailer Tracking, Ocean Freight Shipping, Courier and Delivery etc., This IoT based tracking system provides improved security and precise and clear reports which provides total transparency in the fleet operations and activities to the fleet managers. Various categories of vehicles ranging from cars to trucks can be tracked. Ocean Freight tracking for shipping lines is done through an IoT tracking system through the earth for the better organization, tracking and effective, control of vessel shipments. Smart Contracts ideas are associated with this to facilitate shipping activity safer and smarter. A perfect pick up of courier and delivery operations is being done with the support of instantaneous position tracing and alarms through IoT. The courier service people can able to choose the best route out of available routes, providing an alert on arrival and delivery of courier. Real-time temperature, RH tracking also possible with the integration of cargo monitoring solution and this will be an additional feature. IoT based vehicle tracing solution authorizes fleet managers to reduce fuel consumption, ensure quicker delivery, decrease operational costs, increase safety and reliability and finally which leads to making customers happy.

Personalized Dashboard with IoT based fleet tracking solution provides all the information related to the fleet operation of a company on a single screen. An alert will be given to the truck fleet in case of its entry in the zones which are restricted for their movement. An IoT system that functions as a virtual geographic periphery and an immediate alert is sounded to the driver and supervisors in case any vehicle goes near to that. In case a truck of the fleet is at its abnormal speed or location different from the anticipated/scheduled route, the fleet managers will be alerted immediately. IoT provides the following benefits in this aspect.

    i. Route Management
   ii. Tracking of Vehicle

iii. Monitoring Driver Activity

iv. Goods and Vehicle Monitoring

In order to manage the transport fleet in a smarter way which is beyond the normal basic facilities IoT based system experience is used which analyse the facet of the fleet in all the aspects like monitoring driver movement, observing vehicle, analysing the consumption of fuel used in the vehicle, in order to improve efficient operation and increase profit in the business. Real-time sensor data and signals are used to augment roads used for product delivery, performance Monitoring, observe the vehicle on a real-time basis, both on-road and off-road and support in making intelligent business decisions. Truck weight measurement includes;

a. Payload Maximization

b. Avoid preventable fines

c. Eradicate guesswork

d. Plug profit leaks

In transportation especially in the logistics industry, it was a real-time challenge to the operators to measure the weight of the Truck. The introduction of IoT came with a solution to this issue. By installing sensors on the axle of the Truck real-time weight data is made available and it can be accessed through mobile application also. This IoT solution eliminates the usage of Unnecessary hardware weighing tools and digital equipment. Monitoring the temperature inside the container and carrying the analytics of the business by using advanced methods. To ensure that the container in which the cargo is transported is maintained with the required temperature and RH. Through sensors, the IoT network gives a real-time status and alerts in case of any deviation of the set level of these parameters. The system comprises an IoT platform, mobile & web applications, temperature/RH sensors and gateways.

12.4.2   Application of Smart Grid (SG) in the Automobile Industry

A Smart Grid is "an electricity network that can intelligently integrate the actions of all users connected to it – generators, consumers and those that do both – in order to efficiently deliver sustainable, economic and secure electricity supplies". The world is facing sweeping changes with the electric power system due to irresistible need. In order to cater for the need, there is a need to replace the machines/equipment with ageing technologies to make the system more effective and reliable. This is being done with the association of developing information and communication technologies (ICTs). Even though ICT is used in electricity transmission voltages, its usage is very little in real-time communication. It is neither in the case with customer nor distribution circuits.

Indian Ministry of Power, during the year 2015 gave the approval for the 'National Smart Grid Mission'. Presently, fourteen Smart Grid pilot projects across India has been allocated and state-owned power dispersal services will execute that. Customers' participation is enabled in the power system operation by which lower voltage electric networks get better prominence with the Smart Grid vision. This is being done with the help of smart homes and smart meters. Better utilization of renewable energy sources is possible with the support of Smart Grid and also enhanced energy efficiency. Across the globe, developed and developing countries are seriously working out with their Research and Development activities in order to identify all the possible potential ways to commercialize this concept in a larger spectrum.

12.4.2.1   Smart Grid Can Change the Face of the Automobile Industry

The concept of electric mobility is concurrently developing with the evolution towards a pollution-free greener and cleaner environment driven by digitalization and automation. The infrastructure for electric vehicle (EV) charging is a major challenge. It is important to have adequate investment and proper infrastructure to assist electric mobility. The services of smart charging will certainly reduce the operating costs and digitalization will enhance the customer experience. With Smart Grid technology, cars will become a crucial aspect of the clean energy value chain. An innovative smart charging method is vehicle-to-grid. It seems like SGs and EVs are made to support one other. No doubt, SGs will play a crucial role in reducing CO_2 emission from road transport. In the long-run, there is a huge prospective for smart-grid technology to allow electric vehicles to be used as distributed storage devices. Based on the penetration rate, EVs may account for a considerable share of total electricity consumption. It is estimated that the total EV fleet will reach 31 million in 2035[2]. Smart-grid technologies are at different levels of development. Smart-grid equipment can allow the reduction in charging load during off-peak periods, thus pulling down the day-to-day load usage. Advanced metering equipment is a vital component, permitting a two-way flow of information, providing

---

[2]The World Energy Outlook, from International Energy Agency (IEA).

customers with actual data and permitting customers to plan to charge in a way that minimises costs to them.

Due to global warming issues, pollution and also to cut the fuel import charges, many countries are promoting Electric vehicles as a means of transportation in their countries. The role of Smart Grid in the automobile sector is in the fast-growing stage. This will intellectually charge the car when there is a low demand for power and at the same time production of renewable energy is high. Energy companies are on the discussion to identify the possibilities to integrate the vehicle batteries as a source of power in the course of high power demand or shutdowns. Smart Grid is the combination of Information and Communications Technologies (ICT) and measurement, control and automation, Sensing technologies. In order to meet the various requirements of Smart Grid, the technologies given below must be developed and executed:

(a) Connectivity is being provided between various components in the power system and loads by two-way communication technologies.

(b) In order to make sure the standards of operation and information security, appropriate software must be there which will provide improvement in communication systems and interoperability of information too.

(c) To provide customers with greater information communications the necessary hardware and software has to be there which enable customers to trade in energy markets and customers to provide demand-side response also.

(d) For plug-and-play of home appliances, electric vehicles and micro-generation open architectures method is used.

(e) To offer innovative shielding relay, measurements, to register faults and event records for the power system, Intelligent Electronic Devices (IED) to be installed.

(f) Phase or Measurement Units (PMU) and Wide Area Monitoring, Protection and Control (WAMPAC) to ensure the security of the power system.

(g) To provide prompt diagnosis and quick reaction to any occurrence in various parts and portions of the power system, communication technologies, integrated sensors, measurements, control and automation systems and information and used. This ensures improved quality management and proficient manoeuver of power system components, to support relieve jamming in transmission and distribution circuits and to avoid or reduce possible outages and empower working autonomously when situations require swift resolution.

(h) Smart appliances, communication, controls and monitors to ensure protection, relief, handiness, and power savings of homes

(i) Smart meters, communication, displays and associated software will provide consumers with exact bills, besides with quicker and stress-free supplier switching, to give consumers precise real-time information on their electricity and gas use and other associated information and to enable demand management and demand-side participation and to allow customers to have greater choice and control over electricity and gas use.

12.4.2.2   Smart Grid and Energy Efficient Mobility System

A lot of research is happening in energy efficiency, electric mobility, lightweight equipment, advance batteries, new combustion engines and component level technologies. The governments are coming with new and stricter regulations to bring decarbonized vehicles. In fact, a massive wave of changes is hitting our transportation system. These changes are expected to bring an enormous impact on the future of the transportation system. Some of the breath-taking innovative changes are the auto-driving Google car and Tesla autopilot. Apart from these, higher levels of automation are coming to more mainstream vehicles. It's the trend of connections between vehicles-to-vehicles, vehicle-to-infrastructure. The impact of technology such as GPS mapping and even online shopping on the transport network is significant. Transportation energy consumption could increase by up to two hundred per cent in 2050[3]. The Smart Grid and industrial IoT are solutions for future energy management issues. Integrating Smart Grids will allow maximum efficiency and sustainability, apart from keeping low energy costs. Vehicle–to–Grid technology will go a long way in energy management.

12.5   Role of IoT and SG in Healthcare Industry

The IoT applications are becoming more common in the medical and healthcare sector. IoT is engaged vastly in monitoring the healthcare

---

[3]Energy Talks – SMART mobility for the future.

equipment and drugs, managing the patients' information, electronic storage of medical records etc. Similarly, Smart Grids and Grid computing are offering hopeful solution to e-health management challenges. The path to achieve a global connectivity between IoT and the medical environments was explored [9]. The IoT has exposed potential application in connecting different medical devices, sensors, and healthcare professionals to offer quality medical services in a remote location [10].

12.5.1   Applications of IoT in Healthcare Sector

IoT with the aid of RFID has started to discover wider applicability in the area of healthcare drugs management. IoT and RFID together can assist in preventing public health issues by helping in the supply chain management of medical and healthcare devices. This leads to high quality health treatments with lower cost. IoT along with RFID is expected to have a vital role in real-time monitoring and tracking of healthcare equipment and medicines and also in regulating the market for healthcare products. The value of fake medicines is more than 10 percent of global drug sales[4]. One the major causes of death is contributed to medical errors. According to John Hopkins study, more than 250,000 people in USA are believed to die in USA due to medical errors. In India, nearly 5 million deaths a year is happening due to medical error[5]. It is widely believed IoT will play a significant role in bring down the error rate in medical field. IoT has an extensive application in the digital healthcare information management which include patient identification, laboratory identification, medical waste management, physician identification etc. IoT in health care is often called as Internet of Medical Things (IoMT). An automatic system to monitor patient's body temperature, heart rate, body movements and blood pressure had been explored [11]. To understand the comprehensive monitoring and management of IoMT devices, it is essential to know the application benefits of these devices. The benefits of IoMT varies from simple mood monitoring to advanced robotic surgery.

Remote monitoring in the medical field is possible today mainly on account of IoT-enabled instruments and devices. These IoT devices unleash the possibility of remote superlative care by keeping the patients safe and healthy. The widespread of health care IoT enabled products offers massive opportunities. The huge amount of data generated by these

---

[4]World Health Organization.
[5]Business-standard.com, dated October 28, 2018.

connected devices hold the potential to transform health care. IoT has also made the interaction with physicians and physiotherapists easier and thereby increases the patient's overall satisfaction. IoT enabled wearables like fitness bands and other wireless equipment help in monitoring the blood pressure, temperature, heart rate, glucose level etc. The patients and health-conscious people can track their health conditions easily and get access to personalized medical attention whenever required. The doctors can also effortlessly track patient's compliance to treatment methods and can offer treatment proactively due to continuous and real-time monitoring. The sensor connected IoT devices assist the hospitals to track the present location of the important equipment like oxygen pumps, nebulizers etc. apart from pharmacy inventory control. There are enormous prospects for health insurance firms through IoT enabled devices. The insurance firms will benefit from the data driven through IoT connected smart devices which will be useful in underwriting process and managing the claims. IoT facilitates effective underwriting, optimum pricing, better risk assessment and efficient claim management. Insurance firms may offer certain premium benefits to their customers for sharing the IoT device generated health data.

Figure 12.5 brings out the benefits of IoT in healthcare. The prominent benefits of IoT in the medical and health care sector are; lower treatment cost, enhanced treatment, faster diagnosis of illness, proactive treatment for illnesses, better management of equipment and medicines, enabling better decision, lesser errors and effective waste management.

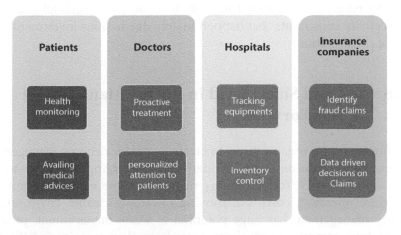

Figure 12.5 IoT beneficiaries in health care.

12.5.2   Application of Smart Grid (SG) in Health Care Sector

Like IoT, SG too offers both advantages and some concerns. Of course, the smart grid brings more concerns than IoT. However, we cannot undermine the benefits offered by Smart Grid. There are some fascinating and convincing motives to favour smart grids. The smart grid is believed to have the potential to reduce air pollution by 30 percent from the electricity sector that in-turn massive number of deaths from air pollution arise out of power plants. Radiotherapy Grid plays an active role in giving treatment to millions of cancer patients across the world. The benefits of smart electric grids are going long way in diagnosing and treating multi factorial disease. Smart Grids also offer huge savings for smart hospitals in terms of energy savings. Application of smart grid and smart meters in health care monitoring systems is phenomenal and involves technological applications that permit an easy integration and better renewable energy penetration. The smart and intelligent power management solutions for healthcare settings provide the necessary devices required to expand working and energy efficiency. Grid Computing is evolving as a hopeful solution to some of the greatest challenges facing e-health [12].

There are arguments about the health hazards posed by smart meters. The smart meters emit radio frequencies (RF) that brings health risk. On the other hand, the smart grids are offering greater environmental benefits viz., integrating solar and wind power, minimizes greenhouse gases and low burning of fossil fuels. Despite making extensive contribution to protecting and improving people health, the widespread use of smart grid and smart meters may be denied if there are adequate evidences proving that smart meters are emitting radio frequencies that are hazardous to health. Another bigger challenge in using the smart devices is technological and connectivity constraints that happen mainly due to poor investments and lack of collaboration.

12.6   IoT and Smart Grid in Energy Management - A Way Forward

It is important for organizations to create a scope for energy management beyond utility consumption by identifying emerging energy management opportunities. Today's energy management necessities are not just to reduce operating costs, but moving towards a cleaner environment. Energy management has huge potential in waste management, product design, transport and supply chain, optimizing plant capacity and effective control of equipment. Business firms should embrace IoT devices, Smart Grid and renewable energy resources for better cost management. The limited rewards of today's energy management products and practices are mainly attributed to just focusing on continuing economic pressure and complying with CO_2 emissions reporting as mandated by the regulators. A chink in renewable energy's armour is that industrial plants require a steady and sustainable energy supply but solar lights and wind power can be erratic. However, this challenge can be overcome through IoT and Smart Grid-based efficient energy management devices and practices. IoT is a technology-enabled network that helps to achieve more with lesser resources. All industries require better energy management. The application of IoT in energy management gives unmatched control and awareness of energy utilization costs. IoT helps to make smart and informed decisions on energy consumption apart from self-optimization and automation in energy management.

The future of IoT in the energy sector is bright as it helps to optimize resources, saves cost, enable preventive maintenance and achieve greater control. The energy managers may not be an expert in deploying IoT based sensors for effective energy management in the organization. In fact, specialized firms are expected to play a prominent role to unlock the potential of IoT in the energy sector. The immediate effect of IoT in the energy sector is to diminish unnecessary waste and pollution by cutting down CO_2 emissions. In an IoT enabled environment, consumers will receive a customized service on demand and society will get benefitted due to optimized use of resources and minimum adverse impact on the atmosphere. IoT has already ushered the technological revolution and grabbing more interest as the globe turns towards higher digitalization. As the world increasingly uses technology, investment in IoT sensor devices is set to increase drastically. No doubt, India is swiftly rising as an IoT hub despite beginning the IoT journey much later compared to developed nations. Apart from the energy sector, IoT applications in transportation and logistics, manufacturing, and automobiles are set to witness unprecedented growth in the days to come. As IoT has become mainstream in numerous areas, the energy sector is no exception to it. A micro-grid is one of the main energy management solutions for the problem of decarbonization. Robots and sensors are expected to play an essential role in the future of automobile industries with a focus on energy optimization. The future moves towards a holistic energy management solution that offers ample possibilities in energy usage, power analytics and IoT enabled smart devices to reduce energy consumption in accordance with demand changes and carbon emission regulations.

More than 50% of India's population and 70% of India's working force belongs to the millennial generation. The challenge for the banking industry is that these millennials have certain expectations on the way bank operates and communicates to them which requires energy-backed solutions. The digitalization of the banking sector depends largely on energy. The applications of IoT, Artificial Intelligence, Blockchain and Machine learning are expected to help the banks in the long-run to achieve complete digitalization in its functioning and to obtain energy optimization. In the automobile sector, enactment of predictive maintenance and deploying robots in the facilities warrants optimum energy use. To conclude, the future of energy management aims to achieve optimal usage of resources, cost control, reducing global warming and to improve the quality of life.

12.7   Conclusion

The IoT and Smart Grid technologies are forefront in bringing a technological revolution in the energy sector. It is very much evident that IoT is the "buzzword of the year". With the introduction of IoT along with other technologies, the automobile industry is thriving in its fleet operation, maintenance management, transparency and safety aspects etc. IoT has brought a tremendous change in car operation also. Apart from car inspection and maintenance, its usage has its wings spread in entertainment, data analytics, vehicular telematics and others. The utility of the internet is redefined by IoT applications in automobile industry. With the development in the technology of the Internet of Things, the automobile sector's use cases will be more popular in the days to come. As far as the banking industry is concerned, the increased use of devices by bank customer at different places in different time period has led to as increased IoT data. Banks can make use of these data to improve customer interactions, design the personalized services and banks can enhance the market share through customer data. The application of IoT would help the banking industry in particular, and the policymakers in general to formulate and design the appropriate policy relating to Bank services. IoT helps the medical and healthcare experts to monitor and control several health problems. In fact, IoT has made a revolutionary change by transforming the medical and health care sector from hospital-centric to patient-centric organization. IoT assists in cost reduction by making resource management easier. Smart Grid technology brings a massive life to plug-in vehicles, as it reduces the cost significantly. Similarly, Smart Grids help the banks to run their branches energy efficiently and leads to drastically reduce power consumption. The potential of IoT and Smart Grids spreads to almost every corner of the business. Smart Grid offers better safety by reducing power failures and fluctuations. Moreover, Smart Grids will provide early warning in case of equipment fault. No doubt, making power grids smarter with energy intelligence generates numerous innovative prospects in the ever changing environment. Although both IoT and Smart Grid have a long way to go in the field of energy management, the prospects are exciting.

References

1. J. Gubbi, R. Buyya, S. Marusic, and M. Palaniswami, *Future Generation Computer Systems*, Vol. 29, No. 7, pp. 1645-1660, 2013.
2. F. Khanboubi, A. Boulmakoul, and M. Tabaa, *Procedia Computer Science*, Vol. 151, pp. 77-84, 2019.
3. M. D. Ramasamy, K. Periasamy, L. Krishnasamy, R. K. Dhanaraj, S. Kadry and Y. Nam, "Multi-Disease Classification Model using Strassen's Half of Threshold (SHoT) Training Algorithm in Healthcare Sector," in IEEE Access,
4. G. Suseendran, E. Chandrasekaran, D. Akila, and A. Sasi kumar, "Banking and FinTech (Financial Technology) Embraced with IoT Device," in Data, Management, Analytics and Innovation, *Springer Singapore*, 2020
5. S. Vijay Kumar, S, IoT applications in Finance and Banking, *International Journal of Research and Analytical Reviews*, Vol.6, No.2, pp.952-954, 2019.
6. M. Salhaoui, A.G. Gonzalez, M. Arioua, F.J. Ortiz, A. E. Oualkadi, and C.L. Torregrosa, Smart Industrial IoT Monitoring and Control System Based on UAV and Cloud Computing Applied to a Concrete Plant, *Sensors*, Vol. 19, p. 3316, 2019.
7. I. Aris, R. Sahbusdin, and A.F.M. Amin, Impacts of IoT and Big data to automotive industry, *10th Asian Control Conference*, 2015, doi: 10.1109/ASCC.2015.7244878.
8. R.K. Bajaj, M. Rao, and H. Agarwal, Internet of Things (IoT) in the Smart Automotive Sector: A Review, *IOSR Journal of Computer Engineering*, pp. 36-44, 2018.
9. Cynthia, J., Sankari, M., Suguna, M., & kumar, D. R. (2018, December). Survey on Disaster Management using VANET. 2018 4th International Conference on Computing Communication and Automation (ICCCA).
10. B. Pradhan, S. Bhattacharya, and K. Pal, IOT-based applications in Healthcare devices, *Journal of HealthCare Engineering*, 2021, doi: 10.1155/2021/6632599.
11. S. Banka, I. Madan, and S.S. Saranys, Smart Healthcare Monitoring using IoT, *International Journal of Applied Engineering Research*, Vol. 13, No. 15, pp. 11984-11989, 2018.

12. Lalitha, K., Kumar, D. R., Poongodi, C., & Arumugam, J. (2021). Healthcare Internet of Things – The Role of Communication Tools and Technologies. In Blockchain, Internet of Things, and Artificial Intelligence (pp. 331–348). Chapman and Hall/CRC.

13

Solar Energy Forecasting for Devices in IoT Smart Grid

K. Tamil Selvi[1]*, S. Mohana Saranya[1] and R. Thamilselvan[2]

[1]*Department of CSE, Kongu Engineering College, Erode, Tamil Nadu, India*
[2]*Department of IT, Kongu Engineering College, Erode, Tamil Nadu, India*

Abstract

Increased energy demands and dependencies on fossil fuels is an important issue in the power sector. Renewable energy sources have a big usage trend in electricity generation. The renewable resources exhibit higher penetration in the energy portfolios of many scenarios, which put emphasis on the need for precise forecasting of variable renewable resources like- solar, wind, and tidal- at different temporal scales to achieve balanced power utilisation in the smart grid. Solar forecasting is an enabling technology for integration of solar resources into the power grid for efficient delivery of power and its consumptions. The existing power system operations need changes with integration of renewable resources. Smart grids allow the integration of smart technologies with the existing power generation system infrastructure. Energy management and demand profile shaping are important concerns in smart grid systems. The solar generation reveals high variability with higher penetration levels in the smart grid poses problems associated with the reservation cost, generation and distribution and reliability of the grid. Hence, there is a need for forecast systems with high precision across multiple time horizons for regulation, dispatching, scheduling the power distribution. The key feature of the smart grid is the ability to utilize the statistics to make optimized operational decisions. With this feature, significant improvement can be made in the smart grid to forecast the behaviour of renewable energy through both short-term and long-term assessments.

Keywords: Smart grid, statistical models, solar energy, deep learning, Internet of Things, stationary models, regressive methods, energy forecasting

Corresponding author: ktamilselvikec@gmail.com

P. Sanjeevikumar, Rajesh Kumar Dhanaraj, Malathy Sathyamoorthy, Jens Bo Holm-Nielsen and Balamurugan Balusamy (eds.) *Smart Grids and Internet of Things: An Energy Perspective*, (365–394) © 2023 Scrivener Publishing LLC

13.1   Introduction

There is a global demand for renewable energy integration into application for efficient power management. Smart grid also uses solar power for its energy resources. It also depends on variability of solar resources, deviation in seasons, and its production and the storage. Solar resource productions are often backed as the auxiliary source of energy which increases the operational and capital efficiency. Hence, there arise a need for efficient forecast of solar energy production for integration into the smart grid. The forecasting can be short-term or long-terms depends on the application scenarios and implementation environment. Probabilistic models [1] can be embedded for forecasting solar power for household and substation levels. Solar power forecast be done in two-time horizons: (i) 6h ahead, and (ii) three days ahead. For grid regulation, solar diffusion grows with solar forecast in multiple horizons of time. In smart grid operation, short-term forecast will be very efficient. Long-term forecast will be mostly used for control performance and scheduling.

Solar forecasting is an empowering technology for solar utilisation and integration into the grid environment to improve the efficiency of energy delivery and minimize the cost associated with the weather aspects. Statistical models and Artificial Intelligence (AI) models is employed to forecast the solar energy in the smart grid for IoT devices [2]. The Pearson product-moment correlation coefficient (PPMCC) provides the correlation coefficient between the solar output and constraint based environmental weather conditions. In system probability distribution function, asymmetry is represented using skewness. The peak magnitude of the distribution is given by Kurtosis. Meta-heuristic algorithms and genetic algorithms provides optimization based on objective functions. The generalized model of forecasting the solar energy is shown in Figure 13.1. The collected data have to be normalized for efficient data analysis and data improvisation can be made for better forecast. The input data is segregated into data for training, data for testing and validation data for model validation. The model is built using training data and tested with test data. The best model can be obtained using parameters like accuracy, error, etc., based on the application domain and task.

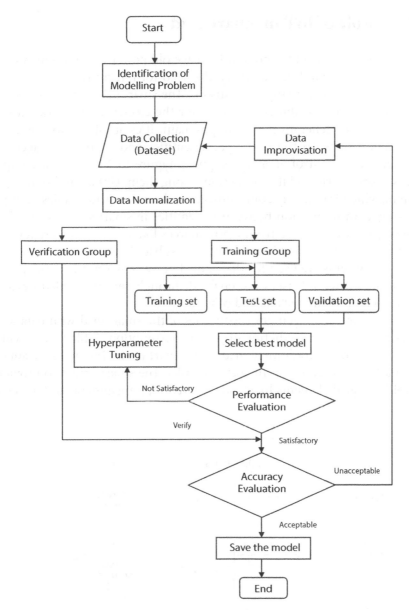

Figure 13.1 Solar energy forecasting model flow.

13.2   Role of IoT in Smart Grid

The outmoded grid environment is an age old power distribution system. For growing demand of electricity, the need for integration of smart grid played a vital role in many domains [3]. The smart grid is a self-sufficient system which is distributed in nature for the electricity network with an efficient power generation and supply chain. It establishes two-way communication between the participating entities and enables management of unpredicted control of energy supplies. Figure 13.2 depicts the components of smart grid and its interaction among them. Unlike traditional grid system, which is one-way communication, the smart grid enables multiple two-way communication between the entities in smart supply chain. The power generation can be from many sources like power plants, renewable sources, etc., The transmission lines with substations and automated distribution systems are used for distributed power environment. The power management by end users are enabled through sensor-enabled devices, smart meters, smart sockets and other devices.

Control and management capabilities of the smart grid with data analytics enables future prediction of power consumption. Table 13.1 provides the comparison of traditional grids with smart grids. The main advantage of smart grid is reduction in cost and risks. The smart grid also provides visibility of grid elements like load, generation, transmission and to detect

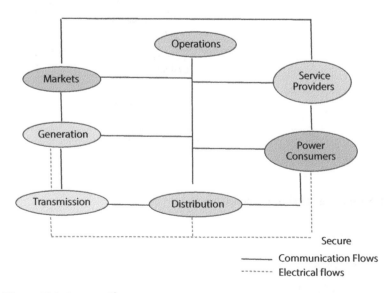

Figure 13.2 Smart grid.

Table 13.1 Tradition grid vs smart grid.

	Traditional grid	**Smart grid**
Metering	Solid state electro-mechanical	Digitalized microprocessor
Communication	Simplex and local duplex communication	Global integrated duplex communication
Customer – interaction	Limited	Extensive
Generation	Global centralized	Both centralized and distributed generation
Power flow control	Restricted protection, monitoring and control systems	Proactive and adaptive protection mechanism
Monitoring	Less visualization	Self-monitoring
Restoration	Works with human intervention	Self-configuring, Self-healing
Operation & Maintenance	Need manual equipment maintenance	Automated remote equipment maintenance
Control	Less possibility of control capabilities	Distributed universal control systems
Reliability	Estimated: Prone to failures and cascading outages	Predictive: Pro-active real-time protection and islanding
Topology	Radial	Network

problems automatically online without outages and downtime. Green energy supply is enabled with smart grid and its associated technology. The basic component of an efficient smart grid is the smart sensors and meters. The energy consumption on the customer side can be tracked with smart grids. The embedded sensors in the environment appliances allows to sense and capture the data enables monitoring and control. The full picture of energy consumption for the aggregated data consumption in the environment with estimated load and cost is obtained using smart meters.

13.3   Clear Sky Models

For predictions of solar energy, three viewpoints are concerned that are accessibility, performance of forecast, and statistical properties. To obtain clear sky irradiance with clear sky models and with time and effort, this combination of factors is termed as accessibility. Mean Square Error scaling used for forecasting performance and static clear-sky index is investigated through statistical properties with time series data. The quantity of solar energy obtained at the land surface under the atmosphere in the mode of free-cloud model is an estimation of clear sky model. Machine learning models are constructed in such a way that the important features like seasonal components have to automatically fetched for efficient prediction. It requires local weather inputs like O_3 content, water vapour content, solar geometry with link turbidity.

13.3.1   REST2 Model

The REST2 Model is a dual band model, which is based on parameters of each extinction layer transmission of the atmosphere. It is dependent on extra-terrestrial spectral distribution and values of solar constants. The input for this model is vertical path length of O3, water vapour content, reduced NO2, surface pressure, zenith angle, surface albedo and Angstrom turbidity coefficient. The basic models like Ineichen-Perez and McClear are less dependent on the parameters [4].

13.3.2   Kasten Model

For accurate estimation of clear sky radiation, Linke turbidity coefficient TL is used to quantify the information. It is dependent on the air mass. Logically it signifies the total proportion of clean and dry cloud environment for the observed quantity. It can be expressed as relation between the normal incidence direct irradiance (NID) and normal incidence extra-terrestrial irradiance (NIE) as written in Equation (13.1).

$$N\ ID = NIE\ .exp\left(\delta_k\ .\ T_L\right) \tag{13.1}$$

The constant δ_k is the Kasten's pyrheliometric constant and it is dependent on factors like molecular scattering and absorption rate in stratospheric layers. Mostly it occurs in the altitudes of 8000 and 2500 m.

13.3.3   Polynomial Fit

The simplest clear sky model is based on the polynomial that is specific to a location. The polynomial is derived based on the cosine of the solar zenith angle θ. It can be expressed as depicted in Equation (13.2)

$$I^{clr} = \sum_{n=0}^{N} c_n \left(cos\ cos\ (\theta)\ \right)^n \tag{13.2}$$

For third order polynomial as proposed by Coimbra and Marquez [5] results in the following expression as shown in Equation (13.3)

$$I_t^{clr} = c_3 (cos\ cos\ (\theta_t))^3 + c_2 (cos\ cos\ (\theta_t))^2 + c_1 (cos\ cos\ (\theta_t))^1 + c_0 \tag{13.3}$$

The coefficients c_n are obtained using dataset by fitting the polynomial. The limitation of the model is the dependency of location specific historic data on clear sky days.

The clear sky index and clearness index are the most common parameters used in solar energy prediction in clear sky model. The fraction of the irradiance obtained (R_t) to ground level model clear sky irradiance (R_t^{clr}) is Clear sky index (k_t) as written in Equation (13.4).

$$k_t = \frac{R_t}{R_t^{clr}} \tag{13.4}$$

Compared to clear sky irradiance, extra-terrestrial irradiance is easier to model because it is independent of the atmospheric dynamic parameters. The extra-terrestrial irradiance can be written as

$$R_t^{EX} = I_0\ cos\ cos(\theta_t) \tag{13.5}$$

Here the solar constant I_0 = 1360 W/m^2, θ_t is the at time t and zenith angle of solar radiation. It is independent of location specific parameters except the zenith angle which is dependent on latitude. The clearness index (c_t) is defined as ratio of irradiance with respect to ground level and extra-terrestrial which can be obtained from Equation (13.4) and (13.5) is depicted in Equation (13.6)

$$c_t = \frac{R_t}{R_t^{EX}} \qquad (13.6)$$

13.4   Persistence Forecasts

The persistence method is the simplest method in the weather forecasting. It assumes that the dynamics are minimal and the prediction of the next series of data in time is equivalent to the current time series data. It is also dependent on (k_t) and clearness index for the prediction of next period solar energy. Based on clear sky index, persistence condition can be defined as shown in Equation (13.7).

$$k_{t+\Delta t} = k_t = \frac{R_t}{R_t^{clr}} \qquad (13.7)$$

Based on clearness index, persistence forecast can be derived as shown in Equation (13.8).

$$c_{t+\Delta t} = c_t = \frac{R_t}{R_t^{EX}} \qquad (13.8)$$

From the clear sky and clearness index, the next step solar irradiance by the persistence forecast is computed as shown in Equation (13.9).

$$F_{t+\Delta t}^{Pers_k} = k_t I_{t+\Delta t}^{clr} \quad \text{and} \quad F_{t+\Delta t}^{Pers_k} = c_t I_{t+\Delta t}^{clr} \qquad (13.9)$$

The most important slighting features of persistence forecast are during the cloudless period, the model works with minimal error and it exhibit delay due to the tenacity of the indices parameters. Various factors affect the solar variability like cover of the cloud, position of solar radiation, etc. The deterministic behaviour of the solar radiation and can be modeled using the clear sky and clearness indices. Hence solar variability provides the information on stochastic components and try to alleviate the fluctuations. It can be derived as step changes of the clear sky and clearness indicies.

13.5   Regressive Methods

Most of the existing stochastic models provides long-term prediction. The long-term prediction is mostly based on environmental factors and ignores the short-term fluctuations and its impact for forecasting. And also, regression models are based on relationship between independent variables and its dependencies are not taken into considerations. The forecasting accuracy can be improved by incorporating the correlation aspects among the features of the prediction data.

For analysis of stationary time series data, Moving Average (MA) and Auto Regression (AR) can be used. Additionally, Auto Regressive Moving Averages (ARMA) and Auto Regressive Integrated Moving Average (ARIMA) is being used for the dynamic time series forecasting.

13.5.1   Auto-Regressive Model

Given a time series data, current observation z_t can be modeled based on previous 'p' observations, $z_{t-1}, z_{t-2}, \ldots z_{t-p}$ with error term ∂_t and Constant C. Thus the Autoregressive (AR) model of order 'p' can be expressed as shown in Equation (13.10).

$$AR(p): z_t = \sum_{i=1}^{p} z_{t-i} + \partial_t + C \tag{13.10}$$

13.5.2   Moving Average Model

The AR model is not only affected by the current error, but also on the previous 'p' error terms, then it is known as Moving Average (AM) model. It can be represented as shown in the Equation (13.11).

$$MA(v): x_t = \partial_t \sum_{i=1}^{v} \partial_{t-i} \tag{13.11}$$

13.5.3   Mixed Auto Regressive Moving Average Model

Auto Regressive Moving Average ($ARMA(p,v)$) integrates $AR(p)$ and $MA(v)$ and can be depicted in Equation (13.12). This model can be used to model the time (hourly) series of solar irradiance based on clearness index c_t. The multiplicative feature of ARMA [6] model enables both forward and backward relationship of time series data.

$$ARMA(p,v): a_t = \sum_{i=1}^{p} a_{t-i} + \partial_t + C + \sum_{i=1}^{v} \partial_{t-i} \qquad (13.12)$$

13.5.4   Mixed Auto Regressive Moving Average Model with Exogeneous Variables

The stationary stochastic models deliberated so for is modeled on univariate basis, hence forecast accuracy is not up to the expected level. To accommodate multivariate time series analysis, $(ARMA(p,v))$ is embedded with the external parameters like evolution of local temperature and its interdependence on the solar radiation forecasting for improved forecasting accuracy. Parameters like humidity, cover of the cloud, wind direction and speed are independent variables for the model but it affects the forecasting value. These variables are called exogeneous variables and the model is termed as Auto Regressive Average model with exogeneous variables (ARMAX).

The model can be expressed [7] as $(ARMAX(p,v,q)$ with p efers to autoregressive model $AR(p)$, v indicates moving average model $MA(v)$ and q be the exogeneous parameters. It is written as shown in Equation (13.13). Here α is parameters of the model and d_{t-i} is the exogeneous input given the model. The overall analysis of the models is shown in Table 13.2.

$$ARMAX(p,v,q): X_t = \sum_{i=1}^{p} X_{t-i} + \partial_t + C + \sum_{i=1}^{v} \partial_{t-i} + \sum_{i=1}^{v} \alpha_i \, d_{t-i}$$

$$(13.13)$$

13.6   Non-Linear Stationary Models

The complex non-linear behaviour of the system like saturation effects, hysteresis, chaos and certain combination of non-linear problems cannot be modeled by linear stationary models as discussed above. The non-linear model explores the hidden complex structures for accurate forecasting. The most common non-linear stationary model is the

Table 13.2 Comparison of regressive models.

AR	MA	ARMA	ARMAX
It is the regression of the variable against itself	Past forecast errors used in a regression-model	Combination of differencing with autoregression and moving average model	It is modeled based on relationship between lagged independent and dependent variables
Variable of interest is forecasted based on the history in the linear combination	Prediction of future values and estimation of trend cycle for the past value is given by average smoothing	It starts with estimation of parameters using likelihood maximization	It is based on lagged variables which are time dependent
Linear predictive modeling technique	Univariate time series modeling technique	Modeling stationary stochastic process with AR and MA	Linear regression model with ARMA to model residuals
Parameters: Error term	Parameters: Error term and average, Order	Parameter: Order of AR, Order of MA	Parameters: Order of AR and MA, external input

Non-linear AR-eXogeneous (NARX) model and can be described using Equation (13.14). This model is relating the current time series value to past time series value, current and past values of exogeneous variables and error term. The function of the model can be wavelet, neural network, sigmoid network and certain non-linear functions.

$$N_t = F(x_{t-2}, x_{t-3}, \ldots v_t, v_{t-1}, v_{t-2}, \ldots) + \delta_t \qquad (13.14)$$

Here x is a variable of interest, v is an external influence variable and δ is the error term.

13.7   Linear Non-Stationary Models

The time dependent nature of non-stationary models results in variation of one or more aspects for the entire time span. Even though, they no fixed mean, it exhibits homogeneity with a part of the series behave like another part of the series which can be local or global. The non-stationary behaviour can be obtained by the suitable variations among the demanding processes.

13.7.1   Auto Regressive Integrated Moving Average Models

The most generalization of ARMA is Auto Regressive Integrated Moving Average (ARIMA) model [8]. The non-stationary mean is converted into stationary mean using differencing mechanism in ARIMA. The variable of interest is regressed based on its past values and indicated by AR part and MA part is denoted by regression error term based on its past values at various time series. Differencing is applied to transform non-stationary time series to the stationary mean. The generalized ARIMA model is represented as

$$N_t = (1 - l)^d X_t \qquad (13.15)$$

Equation (13.15) represents non-stationary model and with differencing operation it is being transformed into stationary aspect model. Equation (13.16) reveals the stationary mode of ARIMA model.

$$ARIMA(p,q,l): \left(1 - \sum_{i=1}^{p} l^i\right) N_t = \left(1 + \sum_{i=1}^{q} l^i\right) \partial_t \qquad (13.16)$$

The parameters l denotes lag order (first), q is the moving average, p is the degree of differencing and ∂ be the error term.

13.7.2   Auto-Regressive Integrated Moving Average Model with Exogenous Variables

The combination of ARIMA model with exogenous variable results in Auto-regressive Integrated moving average model with exogenous variable (ARIMAX) [9]. The Current value of time series is influenced by the exogeneous variable. The difference in lag order is also taken into consideration. ARIMAX model can be represented as shown in Equation (13.17)

$$ARIMAX(p,q,d): y_t = \sum_{i=1}^{p} y_{t-i} + \sum_{j=1}^{q} \partial_{t-j} + \sum_{k=1}^{d} l^i \partial_k \quad (13.17)$$

y_t is the data represented in time, p is the lags in autoregressive method, d is the differencing degree and q is the number of average lags in motion.

13.8   Artificial Intelligence Techniques

13.8.1   Artificial Neural Network

Artificial Intelligence can be applied for solar energy prediction. The most commonly used is Artificial Neural Network (ANN). The basic unit is neuron which receives the input and perform non-linear operations and provides the predicted output. These neurons are connected to adjacent neurons to form a neural network. The simple neuron receives the input, process it and produce the output [10]. Based on the threshold value the neuron will be fired and the output can 1 or 0. This is regulated by bias. The simple artificial neuron structure is shown in Figure 13.3.

13.8.2   Multi-Layer Perceptron

Multi-Layer Perceptron (MLP) performs mapping between input and output variables in non-linear manner [11]. It uses feed forward networks and applies backpropagation for training the model. This model studies the dependencies between input and output information based on the historical statistics [12]. The composed neural network has stacked architecture with input units, hidden units and output units. Figure 13.4 depicts the simplified units of ANN. In addition to layers, each neuron passes the formation to another neuron through the links which are associated with weights.

The parameters in the forecast like wind speed, humidity, temperature, etc., are feed as input for the input layer. The last layer, output layer provides predictions like clearness index, clear sky index for prediction of solar energy. The middle layer hidden neurons provide error propagation

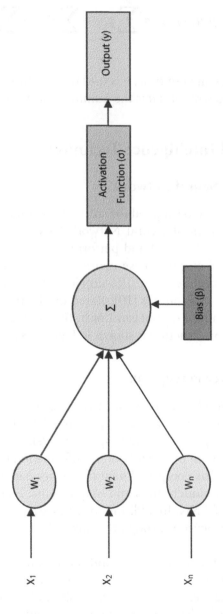

Figure 13.3 Simplified artificial neuron structure.

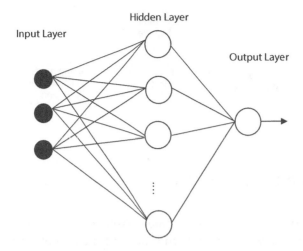

Figure 13.4 Artificial neural network.

for improved prediction accuracy. It is computed using transfer functions like sigmoid, tanh, etc. It is represented as shown in Equation (13.18).

$$f(x_i) = \frac{1}{1 + e^{-x_i}} \qquad (13.18)$$

Here x_i is the weighted sum of the inputs. It is obtained using the input a_j passed to the neuron and the weight w_{ij}, the link between the neuron j and neuron i. Bias β_i is the part of the neuron i as depicted in Equation (13.19). The model learns through the training with the input data. The learning can be supervised or unsupervised. The forecasting of solar radiation belongs to supervised learning. For example, daily clearness index is given as input and the model learns with the measured data and the output value is estimated. The variance between the target value and predicted value (i.e, error) is propagated back to the hidden units. With backpropagation, the weights are updated with bias.

$$x_i = \sum_{j=0}^{n} w_{ij} \, a_j + \beta_i \qquad (13.19)$$

The weights are adjusted based on the backpropagation algorithm. The weights associated with the hidden units to output neurons and hidden

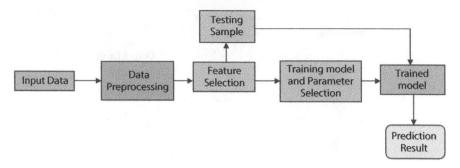

Figure 13.5 ANN based prediction flow.

units to input layer must be updated based on the updation rule. The weight entities between the hidden unit j and the output unit k is depicted as shown in the Equation (13.20).

$$w_{jk} = w_{jk} + \Delta w_{jk} \qquad (13.20)$$

Generally, in ANN based prediction, the input data has to be curated based the model and its dependent elements. Data pre-processing is performed on the input data using statistical modeling and tool based approaches [13]. The contributing features for the forecasting models can be obtained either manually or using feature selection algorithms. Principle Component Analysis (PCA) is the most commonly used for selection of best features and data transformation [14]. From the curated data, training and test samples are segregated and moved into training phase. The model start learning the patterns in the data and based on the parameter supplied, the model is evaluated. The testing samples are validated for model in the real-time accuracy. The overall prediction model and flow is depicted in Figure 13.5.

13.8.3   Deep Learning Model

The artificial intelligence method aforementioned uses shallow model for forecasting renewable energy in its learning process. Mostly backpropagation, support vector machine, boosting algorithm and entropy-based methods are used in shallow training models [15]. It needs huge training phase to acquire the require insight out of the given data. The other limitations of the shallow learning models are manual feature engineering, restricted generalization capability and limited space complexity. To overcome these drawback, deep learning models come into play.

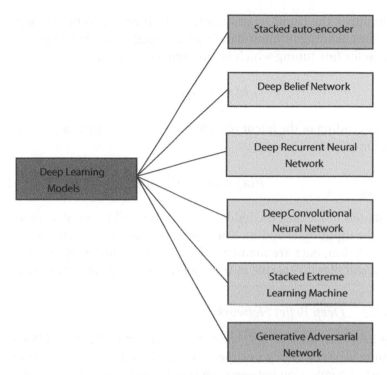

Figure 13.6 Deep learning models for forecasting problems.

The salient features of deep learning models are automatic (unsupervised) feature extraction, well adapted generalization capabilities and big data training samples. The major classification deep learning models are shown in Figure 13.6. These models show an improvement in the accurate prediction of solar energy for smart grid. Further data pre-processing and post error correction techniques has to be incorporated for the dynamic forecasting methods with feature extraction using deep learning models.

13.8.3.1 Stacked Auto-Encoder

Stacked Auto-Encoder (SAE) performs unsupervised feature extraction layer by layer and obtains the initial weights for the given network [16]. In pre-training phase, it obtains the initial weight and performs global labelled learning for fine tuning of the weights. Hence it consists of pre-training phase and fine-tuning phase. SAE consist of layers of sparse of auto-encoders with the hidden unit output is linked to the next hidden unit inputs. It consists of two units namely encoder and decoder. The encoder accomplishes the latent representation which results in hidden layer data $h(x)$. The encoding of input data is represented as the function of weights and bias for fine tuning which is represented in Equation (13.21).

$$h(x) = \sigma(\beta + W_x)$$

(13.21)

The decoding of the latent representation to the output layer is given by Equation (13.22)

$$h(x) = \sigma(c + W^T h(x))$$

(13.22)

With this modelling, the hidden unit maintain all the needed information about the input units and its associated features. Hence, with compressed representation, data are maintained with elimination of redundant information and play a vital role in feature extraction for efficient prediction.

13.8.3.2 Deep Belief Network

Deep Belief Network (DBN) is improved version of Restricted Boltzmann Machine (RBM) which is unsupervised model which has bidirectional and symmetric connection between layers of the network. RBM is a stochastic model consist of visible neurons layers stacked with the layer of hidden neurons. The hidden unit provides the activation probability to the visible layer to calculate the parameters of the neural network. The training of DBN model is based on RBM with its parameters for effective feature extraction [17]. DBN uses greedy based training approach. Stacked RBM can be viewed as DBN with the multi-layer hidden neurons. In greedy based layered unsupervised pre-training, the hierarchical features at each level are identified at a time. This unsupervised feature extraction is combined with the previous learned features with the addition of a layer. This set of layers are combined to give supervised prediction results in deep neural classifier or predictor. The generalized DBN model is represented as

$$P(x, h^1, h^2, \ldots h^n) = P(h^1)P(h^1|h^2) \ldots P(h^{n-1})P(h^{n-1}|h^n)$$

(13.23)

In Equation (13.23), $P(h^{n-1}|h^n)$ is an RBM and $P(h^i|h^{i+1}) = \pi_j P(h^i_j|h^{i+1})$ and the prediction probability is written as

$$P(h^i|h^{i+1}) = \sigma\left(b^i_j + \sum_k^{n(i+1)} W^k_j g^{i+1}_k\right).$$

13.8.3.3   Deep Recurrent Neural Network

Deep Recurrent Neural Network (RNN) captures temporal behaviour exhibited in data by using the history of information. It uses the in-memory to store the previous state information [18]. RNN predicts the random sequences from the input and the previous states. Consider the features a^t be the input and the output prediction variable p^t at time t. Let h^t be the hidden state that can be calculate with previous hidden state h^{t-1} and input feature. Mathematically it is represented as shown in Equation (13.24) at timestep t.

$$h^t = \sigma(U * a^t + W * h^{t-1})$$
$$p^t = softmax(V * h^t) \qquad\qquad (13.24)$$

Between the input and hidden neural unit, the weight is symbolized by U and hidden and the output layer weight is given by V. Between hidden layers, the associated weights are represented by W. The intermediate representation can be obtained by the current hidden representation, $Vh^t + C$. The parameters U, V, W are learnt through backpropagation algorithm. The amount of information that can be propagated can be regulated with additional gating mechanism which is implemented in Long Short-Term Memory (LSTM) and Gated Recurrent Unit (GRU). In smart Grid framework, the previous n days radiation explores the trend information and provides the prediction of next $n + 1$ days. Based on the above exploration, multi-step prediction can be estimated. The error backpropagation works with gradient based aspects and results in minimized prediction errors. Figure 13.7 visualizes the architecture of the RNN. The output of the RNN can be single unit prediction or the multi-unit prediction for the time series data and also for sequence learning problems.

A variant of RNN is Short Long-Term Memory. RNN captures both long-term and short-term dependencies. LSTM helps to avoid long-term dependency [19]. The backpropagation learning avoids vanishing gradient problems. The layers are stacked with the memory units. The state information of the block is maintained using gates. The three gates in each LSTM cell are input, forget and output gate. Figure 13.8 shows the LSTM cell and associated gates. Forget gate determines the amount of information to be neglected based on certain conditions to the next state. The memory states are updated based on input gate and triggered conditions. Only certain state information is given as output which is done by output gate.

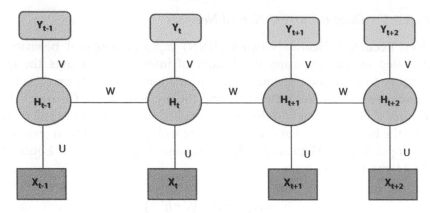

Figure 13.7 Simple recurrent neural network.

Each LSTM maintain cell state C_t, considered as memory unit. The state of the memory is controlled through input gate I_t, forget gate F_t and output gate O_t. It obtains current input X_t and previous memory state C_{t-1}. The overall formulation of LSTM is represented in the Equations (13.25).

$$I_t = \sigma(W_{xi}X_t + W_{hi}H_{t-1} + W_{ci}C_{t-1} + \beta_i)$$
$$F_t = \sigma(W_{xf}X_t + W_{hf}H_{t-1} + W_{cf}C_{t-1} + \beta_f)$$
$$C_t = F_tC_{t-1} + I_t \; tanh \; tanh \; (W_{xc}X_t + W_{hc}H_{t-1} + \beta_c)$$
$$O_t = \sigma(W_{xo}X_t + W_{ho}H_{t-1} + W_{co}C_t + \beta_o)$$
$$H_t = O_t tanh(C_t) \qquad\qquad (13.25)$$

The main advantage of LSTM cell is it stores the accumulated cell stated for the period of time t. This avoids the long-term dependency problems and finds application in time-series analysis and sequence learning problems. It can be further extended with window technique, time steps and memory between batches.

13.8.3.4   Deep Convolutional Neural Network

In Deep Convolutional Neural Network (CNN), convolution operation is performed for mapping between the low-level feature maps to high-level representation of features. For optimized convolution operation, pooling is also done with the adjacent layers of the network [20]. The various types

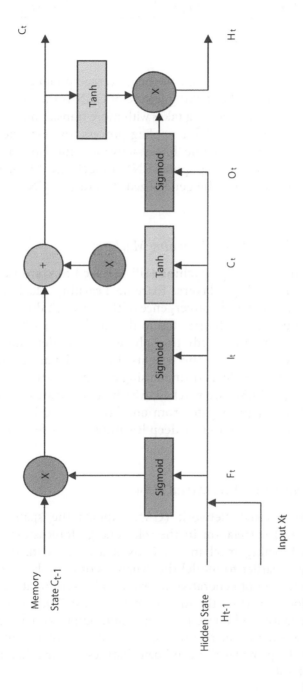

Figure 13.8 A LSTM cell.

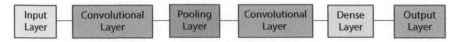

Figure 13.9 A CNN framework.

of pooling like max pooling, min pooling, average pooling, and stacked pooling are performed. The striking feature of CNN is the weight sharing strategy. In CNN, spatial learning takes with more translational invariance through pooling operation. After pooling process, the extracted feature maps are activated through non-linear activation functions like ReLU, tanh, etc. Some of the most popular CNN models are VGG, RESNET, Inception and many more. The generalized structure of CNN is depicted in Figure 13.9.

13.8.3.5   Stacked Extreme Learning Machine

Stacked Extreme Learning Machine (SELM), feed forward neural network stacked on multiple layers. Extreme Learning Machine (ELM) provides fast, efficient and convergence of the network due to randomness of the input weight distributed to the model [21] which remains constant in training and prediction phase. The hidden unit and the output units are linked with the weights that are dynamic and can be learnt very fast. The model is trained using backpropagation algorithm. In SELM, multiple ELMs are stacked, which concentrate only the well-trained weights can propagate from one layer to another. This contributes in feature extraction in deep learning model for solar energy forecasting.

13.8.3.6   Generative Adversarial Network

Generative Adversarial Network (GAN exploits the spatio-temporal (spatial-temporal) correlation in the solar energy forecasting [22] with unsupervised learning mechanism. GAN learns the data distribution that is unknown earlier to model the dynamics of the solar energy forecasts. It is composed of generative network and discriminative network. Generative model provides the joint probability distribution of the input variables. The mapping between the input and output variable are modeled through a function or relation, given by discriminative model. The generative model provides the candidate features and the discriminative model evaluates it.

13.8.3.7   Comparison of Deep Learning Models for Solar Energy Forecast

Based on the application design, different deep learning model exhibits different behaviour and provides intuitive results. Model complexity also increases with increase in automatic feature extraction capabilities, optimizations of the networks and application scenario. The deep learning models predicts the solar energy in short-term manners. For long-term

Table 13.3 Comparison of deep learning models.

Model	Computation efficiency	Feature extraction	Network optimization	Application scenario
SAE	Medium	Unsupervised feature extraction	Difficult to optimize the network	Renewable energy data that needs dimensionality reduction
DBN	High	Unsupervised feature extraction	Difficult to handle multi-dimensional data	Can be applied to renewable energy data, where feature identification is difficult
RNN	High	Unable to describe the features effectively	Less optimized network	The time dependent renewable data can be used
CNN	Low	Strong feature extraction capabilities	Can be optimized	Image based renewable data can be used
SELM	High	Limited feature extraction capability	Difficult to optimize the network	When less data is available for analysis
GAN	Low	Limited feature extraction capability	Can be optimized	Working with data that has lot of missing values

energy forecasting, hardware requirements also play a vital role in the prediction accuracy. Table 13.3 provides overall view of deep learning models and its application scenario. Feature selection is an important task in deep neural network. Irrelevant features have to eliminated to minimize the computational and time complexity. The importance of features can be obtained using the correlation mechanisms and its relevance can be obtained using mechanisms like Pearson, Spearman and XGBoost.

The linear relationship among the features can be obtained using Pearson correlation. -1 represents negative correlation, non-correlated features are given by 0 and perfectly correlated features are given by 1. It provides measure of global synchrony. For n data points, the correlation can be obtained using equation (13.26)

$$Corr_{uv} = \frac{n\sum u_i v_i - \sum u_i \sum v_i}{\sqrt{n\sum u_i^2 - \left(\sum u_i\right)^2}\sqrt{n\sum v_i^2 - \left(\sum v_i\right)^2}} \quad (13.26)$$

The correlation mechanism which is non-parametric in nature is Spearman correlation. It does not consider the data distribution and provides correlation analysis base the scale with which data is measured. For observations of n data, the difference between the ranks of the features is given by r_i. Equation (13.27) provides Spearman correlation coefficient.

$$Corr = 1 - \frac{6\sum r_i^2}{n(n^2 - 1)} \quad (13.27)$$

The importance of the features can be estimated using eXtreme Gradient Boosting (XGBoost) technique. It uses information gain for feature selection. The importance of each feature can be obtained by constructing boosted trees based on importance scores. The score obtained can be used to rank and compare each feature with others. The importance features with splits and weights are obtained using single decision tree.

13.9   Remote Sensing Model

Solar irradiance information can be obtained from Geostationary satellites (GEO) which provides the temporal data [23]. HELIOSAT derives the association between sky clearness index and cloud index at a particular time in space. This generalized method provides the solar irradiance estimation from the images of the satellite. Initially, clear sky irradiance is valued with respect to location and time. Next cloud index is obtained from the satellite image, which provides the solar radiance reflected from the cloud layers. Apart from the physical satellite model, statistical satellite model is also used for solar irradiation estimation. The most commonly used is Perez operational model. It is the improved version of Kasten's Clear sky model which provides coefficient of link turbidity independent of airmass. It provides the regression of global irradiance for an hour, I_t and cloud index C_t [24].

Another simplest statistical satellite forecasting method is Hay-Hanson Model [25]. It provides the statistical regression between the atmospheric absorptivity k_a and clearness index c_t which is represented in Equation (13.28). Here a and b are regression coefficient with values 0.7888 and 1.078 respectively.

$$c_t = a - bk_a \qquad (13.28)$$

13.10   Hybrid Models

The short-term solar energy forecasting for smart grid is proposed using seasonal ARIMA with support vector machines (SVM) [26]. Seasonal ARIMA is used to estimate and analyse the components of generated radiation that are linearly related to each other. The linearity and dynamics of the captured solar data, time varying multiple linear model is designed for forecasting solar energy [27]. Optimized Pruned Extreme Learning Machine (OP-ELM) can provide estimation of clear sky index for solar radiation prediction [28]. To optimize the neural network, the dead neurons can be removed by multi-response sparse regression and leave-one-out cross validation. The optimal weight parameters are obtained using Cuckoo Search meta-heuristic algorithm. LSTM-CNN model is applied for solar radiation forecasting [29]. In this hybrid model, time related features are obtained by LSTM and correlation of spatial relations by CNN. Radial Basis Function combined with auto-regressive analysis is proved to be effective in estimation of solar energy [30]. Mostly hybrid models are proposed for the optimization of network parameters for efficient prediction of solar radiation.

13.11   Performance Metrics for Forecasting Techniques

The prediction model performance is estimated based the difference between the ground truth and the prediction. It is estimated by many measures as shown below.

(i) Mean Bias Error (MBE)

The average forecast error is given by MBE. It represents under forecast or over forecast and gives the forecast error magnitude. The average bias in the forecasting is captured by MBE. It is represented as shown in Equation (13.29) with observed value of X_o and the forecasted value of X_f, N number of input data.

$$MBE = \frac{1}{N} \sum_{i=1}^{N} (X_{f,i} - X_{o,i}) \qquad (13.29)$$

(ii) Root Mean Square Error (RMSE)

RMSE is good indicator to determine the model performance and quality of prediction related to the real behaviour of the system. It is represented in Equation (13.30).

$$RMSE = \sqrt{\frac{1}{N} \sum_{i=1}^{N} (X_{f,i} - X_{o,i})^2} \qquad (13.30)$$

(iii) Mean Absolute Error (MAE)

The average magnitude of prediction error is given by MAE. It is written as shown in Equation (13.31).

$$MAE = \frac{1}{N} \sum_{i=1}^{N} |X_{f,i} - X_{o,i}| \qquad (13.31)$$

(iv) Mean Absolute Percentage Error (MAPE)

MAPE is approximation of MAE and variation is based on the interval with which data is being observed is taken into account. It is shown in Equation (13.32).

$$MAPE = \frac{1}{N} \sum_{i=1}^{N} \frac{\left| X_{f,i} - X_{o,i} \right|}{\left| X_{o,i} \right|} \tag{13.32}$$

(v) RMSE without Systematic Error (SD)

RMSE and MSE give more weightage to larger errors and SD aims to capture the part of RMSE which does not contribute to systematic errors [31]. It is written mathematically as in Equation (13.33).

$$SD = \sqrt{RMSE^2 - MBE^2} \tag{13.33}$$

All the aforementioned measures ac be related with inequalities: $MBE \leq MAE \leq RMSE$. Mostly, MBE is used to determine the average bias of the model to control or correct the bias of the model. For further analysis, RMSE for the verifying analytical measures of the model. For average performance model, RMSE is not an appropriate measure. The errors can also be normalized further for efficient measurement of the model.

13.12   Conclusion

Solar energy forecasting becomes an integral part of smart grid. Accurate prediction of the solar radiation improves the performance of the smart grid operations. Regressive methods explore the correlation among the contributing factors and works well in data intensive and minimal data environment. Non-linear relationship among the data is identified using deep neural models. The features of data related to space and time is obtained with the CNN and RNN models. The networks can further be optimized with hybrid models. Certain model fits well for short-term prediction and another for long-term prediction. An optimal model should be capable of capturing spatial and temporal characteristics with long and short-term prediction of environmental parameters.

The recent trend is towards probabilistic forecasting for short-term prediction. Feature extraction is the important characteristics in which all the prediction algorithms must embed into it. Further unified predictive model can be designed covering all the climatic changes and topographic scenarios.

References

1. Bessa, R.J., *et al.*, *Probabilistic solar power forecasting in smart grids using distributed information.* International Journal of Electrical Power & Energy Systems, 2015. **72**: p. 16-23.
2. Wang, H., *et al.*, *Taxonomy research of artificial intelligence for deterministic solar power forecasting.* Energy Conversion and Management, 2020. **214**: p. 112909.
3. Yun, M. and B. Yuxin. *Research on the architecture and key technology of Internet of Things (IoT) applied on smart grid.* in *2010 International Conference on Advances in Energy Engineering.* 2010. IEEE.
4. Yang, D., *Choice of clear-sky model in solar forecasting.* Journal of Renewable and Sustainable Energy, 2020. **12**(2): p. 026101.
5. Marquez, R. and C.F. Coimbra, *Proposed metric for evaluation of solar forecasting models.* Journal of solar energy engineering, 2013. **135**(1).
6. David, M., *et al.*, *Probabilistic forecasting of the solar irradiance with recursive ARMA and GARCH models.* Solar Energy, 2016. **133**: p. 55-72.
7. Krishnamoorthi, S., Jayapaul, P., Dhanaraj, R.K. et al. Design of pseudo-random number generator from turbulence padded chaotic map. Nonlinear Dyn (2021).
8. Alsharif, M.H., M.K. Younes, and J. Kim, *Time series ARIMA model for prediction of daily and monthly average global solar radiation: The case study of Seoul, South Korea.* Symmetry, 2019. **11**(2): p. 240.
9. Neshat, N., H. Hadian, and M. Behzad, *Nonlinear ARIMAX model for long-term sectoral demand forecasting.* Management Science Letters, 2018. **8**(6): p. 581-592.
10. Voyant, C., *et al.*, *Twenty four hours ahead global irradiation forecasting using multi-layer perceptron.* Meteorological Applications, 2014. **21**(3): p. 644-655.
11. Voyant, C., *et al.*, *Uncertainties in global radiation time series forecasting using machine learning: The multilayer perceptron case.* Energy, 2017. **125**: p. 248-257.
12. Yu, W., *et al.*, *Towards statistical modeling and machine learning based energy usage forecasting in smart grid.* ACM SIGAPP Applied Computing Review, 2015. **15**(1): p. 6-16.
13. Huang, J. and M. Perry, *A semi-empirical approach using gradient boosting and k-nearest neighbors regression for GEFCom2014 probabilistic solar power forecasting.* International Journal of Forecasting, 2016. **32**(3): p. 1081-1086.

14. Gonzalez-Vidal, A., F. Jimenez, and A.F. Gomez-Skarmeta, *A methodology for energy multivariate time series forecasting in smart buildings based on feature selection.* Energy and Buildings, 2019. **196**: p. 71-82.
15. Liu, H., *et al., Deterministic wind energy forecasting: A review of intelligent predictors and auxiliary methods.* Energy Conversion and Management, 2019. **195**: p. 328-345.
16. Jiao, R., *et al., A model combining stacked auto encoder and back propagation algorithm for short-term wind power forecasting.* Ieee Access, 2018. **6**: p. 17851-17858.
17. Neo, Y., *et al. Forecasting of photovoltaic power using deep belief network. in Tencon 2017-2017 IEEE Region 10 Conference.* 2017. IEEE.
18. Alzahrani, A., *et al. Solar irradiance forecasting using deep recurrent neural networks. in 2017 IEEE 6th international conference on renewable energy research and applications (ICRERA).* 2017. IEEE.
19. Abdel-Nasser, M. and K. Mahmoud, *Accurate photovoltaic power forecasting models using deep LSTM-RNN.* Neural Computing and Applications, 2019. **31**(7): p. 2727-2740.
20. M. D. Ramasamy, K. Periasamy, L. Krishnasamy, R. K. Dhanaraj, S. Kadry and Y. Nam, "Multi-Disease Classification Model using Strassen's Half of Threshold (SHoT) Training Algorithm in Healthcare Sector," in IEEE Access,
21. Behera, M.K., I. Majumder, and N. Nayak, *Solar photovoltaic power forecasting using optimized modified extreme learning machine technique.* Engineering Science and Technology, an International Journal, 2018. **21**(3): p. 428-438.
22. Jiang, C., *et al., Day-ahead renewable scenario forecasts based on generative adversarial networks.* International Journal of Energy Research, 2020.
23. Hammer, A., *et al., Solar energy assessment using remote sensing technologies.* Remote Sensing of Environment, 2003. **86**(3): p. 423-432.
24. André, M., *et al., Preliminary assessment of two spatio-temporal forecasting technics for hourly satellite-derived irradiance in a complex meteorological context.* Solar Energy, 2019. **177**: p. 703-712.
25. Chaturvedi, D. and I. Isha, *Solar power forecasting: A review.* International Journal of Computer Applications, 2016. **145**(6): p. 28-50.
26. Bouzerdoum, M., A. Mellit, and A.M. Pavan, *A hybrid model (SARIMA–SVM) for short-term power forecasting of a small-scale grid-connected photovoltaic plant.* Solar Energy, 2013. **98**: p. 226-235.
27. Gandelli, A., *et al. Hybrid model analysis and validation for PV energy production forecasting. in 2014 international joint conference on neural networks (IJCNN).* 2014. IEEE.
28. Wang, J., *et al., Forecasting solar radiation using an optimized hybrid model by Cuckoo Search algorithm.* Energy, 2015. **81**: p. 627-644.
29. Wang, K., X. Qi, and H. Liu, *Photovoltaic power forecasting based LSTM-Convolutional Network.* Energy, 2019. **189**: p. 116225.

30. Krishnasamy, L., Ramasamy, T., Dhanaraj, R., & Chinnasamy, P. (2021). A geodesic deployment and radial shaped clustering (RSC) algorithm with statistical aggregation in sensor networks. *Turkish Journal of Electrical Engineering & Computer Sciences, 29*(3).
31. Rodríguez, F., *et al.*, *Predicting solar energy generation through artificial neural networks using weather forecasts for microgrid control.* Renewable Energy, 2018. **126**: p. 855-864.

14

Utilization of Wireless Technologies in IoTSG for Energy Monitoring in Smart Devices

S. Suresh Kumar[1]*, A. Prakash[2], O. Vignesh[3]
and M. Yogesh Iggalore[4]

[1]*Department of ECE, QIS College of Engineering and Technology, Ongole,
Andhra Pradesh, India*
[2]*Department of EEE, QIS College of Engineering and Technology, Ongole,
Andhra Pradesh, India*
[3]*Department of ECE, Easwari Engineering College, Chennai, Tamil Nadu, India*
[4]*METI M2M India Private Limited, Mysore, Karnataka, India*

Abstract

Nowadays all home appliance needs care and monitoring since most of these devices are AC devices. There is a need to monitor its energy consumption so that it is possible to track its performance over the period. By doing energy monitoring and controlling, it is important to predict the device failure or whether it needs any maintenance or not. By doing energy monitoring properly then it is easy to do predictive maintenance. Before getting into the monitor, it's imperative to have a portable device that is easily installable and replaceable from one appliance to another appliance. A current transformer of a minimum of 30A is required. Need to design a device capable of providing voltage, current, power, kWh, frequency and power factor, along with these parameters a relay to be provided for appliance power on and off controlling purpose. For data analysis and monitor, this energy parameter has to be stored in the cloud platform. By adding the facilities like monitoring, controlling and analysing the energy behaviour of an appliance so that it achieves greater performance.

Keywords: IoT, smart energy meter, voltage, current, power, units, cloud, data analysis

Corresponding author: sureshkumar.sundaram@yahoo.com

P. Sanjeevikumar, Rajesh Kumar Dhanaraj, Malathy Sathyamoorthy, Jens Bo Holm-Nielsen
and Balamurugan Balusamy (eds.) Smart Grids and Internet of Things: An Energy Perspective,
(395–430) © 2023 Scrivener Publishing LLC

14.1   Introduction to Internet of Things

During a presentation to P&G (Proctor and Gamble) in 1999, Kevin Ashton developed the word IoT ("Internet of Things"). It produced RFID for the area of supply chain management, which was used in the Universal Product Code, bar code detector. He then began Zensi, which creates technology for energy monitoring and sensing.

If we had computers which knew everything, we would be able to monitor, count everything, and significantly reduce waste, loss, and costs using information which we collected without help from us. When items needed to be replaced, repaired, or remembered, and whether they were new or past, we would know. In order to see, hear, and smell the world, in all its random beauty, computers must be empowered by their own means of gathering knowledge [9].

The 'Thing' in IoT is a system with all types of integrated sensors which can collect and transmit data through a network without any manual interference. The embedded technology within the object enables it to communicate with internal states and thus with the outside world that helps to take decisions is shown in Figure 14.1.

The Internet of Things is a concept which links all devices to the cloud and allows them to communicate over the internet [1]. It is a huge network

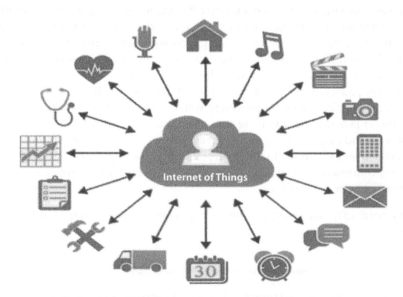

Figure 14.1 IoT - Internet of Things.

Figure 14.2 Connecting multiple devices using IoT.

of connected devices – all of which collect and exchange information about their use and, consequently, their environments is shown in Figure 14.2.

A developer has sent a request for a document that provides the tester with all the information. Tester tells the developer to return if there is a problem. It takes multiple iterations and an IoT application is generated in this way.

For example, a temperature sensor placed in the room collects and transmits information over the network, then used to modify their temperatures by multiple system sensors. The sensor connected to the refrigerator collects the outside temperature information and then changes the temperature of the refrigerator. The devices will communicate, contribute and work together in this process [2].

IoT uses several protocols and technologies to connect with devices according to the need. The protocols & technologies which includes majorly are RFID, radio protocols, Bluetooth, WiFi-Direct, NFC and wireless.

14.2   IoT Working Principle

An IoT ecosystem comprises web-enabled intelligent devices that collect data from their environments using embedded processors, sensors and communications hardware. IoT devices exchange their collected sensor data through the IoT port or other border system through which data is either sent to the cloud to be analyzed or locally analyzed is shown in Figure 14.3. Often these devices communicate with other similar devices and use each other's information. Most devices operate without human involvement, although people can communicate with devices — e.g. setup, instruction or data access. Connectivity, network and communication protocols are mainly based on the same IoT applications that are used for these web-enabled devices.

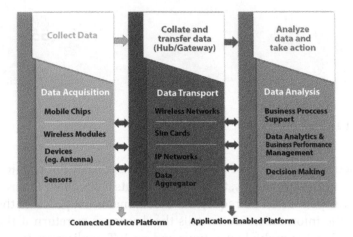

Figure 14.3 IoT architecture.

14.3   Benefits of IoT

IoT is used to monitor devices from the internet remotely, thereby creating ways of directly connecting to computer systems via internet & sensors and integrating them into the physical environment. The interlinkage of these various embedded devices in many areas leads to automation and help advanced applications, resulting in economic benefits, increased performance and precision with less intervention by humans. It covers developments like intelligent homes, intelligent city smart grids and smart transport. IoT's advantages are:

- **Enhanced Customer Engagement**:
  It helps in improving experience of the customer by automating the action. For example, if there is any problem in the vehicle then the fault will be detected and sent to owner and manufacturer.
- **Technical Optimization**:
  It contributes tremendously to technology improvement and improvement. In order to enhancing the design and performance of all sensors, the manufacturing team should collect information.
- **Reduced Waste**:
  It provides real-time information resulting in effective management of resources & decision making.

14.4 IoT Applications

There are numerous real-world applications of the Internet of Things ranging from Consumer & Enterprise IoT to Manufacturing & Industrial IoT is shown in Figure 14.4. A few applications of IoT can be elaborated as follows.

14.5 Introduction to Smart Home

A clever home means that devices and appliances are automatically operated even remotely with a web link with an android device. With an intelligent home computer, the internet is linked, allowing the user to monitor temperature and lighting, home theatre and security access to the home from a distance. All smart home devices can be accessed through a laptop, tablet or smartphone. A single-home automation system can also operate cameras, home controls, door lockers, thermostats, lamps, television and air-conditioning, refrigerator. Any modifications can be made on schedules by the customer [3, 4].

Smart home equipment accompanies self-learning skills to learn the schedules of the home-owner and to modify them as required. Intelligent households assisted by lighting controls that enable the owners of homes to minimize electricity consumption and help reduce energy costs. Any home automation devices alert the house owner if any motion is detected at home when others are away, while in the event of an emergency, the authorities concerned may be called by the police or the fire department. Once linked, IoT technology, the physical objects network that collects

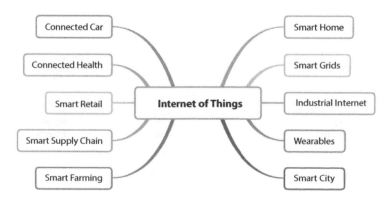

Figure 14.4 Applications of IoT.

and transmits electronic information, includes services including a smart doorbell, a smart protection system and smart devices. Intelligent homes may have hardwired/wireless systems or both. Simple and easy installation of wireless systems. Wireless home automation with features such as safety, climate control and intelligent lighting make it economic.

14.5.1   Benefits of Smart Homes

Smart home technology system provides comfortable home owners. The household owners can monitor them all with a single devise, usually a smartphone/tablet, rather than control equipment, lighting, thermostats and other functions with other devices [5, 7].

Because they are linked to a mobile device, users can obtain alerts and notifications about any issues at home is shown in Figure 14.5. For example, intelligent door clockwork allows homeowners, when they are not at home, to communication and see people who come close to the door. Lighting, internal temperature and every other home appliance can be regulated and set by the users.

An intelligent home can include accessibility devices for elderly or disabled people who stay at home. Control lighting, doors lock, operate telephone or use a computer can be used by Voice Command systems [6]. Home automation enables an individual to set an automated schedule for work such as the watering of the lawn, the heater switch, etc.

Figure 14.5 Benefits of smart home.

14.6   Problem Statement

Most traditional energy metres in homes currently only display the over-all real-time power consumption and the available amount of electricity. There are no days on which full energy parameters can be tracked back-ward. These energy metres frequently find themselves in an uncomfortable position that makes daily checking uncomfortable.

Electricity has become an essential social need and an institution that is essential to our present world's socioeconomic growth. Primary elec-tricity sources are currently small and comparatively costly. Coal, oil and gas prices are rising every year. Energy monitoring and controlling along with the consumed energy tracking will help in energy saving. Energy con-sumption control along with the consumed energy monitoring through smart devices will results in energy saving. This chapter focusses on the following objectives.

a) To monitor the real time domestic energy consumption, in order to keep track of everyday consumption of electricity using industry 4.0.
b) To design and develop efficient IOT based electronic energy meter which is used to monitor energy consumption.
c) To design user friendly, safe system to control home appli-ances such as fan, lights etc
d) Controlling home appliances such as fan, lights etc using smart phone.
e) Power saving and improving overall power efficiency.

14.6.1   Methodology

The following are the various steps involved in IoT product development.

a) Study of communication protocols such as MODBUS, Wi Fi, MQTT, I2C
b) Designing the system architecture for IoT based electronic energy meter and AC control system
c) Design of hardware for implementing the system architecture
d) Development of the designed hardware
e) Defining packet structure for communication protocol

    f)   Developing firmware according to the work-flow of the system
    g)   Deployment/Integration of the firmware with the system designed
    h)   Testing and validation
    i)   Results

14.7   Introduction to Wireless Communication

Without the use of wires, cables or other electric drives, wireless information is transmitted over the entire distance. Wireless communications are the widely known term which encompasses all forms of interconnection and communication, through wireless communication technologies and devices, between two or more devices using a wireless signal.

    a)   With its successful features, the development of wireless technology has brought much progress. The transmitted journey can be between a few metres and thousands of kilometres (e.g., a remote control and radio communication).
    b)   Mobile telephony, wireless internet access, wireless home networking and so on can be used for wireless communication.
    c)   Others include GPS, opening doors, portable computer mice, keyboards and headsets, headphones, radio receivers, Satellite TV and cable telephones. Other examples of radio wireless technology implementations include GPS.

14.7.1   Merits of Wireless

Wireless communication requires the transmission of information between two or more points without any physical link. Due to this lack of a "physical infrastructure" there are many benefits of wireless communication. Sometimes this involves collapse of distance or room. The most critical benefits of wireless communication can be found in the following:

    a)   Cost efficiency
    b)   Flexibility
    c)   Convenience
    d)   Speed

e) Accessibility
f) Constant connectivity

14.8   How Modbus Communication Works

Modbus is a serial communication protocol designed for use with its programmable programmers in Modicon® by Modicon® in 1979. (PLCs). For Modicon+ fieldbus, Modbus stands. It is simply a system used to relay information between electronic devices over serial lines. The data requesting machine is referred to as a Modbus master and Modbus slaves are the information requesting units. In a typical Modbus network, there are one master and up to 247 slaves, each having a unique slave address from 1 through 247. The Master may also provide the Slaves with details.

MODBUS Serial Line Protocol is a Master-Slave Protocol, and one-bit data is sent or received at the time. This is done at level 2 (i.e. Data Link layer) of the model OSI Open System Interconnection. A master-slave system has a master computer that commands and answers one of the "slave" devices. Without a request from the master computer, slave devices will not send any data, and slave devices will not communicate. The MODBUS serial communication stack is generally represented in the 7 layers of the OSI model in Figure 14.6.

The Modbus Application Layer Message Protocol, placed on Level 7 of the OSI model, provides customer-server communication between bus- or networking connected devices. The serial bus master and the slave nodes are used to play client roles on the MODBUS serial line.

Layer	ISO/OSI Model	
7	Application	MODBUS Application Protocol
6	Presentation	Empty
5	Session	Empty
4	Transport	Empty
3	Network	Empty
2	Data Link	MODBUS Serial Line Protocol
1	Physical	EIA/TIA-485 (or EIA/TIA-232)

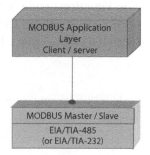

Figure 14.6 Modbus proprieties and ISO/OSI model.

14.8.1   Rules for Modbus Addressing

The address area of Modbus consists of 256 unique addresses. For the broadcast reason the 0th address is reserved. The broadcast address should be identified by all slave devices. No special ID/address should be provided to the Modbus Master device, only slave devices should. This address should be a serial bus unique address.

0	From 1 to 247	From 248 to 255
Broadcast Address	Slave Individual Addresses	Reserved

14.8.2   Modbus Framework Description

A basic Protocol Data Unit (PDU) is determined via the Modbus protocol, regardless of communication layers. There are some additional fields in the PDU for a particular network/bus map of the Modbus protocol is shown in Figure 14.7. The customer who initialises the Modbus process generates the Modbus PDU and then adds fields to create the right communication PDU.

Only the slave address is found in the address field of the Modbus Serial Line. A slave node is adjusted if the slave identification is inserted in the message address field. If the slave node returns its reply, it inserts its own ID into the reply field to let the master node know which slave node it replies. The code of the function specifies the process on the server. A data field that includes request and answering parameters can be followed by the function code. Then the error check box leads to a redundancy check (CRC).

14.8.2.1   Function Code

The Functions code is the second byte directed by the Master node. This code communicates the slave node what on the way to enter, write or read from the table. Table 14.1 displays slave accessed function code table.

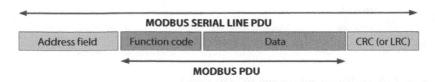

Figure 14.7 Format of MODBUS PDU and serial line PDU.

Table 14.1 Function code table.

Function code	Action	Table name
01 (01 hex)	Read	Discrete Output Coils
05 (05 hex)	Write Single	Discrete Output Coil
15 (0F hex)	Write Multiple	Discrete Output Coils
02 (02 hex)	Read	Discrete Input Contacts
04 (04 hex)	Read	Analog Input Registers
03 (03 hex)	Read	Analog Output Holding Registers
06 (06 hex)	Write Single	Analog Output Holding Register
06 (10 hex)	Write Multiple	Analog Output Holding Registers

14.8.2.2   Cyclic Redundancy Check

At the end of each letter, 2 bytes are added for error detection. Every byte in the message is used for the calculation of the CRC. And if the message receives 1 bit incorrectly, the CRC is different and error occurs.

14.8.2.3   Data Storage in Modbus

In a slave node, the data is stored in four tables as shown in Table 14.2. 2 ON or OFF tables and 2 Register Shop Tables (discrete value) (Numerical values). Read-write table & read-only table are given for both registers and coils. There is a total of 9,999 values in every row, a 1-bit bucket or

Table 14.2 Function code table.

Coil/register numbers	Data addresses	Type	Table name
1-9999	0000 to 270E	Read-Write	Discrete Output coils
10001-19999	0000 to 270E	Read-Only	Discrete Input coils
30001 – 39999	0000 to 270E	Read-Only	Analog Input Registers
40001 - 49999	0000 to 270E	Read-Write	Analog Output Holding Registers

communication is allocated between 0000 to 270E, a 1-word (16-bit = 2-bit) register and a data address between 0000 to 270 E. Every table is allotted.

14.9   MQTT Protocol

MQTT stands for Message Queuing Telemetry Transport protocol, in the year 1999, IBM employee Andy and Eurotech employee Nipper developed the first version of MQTT for monitoring and controlling oil pipeline in desert. As HTTP protocol is heavy for small hardware devices and also the devices that are connected via satellite link; the requirement of this monitoring hardware is that, it should use low bandwidth, low power and it should be lightweight. Hence MQTT. In the year 2013 IBM made MQTT open source. MQTT is an email transportation protocol publish/subscribe for Client Server. It is lightweight, open, easy to use and easy to use. These features are suitable for use in many circumstances and in constraints such as machine-to-machine (M2M) or IoT environments in which a limited footprint and/or a premium network bandwidth are needed.

As it is mentioned in definition, MQTT is a protocol for client servers which publishes/subscribes messaging, meaning all clients with MQTT connections and communications will have a centralized server. There can be multiple MQTT clients connected to a single server.

14.9.1   Pub/Sub Architecture

MQTT works on Pub/Sub architecture which means Publish and subscribe architecture. This is different from traditional client server architecture as shown in Figure 14.8. In client server architecture client directly talks to

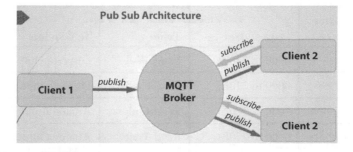

Figure 14.8 Pub/Sub architecture.

end server whereas in MQTT publisher and subscriber never contact each other directly.

14.9.2   MQTT Client Broker Communication

MQTT protocol works on top of TCP/IP protocol. As shown in Figure 14.9, the client always sends connect packets to the server first. Here the broker will never initiate the connection. The connection is always initiated by the client. Broker acknowledges the connection request. Once the connection is established, the client can publish as many messages as it wants and every publish massage will be acknowledged by the broker. If the client is interested in any messages, then it can subscribe to that message and the broker sends back subscribe acknowledgement. Whenever the broker receives a related subscribe message from any another client, it will forward the same to this client. The client can then disconnect from broker, whenever it wants and it will receive a disconnect acknowledgement. (This feature is only available in MQTT 5 but not MQTT 3.)

14.9.3   MQTT Standard Header Packet

MQTT works with exchanging series of packets, Figure 14.10 shows the standard packet structure. Each packet contains 3 sections:

1. Fixed Header (Which is always present in all MQTT packets)
2. Variable Header
3. Payload

Variable Header and Payload are not always present in all the packets.

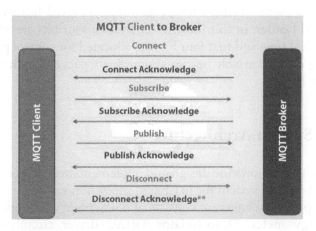

Figure 14.9 MQTT client to broker connection.

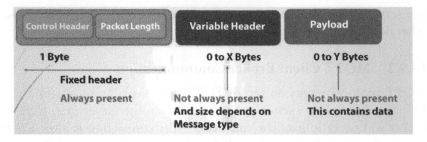

Figure 14.10 MQTT standard packet structure.

Control Packet		Bit-7	Bit-6	Bit-5	Bit-4	Bit-3	Bit-2	Bit-1	Bit-0
		Control packet type				Control packet flags			
Name	value	direction	description			Flags			
CONNECT	1	Client to server	Client request server to connect			0	0	0	0
CONNACK	2	Server to client	Connect acknowledge			0	0	0	0
PUBLISH	3	Client to server	Publish message			DUP	QoS	QoS	RETN
PUBACK	4	Server to client	Publish acknowledge			0	0	0	0
PUBREC	5	C to S or S to C	Publish received			0	0	0	0
PUBREL	6	C to S or S to C	Publish release			0	0	1	0
PUBCOMP	7	C to S or S to C	Publish complete			0	0	0	0
SUBSCRIBE	8	Client to server	Client subscribe request			0	0	1	0
SUBACK	9	Server to client	Subscribe acknowledge			0	0	0	0
UNSUBSCRIBE	10	Client to server	Client unsubscribe request			0	0	1	0
UNSUBACK	11	Server to client	Unsubscribe acknowledge			0	0	0	0
PINGREQ	12	Client to server	Ping request			0	0	0	0
PINGRESP	13	Server to client	Ping response			0	0	0	0
DISCONNECT	14	Client to server	Client disconnecting			0	0	0	0

Figure 14.11 Control packet.

14.9.3.1 Fixed Header

As shown in Figure 14.11, each packet includes fixed header controller byte in fixed header. In this illustration, the last four bits are allocated for control packet type and first four bits are allocated for control packet flags. Depending on the variable header and payload, packet length varies from one to four bytes.

14.10 System Architecture

The Figure 14.12 shows the design and implementation of an energy monitoring and control system for IoT based smart home.

The proposed architecture consists of ESP8266-Wi-Fi module, PZEM-004T energy meter, Opto-isolator TRIAC driver circuit, Real Time

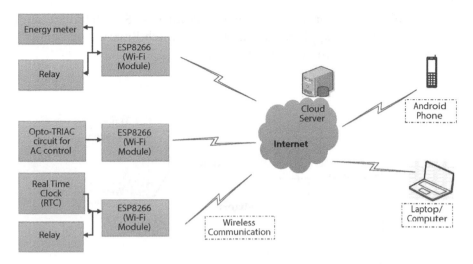

Figure 14.12 Proposed architecture.

Clock (RTC) and SPDT Relays. The 3 products were developed, IoT based electronic energy meter (this product is named as eNtroL), AC Control System for smart home (this product is named as Switch2Smart) and Scheduling Home appliances using timer (this product is named as Switch Binary). Here ESP8266 is used as the controller in all the 3 devices, this ESP module sends the data to the cloud using Wi-Fi communication protocol. And data is visible in the web page and also in android phone. We can also control the home appliance in AC control system through web page or through mobile phones [10].

Here PZEM-004T energy meter is interfaced with esp8266 module to monitor the consumed energy and also a spdt relay is interfaced with esp8266, when the command is given by the user to switch of the power supply then the relay will connect to NO terminal and cuts off the supply [15]. Control of fan, light and other home appliances is done using Opto-isolator TRIAC driver circuit. RTC is used to set the time or alarm in which a particular home appliance is switched on or off at the specified time.

The Modbus protocol is used for communication between the energy meter and wifi module, this Wi-Fi module which collects the data and send it to the cloud server. The modes of communications used here is Wi-Fi (wireless fidelity). That collected data can be viewed in Web application/ Mobile application from any place and at any time.

The proposed system is shown in Figure 14.13 which is divided into three different subsystems such as: energy monitoring device -eNtroL,

AC ontrol system for home appliance control – Switch2Smart and Scheduling of home appliance using timer – Switch Binary.

The three subsystems are explained in detail:

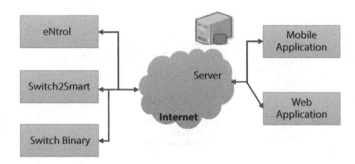

Figure 14.13 Block diagram of the proposed system.

14.11   IoT Based Electronic Energy Meter-eNtroL

eNtroL device is developed to keep track of day to day consumption of energy is shown in Figure 14.14. The consumer can display energy parameters like Current (Ampere-A), Voltage (Volts-V), Energy (KWH), Power (kW), Power-Factor (PF), Frequency (Hz). This information is extracted from the pzem-004t energy meter using Modbus communication protocol. This will help the user to keep track of day to day energy consumption rate i.e., user will be able to know during which time in a day the consumption was more/less. This will help the user to manage the energy consumption during peak hours, thereby saving money.

Figure 14.14 Block diagram of eNtroL.

14.11.1   Components Used in eNtroL

The following components are used to construct the eNtrol system.

- PZEM-004t Energy Meter
- ESP8266 Wi-Fi module
- Switching Device
- 230V AC to 5V Dc Converter
- LM1117 IC- 5V to 3.3V converter

14.11.2   PZEM-004t Energy Meter

Energy Meter/watt meter is an instrument that measures the amount of electrical energy consumed. The SI unit of power is watts (W) which is named after a scientist James Watt and it's measured by employing a watt meter or an energy meter.

This module is used for measuring parameters such as AC current, voltage, frequency, active power, power factor and active energy as shown in Figure 14.15. This module doesn't have any LED/LCD display, the data from this module is read through the TTL (Transistor- Transistor logic) interface [14]. Communication interface: RS485 interface. In the 7th layer of OSI model i.e., The application layer uses to communicate with the Modbus-RTU protocol. Just a few function codes such as 0x03, 0x04, 0x06, 0x41, 0x42 are supported. The code for the function 0x03 for read holder, the code for the function 0x04 for the reading input, the function code 0x06 for the single write register, the function code 0x41 for calibration, 0x42 for reset energy, etc. for calibration, are the function codes. There can be 248 slaves whose address start from 0x01 to 0xF7. The address for the broadcast is 0x00, in this case the slave need not reply to the master. The address 0xF8 can be used for calibration operation.

Functions:

a) It measures Electrical parameter such as current, energy, voltage, frequency, active power.
b) Alarm function during overload
c) Power alarm threshold can be set.
d) The energy value can be reset.
e) Even when the power is off the data will be stored.
f) Function of serial communication

Figure 14.15 PZEM-004T energy meter module.

14.11.3   Wi-Fi Module

ESP8266 Wi-Fi module is a device on chip (SOC) with a protocol stack (TCP/IP), which provides access to the network of every microcontroller. The esp8266 module offers an application and all networking features from a different application processor. Each module features a firmware pre-programmed AT (Attention) command collection. The module ESP8266 has a significant advance in cost-effectiveness [12]. This module has the ability to store and process on board to integrate it through its displayed GPIOs General Purpose Input Output with the necessary sensors and other

Figure 14.16 ESP8266 module.

application-specific devices as shown in Figure 14.16. The module has a minimal PCB region and makes a minimum external circuit. It is composed of an automatic RF-Radio frequency allowing VoIP-Voice to operate in all operating conditions and it does not have to have external RF-Parts. ESP8266 supports VoIP Voice over IP applications and Bluetooth interfaces for automatic delivery and coexistence.

14.11.4   Switching Device

In the proposed systems, we are using 30A Relay as a switching device. This Relay is used to switch the energy meter. Single Pole Double Throw (SPDT) Relay contains 5 terminals, two switching terminals N/O (Normally Open), N/C (Normally Close), one common terminal, and two coil terminals as shown in the Figure 14.17.

Connection to the relay is done by connecting the supply to the coil terminals i.e., one of the coil terminals is connected to positive voltage and another coil terminal is connected to ground. And the common terminal is connected to the supply. When there is no supply to the coil terminals then coil doesn't get energized and the common terminal remains connected with N/C terminal, this condition is called as idle condition. When there is enough supply to the coil terminals ten coil gets magnetically energized

Figure 14.17 30A SPDT relay.

and the flux forces common terminal to connect with N/O terminal and N/C will be open now. By using this mechanism, we can switch.

14.11.5   230V AC to 5V Dc Converter

5V supply is needed to power on Relay and LED. Here the proposed system uses 230v to 5v power supply from easy power as shown in Figure 14.18.

14.11.6   LM1117 IC- 5V to 3.3V Converter

3.3V supply is required to power on ESP8266 module, energy meter module, and for programming the Wi-Fi module. LM1117 is an IC which takes

Figure 14.18 230V AC to 5V DC converter.

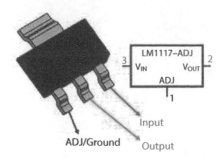

Figure 14.19 LM1117 IC- 5v to 3.3v converter.

5V DC as input and converts it into 3.3V DC as output. It is a 3-pin IC as shown in the Figure 14.19, 1-GND (ground), 2-Vout (in this pin 3.3v output is driven) and 3-Vin (in this pin 5v input is given).

14.12   AC Control System for Home Appliances – Switch2Smart

Switch2Smart device is designed and developed for on and off control along with phase angle control of the AC voltage. On and off control is used to switch on and off the home appliances, whereas phase angle control of the AC voltage is done in order to vary the intensity of light, to control the speed of fan and motor, etc. This AC control system is designed with zero-crossing Opto-isolator TRIAC driver which will drive the TRIAC for AC voltage control.

14.12.1   Opto-Coupler- H11AA1 IC

The H11AA1 is a two-directional optically coupled intake isolator consisting of two reverse parallel infrared gallium arsenide LEDs combined in the 6-pin DIP Figure 14.20 with a silicone NPN photo transistor. The H11AA1 is optimised for applications involving AC signals detection or monitoring and has a minimum CTR of 20 percent, a CTR symmetry that is 1:3.

When the AC voltage goes from zero to peak, the opto-coupler is active and thus it activates the output side [13]. The ESP pin connected to the output of the opto-coupler senses a HIGH voltage. When the pin reads a low it means we are approaching at a zero crossing of the AC mains voltage and depending upon the timing, the ESP will activate the TRIAC driver i.e., opto-coupler MOC3021M that will further activate the TRIAC providing the power to the home appliances such as bulb, fan etc.

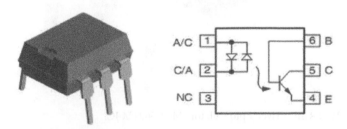

Figure 14.20 Optocoupler-H11AA1 IC.

14.12.2   TRIAC Driven Opto Isolator- MOC3021M IC

The MOC3021M is a Zero-Crossing TRIAC driven Opto-coupler/Opto-isolator is shown in Figure 14.21. Opto-coupler/opto-isolater is the device which transmits electrical signal between two circuits using light. The specialty of MOC3021M is that it has the ability of Zero-Crossing and is TRIAC driven. The output is controlled by a TRIAC and can therefore manage the AC loads in both directions without any problems. Using TRIAC, you can drive up to 400V. Since the AC load is on for the 1st time the TRIAC is only able to run after the AC wave is 0V, this prevents direct peak voltages from being transferred to load and prevents it from being damaged. The load is then on for the first time. As the performance is adjusted, the light luminosity or the speed of a ceiling ventilator and AC engine can be controlled. This IC is the best way to monitor an AC unit. In general, the MOC3021M is used for controlling AC devices, such as bulb strength, speed of a fan, electric motor etc.

14.12.3   TRIAC, BT136-600 IC

TRIAC – Triode for AC (Alternating Current) is a component that conducts current in both the directions. The BT136 IC is a TRIAC with terminal current of maximum 4A. The threshold voltage of gate in the BT136 IC

Figure 14.21 TRIAC driven opto isolator- MOC3021M IC.

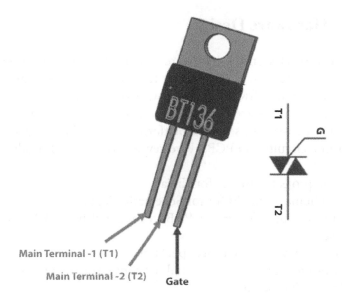

Figure 14.22 TRIAC, BT136-600 IC.

is less so that it can be driven by digital circuits. TRIACs are bi-directional switching devices thus, they are used for switching of AC appliances. Thus, for controlling (i.e., speed control, dimmer) an AC load which will consume less than 6A of current then BT136 TRIAC is used and is showed in Figure 14.22.

14.13 Scheduling Home Appliance Using Timer – Switch Binary

Switch Binary device is designed and developed for switching on and off of the AC appliance at specified time. There is an RTC placed in it, for example if a device needs to be switched on at 1 am and to be turned off at 2 pm, then the timer can be set and even we can set the device to on or off only on some particular days in a week at a particular time. A relay is used here to switch on and off the devices. And the web page is designed to set the timer for the devices, the commands from the web server is sent to the device through wifi communication protocol. RTC uses I2C communication protocol. Also using MQTT protocol the timer can be set to on the device. This product is also integrated with Alexa.

14.14   Hardware Design

This section focuses on the hardware construction of control board. The design of the hardware is done using KiCad software. It is an electronic design automation software package with open source (EDA). It facilitates the design and conversion to PCBs of schemes for electronic circuits. KiCad is an open-source software platform used for the design of schemes for electronic circuits and PCBs. Five key sections are in KiCad:

1. The project manager for KiCad
2. Eschema – The Editor for Schematic Capture
3. The layout software for PCBs, Pcbnew. It has a 3D view as well.
4. GerbView – The Gerber spectator.
5. Component Bitmap 2 – tool for converting images to PCB artwork footprints.

The KiCad is used for composite electronic boards design and production. KiCad has no board-size restrictions and up to 32 copper-layers can be used.

14.14.1   Kaicad Overview

KiCad's workflow consists of two main tasks: drawing the pattern and drawing the table. For these two tasks it is important to have both a schematic component library and a footprint library for PCB. KiCad has several components and footprints as well as new methods for creating them [8]. The flowchart of the workflow of KiCad is shown in Figure 14.23.

14.14.2   PCB Designing Using Kaicad

Using this software, design of all three devices which were mentioned in the previous chapter is carried out. In the hardware designing a PCB board for IoT based electronic energy meter, and an AC control system for smart home was designed using Kaicad software.

14.14.2.1   Designing of eNtroL Board Using Kaicad

Figure 14.24 shows the eNtroL board design with switching unit (SPDT Relay), Voltage conversion unit, ESP8266. All the modules which are

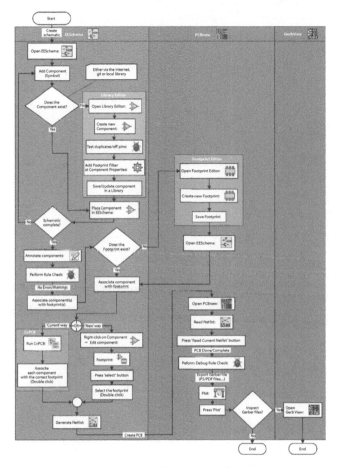

Figure 14.23 Overview of Kaicad.

available as components in KiCad is being placed and mapped to GPIO pins of ESP8266. Once the schematic is complete, components are annotated to assign the names for each component taken in schematic. Next step is to assign footprint for each of the component. Depending on the PCB layers the footprints are matched. If the PCB is being designed for single layer through-hole components are assigned, whereas for two or more-layer design through-hole along with SMD components are assigned. Next step is to generate the Netlist. Once the Netlist is generated, it is read in the Pcbnew program and it is routed by selecting required track width. Once the routing is done with front and back copper, depending on the layer, the design is ready for etching process or if the gerber is generated, it's given for manufacturing.

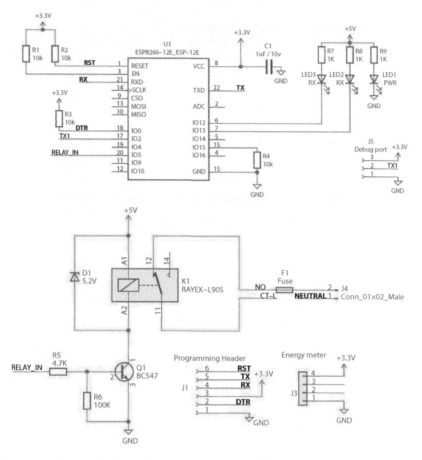

Figure 14.24 Schematic of IoT based energy meter (eNtroL).

14.14.2.2   Designing of Switch2smart Board Using Kaicad

The switch2smart board is designed with switching unit (SPDT Relay), Voltage conversion unit, ESP8266, zero-crossing Opto-isolator TRIAC driven circuit as shown in the Figure 14.25. All the modules which are available as components in KiCad is being placed and mapped to GPIO pins of ESP8266. Once the schematic is complete components are annotated to assign the names for each component taken in schematic. Next step is to assign footprint for each of the component. Depending on the PCB layers the footprints are matched. If the PCB is being designed for single layer through-hole components are assigned, whereas for two layer or more layer design through hole along with SMD components are assigned.

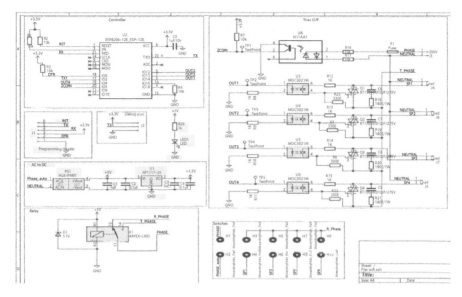

Figure 14.25 Schematic of AC control system (switch2smart).

This is 2-layer board. Next step is to generate the Netlist. Once the Netlist is generated, it is read in the PCB new program and it is routed by selecting required track width. Once the routing is done with front and back copper, depending on the layer of design, design is ready for etching process or if the gerber is generated, it's given for manufacturing.

14.14.2.3   Designing of Switch Binary Board Using Kaicad

The schematic of Switch binary is shown in Figure 14.26. the switch binary board is designed with switching unit (SPDT Relay), Voltage conversion unit, ESP8266, RTC. All the modules which are available as components in KiCad is being placed and mapped to GPIO pins of ESP8266. Once the schematic is complete components are annotated to assign the names for each component taken in schematic. Next step is to assign footprint for each of the component. Depending on the PCB layers the footprints are matched. If the PCB is being designed for single layer through hole components are assigned, whereas for two layer or more layer design through hole along with SMD components are assigned. Next step is to generate the Netlist. Once the Netlist is generated, it is read in the PCB new program and it is routed by selecting required track width. Once the routing is done with front and back copper, depending on the layer of design,

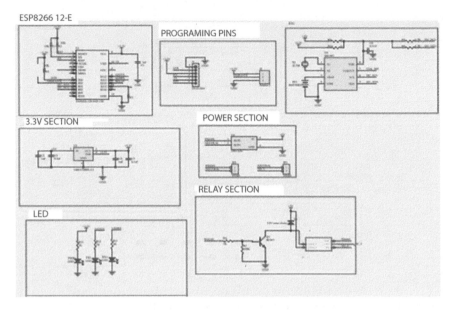

Figure 14.26 Schematic of Switching AC devices using timer (switch binary).

design is ready for etching process or if the gerber is generated, it's given for manufacturing.

14.15   Implementation of the Proposed System

A prototype of the proposed system was designed, developed and tested in the laboratory. 3 individual prototypes were developed and tested. The implementation of the system is done using Visual Studio Code software and Platform IO (IDE). It is an open-source software which makes easy to code and easy uploading to the ESP8266 controller board.

An IoT based electronic energy meter is designed and developed, the developed device gets electricity supply from the main power station to the input terminals of the watt meter. Energy meter has 2 input terminals and two output terminals. The input terminals of the energy metre are connected to the central supply and the same input is provided by cutting both ac converter and energy metre input terminals (230 to 5v). This converter converts 230V AC to 5V DC. The 5V DC supply is output of the converter. This 5V DC output is given as input to the LM1117 IC to convert 5V to 3.3V. This 3.3V is given as a supply to esp8266 module. The output of the

230v to 5v converter is given to relay to energize the coil. Energy meter is connected to esp8266 module.

ESP8266 module passes the Modbus command to energy meter to transmit the current reading. Then, energy meter transmits data to esp8266 which in turn sends to the server. Through ESP8266 module we can also control the supply using relay. And there should be a good Wi-Fi network to get uninterrupted communication between the server i.e., web page/ mobile application and the device [11]. A web page is designed where the user can see the real-time consumption of energy in the home and also through web page user can control the supply by switching relay on and off. This product is developed for real-time energy monitoring and controlling the main supply of the house. The user will be able to view energy param-eters such as voltage (V), current (A), power factor (PF), power (kW), energy (KWH), and frequency (Hz).

This device is integrated with MQTT and ALEXA. That is we can see the real time data in MQTT dashboard and user can power on and off the device using Alexa App which is installed in android mobile phones. For setting up of Alexa, first we have register with the website- sinric.com and after we login there will be an API key, this is used for alexa configuration through web page. And then we have to add the device by giving required name then we get the unique device ID for all the devices which we have added. Then in the android mobile, install Amazon Alexa app and login into that and enable sinric in the app. Then we can find all the devices which are integrated with alexa in this app, and we can control any smart device using this app.

For setting up of MQTT dashboard, we need a server. In the android mobile install an app called as MQTT Dashboard, login by giving the server details. Then we to subscribe to the topic by giving a unique ID which we will get when the device is ON, same way we can publish to the device. Subscribe means getting/reading the data from the device, Publish means writing the data to the device. Web pages for Alexa Configuration, MQTT Configuration, and Wi-Fi Configuration is designed individually.

To achieve remote controlling of AC devices or home appliances an AC control system is developed for smart home. This system is designed and developed for on and off control along with phase angle control of the AC voltage. On and off control is used to switch on and off the home appli-ances, whereas phase angle control of the AC voltage is done in order to vary the intensity of light, to control the speed of fan and motor etc. This AC control system is designed with zero-crossing Opto-isolator TRIAC driver which will drive the TRIAC for AC voltage control. TRIAC, triode for AC, is a generic trademark for a 3-terminal electronic component that conducts current in either direction when triggered. TRIAC based AC control system is designed because of the bidirectional current conduction characteristics. We can switch on and off the devices using web page, alexa or MQTT dashboard. And we can also increase or decrease the brightness of the lights and speed of the fan etc. We can connect 4 AC devices to this product. If we don't want to control the devices using internet then there is an option to control it in manual mode, for that there is an Auto/ Manual switch provided in the product, put the switch in manual mode and then we can control the AC devices using the other 4 switches in the product. When the Auto/Manual switch is in Auto mode then we can control devices using internet i.e., web page, MQTT dashboard or alexa. And the web page is designed to view and control the devices i.e., switch on and off or increase/decrease brightness of bulb, speed of fan etc., and the controlling is done through Wi-Fi communication protocol. Using MQTT protocol the controlling is done using an app in mobile and controlling is also done using alexa.

Scheduling AC devices using timer product is developed for switching on and off the devices using the timer. There is an RTC placed in it, for example if a device needs to be switched on at 1 am and to be turned off at 2 pm, then the timer can be set and even we can set the device to on or off only on some particular days in a week at a particular time. There is an option to schedule a device to on or off only once and it can be scheduled in such a way that once the time is set, every day that particular device will turn on or off at the specified time. A relay is used here to switch on and off the devices. And the web page is designed to set the timer for the devices, the commands from the web server is sent to the device through Wi-Fi communication protocol. Also using MQTT protocol the timer can be set to on the device.

14.16   Testing and Results

The system has been assembled as per the requirement and deployed for testing and validation. The PCB boards were manufactured and the components were soldered to the PCB and the firmware was programmed to the devices. Coding is done using Visual studio code software and Platform IO IDE, it is open source and easy to code. There is programming header in all the products, through which we upload the code.

14.16.1   Testing of eNtrol

The gerber file was generated and it was sent to manufacturing. After the PCB is manufactured then the components are soldered using soldering gun. Figure 14.27 shows the eNtrol board after soldering the components.

The Figure 14.28 shows the end product of entrol, here the input supply from power station is connected to Line and Neutral of the Line terminals and the load is connected to L and N terminals of 230V AC Load from which the power is transmitted to the home appliances. There is also 3 LED indications present in the product - Power, Load & Wi-Fi. Power led indicates whether the power is on or not, Load led indicates whether the load is connected to energy meter or not and wifi led indicates whether there is good internet.

When the device is connected to the supply and is connected to internet, then we can see the real time energy consumption with all the energy parameters such as voltage, current etc., in the above Figure 14.29 no. of units consumed is 0.4 and current is 2.1A, frequency is 50.1 Hz etc. Also Wi-Fi signal strength is visible in this page, user can control relay using the toggle switch provided and MQTT, alexa status is seen, here both are offline. And status indication Led are added. User can also configure Wi-Fi, MQTT and Alexa by clicking on the buttons present in this page. A Reset button is added to reset the device.

Figure 14.27 eNtroL after soldering the components.

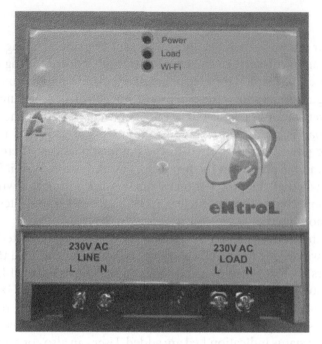

Figure 14.28 eNtroL end product with enclosure and sticker.

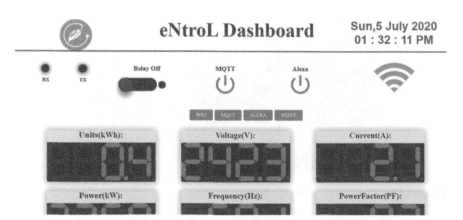

Figure 14.29 Web page for eNtroL.

14.16.2   Testing of Switch2Smart

The Figure 14.30 shows the end product of switch2smart, here the input supply is connected to Line and Neutral of the Line terminals and 4 appliances can be connected to load terminals. There are 5 switches, one is Auto/Manual switch which is used to put the device either in auto mode or manual mode. And other 4 switches are used for controlling 4 loads which are connected to the device when it is in manual mode.

When the device is connected to the supply and is connected to internet, then we can control the AC home appliances which are connected to the device, we can switch on or off appliance using the web page and also,

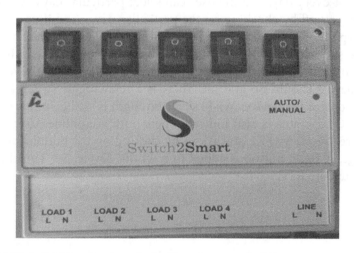

Figure 14.30 Switch2Smart end product with enclosure and sticker.

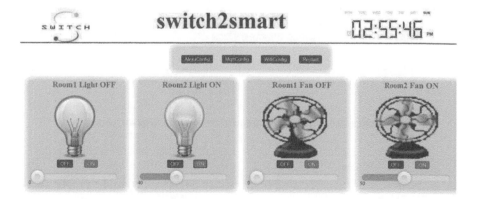

Figure 14.31 Web page for switch2smart.

we can increase or decrease the intensity of light, speed of fan etc. User can also configure Wi-Fi, MQTT and Alexa by clicking on the buttons present in this page as shown in Figure 14.31. A Reset button is added to reset the device.

14.16.3   Testing of SwitchBinary

Using the web page, the user can set the alarm/time at which the connected home appliance should switch on or off. For example if the user wants to switch on the heater every day at morning 6 am and it should switch off at 8 am they should set the start time and end time so that this process will repeat every day, and the user can select particular days in a week to switch on or off by checking on the particular days. And if user wants to on the appliance only once and it should not repeat it again then we can give the start and end time in onetime start and onetime end blocks as shown in Figure 14.32. The table in the web page displays Active time in which device should on and off. There is a relay toggle switch by which we can control the device. Wi-Fi signal strength is visible in this page and alexa, MQTT status is also indicated here both are online. User can also configure Wi-Fi, MQTT and Alexa by clicking on the buttons present in this page. A Reset button is added to reset the device. Set Time button is used to update RTC.

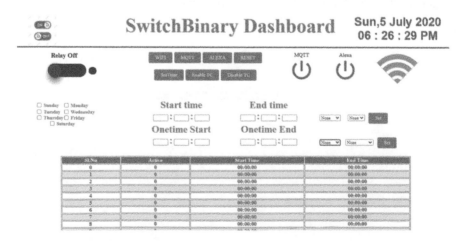

Figure 14.32 Web page for switch binary.

14.17   Conclusion

The implementation of IoT based energy meter helps in monitoring and controlling the energy consumption, also we can back track the energy consumption and AC control system helps in controlling the AC devices which leads to saving of energy usage in our daily life and switch binary helps us to schedule the device on and off time which helps us to save energy. The mobile application development has played a major role in monitoring all these activities and as the usage of mobile phones is intense in this present era, this application will become a user-friendly system. The AC control system is designed with manual as well as auto control of the appliances or Fans/light. In manual mode, control of appliances or fan/light such as switching on/off is done based on the input given by the switches present in the product. In auto mode, control decision of appliances is done by the user through mobile app. As the appliances will switch on/off based on the scheduled time in Switch Binary, this ultimately reduces the power consumption which will lead towards saving power for the next generation. The designed system can be incorporated in the existing home system with ease, because the framework used for the designed system is wireless. Most of the operations and controlling aspects are carried out by wireless modules so installation cost and maintenance cost will be less.

References

1. Abhishek Bhat, Satvik Sharma, Pranav K.R, Monika Rani H.G," Home Automation Using Internet of Things" International Journal of Engineering and Technology, Vol 4, No 7, 2017.
2. Agnetis, Alessandro & Dellino, Gabriella & Detti, Paolo & Innocenti, Giacomo & Pascale, Gianluca & Vicino, Antonio, "Appliance operation scheduling for electricity consumption optimization" Proceedings of the IEEE Conference on Decision and Control, pp. 5899-5904, 2011.
3. N. Skeledzija, J. Cesic, E. Koco, V. Bachler, H. N. Vucemilo and H. Džapo, "Smart home automation system for energy efficient housing," 2014 37th International Convention on Information and Communication Technology, Electronics and Microelectronics (MIPRO), pp. 166-171, 2014.
4. D. Pavithra and R. Balakrishnan, "IoT based monitoring and control system for home automation," 2015 Global Conference on Communication Technologies (GCCT), pp. 169-173, 2015.
5. P. Gupta and J. Chhabra, "IoT based Smart Home design using power and security management," 2016 International Conference on Innovation and Challenges in Cyber Security (ICICCS-INBUSH), pp. 6-10, 2016.

6. C. Lien, Y. Bai, H. Chen and C. Hung, "Home appliance energy monitoring and controlling based on Power Line Communication," 2009 Digest of Technical Papers International Conference on Consumer Electronics, pp. 1-2, 2009.

7. P. Gupta and J. Chhabra, "IoT based Smart Home design using power and security management," 2016 International Conference on Innovation and Challenges in Cyber Security (ICICCS-INBUSH), pp. 6-10, 2016.

8. A. Prakash, S. S. Kumar, O. Vignesh and K. Vasudevan, "Reverse Pumping Based Smart Agricultural system," 7th International Conference on Electrical Energy Systems (ICEES), pp. 284-287, 2021.

9. W. A. Jabbar et al., "Design and Fabrication of Smart Home With Internet of Things Enabled Automation System," in IEEE Access, vol. 7, pp. 144059-144074, 2019.

10. Prakash Arumugam and Vasudevan Kuppan, "A GBDT-SOA approach for the system modelling of optimal energy management in grid-connected micro-grid system," Int J Energy Res, vol.45, pp.6765– 6783, 2021.

11. Kumar, R. N., Chandran, V., Valarmathi, R. S., & Kumar, D. R. (2018). Bitstream Compression for High Speed Embedded Systems Using Separated Split Look Up Tables (LUTs). Journal of Computational and Theoretical Nanoscience, 15(5), 1719–1727.

12. A. Jain, P. Tanwar and S. Mehra, "Home Automation System using Internet of Things (IOT)," 2019 International Conference on Machine Learning, Big Data, Cloud and Parallel Computing (COMITCon), pp. 300-305, 2019.

13. DB Avancini, JJPC.Rodrigues, RAL.Rabêlo, AK.Das, S.Kozlov, and P.Solic, "A new IoT-based smart energy meter for smart grids. Int J Energy Res, vol.45, pp.189– 202, 2021.

14. Krishnasamy, L., Dhanaraj, R. K., Ganesh Gopal, D., Reddy Gadekallu, T., Aboudaif, M. K., & Abouel Nasr, E. (2020). A Heuristic Angular Clustering Framework for Secured Statistical Data Aggregation in Sensor Networks. Sensors, 20(17), 4937.

15. Shishir Muralidhara, Niharika Hegde and PM.Rekha, "An internet of things-based smart energy meter for monitoring device-level consumption of energy", Computers & Electrical Engineering, vol.87, No.106772, 2020.

15

Smart Grid IoT: An Intelligent Energy Management in Emerging Smart Cities

R. S. Shudapreyaa[1]*, G. K. Kamalam[2], P. Suresh[3] and K. Sentamilselvan[4]

[1]Department of Computer Science and Engineering, Kongu Engineering College, Perundurai, Tamil Nadu, India
[2]Department of Information Technology, Kongu Engineering College, Perundurai, Tamil Nadu, India
[3]School of Computer Science and Engineering, Vellore Institute of Technology, Vellore, Tamil Nadu, India
[4]Sir Isaac Newton College of Engineering and Technology, Nagapattinam, Tamil Nadu, India

Abstract

Internet of Things enabled smaller objects are networked, linked, and connected via Internet to have advanced tracking and monitoring services. Through using sophisticated automatic monitoring and networking techniques and other aspects of information technology, the Smart Grid (SG) is a concept for changing electric power grid. SG is a set of computers, applications, networking and communications infrastructure for energy management and tracking built in households, industries and in the grid of electricity delivery. Advanced IoT sensing and networking systems can effectively eliminate or mitigate the disruption to transmission lines caused by natural disasters, boost power transmission efficiency and reduce economic losses. Over an environment where electricity consumption is rising, power generation can also increase to meet consumer requirements and facilitate their daily lives. Because while the number of customers is growing, and also because of the unpredictability of the energy load, the demand for electricity will create difficulties for electricity providers and energy producers. Constant power requirements are extremely likely to arise in certain cycles and can be a challenge to the reliability of the device. An efficient scheme for managing energy is needed to satisfy the demand for energy by the residential consumers. Home applicants are encouraged by utility organizations to participate in the scheme of residential

*Corresponding author: shudapreyaa@gmail.com

P. Sanjeevikumar, Rajesh Kumar Dhanaraj, Malathy Sathyamoorthy, Jens Bo Holm-Nielsen and Balamurugan Balusamy (eds.) Smart Grids and Internet of Things: An Energy Perspective, (431–454) © 2023 Scrivener Publishing LLC

energy management (REM). The system, home energy management would make electricity consumption smarter and more productive. The primary intent of power utility is to lessen the load demand at peak time in the grid as the customer wants to reduce energy costs. Energy-efficient technologies for low-power sensors are also emerging due to the implementation of IoT for building smart cities. The energy regulation is seen as a crucial framework for the realization in smart cities of complex energy systems. We offer a short description of energy efficiency and issues of smart cities in this chapter. Any energy-efficient technologies exist that can either reduce energy usage or maximize the use of resources. Smart city strategies must also have the potential to use electricity effectively to manage the associated problems. To optimize energy conservation of residential buildings in this chapter we focus on the Wind-driven Bacterial Foraging Algorithm (WBFA)-based approach and benchmark strategies such as Binary Particle Swarm Optimization (BPSO), Bacterial Foraging Optimization (BFO), Wind-Driven Optimization (WDO), Genetic Algorithm (GA), Genetic Wind Driven Optimization (GWDO), and Genetic Binary Particle Swarm Optimization (GBPSO).

Keywords: Smart grid, smart meters, smart cities, Internet of Things, energy management system, optimization algorithms

15.1   Overview of Smart Grid and IoT

The electrical network that serves any person, corporation, and infrastructure utility in a city is referred to as the "grid." Wireless devices such as sensors, radio modules, gateways, and routers are among the innovations that make today's IoT-enabled energy grid "smart." In traditional power grids, power quality and reliability are major challenges for both energy providers and customers. The Internet of Things (IoT) era's ongoing technical advances offer better solutions for enhancing the management of these problems and enforcing Smart Grid (SG) initiatives.

15.1.1   Smart Grid

Smart Grids (SG) include technology that digitizes electric utility grid to bring out communication that is digitalized between grid components. In conventional manner of grid, power utilities send the workers to manually read meter readings from the consumer, measure the voltage and various

Table 15.1 Components of smart grid and its roles.

SG components	Roles
Electric power generators	Electric power generators control the electric power generation and electric power flow through the electronic controllers.
Electric power substations	Electric power substations control the electric power generation and electric power flow through the electronic controllers.
transmission and distribution lines	It connects power generation plant and the consumers. It is a network of lines that transmits the power between base stations to the consumers. This network consists of numerous wires that are attached to the towers. Power generated at power utilities is of low voltage and before transmitted to the customer it is stepped up to the high voltage and transmitted. At the customer it is again steeped down to the consumer requirement.
Controllers	It makes use of the measurement of power, finds out the functioning of domestic devices and disconnects the power. It again reconnects the power if start signal is received by the active demand system or the time deadline of the user is arrived.
Smart meters	It is an electronic device that stores the details like electric energy consumption, level of voltage, current, power factor. Consumer can get the detail of electricity consumption through smart meters. Suppliers can use smart meters for monitoring the electricity consumption behavior of consumers and for customer billing. It enables smart meter and the central system a communication in two-way. Communication is established through wireless or wired. Smart meter setup made over buildings and enables communication in both side among utility and consumer. It supports continuous communication thus leads to monitoring loads form numerous customers in real-time. Smart meters provides a gate way between smart sockets and demand response-aware devices

(*Continued*)

Table 15.1 Components of smart grid and its roles. (*Continued*)

SG components	Roles
Collector nodes	Collector nodes communication is through Zigbee, mesh wireless two-way communication network. Two-way communication path is established between utility and collector nodes. AMI (Advanced Metering Infrastructure) through internet used to establish the communication between the collector nodes and the utility. DMZ (Demilitarized Zone) is used to provide extra protection during communication.
distribution and transmission control centers	distribution control center provides uninterrupted power supplies to the consumers. SG control center integrates Information Technology (IT) and Operation Technology (OT) to improve the value of business and delivers high reliability. Thus, SG achieves efficient, reliable and flexible operation.
Energy subsystem	Power generation, transmission and distribution
Communication layer	communication technology includes both wired and wireless technology and enables to exchange information among various SG components
Metering devices	records both electrical and non-electrical measurement values
Computational intelligence	extracts knowledge from the data and perform decision making
Applications and services	includes numerous software that provides visualization, monitoring and/or control to service the needs of the consumers

data. In SG, the components through integrated sensors carries data in two-way capability of communication between the devices placed in the consumer and the power utility operation centre. Table 15.1 lists the SG components and their roles.

15.1.2   Smart Grid Data Properties

Smart Grids is referred as next generation power grid. Integrating IoT and SG enable the two-way communication in an efficient manner. The communication is reliable, and also provides secured communication. The flow of data in SG is in the order from power plant and then to the physical devices like smart meters, intelligent monitors and electrical devices [9]. The data is then streamed to the control systems. The control system monitors the real-time streamed data to know grid status and stores data for later processing. The streamed data is used for forecasting or historical explorations [36]. While generating the data, a physical device associate a time stamp with the data and streams the data through the communication infrastructure. The data generated by the physical devices are termed as time series data or data stream. Data stream consists of an infinite sequence of time-stamped data records. The properties of SG data are:

Heterogeneous – diverse nature of data due to various physical devices, interfaces, capabilities
Time-stamp- it represents the time and date and the time-stamp is associated with the data generated by the physical devices and send along with the data stream.
Generation rate of data is high- In SG, the rate of data generated by the physical devices is so high [10]. To cope up with the data generation rate the data have to be considered in the order of time-stamp and time-stamp of the data is found through a single scan of the entire data stream.
Unboundedness-There is no bound on the volume of data generated by the physical devices. It is very difficult to store the infinite amount of data stream utterly
Evolving nature- streamed data characteristics change over time and this characteristic termed as temporal locality and in the stream mining process it includes an inherent component along with the data stream. To adapt the changes in the characteristics of stream data, stream elements have to be examined in a time-aware manner. Attacks or malware may cause a structural break in the data streamed.
Unordered Data- though the data generated by the physical devices is time-stamped, the data streamed through the communication interface is not in the order it was generated.

15.1.3 Operations on Smart Grid Data

The cloud environment should possess the s operations in the cloud to process SG data:

Storage- clouds have to provide a storage place for storing the stream data based upon the rate at which the data is generated by the physical devices [12]. Cloud system should provide space for archival of data and also it should provide a methodology for deleting the unwanted data to maintain data consistency.

Indexing- to perform search operation efficiently in a large volume of data stream, indexing algorithm is implemented.

Aggregation- The volume of data generated by the physical devices is large. The infinite data stream can be processed in a batch-order. The computation process is carried out in aggregation to handle the large volume of data stream.

Clustering- clustering algorithm is required to process the large volume of SG data. It is used to redue the time complexity and space complexity in processing the data.

Sampling- it returns a sample of data stream efficiently in view of an illegal attack or damage of data.

Searching- the most important operation performed on the stream data is mining. In SG, this operation has to be carried out efficiently and also in a secure manner, because the data stored in the cloud contains valuable sensitive information.

Auditing- It is required in the prevention and detection of the data stream from the harmful attacks and from unauthorized access.

15.2   IoT Application in Smart Grid Technologies

IoT is a network and its service enables people and things communicate at any time, in any place, with anyone, and everything [13]. As a result, IoT provides huge global dynamic network system of Internet-enabled organizations that use web applications. SG is a significant IoT applications and a data communications network. SG integrated along with power grid and captures and analyzes data generated from transmission lines, SG customers, and distribution substations.

15.2.1   Power Transmission Line - Online Monitoring

Significant application of IoT in SG is power transmission online monitoring, especially in prevention during disaster, and mitigation in system of transmission of power. Natural disasters have posed numerous issues in high voltage transmission of power in recent years, comprising stability, protection, and reliability [14]. Furthermore, the new transmission power line control system is primarily operated manually. On 220kv and 500kv high voltage transmission power lines, required sensors for conductor gallop, wind vibration, micrometeorology, and conductor temperature deployed enables online monitoring of power transmission systems. It comprises two components. To track power transmission lines condition, one pan is mounted alongside them. Its other pan is placed on the transmission lines to keep an eye on the atmosphere and its current condition [15]. Wireless networks are commonly used to communicate between IoT enabled devices, transmission lines, and transmission power. Master station device could send data over a cellular network, as well as a fiber optic network and/or a wireless broad band system.

15.2.2 Smart Patrol

The patrol for transmission of power, transformation of power, and distribution mainly depends on manual operation of staffs. Due to climatic conditions, environmental factors, and other factors, the quality and in-place-rate of patrol cannot be guaranteed rigorously. Moreover, the patrol of unattended substation equipment is difficult for the power workers to examine [16]. In order to provide efficient solution for the above problems, the patrol system of power transmission, transformation and distribution system needs to be upgraded by IoT technology. RHO tags could be used to locate the power equipment which could supervise and guide the patrol staff with standardization and regulation of the workflow execution [17]. With the help of RHO, smart patrol can enhance the quality and the efficiency of power transmission line patrol, guarantee the stability of power grid system and improve the power supply reliability.

15.2.3 Smart Home Service

Smart power utilization service includes hybrid smart AMR system, smart sensor network system, smart home system, security system, and energy information collection system, etc. There are three functions for the smart power utilization service system: reliable electricity supply, smart home experience for users and smart management and efficient use of energy [18]. As shown in Figure 15.3, the communication of the hybrid smart AMR system is mostly based on Power Line Carrier (PLC), Fiber to the Home (FTTH), broadband wireless communication, and other broadband communication network. Through this system, real-time communication between the power grid and users can be realized. The capacity of integrated services of power grid can be enhanced. The interactive marketing demands can be met. The quality of service can be improved [19]. The user's energy efficiency can be enhanced significantly by applying the smart interactive terminal in smart home services.

15.2.4   Information System for Electric Vehicle

Electric vehicles (EV) provides an intelligent SG opportunity in addition to eco-friendly transportation. It stores energy. EV charging station is composed of four different facets: system for power supply, equipment for charging, monitoring system shown in Figure 15.4. The system for power supply is solely accountable for safety output and electricity management. Charging and discharging of EVs are implemented in the charging equipment, including DC charger and AC charger [20]. AC charger provides slow charging for the EVs, while DC charger provides fast charging mode and function for billing. Monitoring system solely accountable for the real-time monitoring and provides security for the charging environment.

EV can be considered as the mobile power' storage device of SG and helps power grid to mitigate effect of peak-valley. This new potential leads to efficient resource management and also provides friendly environment. Consumers acquire the benefit irrespective of the utility with cost efficient electricity at no peak duration. In order to realize the interconnection of EV and power grid, it is required to develop EV industry communication supporting facility and management platform simultaneously [21]. Based on smart sensing and high capacity transmitting device, loT technology could provide smart sensing and efficient interaction for EVs, batteries, and charging stations. Smart sensing devices include wireless sensors. RFID tags and GPS are high capacity transmitting devices. In addition on-line monitoring centralized control, optimal resource allocation and entire lifecycle management of the equipments could be achieved through comprehensive information analysis [22]. By perceiving the available resources and the state of the resources in using, unified resources allocation and efficient service can be provided for charging station and the customers.

15.3   Technical Challenges of Smart Grid

15.3.1   Inadequacies in Grid Infrastructure

Grid infrastructure still exists to be in the evolving stage. Existing grid network in not sufficient enough to satisfy the forthcoming requirements of achieving efficient energy utilization and generation of power in distributed environment [23]. Apart from indulging towards SG, it becomes essential in addressing the problem of improving the grid distributed infrastructure. In India, electrical components are not evenly linked with grid present in the nation. It should be evenly connected to make it most favorable to expel huge wind farms that require efficient installation of the complete infrastructure.

15.3.2 Cyber Security

Integrating grid with cyber network emerges various vulnerabilities in the system. Identifying and avoiding the gap before the security violation occurs is quite important. Main objective of cyber security feature addressed [11], is availability, confidentiality and integrity. Availability in the context points to reliable, well-timed information gathering from database. Integrity refers to the protection of valuable information from any security breach such as modification or destruction of information. Confidentiality, meaning in the context points to protecting the information from accessing using someone else's account. Cyber security becomes a fundamental issue, even a gap brings the chance of making a probable threat leads to disaster for power utilities and also for the consumers involved with grid infrastructure. Security feature is inadequate to overcome the cyber threats like logic bomb on grid, zero day, malware, etc. [37]. SG is a multilayer structure and hence requires advanced security techniques to overcome the ever-arising cyber threats.

15.3.3 Storage Concerns

SG uses renewable for generation huge power in a distributed manner. Storage of power is essential because the power generated from various renewable is variable in quantity. Usually storage requirement opted is battery and its duration of life is from four to five years. Storage techniques like flywheels, storage of hydrogen, storage of thermal power, etc. comes with their specific concern. Storage technique such as pumped storage efficiency ranges from seventy to eight five percentage [35]. Disadvantage of this technique is that it needs vast reservoirs for storage. Flywheel absorbs and delivers energy quickly within few seconds. Flywheels withstand grid frequency in seconds and not suitable for longer time period. Specific electricity storage technology is battery and lead-acid is the significant one. Advantage of flywheels is portable, but insufficiency of raw material for making batteries and expensive is the serious issue while considering battery as storage technique.

15.3.4   Data Management

SG establishes a heterogeneous power network comprising quantum of smart meters, sensors and controllers. Information from these devices are huge volume and analyzing these data will suffice in prediction before breakdown or damage occurrence. Smart meter reads data every fifteen minutes, the large volume of data from this device results in difficult for storage and retrieval [34]. Large volume of data will lead to more time in data analysis and report generation. To overcome this issue, cloud provides efficient storage for voluminous data and also data analysis is very faster and retrieval of data is also quicker.

15.3.5   Communication Issues

Communication technologies are available in wide range for deployment in SG. Each technology has its own limitations. First technology supports limited bandwidth, second technology covers minimum distance, third technology leads to higher loss in data, and other technology comes with bounded success in underground installations [30]. Technologies defined in SG are ZigBee, GSM, GPRS, etc. GSM and GPRS coverage range is within 10 km and lacks in data rates. ZigBee covers thirty to fifty meter only.

15.3.6   Stability Concerns

SG comprises on a very big scale the renewable and Micro Grids (MG). In distributed generation, the flow of power is bidirectional. Distributed power generation contains numerous advantages over traditional and nuclear sources of energy [29]. Huge penetration of renewable and MG would increase.

i)   Angular stability because of smaller inertia
ii)   Voltage stability because of the support for power sharing is smaller

15.3.7   Energy Management and Electric Vehicle

Electric vehicle batteries can be charged in idle time and is used for the functioning of the vehicle during peak hours [28]. The basic controls that is required for managing the EV energy is as follows:

i)   Power flows form Vehicle to Grid (V2G), Grid to Vehicle (G2V), Vehicle to Vehicle (V2V)
ii)   Reactive power and DC link voltage control.

15.4 Energy Efficient Solutions for Smart Cities

15.4.1 Lightweight Protocols

It leads to lesser overhead. In IoT integrated smart cities communication is achieved through various lightweight protocols [27]. The lightweight protocol Message Queue Telemetry Transport (MQTT) fetches the information generated in IoT devices and forwards to servers. The networks and devices that are working under some constraints for web transfer is handled efficiently by CoAP protocol [8]. Numerous communication protocols are designed to support specific scenarios and the applications it could suit well. Protocol conversion is essential in IoT, because the IoT devices are form various manufacturers or using different protocols and has to be adapted to the distributed heterogeneous environment.

15.4.2 Scheduling Optimization

The main objective is to optimize the resource to lessen energy consumption ultimately reduces electricity usage [26]. Demand-side management (DSM) manipulates electrical utilization in the residential area through optimally scheduling the system load and consequently cost is reduced. DSM performs tasks like shifting of load, conversation of energy. Transferring customers load from the level of high-peak to low-peak is termed shifting of load [38]. Through the technique, the energy is conserved and can be used by other customers.

15.4.3 Energy Consumption

IoT-integrated city requires prognostic model for consumption of energy. Numerous applications in smart city require a predictive model like model for traffic, travel, controlling temperature and humidity. Predictive models like neural networks, Markov decision process can be used. Making use of the predictive models not only reduces energy consumption in smart cities but also provides significant social benefits.

15.4.4 Cloud Based Approach

Cloud to cater to the needs of IoT-enabled smart cities, computing and storage facility is enhanced so that they can be used to provide efficient solution for energy consumption. Cloud enables to store and process a massive amount of data by managing the data stored in distributed data centers in an energy-efficient way.

15.4.5   Low Power Transceivers

In smart-city applications, Internet-of-Things (IoT) devices work with bounded batteries. For efficient energy management or efficient consumption of energy requires a low-power design framework. Existing architecture for IoT devices lacks in energy management. In energy efficiency, the important parameter considered is radio duty cycle in IoT devices. Researchers are still exploring efficient design architecture to reduce radio duty cycle in IoT devices.

15.4.6   Cognitive Management Framework

The heterogeneous nature of IoT devices makes the service provided by the IoT devices as unreliable [7]. Exploring a framework that is cognitive in nature becomes important and it incorporates both intelligent and cognitive approach in smart cities. Cognitive structure indulges learning and sensible or logical way of thinking in order to bring out efficient conclusion for IoT networks. Context-aware structure, based on the contextual background the efficient decisions are made in IoT-enabled smart cities.

15.5   Energy Conservation Based Algorithms

15.5.1   Genetic Algorithm (GA)

Electric cost is minimized by GA based approach. It effectively allocates the smart devices of residential building. Input parameters considered for the GA algorithm is operational parameters of smart appliances, power grid energy. From these inputs, the GA algorithm generates the input chromosomes [5]. Each chromosome is termed as the candidate solution. Then the algorithm estimates the fitness function from the randomly generated population and the best result of the evaluation is stored. The bets result obtained is given as input ti=o the cross over and mutation phase and acquires the global optimal result [6]. The global optimal value provides efficient schedule of utilization of power for smart devices. The controlling variables of GA is cross over and mutation probability. The cross

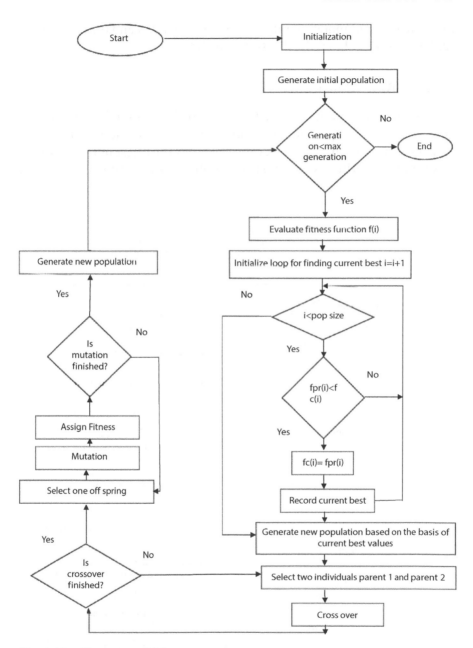

Figure 15.1 Illustration of GA.

over rate (cr) and mutation rate (pm) is defined as 0.9 and 0.1 respectively [25]. Figure 15.1 shows the illustration of GA.

15.5.2   BFO Algorithm

BFO algorithm functionality is based on the behavior of bacterium. To get maximum energy, the bacterium swims to find the best nutrients [4]. The optimal solution is the one which has the fittest nutrients value. BFO comprises three steps: first step is elimination-dispersion, second

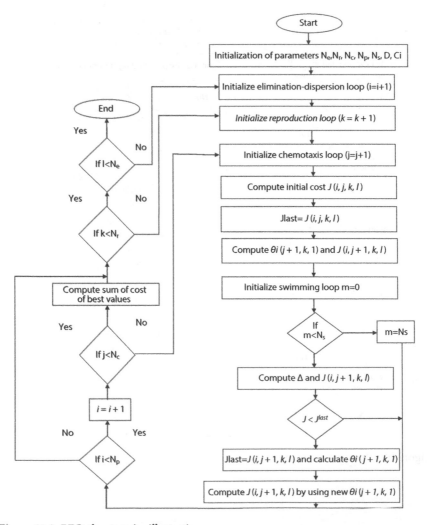

Figure 15.2 BFO-the stepwise illustration.

step is reproduction and third step is chemotaxes. Required parameters are initialized. The chemotaxes process is then carried out. During this phase, bacteria population matrix is generated based on random method [39]. Bacterium position is referred as candidate solution. Bacterium tumbling, swimming is related to convergence and divergence. Population matrix obtained after fitness evaluation forms the local best solution. Step size and position of bacterium is represented as $\theta(i,:)$ and c_i respectively. Step size of the bacterium controls the rate of convergence [24]. Lower step size and higher step size converges and diverges to form local minima and global optima. Irrelevant and redundant nature of information is eliminated in the elimination-dispersion step and provides a global optimal solution which makes the power utilization schedule an optimal one for smart devices. The stepwise illustration is shown in Figure 15.2.

15.5.3   BPSO Algorithm

BPSO is binary equable algorithm to PSO [3]. The logic is similar to the foraging behavior of birds. To gather food the birds move in flock with particular position and velocity. Similar to the behavior of birds, the algorithm has two controlling parameters position and velocity. Particle velocity controls the population matrix and particle position controls the candidate solution. Particle velocity is represented as follows:

$$V_i = 2 * V_{max} * ((rand\,(swarm,\,n)) - (1 * 0.5)) \qquad (15.1)$$

Value present in matrix position specifies the ON or OFF condition of the smart devices. Initially the position matrix values are generated using random values and updated based on the fitness function evaluation [31]. Once when the fitness function evaluation is completed, local best solution (pbest) is obtained. Termination condition identifies the global best solution (gbest). Effectively the energy management is achieved by the BPSO algorithm. gbest provides the optimal utilization power allocation of smart devices connected in residential buildings. Sigmoidal function used along with the velocity function to acquire binary equable. Sigmoidal function is stated as follows:

$$Sigmoid(j,\,i) = 11 + e - V_{new} \qquad (15.2)$$

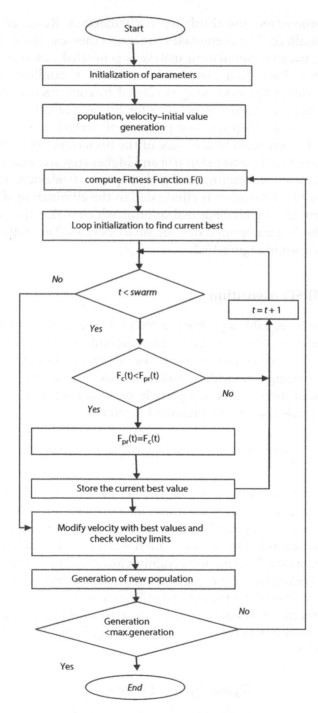

Figure 15.3 Illustration of binary particle swarm optimization.

Binary equable of position matrix is stated as follows:

$$X_{new} = 1_i \, frand(1) \leq Sigmoid(j, i) \tag{15.3}$$

$$X_{new} = 0i \, frand(1) > Sigmoid(j, i) \tag{15.4}$$

Fitness evaluation phase input value is binary equable of position matrix. The step is iterated a number of time span and reaches the global best solution. BPSO algorithm operation procedure is shown in Figure 15.3.

15.5.4   WDO Algorithm

It is nature-inspired algorithm. The logic behind this algorithm is atmospheric motion of wind principal. Two functions are air parcel position and velocity. Solution matrix is air parcel matrix. Initialization of control parameters is done and then the parcel position matrix is randomly generated [2]. Each value in the random matrix is providing the status of smart devices of residential area. Velocity initial value is computed as follows:

$$V_i = V_{max} * 2 * (rand \, (populationsize, n) - 0.5) \tag{15.5}$$

Values in the parcel position matrix updates based on fitness function evaluation. Changed value provides the optimal utilization power allocation of smart devices connected in residential buildings [32]. Updating of velocity value is also performed. Updating of parcel position matrix is done as follows:

$$X_{new} = X_{cur} + U_{new} \, \Delta t \tag{15.6}$$

Updating of position and velocity process is iterated till end case is occurred or optimal value is reached. WDO outputs a global best solution gbest and it provides the optimal utilization power allocation of smart devices connected in residential buildings [40]. The logic of the GWDO algorithm is represented in Figure 15.4.

15.5.5   GWDO Algorithm

GWDO a hybrid algorithm plunging algorithm WDO, crossover and mutation of GA. Plunging is required because GA efficiently reduces PAR and WDO algorithm efficiently minimizes coat and maximizes UC [1]. The logic of the GWDO algorithm is represented in Figure 15.5.

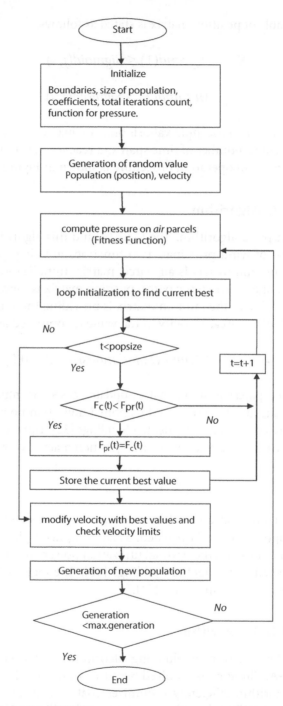

Figure 15.4 Illustration of WDO.

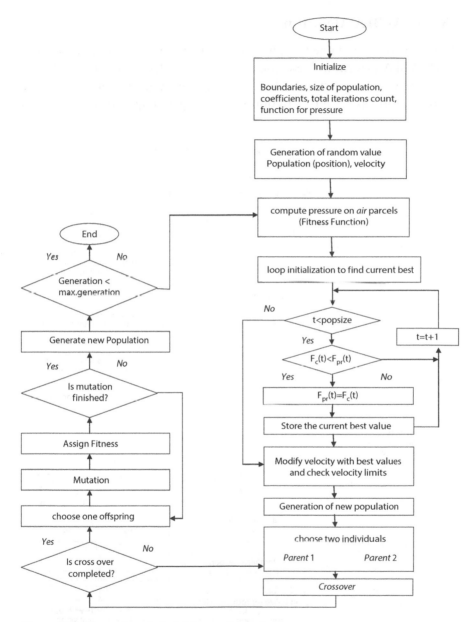

Figure 15.5 Illustration of wind-driven optimization.

15.5.6 WBFA Algorithm

The algorithm is obtained by plunging the heuristic algorithms WDO and BFO. WBFA algorithm logic considers the complete procedure of WDO and in BFO it considers the elimination-dispersion, chemotaxis, and the reproduction operation procedures. Plunging is required because BFO

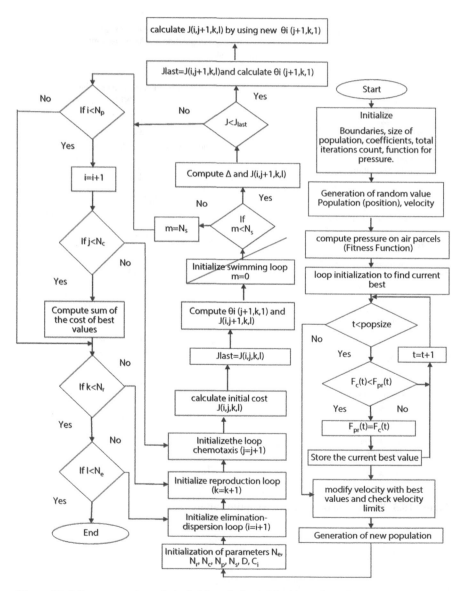

Figure 15.6 Representation of wind-driven bacterial foraging algorithm.

efficiently reduces PAR and WDO algorithm efficiently minimizes coat and maximizes UC [33]. WBFA comprises four stages. First stage is WDO algorithm. The second stage is elimination-dispersion procedure. The third stage is reproduction procedure. Finally, the fourth stage of the algorithm represents the chemotaxis procedure. More number of control parameters and the deeper layer layout of the algorithm provide an excellent striking performance. More number of control parameters and the deeper layer layout of the algorithm enable to meet the required objectives but leads to more execution time. WBFA algorithm steps are illustrated in Figure 15.6.

15.6 Conclusion

The current paper demonstrated the importance of Global energy system is undergoing rapid change, with "potentially far-reaching consequences that will unfold over the next decades," according to the study. Today, the position of energy manager is extremely broad and often ambiguous. Instead of being seen as task managers, energy managers are viewed as business associates. In reality, various countries have different approaches to hiring managers in the renewable energy. The significance of smart water grids in creation of smart cities aims in using water efficiently. The importance of providing real-time data to end-users, as well as detecting leakage and contamination, has been highlighted various researcher conducted.

References

1. Nadeem, J.; Hafeez, G.; Iqbal, S.; Alrajeh, N.; Alabed, M.S.; Guizani, M. Energy efficient integration of renewable energy sources in the smart grid for demand side management. IEEE Access 2018, 6, 77077–77096.
2. Zikri, B.; Komurcu, M.; Bossard, J.A.; Werner, D.H. The wind driven optimization technique and its application in electromagnetics. IEEE Trans. Antennas Propag. 2013, 61, 2745–2757.
3. Poli, R.; Kennedy, J.; Blackwell, T. Particle swarm optimization. Swarm Intell. 2007, 1, 33–57.
4. Ali, E.S.; Abd-Elazim, S.M. Bacteria foraging optimization algorithm based load frequency controller for interconnected power system. Int. J. Electr. Power Energy Syst. 2011, 33, 633–638.
5. Xin, J.; Xiao, C. Household Energy Demand Management Strategy Based on Operating Power by Genetic Algorithm. IEEE Access 2019, 7, 96414–96423.

6. Zhuang, Z.; Lee, W.C.; Shin, Y.; Song, K.B. An optimal power scheduling method for demand response in home energy management system. IEEE Trans. Smart Grid 2013, 4, 1391–1400.

7. P. Vlacheas et al., "Enabling Smart Cities through a Cognitive Management Framework for the internet of Things", IEEE Commun. Mag., vol. 51, no. 6, pp. 102-11, June 2013.

8. AI-Fuqaha et al., "Internet of Things: A Survey on Enabling Technologies Protocols and Applications", IEEE Commun. Surveys & Tutorials, vol. 17, no. 4, pp. 2347-76, Nov. 2015.

9. Tsoukalas, L., and R. Gao, From Smart Grids to an Energy Internet Assumptions, Architectures and Requirements, IEEE DRPT Conference, April, 2008.

10. Pipattanasomporn A., and A. Rahman, Multi-Agent Systems in a Distributed Smart Grid: Design and Implementation, Proc. IEEE PES 2009 Power Systems Conference and Exposition, Mar. 2009.

11. Chuang, J., and M. McGranaghan, Functions of a Local Controller to Coordinate Distributed Resources in a Smart Grid Angela Chuang, IEEE, 2008.

12. McDonald, J., Leader or Follower: Developing the Smart Grid Business Case, IEEE Power &Energy, p. 18-24, Nov-Dec, 2008.

13. Hamlyn, A., H. Cheung, T. Mander, L. Wang, C. Yang, R. Cheung, Computer Network Security Management and Authentication of Smart Grids Operations, IEEE, 2008.

14. Silva, B.N.; Khan, M.; Han, K. Towards sustainable smart cities: A review of trends, architectures, components, and open challenges in smart cities. Sustain. Cities Soc. 2018, 38, 697–713.

15. Ejaz, W.; Naeem, M.; Shahid, A.; Anpalagan, A.; Jo, M. Efficient Energy Management for the Internet of Things in Smart Cities. IEEE Commun. Mag. 2017, 55, 84–91.

16. Zanella, A.; Bui, N.; Castellani, A.; Vangelista, L.; Zorzi, M. Internet of Things for Smart Cities. IEEE Internet Things J. 2014, 1, 22–32.

17. Gungor, V.C.; Sahin, D.; Kocak, T.; Ergut, S.; Buccella, C.; Cecati, C.; Hancke, G.P. Smart Grid and Smart Homes: Key Players and Pilot Projects. IEEE Ind. Electron. Mag. 2012, 6, 18–34

18. Masera, M.; Bompard, E.F.; Profumo, F.; Hadjsaid, N. Smart (Electricity) Grids for Smart Cities: Assessing Roles and Societal Impacts. Proc. IEEE 2018, 106, 613–625

19. Liserre, M.; Sauter, T.; Hung, J.Y. Future Energy Systems: Integrating Renewable Energy Sources into the Smart Power Grid Through Industrial Electronics. IEEE Ind. Electron. Mag. 2010, 4, 18–37.

20. Hernandez, L.; Baladron, C.; Aguiar, J.M.; Carro, B.; Sanchez-Esguevillas, A.J.; Lloret, J.; Massana, J. A Survey on Electric Power Demand Forecasting: Future Trends in Smart Grids, Microgrids and Smart Buildings. IEEE Commun. Surv. Tutor. 2014, 16, 1460–1495.

21. Bulkeley, H.; McGuirk, P.M.; Dowling, R. Making a smart city for the smart grid? The urban material politics of actualising smart electricity networks. Environ. Plan. A 2016, 48, 1709–1726.

22. Nguyen, C.P.; Flueck, A.J. Agent based restoration with distributed energy storage support in smart grids. IEEE Trans. Smart Grid 2012, 3, 1029–1038.

23. Mohd, A.; Ortjohann, E.; Schmelter, A.; Hamsic, N.; Morton, D. Challenges in integrating distributed energy storage systems into future smart grid. In Proceedings of the IEEE International Symposium on Industrial Electronics, Cambridge, UK, 30 June–2 July 2008; pp. 1627–1632.

24. Lucas, A.; Chondrogiannis, S. Smart grid energy storage controller for frequency regulation and peak shaving, using a vanadium redox flow battery. Int. J. Electr. Power Energy Syst. 2016, 80, 26–36.

25. L. Atzori, A. Lera and G. Morabito, "The internet of things: a survey [J]", Computer Networks, vol. 54, no. 15, pp. 2787-2805, 2010.

26. R. Khan, S. U. Khan, R. Zzheer and S. Khan, "Future internet: The internet of things architecture possible applications and key challenges[C]", 10th international Conference on Frontiers of Information Technolozv, pp. 257-260, 2012.

27. D. Bandyopadhyay and J. Sen, "Internet of Things: Applications and Challenges in Technology and Standardization [J]", Wireless Personal Communications, vol. 58, no. 1, pp. 49-69, 2011.

28. J. B. Ling and T. Liu, "Analyzing of Smart Grid Networking Technology and Application [J]", Mechanical & Electrical Engineering Technology, vol. 43, no. 1, pp. 67-69, 2013.

29. V.C. Gungor, D. Sahin, T. Kocak and S. Ergut, "Smart grid technologies: Communication Technologies and Standards [J]", IEEE trans.on Industrial Informatics, vol. 7, no. 4, pp. 529-539, 2011.

30. P. McDaniel and S. Mclaughlin,"Security and Privacy Challenges in the Smart Grid [J]",IEEE Security&Privacy, vol. 7, no. 3, pp. 75-77, 2009.

31. Zou, H.; Mao, S.; Wang, Y.; Zhang, F.; Chen, X.; Cheng, L. A survey of energy management in interconnected multi-microgrids. IEEE Access 2019, 7, 72158–72169.

32. Choi, J.S. A Hierarchical Distributed Energy Management Agent Framework for Smart Homes, Grids, and Cities. IEEE Commun. Mag. 2019, 57, 113–119.

33. Rodríguez-Molina, J.; Kammen, D.M. Middleware Architectures for the Smart Grid: A Survey on the State-of-the-Art. Taxonomy and Main Open Issues. IEEE Commun. Surv. Tutor. 2018, 20, 2992–3033.

34. Schmutzler, J.; Gröning, S.; Wietfeld, C. Management of distributed energy resources in IEC 61850 using web services on devices. In Proceedings of the IEEE International Conference on Smart Grid Communications (SmartGridComm), Brussels, Belgium, 17–20 October 2011; pp. 315–320.

35. Daoud, M.; Fernando, X. On the communication requirements for the smart grid. Energy Power Eng. 2011, 3, 53.

36. Hossain, E.; Han, Z.; Poor, H.V. Smart grid communications and networking; Cambridge University Press: Cambridge, UK, 2012.
37. Shu-wen, W. Research on the key technologies of IOT applied on smart grid. In Proceedings of the International Conference on Electronics, Communications and Control (ICECC), Ningbo, China, 9–11 September 2011; pp. 2809–2812.
38. Rahman, M.G.; Chowdhury, M.F.B.R.; Al Mamun, M.A.; Hasan, M.R.; Mahfuz, S. Summary of smart grid: Benefits and issues. Int. J. Sci. Eng. Res. 2013, 4, 1–5.
39. Reka, S.S.; Dragicevic, T. Future effectual role of energy delivery: A comprehensive review of Internet of Things and smart grid. Renew. Sustain. Energy Rev. 2018, 91, 90–108.
40. Collier, S.E. The Emerging Enernet: Convergence of the Smart Grid with the Internet of Things. IEEE Ind. Appl. Mag. 2017, 23, 12–16.

Index

Also of Interest

Check out these other related titles from Scrivener Publishing

SMART GRIDS AND GREEN ENERGY SYSTEMS, Edited by A. Chitra, V. Indragandhi and W. Razia Sultana, ISBN: 9781119872030. Presenting the concepts and advances of smart grids within the context of "green" energy systems, this volume, written and edited by a global team of experts, goes into the practical applications that can be utilized across multiple disciplines and industries, for both the engineer and the student.

SMART GRIDS AND MICROGRIDS: Concepts and Applications, Edited by P. Prajof, S. Mohan Krishna, J. L. Febin Daya, Umashankar Subramaniam, and P. V. Brijesh, ISBN: 9781119760559. Written and edited by a team of experts in the field, this is the most comprehensive and up to date study of smart grids and microgrids for engineers, scientists, students, and other professionals.

MICROGRID TECHNOLOGIES, Edited by C. Sharmeela, P. Sivaraman, P. Sanjeevikumar, and Jens Bo Holm-Nielsen, ISBN 9781119710790. Covering the concepts and fundamentals of microgrid technologies, this volume, written and edited by a global team of experts, also goes into the practical applications that can be utilized across multiple industries, for both the engineer and the student.

INTEGRATION OF RENEWABLE ENERGY SOURCES WITH SMART GRIDS, Edited by A. Mahaboob Subahani, M. Kathiresh and G. R. Kanagachidambaresan, ISBN: 9781119750420. Provides comprehensive coverage of renewable energy and its integration with smart grid technologies.

Encyclopedia of Renewable Energy, by James G. Speight, ISBN 9781119363675. Written by a highly respected engineer and prolific author in the energy sector, this is the single most comprehensive, thorough, and up to date reference work on renewable energy.

Green Energy: Solar Energy, Photovoltaics, and Smart Cities, edited by Suman Lata Tripathi and Sanjeevikumar Padmanaban, ISBN 9781119760764. Covering the concepts and fundamentals of green energy, this volume, written and edited by a global team of experts, also goes into the practical applications that can be utilized across multiple industries, for both the engineer and the student.

Energy Storage, edited by Umakanta Sahoo, ISBN 9781119555513. Written and edited by a team of well-known and respected experts in the field, this new volume on energy storage presents the state-of-the-art developments and challenges in the field of renewable energy systems for sustainability and scalability for engineers, researchers, academicians, industry.

Energy Storage 2nd Edition, by Ralph Zito and Haleh Ardebili, ISBN 9781119083597. A revision of the groundbreaking study of methods for storing energy on a massive scale to be used in wind, solar, and other renewable energy systems.

Hybrid Renewable Energy Systems, edited by Umakanta Sahoo, ISBN 9781119555575. Edited and written by some of the world's top experts in renewable energy, this is the most comprehensive and in-depth volume on hybrid renewable energy systems available, a must-have for any engineer, scientist, or student.

Progress in Solar Energy Technology and Applications, edited by Umakanta Sahoo, ISBN 9781119555605. This first volume in the new groundbreaking series, Advances in Renewable Energy, covers the latest concepts, trends, techniques, processes, and materials in solar energy, focusing on the state-of-the-art for the field and written by a group of world-renowned experts.

A Polygeneration Process Concept for Hybrid Solar and Biomass Power Plants: Simulation, Modeling, and Optimization, by Umakanta Sahoo, ISBN 9781119536093. This is the most comprehensive and in-depth study of the theory and practical applications of a new and groundbreaking method for the energy industry to "go green" with renewable and alternative energy sources.

DESIGN AND DEVELOPMENT OF EFFICIENT ENERGY SYSTEMS, edited by Suman Lata Tripathi, Dushyant Kumar Singh, Sanjeevikumar Padmanaban, and P. Raja, ISBN 9781119781042. Discusses the concepts and fundamentals of efficient energy systems, this volume, written and edited by a global team of experts, also gives the practical applications that can be utilized across multiple industries, for both the engineer and the student.

INTELLIGENT RENEWABLE ENERGY SYSTEMS: Integrating Artificial Intelligence Techniques and Optimization Algorithms, edited by Neeraj Priyadarshi, Akash Kumar Bhoi, Sanjeevikumar Padmanaban, S. Balamurugan, et al., Benjamin Wicker, ISBN 9781119786122. This collection of papers on artificial intelligence and other methods for improving the renewable energy systems, written by industry experts, is a welcome addition to the literature for engineers, scientists, and students and is a must-have for any library on renewable energy systems and technology.

SMART GRIDS FOR SMART CITIES VOLUME 1 AND VOLUME 2, edited by O.V.Gnana Swathika, K. Karthikeyan, Sanjeevikumar Padmanaban, et al., ISBN 9781119768784 and 9781119872030, written by a team of experts in the field this is the first comprehensive two-book set to offer practical solutions for both an electric vehicle in this field, for engineers, scientists, students and their practitioners.

Printed and bound by CPI Group (UK) Ltd, Croydon, CR0 4YY

27/10/2024

14580470-0004